CQ GUIDE TO

CURRENT AMERICAN GOVERNMENT

Spring 1998

D1318708

CQ GUIDE TO

CURRENT AMERICAN GOVERNMENT

Spring 1998

Congressional Quarterly Inc.
Washington, D.C.

Congressional Quarterly Inc.

Congressional Quarterly Inc., an editorial research service and publishing company, serves clients in the fields of news, education, business, and government. It combines the specific coverage of Congress, government, and politics contained in the *Congressional Quarterly Weekly Report* with the more general subject range of an affiliated service, the *CQ Researcher.*

Congressional Quarterly also publishes a variety of books, including college political science textbooks and public affairs paperbacks on developing issues and events under the CQ Press imprint. CQ Books researches, writes, and publishes information directories and reference books on the federal government, national elections, and politics, including *Guide to the Presidency, Guide to Congress, Guide to the U.S. Supreme Court, Guide to U.S. Elections,* and *Politics in America. CQ's Encyclopedia of American Government* is a three-volume reference work providing essential information about the U.S. government. The *CQ Almanac,* a compendium of legislation for one session of Congress, is published each year. *Congress and the Nation,* a record of government for a presidential term, is published every four years.

CQ publishes the *Congressional Monitor,* a daily report on current and future activities of congressional committees, and several newsletters. An electronic online information system, Washington Alert, provides immediate access to CQ's databases of legislative action, votes, schedules, profiles, and analyses.

Printed in the United States of America

ISSN: 0196-612X
ISBN: 1-56802-107-0

Contents

Introduction

Congressional Quarterly's *Guide to Current American Government* is divided into four sections—foundations of American government, political participation, government institutions, and politics and public policy—that correspond with the framework of standard introductory American government textbooks. Articles have been selected from the *Congressional Quarterly Weekly Report* to complement existing texts with up-to-date examinations of current issues and controversies.

Foundations of American Government. Fundamental aspects of the U.S. Constitution are the focus of this section. The fate of affirmative action hangs on the Supreme Court's interpretation of the Fourteenth Amendment, which guarantees equal treatment under the law for all citizens. The line-item veto, the other issue addressed in this section, goes to the heart of the separation of powers, which is a basic principle of American government.

Political Participation. CQ editors review the relevant actors in electoral politics—candidates, voters, and parties—and then turn to interest group politics. Politics is never static; the universe of candidates, issues, and positions is always awhirl. At the moment, both parties are struggling to remain relevant in an age of individual-centered campaigning, antipartisan sentiment, and fragmented electorate. The Democratic Party struggles under the added burdens of a declining labor and urban base. Meanwhile, a traditionally strong lobby—the tobacco industry—reels, and a low-profile home builders lobby nets success.

Government Institutions. Aspects of Congress, the presidency, the judiciary, and the bureaucracy are discussed in turn. CQ editors review the first session of the 105th Congress and look ahead to the second session; presidential leadership in 1998 is a wildcard, given the president's dramatic defeat on trade legislation at the end of the session.

Politics and Public Policy. The *Guide* concludes with a half-dozen in-depth reviews of major policy areas: reform of the IRS and tax code; the enduring problems of hazardous and nuclear waste; a preliminary assessment of welfare reform and the problems still ahead; trade policy; and women in the military.

By reprinting articles largely as they appeared in the *Weekly Report*, the *Guide*'s editors provide a handy source of information about contemporary political issues. The date of original publication is noted with each article to give readers a time frame for the events that are described. Although new developments may have occurred subsequently, updates of the articles are provided only when they are essential to an understanding of the basic operations of American government. Page number references to related and background articles in the *Weekly Report* and *CQ Almanac* are provided to facilitate additional research on topical events. Both are available at many school and public libraries.

Foundations of American Government

The U.S. Constitution was drafted more than two centuries ago to perform several major functions: to guarantee individual liberties from encroachment by the government; to set forth the composition, jurisdiction, and powers of the executive, legislative, and judicial branches of the government; to regulate relations between these branches; and to regulate relations between the federal government and the states.

The written text of the Constitution has been remarkably stable, having been amended only twenty-seven times. But its interpretation has been more variable. The interpreter of the Constitution—the Supreme Court—is not a disconnected body sitting apart from society; its members are generally reflective of the era in which they live. For example, since the adoption of the Fourteenth Amendment in 1868, guaranteeing equal protection under the law for all citizens, the Constitution has been interpreted as both supporting and prohibiting segregation, Jim Crow laws, the poll tax, and the "separate but equal" treatment of minorities. From the 1960s through the 1980s the relatively liberal Supreme Court supported state and federal efforts to ameliorate past discrimination by giving minorities preferential access to education, government contracts and jobs, and other government programs and benefits. As the Court began to turn more conservative in the late 1980s and early 1990s, however, it began to question the constitutionality of race-based government actions. In the first selection, CQ editors take a look at affirmative action in the 1990s as well as other issues likely to come before the Court in the near future.

The next two selections concern the line-item veto. The power to veto select portions of appropriations bills is enjoyed by many state governors and was long sought by U.S. presidents. President Bill Clinton, by virtue of a law passed in 1996, is the first president to have line-item veto power. But its constitutionality is in doubt. In June 1997 the Supreme Court turned away a constitutional challenge on the narrow grounds that the petitioners—members of Congress—had not yet been harmed by the veto and therefore had no standing to bring suit, as discussed in the first of the articles. In August, President Clinton weighed the political and constitutional considerations behind his first line-item vetoes, as reflected in the second of the articles.

1

<u>CONSTITUTIONAL INTERPRETATION</u>

Affirmative Action Issues Top High Court's Docket

Dismissal of white teacher in New Jersey at center of major evaluation of government programs

Note: At press time, the status of the Court cases discussed in this article had been finalized: the Court let stand California's Proposition 209 on November 3, 1997, and on November 21 the *Piscataway* case was settled out of court. Although these cases have been resolved, affirmative action controversies will continue to attract headlines in the months ahead. This article is offered as a backgrounder on the affirmative action debate.

The political wars over affirmative action have been waged until now primarily in statewide ballot initiatives, university admissions offices and other fronts far from Washington. That may be about to change.

The Supreme Court, in its term beginning Oct. 6, is poised to make a major evaluation of the broad array of government programs known as affirmative action, which aims to promote minorities and women in government contracting, hiring and school admissions.

The court already has agreed to take a New Jersey case involving a white teacher who was laid off while an equally qualified black teacher retained her job. And the odds are even that the court will agree to consider a challenge to California's sweeping Proposition 209, passed in 1996, which amends the state Constitution to bar racial and gender preference programs except to comply with a court order.

Any high court ruling would have a major effect on the states: 26 of them are awaiting final word on Proposition 209 before adopting similar laws.

The court's rulings also will affect the congressional landscape. The New Jersey case, *Piscataway Township Board of Education v. Taxman*, in-

CQ Weekly Report Oct. 4, 1997

Title VII 1964 Civil Rights Act
It shall be an unlawful employment practice for an employer to fail or refuse to hire or to discharge any individual...because of such individual's race, color, religion, sex or national origin.

Justice O'Connor

Proposition 209 SEC. 31
(a) The state shall not discriminate against, or grant preferential treatment to, any individual or group on the basis of race, sex...

Rep. Canady

volves a reinterpretation of the landmark 1964 Civil Rights Act (PL 88-352).

The outcome of the Proposition 209 case, *Coalition for Economic Equity v. Wilson*, will affect proposed legislation by conservative lawmakers to adopt Proposition 209 policies nationwide. *(1964 Almanac, p. 338)*

Rep. Charles T. Canady, R-Fla., and Sen. Mitch McConnell, R-Ky., have introduced bills (HR 1909, S 950) that would ban consideration of race and gender in federal hiring and contracting. The House bill already has been approved by the Judiciary Subcommittee on the Constitution.

But the legislation could be stopped dead if the Supreme Court finds the California initiative unconstitutional. If the court upholds the statute, or declines to hear the case, Canady and McConnell could assume they were on safe legal ground. *(Weekly Report, p. 1635)*

"Both cases . . . may end up having a

wide-ranging impact on how our nation continues to grapple with racial problems," says Steven R. Shapiro, national legal director of the American Civil Liberties Union.

Flip-Flop

Piscataway involves two teachers — one black, one white — in the business department of a public high school in Piscataway, N. J.

The white teacher, Sharon Taxman, lost her job when the school decided it needed to eliminate a position but did not want to undercut its efforts to maintain a diverse faculty. The case is particularly unusual because Taxman and the black teacher had exactly the same amount of seniority and had received exactly the same job performance ratings.

The school had a policy to promote diversity but had never used it. The business department was mostly white, but overall the school had no problem attracting qualified minority teachers, making its faculty satisfactorily diverse. In this case, the school used a preference for diversity as a tiebreaker between two otherwise equally qualified teachers.

After her dismissal, Taxman sued, arguing that she had been subject to discrimination. Both the district court and the 3rd U.S. Circuit Court of Appeals, based in Philadelphia, agreed.

At issue in the case is Title VII of the 1964 Civil Rights Act, which barred discrimination on the basis of race, color, religion, sex or national origin; and created the Equal Employment Opportunity Commission to clamp down on discrimination. Over the years Title VII has been amended and expanded through executive order and is considered the legal underpinning of many affirmative action policies throughout the country.

But when the Piscataway case

A Shift to Nuts and Bolts

Affirmative action and First Amendment issues top the agenda of the Supreme Court, which begins hearing cases Oct. 6. During last year's term, which ended in June, the court examined constitutional principles. This term is more focused on nuts-and-bolts issues affecting commerce, politics and the workplace. Among cases that have been taken or are likely to be taken are:

● **Affirmative action.** In *Piscataway Township Board of Education v. Taxman*, the court will examine whether Title VII of the 1964 Civil Rights Act permits affirmative action programs for the broad purpose of promoting racial and gender diversity, or only for the narrower purpose of remedying a case of discrimination.

The court has not yet agreed to hear a challenge to California's Proposition 209, which bars race and gender preferences in state contracting, employment and college admissions. In this case, *Coalition for Economic Equity v. Wilson*, the court would have to decide whether to uphold a lower court ruling that said nothing in the Constitution stops a state from passing such an initiative.

Opponents argue that the initiative violates the equal protection clause of the 14th Amendment. It would prevent the state from using affirmative action even to remedy blatant discrimination. Furthermore, they argue, the Supreme Court has specifically allowed — though increasingly restricted — the use of affirmative action for non-remedial purposes.

● **Campaign finance.** In *Federal Election Commission v. Akins*, the court will examine whether the government should designate any group that contributes $1,000 or more to a candidate as a political action committee, and require the group to disclose its funding sources. The FEC has adopted polices only requiring disclosure from groups whose major purpose is electioneering.

The case involves the American Israel Political Affairs Committee (AIPAC), a pro-Israeli lobbying group. Pro-Arab groups filed suit arguing that AIPAC is heavily in-

FILE PHOTO

The Supreme Court will hear at least one major affirmative action case in its new term, which begins Oct. 6.

volved in election politics, even though it does not qualify as a political action committee under the FEC definition. The D.C. Court of Appeals agreed. The high court may rule on the merits, or it may decide the Arab groups do not have standing to sue because they cannot show they were directly harmed by the FEC policy.

● **Participation in debates.** In *Arkansas Educational Television v. Forbes*, the court will examine whether a public television station can bar from a televised debate a third party congressional candidate the station deems not viable. The case centers on the government-supported nature of public broadcasting. Commercial stations have fairly broad latitude to make such decisions.

● **Sexual harassment.** In *Oncale v. Sundowner Offshore Services Inc.*, the court will examine whether sexual harassment can occur between members of the same sex. The case involves a worker on an offshore oil platform who claimed he was harassed by a male boss.

● **Copyright law.** In *Feltner v. Columbia Pictures Television*, the court will examine whether copyright infringement cases must be heard by a jury.

● **NEA grants.** In *National Endowment for the Arts v. Finley*, the court may rule on requirements that recipients of NEA grants follow "general standards of decency and respect for the diverse beliefs and values of the American public." The 9th U.S. Circuit Court of Appeals, based in San Francisco, ruled against these standards, saying they violate First Amendment rights to free speech. The government has asked for the Supreme Court to take the case, which it is likely to do.

● **School vouchers.** A challenge to school vouchers, which give parents public money to spend at private or parochial schools, is working its way through the courts in Ohio. It could reach the high court this term or next term. Opponents to vouchers argue that they violate the principle of separation of church and state.

reached the 3rd Circuit, that court took a restrictive approach to Title VII, ruling that the statute prohibits consideration of race for any purpose other than to remedy specific cases of discrimination. Discrimination was not the issue at the Piscataway school, the court said; Taxman lost her job because of a desire to promote diversity — and such "nonremedial" racial preferences are

not permitted.

Taxman's attorneys will argue that the 3rd Circuit was correct and that the Piscataway School Board — and other governments — have gone beyond what Title VII permits.

The Piscataway board argues that nothing in Title VII prohibits non-remedial affirmative action programs, adding that the 3rd Circuit opinion infringes on

constitutionally protected behavior. The board argues that its diversity policy enhances the educational experience and better prepares students for life in a pluralistic society.

It will try to show it has a compelling interest in these goals and that a diversity policy is the only way to reach them. If it can do this, it will have met the requirements the court has imposed on affirmative action programs in the past. State or local affirmative action policies must meet "strict scrutiny" by the courts, the toughest level of judicial review: They must take a targeted approach to meet a compelling policy goal.

The case has prompted some government flip-flopping. When it was before the U. S. District Court, the Justice Department under President George Bush sided with Taxman, arguing that a desire for diversity was no justification for dismissing someone.

When Bill Clinton was elected in 1992, his administration turned the government 180 degrees to oppose Taxman and support the school's diversity goals. It has since turned around again, now taking the same position as Bush's in a brief filed with the court.

If the Supreme Court affirms the entire 3rd Circuit ruling, it would be placing a significant restriction on affirmative action programs. The programs would be acceptable only as remedies to discrimination, and not as a way to meet broader social goals.

Most court observers expect something less: a further effort to set the parameters of non-remedial affirmative action programs, without banning them outright.

Proposition 209

Proposition 209 represents an even broader repudiation of affirmative action. It would ban race and gender considerations in all instances, notwithstanding strong evidence of discrimination. The only exception would be if a court-ordered remedial action. The 9th U.S. Circuit Court of Appeals, based in San Francisco, in finding Proposition 209 constitutional, ruled this summer that nothing in the Constitution bars a state from banning racial and gender preferences.

At the Supreme Court, opponents of Proposition 209 see an opportunity to persuade a narrow majority of justices to take their side. In its most recent affirmative action rulings — *City of Richmond v. Croson* and *Adarand Constructors Inc. v. Peña*— the court curtailed racial and gender preferences by eliminating specific numeric set-asides and subjecting all affirmative action programs to strict scrutiny.

But in both cases, the court carefully left open a window for non-remedial affirmative action. Key to winning a narrow majority to overturn Proposition 209, as well as the *Piscataway* ruling, will be Justice Sandra Day O'Connor,

who has often been a swing vote on affirmative action cases. She wrote the 5-4 majority opinion in *Adarand*. *(1995 Almanac, p. 6-38)*

"What 209 does is not just close the window," says Mark Rosenbaum, legal director of the ACLU of Southern California. "It locks it shut."

Opponents of Proposition 209 say their biggest fear is that the case will not be heard. They say they want the

REUTERS

Jesse Jackson, San Francisco Supervisor Mabel Teng and Mayor Willie Brown with protesters of Proposition 209 on Aug. 28.

court to rule on the use of affirmative action, particularly because states and municipalities around the country are gearing up to follow California's lead.

There are some indications, however, that the court may decline to hear the case. This summer it refused to issue a stay to stop Proposition 209 from going into effect while it is under challenge. Some legal scholars argue that denying a stay can indicate that the court does not want to hear a case.

In 1996, the court declined to hear a similar case, *Texas v. Hopwood*, involving an affirmative action program for admissions to the University of Texas.

And some legal scholars say the court will only want to deal with one major affirmative action case in a single term. "Whether they would want to take two big cases in one term, it's extremely hard to call," says Elliot Mincberg, legal director of People for the American Way, a liberal civil liberties group. "I think it could go either way."

A rejection of the case would leave the ultimate constitutionality of anti-preference measures such as Proposition 209 in legal limbo. The 9th Circuit ruling would form the legal precedent, but it would not necessarily mean the Supreme Court approved it or would not issue its own ruling in the future.

The current challenge to Proposition 209 asks the court to reject it on its face. If that fails, opponents are sure to challenge the way it is being implemented.

Nevertheless, if the court rejects the case, 26 states and numerous local governments will move ahead with similar proposals, according to the ACLU. This November, for example, a citywide ban on affirmative action is on the ballot in Houston.

Political Practices

Besides affirmative action programs, the court plans to look this term at several issues involving political practices. In *Arkansas Educational Television Commission v. Forbes*, it will delve into the First Amendment rights of a third-party congressional candidate denied the right to participate in a televised debate.

In *FEC v. Akins*, the court will examine whether a group that contributes more than $1,000 to political candidates should have to register as a political action committee and meet the Federal Election Commission's disclosure requirements.

And in *National Endowment for the Arts v. Finley*, it will likely take up decency standards imposed on grantees of the NEA. A group of grantees argues that the standards violate First Amendment rights to free expression.

What looks unlikely at this point is another re-evaluation of constitutional principles as sweeping as the court made in the 1996-97 term. Last year, the court's rulings on congressional power were its most significant since the New Deal.

In last term's gun law cases, *Printz v. U.S.* and *Mack v. U.S.*, the court said Congress had no right to require local police to conduct background checks on prospective gun buyers. That put teeth back into the 10th Amendment, which limits federal powers to those enumerated in the Constitution. In *City of Boerne v. Flores*, the court restricted Congress' power to enforce individual liberties through the 14th Amendment. *(Weekly Report, p. 1524)*

This term is focused less on the Constitution and more on state, federal and local laws, says University of Virginia Law Professor A.E. Dick Howard. Its docket includes cases on workplace harassment, the legality of high speed chases, even a dispute over the ownership of Ellis Island. "Call it the people's term," Howard said. ∎

SEPARATION OF POWERS

Supreme Court Dismisses Case Against Line-Item Veto Law

In a decision that has the potential to greatly strengthen President Clinton's hand in spending decisions, the Supreme Court has restored, at least for now, the line-item veto law passed last year.

The court on June 26 announced a 7-2 decision that reversed a lower court and dismissed a lawsuit brought by six members of Congress who argued that the Line-Item Veto Act unconstitutionally transferred too much lawmaking power to the president.

The court's majority decision, written by Chief Justice William H. Rehnquist, did not address the constitutional merits of the underlying law. Instead, the waters remain muddy. The case, *Byrd v. Raines*, was dismissed because the court found that the members of Congress who brought it lacked legal standing to sue. They had not suffered any injury under the law (PL 104-130), since the veto has yet to be used.

The court has always held that a plaintiff has standing if his case involves a "case or controversy" in which there has been a concrete personal injury. The plaintiffs, led by Sen. Robert C. Byrd, D-W.Va., argued that the mere existence of the law erodes their power as legislators, in part because the threat of the veto might be used to affect their votes and actions.

The court was not convinced. "Appellees' claim of standing is based on a loss of political power," Rehnquist wrote, adding that the plaintiffs in the case "have alleged no injury to themselves as individuals, the institutional injury they allege is wholly abstract and widely dispersed, and their attempt to litigate this dispute at this time and in this form is contrary to historical experience."

Clinton supported the line-item veto, as have presidents dating back to Ulysses S. Grant. He regains the as-yet-unused power just as the annual appropriations cycle is revving up and just as a bill containing multiple tax breaks — some of which might be eligible to be struck by the veto — passed both the House and Senate.

"I intend to use it whenever appropri-

Clinton

Byrd

ate, and I look forward to using it wisely," Clinton said in a statement. "With it, the president will be able to prevent Congress from enacting special-interest provisions under the cloak of a 500- or 1,000-page bill."

What Congress passed last year was not a true line-item veto. A true line-item veto would permit the president, unless overridden by a two-thirds vote in both House and Senate, to strike certain provisions of bills while letting the rest of the measure become law. But such an explicit veto would require amending the Constitution, a virtually impossible job.

Instead, congressional budget hawks devised an "enhanced rescissions" procedure that would permit the president to "cancel" specific dollar items in appropriations bills, new entitlement spending or certain narrowly targeted tax breaks. Such cancellations would take effect unless Congress passed a bill to reverse them; it is assumed that the president would then veto any such measure.

Even though Clinton has regained the power — which was blocked by U.S. District Court Judge Thomas P. Jackson in April — it is not certain that he will be able to wield it for long. Another lawsuit is certain to be filed once the new power is exercised. But the next lawsuit will likely be filed by a local government, citizen or group that has a direct stake in a spending item killed by the president, rather than a member of Congress, said attorney Alan B. Morrison, who argued Byrd's case.

"Losing on a technicality just delays the time when the court must decide this fundamental issue," said Sen. Carl Levin, D-Mich., another plaintiff.

The Supreme Court's decision came as a bitter pill to Byrd and his colleagues, who had won a resounding victory in April from Jackson. Jackson accepted the lawmakers' argument that the law is unconstitutional because it changes the procedure laid out in the Constitution for making law. *(Weekly Report, p. 833)*

When Congress sends the president a bill for his signature, the president must sign it, veto it or let it become law without his signature. The new "enhanced rescissions" power would, according to Judge Jackson, permit "the president to repeal duly enacted provisions of federal law."

The plaintiffs were Sens. Byrd, Levin, and Daniel Patrick Moynihan, D-N.Y., and former Sen. Mark O. Hatfield, R-Ore. (1967-97); and Reps. Henry A. Waxman, D-Calif., and David E. Skaggs, D-Colo.

Justices John Paul Stevens and Stephen G. Breyer dissented from Rehnquist's opinion. Stevens said he would have found the law unconstitutional; Breyer said the plaintiffs had standing, but he did not express any views on the constitutional merits.

A New Dynamic

The decision has the potential to give Clinton great leverage in the upcoming round of spending bills that are making their way toward the House floor. Most of that leverage will come in September, when the bills are in conference and negotiators split their differences and make trade-offs. After the conference is completed and passed, the president will have the ability to revisit the bill. A threat to veto an item dear to Congress might give Clinton the upper hand.

"It changes the dynamic of last-minute negotiations on appropriations, clearly," said House Appropriations Committee Chairman Robert L. Livingston, R-La., who voted for the bill last year but makes little effort to disguise how much he dislikes it.

On the other hand, the new power is a double-edged sword. Any use of the veto threatens to start fights with Congress that the president might be wise to avoid. And since any vetoed item is

Excerpts of the Opinions

From the majority opinion, written by Chief Justice William H. Rehnquist:

The District Court for the District of Columbia declared the Line Item Veto Act unconstitutional. On this direct appeal, we hold that appellees lack standing to bring this suit, and therefore direct that the judgment of the District Court be vacated and the complaint dismissed. . . .

We have consistently stressed that a plaintiff's complaint must establish that he has a "personal stake" in the alleged dispute, and that the alleged injury suffered is particularized as to him. . . . We have also stressed that the alleged injury must be legally and judicially cognizable. This requires, among other things, that the plaintiff have suffered "an invasion of a legally protected interest which is . . . concrete and particularized," and that the dispute is "traditionally thought to be capable of resolution through the judicial process." . . .

In the light of this overriding and time honored concern about keeping the Judiciary's power within its proper constitutional sphere, we must put aside the natural urge to proceed directly to the merits of this important dispute and to "settle" it for the sake of convenience and efficiency. Instead, we must carefully inquire as to whether appellees have met their burden of establishing that their claimed injury is personal, particularized, concrete, and otherwise judicially cognizable. . . .

They have not alleged that they voted for a specific bill, that there were sufficient votes to pass the bill, and that the bill was nonetheless deemed defeated. In the vote on the Line Item Veto Act, their votes were given full effect. They simply lost that vote. Nor can they allege that the Act will nullify their votes in the future. . . . In the future, a majority of Sena-

Rehnquist

tors and Congressmen can pass or reject appropriations bills; the Act has no effect on this process.

In addition, a majority of Senators and Congressmen can vote to repeal the Act, or to exempt a given appropriations bill (or a given provision in an appropriations bill) from the Act; again, the Act has no effect on this process. . . .

In sum, appellees have alleged no injury to themselves as individuals, the institutional injury they allege is wholly abstract and widely dispersed, and their attempt to litigate this dispute at this time and in this form is contrary to historical experience.

From the dissenting opinion of Justice John Paul Stevens:

The Line Item Veto Act purports to establish a procedure for the creation of laws that are truncated versions of bills that have been passed by the Congress and presented to the President for signature. If the procedure were valid, it would deny every Senator and every Representative any opportunity to vote for or against the truncated measure that survives the exercise of the President's cancellation authority.

Because the opportunity to cast such votes is a right guaranteed by the text of the Constitution, I think it clear that the persons who are deprived of that right by the Act have standing to challenge its constitutionality.

Moreover, because the impairment of that constitutional right has an immediate impact on their official powers, in my judgment they need not wait until after the President has exercised his cancellation authority to bring suit.

Finally, the same reason that the respondents have standing provides a sufficient basis for concluding that the statute is unconstitutional.

---

dedicated to deficit reduction and cannot be spent on other programs, there is incentive all around to avoid the use of the new power.

In addition, there are any number of ways Congress might evade the new power if it chooses. For example, since the new power is granted via an ordinary law, legislative riders could be attached to any spending bill that would exempt certain high-priority or controversial items — or even the entire law.

"Theoretically, we could do that sort of thing" and exempt items from the veto, said Skaggs. "As a practical and political matter, I kind of doubt it."

In any event, if such riders were attached to appropriations bills, they would have to be protected by the House Rules Committee, where Chairman Gerald B.H. Solomon, R-N.Y., is one of the foremost supporters of the veto. Otherwise, they could be stripped on a point of order because they would represent authorizing legislation on an appropriations bill.

The most immediate test of the new law may come on the tax bill currently before both chambers. Both versions (S 949, HR 2014) contain numerous special-interest provisions, some of which might be eligible to be canceled by Clinton.

Under the line-item veto law, any tax break handed out to 100 or fewer beneficiaries can be "canceled" by the president. But in a process that has been compared to the fox guarding the henhouse, any such "limited tax benefit" can be vetoed only after the Joint Tax Committee — whose members comprise the senior members of the tax-writing committees — have determined which provisions, if any, are eligible to be killed. Joint Tax will have to scrutinize the tax bill that is presented to Clinton for any such special-interest tax breaks; if there are none, it must certify that that is the case.

The way the law is worded, there are many ways to write the tax bill to protect tax provisions from the veto pen.

And, while the veto in theory can be used against new or increased spending on entitlements like Medicare and Medicaid, any such spending contained in the budget bills (HR 2015, S 947) that passed the House and Senate on June 25 is unlikely to face a Clinton veto.

Instead, it will likely be the appropriators who will have to wrangle with a resurgent Clinton armed with new power to kill congressional priorities. "I really wonder whether anyone up here realizes how much leverage we've given [Clinton]," said a top Livingston aide. ■

Clinton Weighs Politics, History In Decision To Use Veto Power

While president says he wants to avoid slicing negotiated provisions, several narrow tax benefits make administration's 'hit list'

Ⅰn theory, the line-item veto is simple. It gives President Clinton an unprecedented opportunity to weed out objectionable spending or tax provisions without sacrificing an entire bill.

But in reality, Clinton's historic choice of when and where to use this new power is one of the most complex judgments he has ever faced.

Legal and policy questions plagued Clinton as he reviewed a list of 79 narrowly focused tax provisions eligible for veto in the bill he signed Aug. 5 (PL 105-34). His chief dilemma: whether to use the power to kill any of those tax breaks — and provoke a constitutional challenge on what he understands to be weak legal ground — or to wait until the fall to deploy the veto against a target-rich wave of appropriations bills.

He also faced serious political considerations. Most important, should he pick fights with Congress over tax provisions that, when compared with the size of the huge spending and tax bills, are relatively insignificant? Or if he fails to use the veto, will congressional Republicans view him as weak when he confronts them on the 13 pending appropriations bills for fiscal 1998?

Perhaps the only easy part of Clinton's decision was knowing that, whatever narrow provisions he vetoed, he would win strong public approval. Polls show taxpayers stand ready to applaud the elimination of any special-interest benefit. And any egregious example of "pork barrel" spending knifed from an appropriations bill will clearly give him the upper hand in a public-relations battle with Congress.

CQ Weekly Report Aug. 9, 1997

DOUGLAS GRAHAM

Clinton gives speech on South Lawn before signing budget measures Aug. 5.

Ultimately, the substance of what would fall to the veto paled beside the historic importance of the act itself. If upheld by the courts — and legal experts say that is a big "if" — the line-item veto will stand alongside the powers to declare war and to claim executive privilege as one of the premier prerogatives Clinton is entrusted to nurture and pass along to his successors.

Pen at the Ready

Clinton, who has until midnight Aug. 11 to strike items from the reconciliation bills, appeared eager to wield his new power. Although he had received only cursory briefings on veto options at the time, he said at a press conference Aug. 6 that he expected to use the veto on the tax bill. "I am anticipating that there will be some things that I would want to exercise it on," he said.

Clinton said he wanted to avoid striking any provision that had been agreed to in negotiations with Congress, but he expected there would be one or more items to veto. "I will just go down and evaluate them and decide whether I think that they are sufficiently objectionable that they should be vetoed," Clinton said.

As it turned out, the majority of the 79 "limited tax benefits" identified by the Joint Committee on Taxation proved entirely defensible on policy grounds. The veto law (PL 104-130) charges that panel with isolating provisions that benefit 100 or fewer taxpayers, or "transition rules" that help 10 or fewer taxpayers. *(Weekly Report, p. 1918)*

By Aug. 8, Clinton aides reduced the number of potential targets to a handful. Their hit list included:

● A reduction in the tax on hard apple cider so that it would be taxed at the same rate as beer. It is now taxed at the higher rate levied on wine. Estimated revenue loss over five years: $3 million.

● Permission for the transfer of assets held in a charitable trust to an employee stock ownership plan without paying taxes on the value. This had been pushed for years by the estate of wealthy Texas executive Charles Sammons. Five-year cost: $23 million.

● Deferral of taxes on the sale of food-processing facilities to farmer-owned cooperatives. This was sought by Texas businessman Harold C. Simmons, who had sugar-beet processing plants he wanted to sell. Five-year cost: $84 million.

● A break that would give state and local officials who operate fee-based licensing offices more favorable tax treatment for expenses. The measure, pushed by Senate Majority Leader Trent Lott on behalf of a county clerk in his home state of Mississippi, would apply to taxes paid back to 1987. Five-year cost: $27 million.

● A refund to Amtrak of taxes paid before 1971 by the railroads that merged their passenger operations to form the

'A True Milestone for Our Nation'

On a nearly perfect Washington summer day, with the skies clear, flags flying and a military band playing, President Clinton on Aug. 5 signed the historic spending and tax reconciliation bills that Congress passed on July 30 and 31.

Clinton took the opportunity to present a vision of the United States as, once again, a shining city on a hill and, along with Speaker Newt Gingrich, R-Ga., heralded the bills as a victory for bipartisanship.

The two bills (PL 105-33, PL 105-34) are touted as balancing the budget by 2002 at the same time that they put into effect a $95 billion net tax cut aimed at middle-income families and investors and expand access to children's health care.

Clinton described the bills as "a true milestone for our nation" and then — in rhetoric recalling the 19th century description of the British Empire as a country on which the sun never set — went on to say that the legislation puts the United States in a position of strength as it enters the 21st century. "It wasn't so very long ago that some people looked at our nation and saw a setting sun. . . . The sun is rising on America again," he said.

"For too long, it seemed as if America would not be ready for the new century, that we would be too divided, too wedded to old arrangements and ideas. . . . After years in which too many people doubted whether our nation would ever come together again . . . we set off on a new economic course," Clinton said.

Gingrich hailed the unusual bipartisanship that led to the bills' completion. With striking magnanimity for a man often viewed as a strict partisan, Gingrich gave credit to Clinton, Vice President Al Gore and their families, as well as White

DOUGLAS GRAHAM

House Chief of Staff Erskine Bowles and Treasury Secretary Robert E. Rubin for taking the steps needed to make a deal work. "Their willingness this year, coming off their victory, to reach out a hand and say let's work together, was the key from which everything else grew."

Gingrich went on to promise to work with Clinton on the toughest issue likely to confront the government in coming years: overhauling the federal entitlements of Social Security and Medicare, the federal health insurance for the elderly. And his comments signaled to critics in his own party that Gingrich plans to be in Congress and presumably to be Speaker through 2000.

"I pledge right here, working with the president, that we will . . . enact in 1999 the right savings and the right steps to reform the system for the Baby Boomers and their children," Gingrich said.

One day after the signing ceremony, Clinton announced that his Office of Management and Budget (OMB) had revised its deficit projection for fiscal 1997 to $37 billion, down from the $67 billion projected just last May. And Clinton said that the budget agreement would lead to a $20 billion surplus in fiscal 2002.

The Congressional Budget Office did OMB one better, projecting a 1997 deficit of $34 billion. Either figure would make this year's deficit the lowest in 23 years.

Despite Clinton's announcement, OMB officials said they were not yet ready to release their much-awaited "mid-session review" of the economy, which was due in July. The administration had stalled the report's release during budget negotiations.

now-troubled carrier. Five-year cost: $2.3 billion.

As they pared the list, administration aides fielded phone calls from members of Congress and lobbyists who feared for provisions they had worked hard to get in the bill. It quickly became clear that key Democrats as well as Republicans had much at stake.

"I don't like the line-item veto. . . . I worked hard to put some things in the bill. Who knows better than I do what the people need?" said New York Rep. Charles B. Rangel, the ranking Democrat on the Ways and Means Committee, whose favorites included a provision involving advance refunding of bonds issued by the Virgin Islands.

The provision to help manufacturers of hard cider had the support of senior

Sens. Daniel Patrick Moynihan, D-N.Y., and Patrick J. Leahy, D-Vt., as well as a number of House lawmakers of both parties from apple-growing states.

Caught in the crossfire were the two provisions identified with wealthy Texans. The break for farmers' cooperatives that buy food-processing equipment was portrayed as a hefty tax break to Simmons, who is a big GOP donor. But if Clinton vetoed that, could he let go the provision that would help the Sammons estate transfer assets to an employee stock ownership plan? That was ultimately pushed into the bill by Senate Minority Leader Tom Daschle of South Dakota, which is home to a subsidiary of Sammons Enterprises Inc.

Clinton and his aides also had to confront a larger political dilemma. The

budget deal was approved by overwhelming margins of both parties and has been heralded as the pinnacle of bipartisanship. If Clinton vetoed some provisions in the package, House Speaker Newt Gingrich, R-Ga., and other legislators said, it would cast a pall over the spirit of the budget deal.

"There are some things I didn't like in this deal, but the fact is, I signed on to it," said Frank R. Lautenberg of New Jersey, ranking Democrat on the Senate Budget Committee.

Militating for use of the veto were some Democrats who said this was the ideal opportunity to show Republicans that Clinton will not shrink from appropriations battles to come.

"To the extent that what the president does on the tax bill is a shot across the bow, it may restrain what people put in the appropriations bills over the next few months," said California Rep. Vic Fazio, chairman of the House Democratic Caucus.

Tobacco Not Targeted

The Joint Tax list included a number of popular tax breaks that no one thought of as "limited tax benefits." Furthermore, for all the items that showed up on the list, there were a couple of big ones left off.

A big break to the tobacco industry was not on the list, even though the provision would have the effect of reducing by $50 billion or more the industry's proposed settlement with state attorneys general that is now being reviewed by Congress. The explanation: It has no effect unless and until the tobacco agreement becomes law, according to Kenneth J. Kies, staff director of the Joint Tax Committee.

Also left off the list was a provision that benefits Amway Corp.'s overseas subsidiaries. Kies said that benefit actually accrues to the company's shareholders, of which there are more than 100.

On the list was the popular research and development tax credit, which is designed to make early-stage research more affordable, and the "orphan drug" tax credit, which gives an incentive to companies to manufacture costly drugs for patients with rare diseases.

Why were they on the list? Far fewer than 100 pharmaceutical firms make orphan drugs. And a company can carry forward the research credit for use in future tax years. But since it was renewed for just 13 months, only a handful of companies are likely to be claiming it much beyond that.

The list was based on dozens of similarly technical assumptions by the Joint Tax Committee about how businesses and individuals would use certain measures. Kies insisted that political considerations were not a factor.

Constitutional Quicksand

Experts have profound doubts about the constitutionality of the new line-item law — especially if it is used to kill tax breaks instead of spending items. Opponents of the law say it bestows on the president authority to rewrite laws after Congress has completed action, a legislative power that can only be bestowed by amending the Constitution. The law has already been struck down by a federal judge, only to be revived on a technicality by the Supreme Court. (*Weekly Report, p. 1498*)

Lawyers on all sides agree that the veto is on its shakiest legal ground when applied against tax provisions. When defending the veto, the Justice Department relied heavily on the flexibility the president has had in spending money provided by Congress.

"From the beginning of the Republic, Congress has frequently conferred upon the president substantial discretion over the expenditure of appropriated funds," the Justice Department's brief said.

That has not been the case with tax bills. "On an appropriation, [proponents of the veto] argue that the president has

DOUGLAS GRAHAM

Lott and Gingrich shake hands during Aug. 1 signing ceremony in Statuary Hall.

received the power not to spend money," said attorney David H. Thompson, who worked on the challenge to the law. On tax provisions, "he's essentially going into the U.S. Code and ripping out a page."

The Justice Department is clearly uncomfortable with the idea of defending the veto on the tax side. Its initial brief to the Supreme Court did not mention tax issues; a later "reply brief" said the cancellation of limited tax benefits is a "delegation of discretionary authority." But the same brief argued that, "even if the Act's provisions regarding limited tax benefits were to be found constitutionally deficient, that result would not affect the validity of the rest of the Act."

Students of the veto had predicted that Clinton would threaten its use as a way to win concessions in other parts of the legislation, but sources said the subject never came up during the protract-

ed talks between the administration and Congress over the reconciliation bills.

Rescissions Vs. Vetoes

Clinton was not given a line-item veto as it is traditionally known or as it is used by the 43 governors who are armed with versions of it.

Under a traditional line-item veto, the executive can strike individual items or lines or words from bills that he wants to sign. But amending the Constitution to granting the president such power proved a politically impossible task.

Instead, Republicans devised a way to strengthen the president's ability to propose rescissions of spending from already enacted appropriations bills. Under the framework of the law, presidentially proposed rescissions take effect automatically, unless Congress passes a bill to block them. The president would certainly veto any such bill. (*1996 Almanac, p. 2-28*)

The new power also permits the president to "cancel" limited tax provisions and new entitlement spending.

Furthermore, the new law contains a requirement that any savings from a vetoed item must be used to reduce the deficit and cannot be grabbed by appropriators and spent later. This deficit-reduction "lockbox" creates incentives for Clinton and Congress to work together to avoid many vetoes in order to make full use of the pool of money available for discretionary spending.

The veto is to expire in 2005. ∎

Political Participation

In this section, CQ editors present a range of articles on the major participants in American politics: candidates, voters, political parties, and interest groups.

For many years local political office was a stepping-stone to state-level office, which in turn was the proving ground for candidates to federal office. Seldom did a candidate with no prior political experience run for Congress. By the same token, rarely did a well-known, prospective candidate with a good chance of winning federal office turn down the opportunity to run. But today both the Democratic and Republican Parties are having trouble recruiting strong candidates for U.S. House and Senate races. In the first article in this section, CQ editors delve into the possible causes of this phenomenon.

Candidates and parties appeal to voters on the basis of the positions they take on different issues. With the budget deficit fast nearing zero, Democrats and Republicans are losing a defining issue. Staking out a position on an issue, however, can cost as many votes as it wins, especially when the electorate is of "neither one mind nor one heart."

In a look ahead to the 1998 elections, CQ editors divine a more favorable outlook for the women who were elected to the Senate in 1992.

Money is the taproot of politics, without which candidates and parties could not spread their messages. And nothing engenders as much passion as campaign finance reform, yet it invariably falls victim to zero-sum politics: any reform would necessarily impair one party more than another, rendering compromise all but unattainable. Money problems are only one issue facing the Democratic Party. Its two strongest constituencies historically—the labor movement and urban voters—are declining in strength and numbers. Urban flight to the suburbs has made it critically important to the Democrats that every potential urban voter be counted, hence the importance of the census. To maximize their relevance, both parties are adopting marketing strategies.

The focus of *Guide* editors then turns from electoral politics to interest group politics. The tobacco lobby, long a well-funded powerhouse on Capitol Hill, is being forced by the prevailing political climate to compromise in order to achieve its goals. But lobbying need not be high profile to be effective. The more obscure home builders lobby successfully backed a law to give home builders and property owners direct access to federal courts when their development plans run afoul of local zoning ordinances. The final article in this section turns the traditional lobbying paradigm on its head. Instead of private organizations initiating a lobby campaign against a piece of legislation, congressional opponents of a bill have staked out a position and are hoping to gain the support of the lobbies.

CANDIDATE RECRUITMENT

With Major Issues Fading, Capitol Life Lures Fewer

Both parties are struggling to fill campaign rosters for '98 races as potential candidates find reasons for staying home

Here's a scenario Mark Twain might have found amusing: The 106th Congress could be the first to have two Tom Sawyers — except that one is not sure he wants to leave home just yet.

The House's current Tom Sawyer, an Ohio Democrat, is expected to seek a seventh term in his Akron-based district in 1998. But the prospective second Tom Sawyer, the leader of the Democratic minority in the Kansas House, has been resisting party recruiters' efforts to lure him into federal politics.

After more than a decade in the legislature representing a low-income district in Wichita, Sawyer may have gone about as far as he can go in Kansas (where statewide elections are as Republican as ever). His salary is about $17,000 a year.

So, as he turns 40 in 1998, this particular Tom Sawyer might decide to seek his fortune in the wider world by taking on two-term Republican Todd Tiahrt in the Wichita-based 4th Congressional District. Tiahrt upset longtime Democratic Rep. Dan Glickman (now the secretary of Agriculture) in 1994 but was re-elected with just 50.1 percent of the vote in 1996.

Sawyer, however, has yet to be convinced that his future is in Washington. And in that he is far from alone.

In Washington state, the GOP is eagerly seeking a candidate to succeed Rep. Linda Smith, who is running for the Senate. So far, the one Republican willing to run is the man Smith humbled as a write-in candidate in the 1994 primary.

In Georgia, Democrats think they can

CQ Weekly Report Oct. 25, 1997

Riley **Aderholt** **Shimkus**

Watkins **Hill** **Cannon**

GOP Frosh: Home Free?

Eight of the House Republicans first elected in 1996 captured formerly Democratic districts by close margins (none had more than 52.4 percent of the vote). On the numbers, they would seem natural targets for Democrats in 1998. But six of the eight have yet to draw a Democratic challenger: Bob Riley and Robert B. Aderholt of Alabama, John Shimkus of Illinois, Rick Hill of Montana, Christopher B. Cannon of Utah and Wes Watkins of Oklahoma (who previously served as a Democrat, 1977-1991). The other two, Anne M. Northup of Kentucky and Kenny Hulshof of Missouri, will probably be favored over the opponents who have declared against them to date.

recoup some of the losses they have suffered in the 1990s but are having trouble getting their best horses to run.

In Massachusetts, where Republicans now have no congressional seats, potentially vulnerable Democratic incumbents could go unopposed.

All over the country, both parties are finding that peace, prosperity and divided government have muted the vox populi. At the same time, the idea of life in Congress or on the campaign trail appears to have lost some of its appeal.

The frustration begins on the Senate front, where both Democrats and Re-

publicans are kicking themselves in advance over their inability to field top-flight candidates for seats that are, or ought to be, in play. *(Weekly Report, p. 2048)*

Of the 29 Senate incumbents expected to seek re-election next year, only a handful have as yet drawn a truly threatening rival. The GOP has more than 30 governorships for the first time in a generation, but so far it has persuaded only one current or former governor to run for the Senate in 1998. *(Weekly Report, p. 1590)*

Recruiters for House races are struggling too. First-choice candidates have queued up for the seats to be vacated by retirements, and each party has found some strong second-chance candidates among challengers who came close to beating incumbents in 1996.

But once the obvious targets have been accounted for, the crowd of potential candidates thins out quickly. In at least a dozen districts where the current seat-holder won with 52 percent of the vote or less in 1996, no one has stepped forward to carry the opposition party banner in 1998.

With the peacetime economy still soaring, and with violent crime rates and welfare rolls declining, 1998 is shaping up as a good year to be an incumbent — probably the best since the 1980s.

"There's no sign of any kind of potential political upheaval, and that should serve incumbents of both parties very well," said Gary Jacobson, an expert on House elections at the University of California, San Diego. "When you have divided government in reasonably good times, you're going to have stasis. There's no one to be angry at."

Plenty of time remains for the political landscape to change. But in this cycle thus far, the one overarching event has been the cease-fire in the perennial budget wars.

That midsummer deal struck by Congress and President Clinton still has its loud critics in both parties. Nonetheless, the impending disappearance of the deficit itself (accomplished largely through the growth of the economy and consequent tax revenues) has contributed to a sense of comparatively peaceful coexistence. (*Weekly Report, p. 1831*)

Meanwhile, there has been no issue so salient as the attempted health care overhaul in the 103rd Congress, no gun rights vote, no budget deal to be labeled "the largest tax increase in history" and no House bank scandal or government shutdown. In sum, nothing has occurred that could roil the waters sufficiently to create a national tide in either major party's direction.

"It's going to be very hard for challengers to convince voters to throw the rascals out from either party," Jacobson said.

Throughout the first year of the 105th Congress, there have been issues that appeared to have strong potential as political rallying points. But neither the campaign finance scandals nor the $368.5 billion settlement between the states and the tobacco industry has sparked widespread interest outside the Beltway. The partial-birth abortion issue and campaign finance overhaul are more likely to matter to voters who were already activists on one side or the other.

The GOP thought it had a ready-made winner in the issue of IRS reform, but even that traditional Republican target may now have to be shared with Democrats, who have picked up the anti-tax theme with unusual agility this month.

In an era of similar objectives and forced cooperation, it is hard to imagine an aroused electorate on Election Day.

"Rather than advocating major reforms, both Clinton and the Republican House are recommending incremental change, and incremental change doesn't excite," said Paul S. Herrnson, a government and politics professor at the University of Maryland and author of a standard book on House elections.

Officials in both camps concede that House elections are going to be a series of 435 local races, in contrast to the nationalized cycles of 1994 and 1996. Elections fought at the local level are far less likely to produce the kind of

Marginal Mandates

House Members With Lowest Share of Vote in 1996

Members traditionally have been considered vulnerable if re-elected with less than 55 percent of the vote. By that benchmark, 96 members of the current House would be considered tempting targets. Among them are 51 members (listed below) who received 52 percent of the vote or less, including more than a dozen who received less than 50 percent in multi-candidate contests. The low percentages were particularly common in California (7) and other states where alternative parties receive substantial fractions of the vote. Where members have served non-consecutive terms, their first year of election is noted, followed by the years they were elected as non-incumbents.

Member	District	1996 Vote Share	First Elected
Bob Riley	R-Ala. (3)	50.9	1996
Robert B. Aderholt	R-Ala. (4)	50.0	1996
J.D. Hayworth	R-Ariz. (6)	47.6	1994
Frank Riggs	R-Calif. (1)	49.6	1990/1994
Ellen O. Tauscher	D-Calif. (10)	48.6	1996
Walter Capps	D-Calif. (22)	48.4	1996
Brad Sherman	D-Calif (24)	50.4	1996
James E. Rogan	R-Calif. (27)	49.9	1996
George E. Brown Jr.	D-Calif. (42)	50.5	1962/1972
Loretta Sanchez	D-Calif. (46)	46.8	1996
Sam Gejdenson	D-Conn. (2)	51.6	1980
Jim Maloney	D-Conn. (5)	52.0	1996
Nancy L. Johnson	R-Conn. (6)	49.6	1982
Dave Weldon	R-Fla. (15)	51.4	1994
Neil Abercrombie	D-Hawaii (1)	50.4	1990
Helen Chenoweth	R-Idaho (1)	50.0	1994
Jerry Weller	R-Ill. (11)	51.8	1994
Lane Evans	D-Ill. (17)	51.9	1982
John Shimkus	R-Ill. (20)	50.3	1996
John Hostettler	R-Ind. (8)	50.0	1994
Leonard L. Boswell	D-Iowa (3)	49.4	1996
Greg Ganske	R-Iowa (4)	52.0	1994
Vince Snowbarger	R-Kan. (3)	49.8	1996
Todd Tiahrt	R-Kan. (4)	50.1	1994
Anne M. Northup	R-Ky. (3)	50.3	1996
John F. Tierney	D-Mass. (6)	48.1	1996
Jo Ann Emerson	R-Mo. (8)	50.5	1996
Kenny Hulshof	R-Mo. (9)	49.4	1996
John Ensign	R-Nev. (1)	50.1	1994
John E. Sununu	R-N.H. (1)	50.0	1996
Charles Bass	R-N.H. (2)	50.5	1994
Bill Pascrell Jr.	D-N.J. (8)	51.2	1996
Michael Pappas	R-N.J. (12)	50.4	1996
Sue W. Kelly	R-N.Y. (19)	46.3	1994
Ted Strickland	D-Ohio (6)	51.3	1992/1996
Dennis J. Kucinich	D-Ohio (10)	49.1	1996
Bob Ney	R-Ohio (18)	50.2	1994
Wes Watkins	R-Okla. (3)	51.4	1976/1996
Elizabeth Furse	D-Ore. (1)	51.9	1992
Darlene Hooley	D-Ore. (5)	51.2	1996
Jon D. Fox	R-Pa. (13)	48.9	1994
Phil English	R-Pa. (21)	50.7	1994
Max Sandlin	D-Texas (1)	51.6	1996
Ron Paul	R-Texas (14)	51.1	1976/1984/1996
Charles W. Stenholm	D-Texas (17)	51.6	1978
Christopher B. Cannon	R-Utah (3)	51.1	1996
Jack Metcalf	R-Wash. (2)	48.5	1994
Linda Smith*	R-Wash. (3)	50.2	1994
Adam Smith	D-Wash. (9)	50.1	1996
Mark W. Neumann*	R-Wis. (1)	50.9	1994
Jay W. Johnson	D-Wis. (8)	52.0	1996

Running for the Senate in 1998

1998 Congressional Primary Dates . . .

State	Primary Date (Runoff)	Filing Deadlines		
		Major Party Primary	Third Party Primary	Independents
Alabama	June 2 (June 30)	April 3	July 6	July 6
Alaska	Aug. 25	June 1	June 1	June 1
Am. Samoa	Nov. 3 (Nov. 17)	Sept. 1	Sept. 1	Sept. 1
Arizona	Sept. 8	June 25	June 25	June 25
Arkansas	May 19 (June 9)	March 31	Aug. 3	May 1
California	June 2	March 6	March 6	Aug. 7
Colorado	Aug. 11	June 8	July 14	July 14
Connecticut*	Sept. 15	Aug. 12	Aug. 12 (Third) Sept. 9 (Minor)	Aug. 12
Delaware	Sept. 12	July 31	Sept. 1	Sept. 1
D.C.	Sept. 15	July 8	Aug. 26	Aug. 26
Florida	Sept. 1 (Oct. 1)	May 8 (noon)	July 13	July 17
Georgia	July 21 (Aug. 11)	May 1	July 14 (noon)	July 14 (noon)
Guam	Sept. 5	July 7	n/a	July 7
Hawaii	Sept. 19	July 21	July 21	July 21
Idaho	May 26	April 3	April 3	April 3
Illinois	March 17	Dec. 15, 1997	Aug. 3	Dec. 15, 1997
Indiana	May 5	Feb. 20 (noon)	Aug. 3 (noon)	Aug. 3 (noon)
Iowa	June 2	March 13	Aug. 14	Aug. 14
Kansas	Aug. 4	June 10 (noon)	June 10 (noon)	Aug. 3 (noon)
Kentucky	May 26	Jan. 27	Aug. 11	Aug. 11
Louisiana	Oct. 3 (Nov. 3)	Aug. 21	Aug. 21	Aug. 21
Maine	June 9	March 15 (5 pm)	n/a	June 1 (5 pm)
Maryland	Sept. 15	July 6 (9 pm)	Aug. 3 (5 pm)	Aug. 3 (5 pm)
Massachusetts	Sept. 15	June 2	Aug. 25	Aug. 25
Michigan	Aug. 4	May 12 (4 pm)	Aug. 4	July 16 (4 pm)
Minnesota	Sept. 15	July 21	July 21	July 21
Mississippi	June 2 (June 23)	April 3	April 3	April 3
Missouri	Aug. 4	March 31 (5 pm)	July 27 (5 pm)	July 27 (5 pm)
Montana*	June 2	March 19	March 19 (Third) June 1 (Minor)	June 1

n/a Not applicable.

* A "third party" is one with regular ballot status and primaries akin to those of the two major parties.

turnover seen in the last three cycles — although there will be plenty of full-throttle races here and there.

Many will take place in districts with no incumbent. Idaho Republican Rep. Michael D. Crapo's Oct. 20 announcement that he will run for the Senate brings the total number of House members retiring or seeking other offices to 16. (*Weekly Report, p. 2561*)

In the past two election cycles, House retirements began with a similarly modest number: 16 as of Oct. 24, 1995 and 17 as of Oct. 24, 1993. In both cycles, however, the number of voluntary departees tripled before Election Day.

The retirement number appears less likely to balloon in 1998, due to the relatively short tenure of most current members. After years of upheaval — more than 60 percent of the current House is new in the 1990s — members are settling into their jobs. The next big turnover may come in the presidential election year of 2000, when some of the

more ardent supporters of term limits in the Republican Class of 1994 will hit their self-imposed six-year ceiling.

Having held their House majority into a second term for the first time since 1928, Republicans feel the wind of history at their backs. The New Deal election of 1934 was the only midterm cycle since the Civil War in which the president's party improved its standing in the House.

Still, Clinton's coattails proved short in 1996 — 91 districts that he carried sent a Republican to Congress — so comparatively few Democrats "lucked into" seats from which they can be easily ejected.

"I don't see the presidential party losing the number of seats the presidential party normally loses," predicted Sandy Maisel, chairman of the government department at Colby College in Maine and co-leader of a National Science Foundation study on candidate recruiting.

"I think it's going to be very hard to unseat many candidates this time around

and there will be a smaller number of retirements this year."

Where vacancies do occur, they often offer little chance of a takeover. Several of the districts that are being vacated in 1998 are so strongly partisan that even party officials grudgingly concede they are hopeless. For instance, the two Chicagoland seats that are being vacated by Republican Harris W. Fawell and Democrat Sidney R. Yates will almost certainly be retained by the party that currently holds them.

Nonetheless, the two parties will seek to gain ground where previous defenders have decamped. The two parties will make strong runs for each other's open seats in Kentucky, where Democrat Scotty Baesler and Republican Jim Bunning are giving up their House careers in favor of a shot at the Senate.

Democrats have their hearts set on capturing the Wisconsin seats being vacated by Republicans Scott L. Klug and Mark W. Neumann (who is running for

. . . And Filing Deadlines

State	Primary Date (Runoff)	Filing Deadlines		
		Major Party Primary	Third Party Primary	Independents
Nebraska	May 12	Feb. 15 (incumbents) March 1 (others)	Sept. 1	Sept. 1
Nevada	Sept. 1	May 18	June 26	Aug. 17 (5 pm)
New Hampshire	Sept. 8	June 12	Sept. 2	Sept. 2
New Jersey	June 2	April 9	n/a	April 9
New Mexico	June 2	March 25	July 14 (Minor)	July 14
New York	Sept. 15	July 16	July 16	Aug. 18
North Carolina	May 5 (June 2)	Feb. 2	n/a	June 26
North Dakota	June 9	April 10	March 31	Sept. 4
Ohio	May 5	Feb. 19	n/a	May 9
Oklahoma	Aug. 25 (Sept. 15)	Aug. 8 (5 pm)	n/a	Aug. 8 (5 pm)
Oregon	May 19	March 10	Aug. 25	Aug. 25
Pennsylvania	May 19	March 10	Aug. 3	Aug. 3
Puerto Rico**				
Rhode Island	Sept. 15	June 24	n/a	June 24
South Carolina	June 9 (June 23)	March 30 (noon)	n/a	Aug. 1
South Dakota	June 2 (June 16)	April 7	n/a	Aug. 4
Tennessee	Aug. 6	May 21 (noon)	n/a	May 21
Texas	March 10 (April 14)	Jan. 2	May 26	May 14
Utah	June 23	March 17	March 17	March 17
Vermont	Sept. 8	July 20	Sept. 17	Sept. 17
Virginia***	June 9	April 10	June 9	June 9
Virgin Islands	Sept. 8	Aug. 11	Aug. 11	Aug. 11
Washington	Sept. 15	July 31	July 10	July 10
West Virginia	May 12	Feb. 7	May 11	May 11
Wisconsin	Sept. 8	July 14	July 14	July 14
Wyoming	Aug. 18	June 5	Aug. 17	Aug. 25

** The election for Resident Commissioner to the House for Puerto Rico is held every four years, coinciding with presidential elections.

*** Virginia Republicans and Democrats usually nominate House and Senate candidates by convention rather than by primary.

Source: Federal Election Commission

Senate). Lydia C. Spottswood, who lost to Neumann by 2 percentage points in 1996, will take another shot at the open seat, which has also attracted interest from nearly a half-dozen Republicans.

In a similar case in Washington state, psychologist Brian Baird will run for the seat being vacated by Republican Rep. Linda Smith, another Senate candidate. Baird barely lost to Smith in 1996. But here, Republican recruiters are still beating the bushes around southwestern Washington for a top-tier opponent for Baird. So far, the field consists of Paul J. Phillips, a fill-in candidate who had the party ballot line in 1994 but still lost to late-starting Smith.

Republicans are also looking with longing at the downstate Illinois seat being vacated by Democrat Glenn Poshard, who is running for governor. But Democrats may be able hold the seat with state Rep. David D. Phelps, a longtime Poshard friend.

Like Poshard, Phelps takes a conservative line on social issues (both oppose abortion, and Phelps is a traveling gospel singer). And, even when he sounds familiar Democratic themes such as improving public schools and access to health care, he sounds like a Main Street Republican, stressing economic development over big government solutions.

"When you ask, how do we help health care and education, it doesn't take a rocket scientist to know that if you have a good economy you'll have good health care and schools," Phelps said.

Scandals and Rematches

Another soft spot in the armor of incumbency may be found where members are weakened by association with scandal. The Illinois GOP sees 1998 as their year to defeat Democrat Jerry F. Costello. Although his southern Illinois district takes in strongly Democratic territory in East St. Louis, Costello has been tarnished by the

conviction of his childhood friend and former business partner Amiel Cueto. Costello was named an "unindicted co-conspirator" in Cueto's obstruction of justice trial, and the investigation continues.

Bill Price, a physician and son of Costello's Democratic predecessor, Melvin Price (1945-1988), is pursuing the GOP nomination in Illinois' 12th District, as is former nurse Gail Kohlmeier.

The only other House member currently in hot water over ethics is California Republican Jay C. Kim. A number of Republicans have lined up to hold his staunchly GOP district, assuming despite his protestations to the contrary that he will step down following his January sentencing for campaign finance violations.

Even incumbents who have not suffered from missteps on ethics may be viewed as damaged goods if their last margin of victory was harrowing. The 1996 cycle produced a large number of narrow margins, including four of less than a thousand votes. *(Chart, p. 13)*

In such instances, a party may ask the near-winner to run again, assuming that name recognition will be high and fundraising easier. In Connecticut, for example, Democratic lawyer Charlotte Koskoff is running for a third time against Republican Nancy L. Johnson, having come within a percentage point of upsetting her in 1996. Koskoff hopes Johnson will be wounded by news reports that she sponsored a tax provision that benefited a local company in which she holds stock.

But it is also common for recruiters to favor a fresh face over a rematch, theorizing that a better candidate might have won the last time. For example, Republicans like their chances for the seat of retiring 17-term Democrat Lee H. Hamilton in southeastern Indiana's 9th District. But so far they have scrambled without success to recruit an alternative to former state Sen. Jean Leising, who lost twice to Hamilton and has ruffled many feathers in the Hoosier aviary.

Leising may not find the going much easier in 1998, as 9th District Democrats were able to recruit former state Rep. Baron P. Hill, who carried the district in an unsuccessful 1990 Senate bid.

Wide-Open California

Similarly, California Democrats hope to make further gains after their three-seat net pickup in 1996 by focusing on Republican Frank Riggs in the 1st District. Their top prospect in that northern coastal area, state Sen. Mike Thompson, would not run in 1996 but has announced he will do so in 1998. The problem is that the 1996 nominee, Michela Alioto, wants a rematch with Riggs and is raising money for a primary. When such a situation produces a primary, it can wind up strengthening the incumbent for the rematch.

Republicans hope to avoid primaries and concentrate on avenging close losses in several other Southern California districts, including the San Bernardino-based 42nd District, where veteran Democrat George E. Brown Jr. eclipsed Superior Court Judge Linda M. Wilde by 996 votes in 1996. Wilde is considering a rematch.

In the 46th District, former GOP Rep. Robert K. Dornan has filed preliminary papers for a challenge to Democrat Loretta Sanchez, who unseated him in a disputed election that is still under investigation. Dornan faces a

large field of other Republicans eager for a shot at Sanchez.

Looking at a map of congressional districts, it's easy to see why fewer seats are up for grabs this time around. The increasingly strong regional bases of the two parties have given them a strong fallback position but limited their forays beyond.

Costello   **Kim**

Under Ethics Clouds

The reconstituted House ethics committee has met only once in the 105th Congress, but two members have been enmeshed in legal difficulties during the months of moratorium on new ethics complaints. Third-term Republican Jay C. Kim of California has pleaded guilty to two misdemeanors in connection with an investigation of fundraising for his 1992 campaign. He will be sentenced in January, and could face six months in prison as well as substantial fines. Veteran Democrat Jerry F. Costello of Illinois, now in his fifth full term, was named an unindicted co-conspirator during the trial of a childhood friend and former business partner, who was convicted of obstruction of justice.

Northeastern Republicans, wishing to recoup some losses, dream of defeating either of the two Democrats who unseated Massachusetts Republicans in 1996, Jim McGovern and John F. Tierney. Former Republican Rep. Peter G. Torkildsen (1993-97) has already begun plotting his revenge bid against Tierney, while state Sen. Matthew J. Amorello is gunning for McGovern. But Bay State Republicans are still fishing for candidates against potentially vulnerable Democrats John W. Olver and Bill Delahunt.

Conversely, Republicans already own all but three seats in the interior West, urban districts in Phoenix and Tucson, Ariz., and Boulder and Denver, Colo. The GOP intends to make a serious if long shot run after the Boulder seat, being vacated by David E. Skaggs.

Meanwhile, Democrats are pining to regain the northern New Mexico seat they lost to Republican Rep. Bill Redmond following Bill Richardson's ap-

pointment as United Nations ambassador. They will also make a strong run for the Nevada seat of GOP Rep. John Ensign, assuming he decides to run for the Senate.

Democrats call former state Rep. Shelley Berkley, who has close ties to the gambling industry, "a recruitment success," and House Minority Leader Richard A. Gephardt, D-Mo., has reportedly promised her a seat on the Ways and Means Committee.

Similarly in the South, the GOP's greatest area of growth since Clinton's election in 1992, there are fewer seats ripe for the party's picking. With the exception of a few seats awaiting the eventual retirement of popular, or at least sturdy, Democratic incumbents, Republicans have already won the easy ones.

"Outside of Texas, what you're down to is one or two per state" that are live pickup possibilities, said Ed Brookover, political director of the National Republican Congressional Committee (NRCC). That contrasts, he said, with 1994, when a state such as North Carolina gave the GOP a net gain of four seats.

Democrats have hopes of regaining some of the ground they have lost in their old Southern base, and they plan to go after such targets as Alabama Republicans Robert B. Aderholt and Bob Riley — freshmen who won with about half the vote in 1996. But they have no announced candidate, as yet, against either.

They will also launch repeat attacks on such potentially vulnerable Republicans as Georgians Saxby Chambliss and Charlie Norwood, both members of the Class of 1994. Each finished with less than 53 percent of the vote or less in 1996, running in largely unfamiliar districts that had been freshly redrawn in answer to Supreme Court complaints about racial gerrymandering.

David Bell, Norwood's 1996 opponent, is considering a rematch, and national Democrats are high on the potential challenge state court Judge John Ellington is considering bringing against Chambliss.

But neither man has committed as yet. Democratic recruiters are having difficulty closing the sale with such potential candidates as Ellington and Sawyer of Kansas. A takeaway of just a dozen seats would return the Democrats to majority control, but the kind of people the recruiters look for often have something to lose if they run. Why not wait until the playing field may be more favorable, in 2000 or beyond? ■

A Balanced-Budget Deal Won, A Defining Issue Lost

Without the deficit as a rallying point, parties may be impelled to rethink their agendas and political rhetoric

Congress has decamped for its August recess having cleared legislation to balance the federal budget by 2002 and provide the first broad-based tax cut since 1981. Members will face a daunting question upon their return in September: What's left to fight over?

Republican majorities first elected in 1994 have achieved the centerpiece of their fiscal agenda — a balanced budget — and added their "crown jewel" of a $95 billion net tax cut over five years as well. They can tout a $500-per-child tax credit, a cut in the top individual tax rate on profits from the sale of stocks and other assets, and a significant increase in the estate tax exemption.

At the same time, President Clinton has what may be his greatest legislative triumph — perhaps his monument. Not only can he claim to have "set the nation's fiscal house in order," as he said July 29, but he can say he negotiated a winning deal in the bargain.

Clinton's team left the table with what he wanted on more of the details — the scope of the child tax credit, a new children's health initiative, restoration of welfare benefits for disabled legal immigrants and a score of other issues — than most in Congress expected when the overall compromise was roughed out in May. *(Weekly Report, p. 993)*

It is difficult to overestimate the psychological importance of bringing the budget towards balance for the first time in three decades, both for politicians in Washington and the nation at large. Economists may debate its significance in the overall economy, but deficit reduction has been the foremost political and policy challenge of the past decade.

This deal will doubtless be amended over the next five years of budget resolutions and reconciliation, and appropriations bills. If it retains a recognizable shape, today's dealmakers will have been vindicated. And if the deficit stays in its cage through the next recession or national

DOUGLAS GRAHAM

Clinton announces the balanced-budget agreement at the White House on July 29 as Gore, left, and Democratic lawmakers applaud.

emergency, policy will have shown its mastery of circumstance.

But while Washington awaits history's judgment of these questions, Congress must decide how to order its calendar and its priorities without the perennial preoccupation with the deficit.

From the standpoint of partisan politics, who will miss deficit spending more: those who wish they had more money to spend or those who wish they still had the deficit as an issue?

"It's going to be kind of tough to be a Republican, in a way," says former Rep. Fred Grandy (1987-95), an Iowa Republican who now heads Goodwill Industries International. "We stand to lose a major shibboleth in the 'tax-and-spend' issue."

Coupled with the end of the Cold War, which leaves few opportunities to hammer on foreign affairs, party-defining issues are getting harder to find. "It's been years now since the Berlin Wall has fallen," Grandy said. "That means going more into the social agenda for issues. It means going into local and personal issues that are by nature divisive."

Gerald Pomper, a professor of political science at Rutgers University's Eagleton Institute, sees a bipartisan paradox in the aftermath of a successful budget deal.

"It makes it tough to run a campaign for both parties," said Pomper. "It's hard to do the usual line about 'liberal big spenders,' and it's hard for the Democrats to talk about 'oppressors of the poor and the middle class' when, if anything, they've helped in the oppressing."

In the short run, Pomper said, the deal should help Republicans divert attention from recent leadership struggles and refocus their drive for more seats in the House in 1998.

"But for the long run it may be good for the Democratic Party," he added, "because what Clinton's been doing is taking away major issues for Republicans to run on — crime, welfare, wasteful spending."

Differences Among Democrats?

Certainly that is the way Vice President Al Gore will want to read the portents, having bet his political future in 2000 on

CQ Weekly Report Aug. 2, 1997

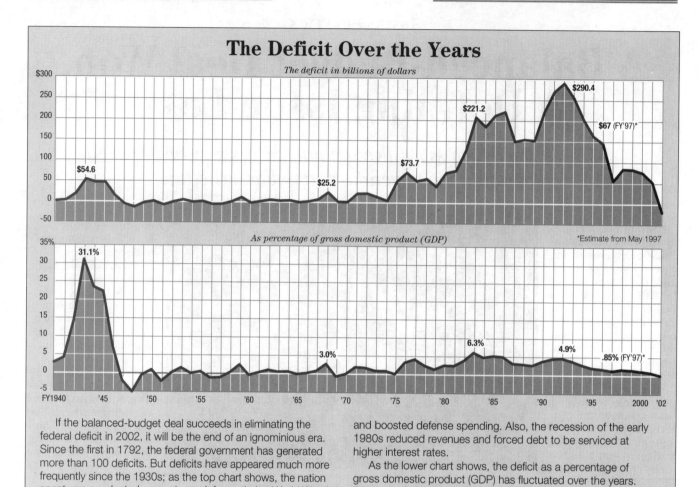

The Deficit Over the Years

The deficit in billions of dollars

$54.6

$25.2

$73.7

$221.2

$290.4

$67 (FY'97)*

*Estimate from May 1997

As percentage of gross domestic product (GDP)

31.1%

3.0%

6.3%

4.9%

.85% (FY'97)*

FY1940 '45 '50 '55 '60 '65 '70 '75 '80 '85 '90 '95 2000 '02

If the balanced-budget deal succeeds in eliminating the federal deficit in 2002, it will be the end of an ignominious era. Since the first in 1792, the federal government has generated more than 100 deficits. But deficits have appeared much more frequently since the 1930s; as the top chart shows, the nation spent unprecedented amounts on defense during World War II.

Deficits soared in the 1980s as the government cut taxes and boosted defense spending. Also, the recession of the early 1980s reduced revenues and forced debt to be serviced at higher interest rates.

As the lower chart shows, the deficit as a percentage of gross domestic product (GDP) has fluctuated over the years. That measure reflects the economy's ability to absorb the effects of deficit spending.

SOURCES: Congressional Budget Office, CQ calculations

Clinton's success. But there well may be other Democratic views on this score, including those of House Minority Leader Richard A. Gephardt, D-Mo., who has been conspicuously absent in the celebrations of the budget deal.

Gephardt, and perhaps other potential bidders for the 2000 presidential nomination, well may contend that Clinton and Gore purchased peace with the GOP at the expense of traditional Democratic constituencies.

GOP leaders, too, dispute the notion that Clinton stole their clothes. And they vow to unveil a substantial agenda in the coming months that will address issues of education and the workplace, as well as tax simplification, in hopes of appealing to families and owners of small businesses.

But it may be difficult in either the short-term or the long to arrive at anything as momentous as a balanced budget or as consensus-building as a tax cut.

"I'm not sure there is any overriding issue at this point," said James Campbell, a professor of political science at Louisiana State University. "This would have been the time for Jimmy Carter's 'malaise' speech. People are tuning out completely."

Well, not everyone. Among those who have not tuned out are the many social-conservative activists who have languished for years in the shadow of the fiscal issue. Ralph Reed, the former executive director of the Christian Coali-

tion, often warned that while religious conservatives supported a balanced budget and tax cuts, they expected reciprocal attention to their own agenda once the money matters were resolved.

Meanwhile, more secular conservatives who regard the budget deal as a sellout on principle will not sit idly by while the discussion moves on to other issues they find less compelling.

Stephen Moore, director of fiscal policy studies at the libertarian Cato Institute, has objected in the National Review to "the ludicrous statements by [Senate Majority Leader Trent] Lott and [Speaker Newt] Gingrich that 'Now that the budget is behind us we can move on to other issues.' " Moore compares this to a couple rushing through lovemaking so they can watch late-night television.

Campbell reads the "lesson of the 1990s elections" as a warning against overreaching or overpromising on the part of either party. Given this national mood, Campbell sees obvious risk in either party pressing its wish list.

"Of course, there are people who are not willing to lie low until things get clarified, people who don't want to bide their time," said Campbell. "But Newt realizes that is not a winning strategy. The party ought to be stronger after 1998, and maybe after 2000 it will have a president who will be more sympathetic."

THE DEFICIT DEAL

Looking to 2000 is a recurrent theme in some GOP leaders' public statements. Gingrich, R-Ga., has called for a comprehensive debate on ways to reduce the role of the federal government and to overhaul its tax system as part of the 2000 presidential campaign.

But defining the party's direction by means of a debate has its dangers too.

"There is peril in success," said Grandy. "To some degree we are victims of our own success right now. Without a major cause to champion, the factions of a party tend to fight among themselves."

The Foundation of Success

The relative ease with which Clinton and Congress produced the final piece of the balanced-budget effort makes it easy to forget the tortuous path that brought them to this point.

The budgeteers of 1997 were able only to draft a plan that satisfies staunch conservatives such as House Ways and Means Chairman Bill Archer, R-Texas, and liberals such as Sen. Edward M. Kennedy, D-Mass., because of the groundwork laid by the politically wrenching anti-deficit battles of 1990 and 1993.

DOUGLAS GRAHAM

Ohio Republican John R. Kasich, chairman of the House Budget Committee, talks about passage of the budget deal at a news conference July 30.

"When this administration took office, America's budget deficit was $290 billion and rising. We put in place a comprehensive economic strategy to cut the deficit and invest in our people," Clinton told the cheering gathering of Democrats on the White House's sunny lawn. "The budget plan adopted in 1993 made a large contribution to today's conditions in America: a strong economy, low inflationand a deficit that has already shrunk by more than 80 percent."

For Republicans, the agreement caps a balanced-budget and tax-cutting drive that has consumed them since they took over Congress in 1995, though it came through incremental change, not revolution.

"We are reversing the decades-old trend of bigger government, bigger taxes and bigger spending," said Senate Finance Committee Chairman William V. Roth Jr., R-Del. "Balancing the budget and cutting taxes are Republican ideas — make no mistake about that."

Banking on Economic Projections

And without a roaring economy churning out revenue greater than anyone expected, the separate, back-to-back celebrations by Democrats at the White House and by Republicans on the steps of the Capitol on July 29 would not have been possible. (A bipartisan signing ceremony is expected the week of Aug. 4.)

"The true hero is this stupendous economy. . . . The economy has done more to reduce the deficit than the politicians have," said Martha Phillips, executive director of the Concord Coalition, a balanced-budget advocacy group. Referring to the 1990 and 1993 packages, she adds, "This is probably No. 3 in terms of size and momentousness, but it's the last little piece."

For budget purists, the final product puts off until tomorrow the tough choices needed to address the crisis that will occur when the Baby Boomers begin to retire and claim Social Security and health care benefits. (While the Senate had voted to increase from 65 to 67 the eligibility age for Medicare coverage and take other dramatic cost-saving steps, the final bill does none of that, deferring to a bipartisan study commission.)

But for the overwhelming majority in Congress, which has been obsessed with the deficit since the 1980s, such long-term concerns were secondary to getting the deficit monkey off its back.

This budget pact, like many preceding it, is facing criticism for relying on economic predictions that there will not be a recession in the next five years, savings from discretionary appropriations that really do not bite until after the 2000 elections and one-time (and perhaps illusory) savings from auctions of the electromagnetic spectrum. The agreement will produce projected savings of $263 billion through 2002.

The real credit for bringing the budget near balance, say budget gurus of all stripes, rests with earlier efforts, including the much-maligned 1990 deal that helped send President George Bush home to Houston and the Democrats-only effort of 1993 that led to the GOP takeover of Congress. *(1990 Almanac, p. 111; 1993 Almanac, p. 85)*

When a Republican majority stormed the Capitol in 1995, the deficit stood at about $200 billion. To reach balance, they proposed to cut projected spending by $894 billion and cut taxes by $245 billion over seven years. At the end of the landmark 104th Congress, Republicans could point to two principal areas of savings: $49 billion from reduced domestic appropriations and another $55 billion estimated to flow from the welfare overhaul law (PL 104-193). About $16 billion in those welfare savings would be restored under this year's spending bill. *(1996 Almanac, p. 6-3)*

When Clinton and Congress returned to the budget after the 1996 election, they confronted an easier job, as well as a better sense of each other's boundaries. When 1997 began, the Office of Management and Budget (OMB) estimated the deficit for the current fiscal year at $126 billion. Now, the deficit could dip below $40 billion, fueled by an economy on overdrive.

Simply put, the final deal comes at a juncture in deficit politics at which it is possible to balance the budget with relatively little pain. And, at a critical juncture just before negotiators closed out their talks May 2, the Congressional Budget Office (CBO) adjusted its revenue estimates to make negotiators' jobs easier by assuming $225 billion more in revenues over five years than under prior estimates.

Ironically, among the politicians who stand to benefit most from the deal is Gingrich, who ascended through the GOP ranks in part by vilifying the politically wrenching 1990 and 1993 budget bills.

While those earlier deals did much of the heavy lifting, the GOP revolution changed the political dialogue. Clinton vetoed their balanced-budget bills and adroitly exploited their admitted over-aggressiveness, but Republicans clearly pulled him in their direction.

Satisfaction on Both Sides

In the end, both sides could claim significant victories. For Republicans, their list included:

● **Taxes.** Just getting a tax-cut bill signed by Clinton represents a major win for Republicans. But as Clinton noted, this tax package is small in comparison to President Ronald Reagan's 1981 tax cut, about one-tenth of the size after adjusting for inflation. But Republicans are able to reward key elements of their constituency. The pro-family wing gets the lion's share, the $500-per-child tax credit for families with adjusted gross incomes of up to $110,000 per year, estimated to cost $84 billion over five years.

Supply-siders received the crown jewel of the GOP agenda, a cut from 28 percent to 20 percent in the top individual rate for capital gains. While Republicans had to give up their proposal for discounting long-term profits to account for inflation while the asset was held, they won an even lower rate of 18 percent for assets held for five years.

Republicans also prevailed on provisions to ease inheritance taxes, a critical demand of small businesses and family farmers who have complained that estate taxes make it difficult to pass their businesses on to their heirs.

● **Medicare.** Republicans came under withering political attacks for their 1995 Medicare plan, which, among other things, would have capped total Medicare spending. This year's agreement takes a more gradual approach — but still

"It is a quick fix for the next few years, not a reliable blueprint for our nation's future."

— Richard A. Gephardt, D-Mo., House minority leader

represents some of the most important changes since the program started in 1965. Republicans retained many of the elements of their vetoed 1995 plan, such as opportunities for the elderly to establish "medical savings accounts." Most of the $115 billion in Medicare-related savings would come from reducing payments to hospitals and other health care providers and by integrating more managed care into the program.

For Clinton and congressional Democrats, the biggest victories included:

● **Taxes.** As expected, Clinton succeeded in killing a House drive to exempt from tax the portion of capital gains attributable to inflation. And he also succeeded in extending the $500-per-child tax credit to low-income workers who pay no federal income tax because of generous Earned Income Tax Credit benefits. They will be able to claim it against their payroll taxes for Social Security.

● **Children's health.** This expansion of health coverage for the children of low-income, uninsured parents was not included in Clinton's budget. But it was pushed hard by Kennedy, Senate Minority Leader Tom Daschle, D-S.D., and prominent Republicans such as Sen. Orrin G. Hatch, R-Utah. The May 2 budget agreement called for a $16 billion initiative, but the final spending bill will provide $24 billion, financed by a 10 to 15-cents-per-pack increase in the cigarette tax.

Unfinished Business

Even as lawmakers raced to go home and tout their accomplishments to their constituents, there were a few skunks at the picnic.

Gephardt attacked the final bills as unfairly tilted towards the wealthy and insufficiently aggressive on the deficit. "It is a quick fix for the next few years, not a reliable blueprint for our nation's future," Gephardt said July 29.

A handful of deficit hawks attacked the end result as a missed opportunity to address demographic and generational problems that loom when Baby Boomers start to retire. Three controversial Senate Medicare provisions — to gradually raise the eligibility age from 65 to 67, increase premiums for wealthier beneficiaries and impose a $5-per-visit co-payment on certain home health care benefits — all were dropped. Instead, Congress and Clinton agreed on a 17-member bipartisan commission to recommend the changes required to prepare Medicare for the next generation.

At the end of the day, however, the final measures were shaped by the politics of 1997: a Democratic president at the height of his popularity and a chastened Republican Congress that reads the split decision of last year's election as a mandate for incremental change. ∎

THE ELECTORATE

America's Heartland: Neither One Mind nor One Heart

Romanticized views aside, rural voters remain among least predictable as they struggle with economic pressures and divisive social issues

The mere mention of rural America conjures up images of furrowed fields and village squares, but this huge geographic sector of the country is hardly monolithic.

The variety can be seen in the differing profiles of a few representative counties stretched from the Eastern piedmont to the Ozarks to the Sierra Nevada. Virginia's Clarke County was in the vanguard of the transformation from the old Democratic South to the new Republican South, but it is struggling against being absorbed into the Northern Virginia suburbs nearby. *(Story, p. 25)*

Iowa's Madison County represents the rural heartland at its most romantic but like much of rural America faces a basic problem of keeping its young at home. *(Story, p. 24)*

Arkansas' Baxter County, on the Missouri state line, has experienced the kind of robust growth associated with recreation and retirement industries in the affluent 1990s. As the proportion of retired Americans escalates rapidly after the year 2010, any hope that rural venues will have a comeback will depend on communities such as these.

California's Lassen County has the open spaces of the frontier West and an abundance of timber, but it has depended on the presence of two large prisons to keep the local economy thriving. *(Story, p. 26)*

There are some common characteristics of rural America, however. People who live here are generally less affluent, more likely to be white and politically more conservative than the rest of the nation, particularly on social issues such as abortion and gun control.

Much of rural America usually is disposed to vote Republican, especially now that the Democratic hold on the rural South has been broken. In the current Congress, Republicans hold nearly two-thirds of the districts in which at least 60

Rural areas may regain some population and political clout by luring retiring baby boomers.

percent of the population lives outside a metropolitan area.

At the same time, rural America may be called the least predictable of the nation's demographic or geographic blocs. While most rural districts elected Republicans to the House, a clear majority of the rural districts also voted for President Clinton.

And it is this willingness to split ballots and make quick partisan turnarounds that enables the rural voter to

retain some measure of political importance. Unlike the cities, which for decades have voted overwhelmingly Democratic in federal elections, rural America is often up for grabs.

Throughout the nation's history, rural discontent with the status quo has been a cornerstone of congressional upheaval, and that was the case in 1994, when Republicans gained control of Congress. The GOP has picked up a net 15 House seats in rural America since Clinton's first inauguration, including 11 in the South alone. Seats formerly held by such Democratic lions as Tom Bevill of Alabama, William H. Natcher of Kentucky, and Jamie L. Whitten and G. V. "Sonny" Montgomery of Mississippi have fallen to Republicans who are not likely to give them back soon.

Many of the Democrats who have been successful in recent years in rural America have been traditional conservatives — Dixiecrats, or "Tory" Democrats in Texas, or "Pinto" Democrats elsewhere in the Southwest. Now they are more likely to call themselves "Blue Dogs," a group dedicated to resisting leftward impulses within the House Democratic caucus.

They have been fiscally conservative and positioned to the right of the mainstream of their national party on social issues. But that does make them functional Republicans. While most rural GOP House members drew ratings in 1996 from the liberal Americans for Democratic Action (ADA) that were in the single digits (on a 100-point scale), prominent "Blue Dog" Democrats such as Collin C. Peterson of Minnesota and Charles W. Stenholm of Texas had ADA scores last year of at least 50 percent.

By and large, rural Democratic congressmen find themselves in agreement with the Clinton administration much of the time. "My constituents are closer to this administration than most of them would even think on policy issues" such as health care, education

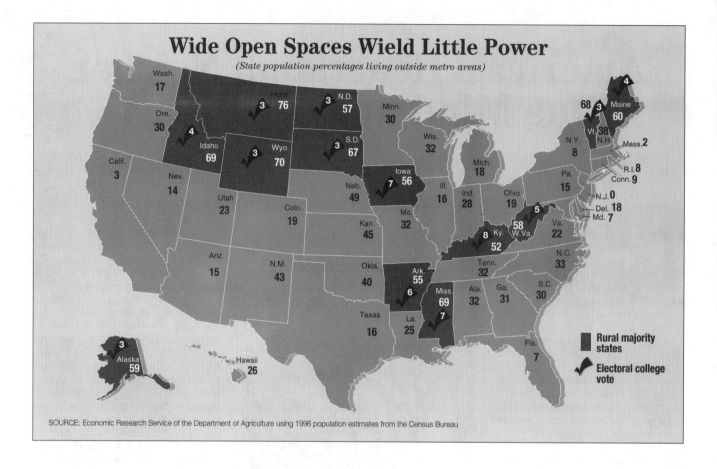

Wide Open Spaces Wield Little Power

(State population percentages living outside metro areas)

Wash. **17**
Ore. **30**
Calif. **3**
Nev. **14**
Idaho **69**
Utah **23**
Ariz. **15**
Mont. **76**
Wyo. **70**
Colo. **19**
N.M. **43**
N.D. **57**
S.D. **67**
Neb. **49**
Kan. **45**
Okla. **40**
Texas **16**
Minn. **30**
Iowa **56**
Mo. **32**
Ark. **55**
La. **25**
Wis. **32**
Ill. **16**
Ind. **28**
Mich. **18**
Ohio **19**
Ky. **52**
Tenn. **32**
Miss. **69**
Ala. **32**
Ga. **31**
N.C. **33**
S.C. **30**
Fla. **7**
W.Va. **58**
Va. **22**
Pa. **15**
N.Y. **8**
Maine **60**
Vt. **38**
N.H. **68**
Mass. **2**
R.I. **8**
Conn. **9**
N.J. **0**
Del. **18**
Md. **7**
Alaska **59**
Hawaii **26**

■ Rural majority states
✔ Electoral college vote

SOURCE: Economic Research Service of the Department of Agriculture using 1996 population estimates from the Census Bureau

and taxes, says Democratic Rep. Ted Strickland, who represents a rural district in southern Ohio. Problems with the administration, he says, have tended to come on "socially divisive issues."

Losing Strength

Through much of the 19th century, the United States was an agrarian nation. But in the 20th, the country has gone through two transformations. Early in the century, the cities gained ascendancy over the countryside. But that era gave way gradually after World War II, with the suburbs establishing hegemony. *(Weekly Report, p. 1209, 1645)*

Through much of this century, rural America was able to maintain bastions of political might in malapportioned legislatures — at both the state and national level. But that grip was weakened by population shifts and finally broken by the court-ordered "one-person, one-vote" decisions made by the Supreme Court in the 1960s. Since then, the demographic trends that forced the law to change have accelerated.

Currently, nearly four out of every five Americans live in cities or suburbs. Barely one out of five lives in small towns or the countryside, and the rural share of congressional seats is even smaller. As

recently as 1966, there were 181 districts (or 42 percent of the entire House) with a population that was majority rural; by 1993, that number was down to 77 districts (18 percent). And using Congressional Quarterly's traditional definition, which classifies a district as rural only when its non-metro population reaches 60 percent, just 57 districts in the 105th Congress could be considered rural (13 percent of the House).

Geographically, most of the rural districts are in the South and Midwest (21 apiece), with the rest almost evenly split between the East (eight) and the West (seven).

Demographically, rural America is overwhelmingly white. The bulk of the rural districts have a non-Hispanic white population in excess of 90 percent. Only a handful are predominantly minority, and they are clustered in the Sun Belt — in the old Cotton Belt states and in areas of the Southwest where Latino immigrants have been concentrated.

Economically, rural America is comparatively poor. It may possess most of the nation's natural resources, but that is not reflected in the personal income of the people who live there. According to a 1993 study by the Congressional Research Service, no rural district was

ranked in the top 100 in terms of median family income (based on 1990 Census data); only two districts (both in New England) were in the top 200. Most rural districts were among the bottom 100 in this measurement of personal affluence.

Although the cost of living tends to be lower in rural America, says Calvin L. Beale, a demographer with the Department of Agriculture, all rural areas are "concerned about jobs" and many suffer chronically high rates of unemployment.

According to 1996 population estimates, 13 states have a rural majority, a number that includes the president's home state of Arkansas as well as Iowa, the traditional kick-off point for the quadrennial presidential nominating process. But this baker's dozen offers only 59 electoral votes to a presidential candidate fortunate enough to win them all. That is just five more electoral votes than are available in California alone. *(Rural America map, this page)*

In some large battleground states such as California, the rural vote is almost an afterthought. Only 3 percent of California's residents live outside metro areas. In Massachusetts and New Jersey, the rural population is less than 5 percent. In Florida and New York, it is less than 10 percent, and it is less than 20

Decline in Rural Congressional Districts

Population shifts and the application of the "one person, one vote" principle by the Supreme Court in the early 1960s have caused the number of rural congressional districts to decline over the last three decades. As recently as the mid-1960s, rural America had more seats in the House than either the suburbs or the cities. Now, it has less than either. The majority and "dominant" measurements featured here are explained further in the chart below.

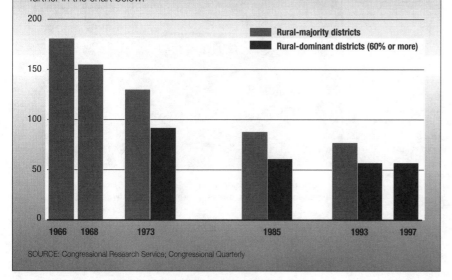

■ Rural-majority districts
■ Rural-dominant districts (60% or more)

SOURCE: Congressional Research Service; Congressional Quarterly

Rural America Up for Grabs

In the mid-1990s, the allegiance of rural voters has been in flux. President Clinton carried a majority of rural congressional districts in 1996, as well as a majority of urban, suburban and "mixed" districts. But at the same time, Republican House candidates also were winning a majority of the districts in each category.

According to the definition traditionally used by Congressional Quarterly, districts are urban when at least 60 percent of their residents live within central cities of a metropolitan area. Districts are suburban when at least 60 percent of their residents live within a metropolitan area but outside a central city. Districts are rural when at least 60 percent of their residents live outside a metropolitan area (and outside towns with populations of 25,000 or more), while "mixed" districts are those where none of the categories accounts for 60 percent of the population.

By this definition, 37 percent of all districts are suburban, 35 percent are "mixed," 15 percent are urban, and 13 percent are rural. The chart below compares the 1996 presidential voting with the composition of the House at full strength this summer (before Republican Susan Molinari of New York resigned her seat but after Republican Bill Redmond picked up the rural New Mexico seat vacated by Democrat Bill Richardson). One rural House seat (Vermont) is held by an independent.

	Total Districts	'96 Presidential Clinton / Dole		House Seats Dem. / GOP		House Democrats Lag Behind Clinton
Urban	67	61	6	58	9	– 3
Suburban	160	105	55	68	92	– 37
Rural	57	33	24	19	37	– 14
Mixed	151	81	70	61	90	– 20
TOTAL	**435**	**280**	**155**	**206**	**228**	**– 74**

SOURCE: Congressional Quarterly

percent in Illinois, Michigan, Ohio, Pennsylvania and Texas. The non-metro population is even under 20 percent in the vast Western states of Arizona, Colorado and Nevada, where most residents live in large metro centers such as Phoenix, Denver and Las Vegas.

But voting power aside, rural America retains significance because its mystique refuses to recede. Even as the nation has become citified and suburbanized, national politicians have tended to become more and more deliberate in their identification with small-town America.

President Dwight D. Eisenhower, a career military man who entered politics from an address in Manhattan, always insisted his hometown was Abilene, Kan. (which he had left while still a boy). President Richard M. Nixon harked back to a pre-suburban Whittier, Calif. Jimmy Carter went home to the farm at Plains, Ga., and Ronald Reagan shunned images of Hollywood for those of the Illinois towns of Dixon and Tampico.

Country Charm

Clinton has yielded to no one on this score. As he moved onto the national stage in 1992, it was as the candidate from "a place called Hope." The expression had dual meeting. It struck an optimistic chord in a year when many voters thought the economy was mired in recession. It also accented his roots in small-town Arkansas and linked him with traditional family values at a time when his personal character was already under attack.

Clinton underscored his identification with small-town America in the 1992 campaign with a series of bus trips across the rural heartland. And he made a well-publicized train trip on the eve of the 1996 Democratic convention that traversed rural Ohio and Michigan. As a consequence, while liberal Democrats such as George S. McGovern, Walter F. Mondale and Michael S. Dukakis were buried in the rural voting when they ran for president, Carter and Clinton made deep inroads into the rural electorate.

Carter more completely dominated the rural South in his successful run for the White House in 1976, but Clinton more deeply penetrated the rural vote in other parts of the country. In Illinois, for instance, he won more than two dozen downstate counties in 1992 that no Democratic presidential candidate had carried at least since Lyndon B. Johnson's landslide victory over Barry M. Goldwater in 1964. Clinton carried most of those counties again in 1996.

The rural sector goes by different

The Traits of Madison County

Probably no county is as closely identified with the romantic image of rural America as Madison County, Iowa. Even before the popular novel and movie, "The Bridges of Madison County," the county was known as the birthplace of actor John Wayne.

That provides Madison with something most other rural counties do not have, a thriving tourist trade. Visitors can take in the "Duke's" birthplace in the county seat of Winterset (where he was born in 1907 as Marion Michael Morrison), or head out to Roseman Bridge, where the fictional National Geographic photographer Robert Kincaid and farm housewife Francesca Johnson got better acquainted with each other in Robert James Waller's best-seller. Tourist dollars, says Ted C. Gorman, the publisher of the Winterset Madisonian, add "a little cream" to the local economy.

Like other prospering counties in the agrarian Midwest, Madison County is economically diverse. It has a sizable commuting population that drives to jobs in nearby Des Moines, several local manufacturing concerns that make appliance accessories, furniture and wooden bird houses, and a fairly vibrant farm economy focused on corn and beans.

"Right now times are pretty good," says Republican Rep. Greg Ganske, whose district includes Madison County. "Small-town merchants rely on the farm economy. When the farm economy is doing well, merchants are doing OK."

Yet while Madison County in recent years has reversed the population slide that affected much of rural America in the recession-tinged 1980s, its 1995 estimated population of 13,490 is barely 350 higher than it was in 1950.

"There's a brain drain," says Gorman. "When (young people) graduate, they're gone. Old people control the

WINTERSET MADISONIAN PHOTO

'Bridges of Madison County' director and co-star Clint Eastwood, under umbrella, during filming in Iowa in 1994.

wealth and land. Young people are pretty well shut out of farming and business."

Politically, Madison is a classic swing county. Democrats have carried it in the last three presidential elections, with the county's 1996 totals almost identical to the national totals: 49 percent for President Clinton, 40 percent for Republican Bob Dole and 10 percent for Ross Perot. But Ganske has won Madison County both times he has run for Congress (in 1994, he unseated 36-year Democratic veteran, Neal Smith). And Republicans have recently wrest control of county government from the Democrats. "Politically," says Gorman, "it's a tough county to figure out."

---

names in different states. In Illinois, it is downstate. In New York, it is upstate. In Pennsylvania, it is the "T" (a reference to the shape the rural counties make on the map). But in virtually every major state, the rural vote is variegated. "It's difficult to talk about rural areas in the singular," says Republican consultant David Hill about his home state of Texas.

The same can be said about other battleground states as well. Paul M. Green, an Illinois political analyst at Governors State University, sees his state's huge downstate divided into three different sectors by its major east-west interstate highways. South of Interstate 70, he says, the land is not particularly prosperous and prisons are a basic growth industry. The area is populated by "traditional good old boy downstate Democrats," says Green. "It's the only place in Illinois that thinks Clinton doesn't talk with an accent."

A bit to the north between Interstates 70 and 80, says Green, the soil is rich and deep. This is "the heart of Re-

publican central Illinois" and for years was the bailiwick of House Minority Leader Robert H. Michel.

Meanwhile, the rural portion of Illinois north of Interstate 80, says Green, is being eaten up by the westward expansion of the Chicago suburbs. It is moving five miles westward each decade, he says. "In our lifetime, the suburbs will sprawl from Chicago to Rock Island (on the Iowa border)."

Hoosier vs. Appalachian

University of Akron political scientist John C. Green talks of a similar division within Ohio's rural sector. There is "Hoosier Ohio" and "Appalachian Ohio," he says. The latter covers the southern part of the state. It is not economically prosperous, depends on government aid and is apt to vote Democratic — especially if a Southerner such as Carter or Clinton tops the ticket.

"Hoosier Ohio" covers much of the central and northern parts of the state and is Republican corn country. "Farm-

ers there are small business people," says Green. "While Appalachian [Ohio] feels left behind," Hoosier Ohio is "more prosperous and feels integrated into the modern economy."

That distinction recurs throughout rural America. On one hand, there are energetic, growing rural areas. On the other hand, there are rural areas that are isolated and dying. G. Terry Madonna, a political scientist at Millersville University (Pa.), has seen plenty of these less fortunate communities in the hills and hollows of Pennsylvania. They seem "locked in time and space," says Madonna, and there is little immigration. "The values that exist there are the values that have been held [there] for generations."

It is not uncommon for former residents to return to small towns and wonder at how many things remain as they were decades earlier — with perhaps the addition of a McDonald's franchise. If time does not stand still, it at least moves far more slowly.

Politically, that often means that po-

In Virginia, Suburbs Come Calling

Virginia's Clarke County is barely an hour's drive northwest of the nation's capital, but in temperament it seems a world apart.

Outside the small county courthouse in Berryville is a statue to Confederate war dead. In warm weather, the town's main intersection features a large produce stand, and the fairgrounds at the outskirts of town bustles in late summer as local farmers display their livestock and poultry.

Jesse Russell, the county zoning administrator, left the area after he graduated from high school. But after military service and college, he returned. "Then, I was old enough to appreciate where I came from," he says.

With a population of barely 12,000, Clarke County is hardly a political powerhouse. Clout lives just over the foothills of the Blue Ridge Mountains in the vote-rich suburbs of Northern Virginia. First, the people left for the city; then they came part of the way back to live in the suburbs. Only a handful like Russell have come all the way back to the country.

The spectre of suburban sprawl is almost palpable in Clarke County, where a major concern is how to manage the population growth that has overwhelmed counties such as Loudoun and Fairfax to the east. From 1850 to 1950, Clarke had a population of roughly 7,000. Since, then, the population of the county has nearly doubled.

Yet Clarke retains its rural flavor and local leaders want to keep it that way. In the early 1980s, Clarke was one of the first counties in the state to institute "sliding scale zoning" in an effort to protect open space. Only one house is permitted to be built on a 10-acre parcel; only four houses on 100 acres; only 14 houses on 1,000 acres.

The county is trying to keep any large new subdivisions

RHODES COOK

Historic Clark County added an "e" to its name as its population grew.

clustered around Berryville, where there is already an existing infrastructure. "We want to keep (Clarke County) basically the same without closing the gates," says Russell. "There will be growth but nothing staggering or overwhelming."

One aspect of the county that has changed dramatically over the years is its partisan political allegiance. For years, Clarke County was known as the home of Democratic Sen. Harry F. Byrd (1933-65); now its most famous political citizen is former GOP Senate candidate, Oliver L. North.

The symbolic change seems fitting. For a century after the Civil War, Clarke County was part of the northern flank of the rural Democratic South. But like much of the rest of the region, it temporarily abandoned the Democrats to vote for Dwight D. Eisenhower in the 1950s, and then left the party for good after the Democrats' liberal Great Society initiatives a decade later. Clarke County has not voted for a Democratic presidential candidate since 1964.

The Republican ascendancy in the county, though, has not required any philosophical transformation on the part of local voters. Democratic and Republican voters in the county "see eye to eye on many things," says Doug Sours, a college student and local Democratic activist. "We're both pretty conservative."

That could be guessed from looking at the inscription on the Civil War monument in front of the courthouse. "Erected to the memory of the sons of Clarke who gave their lives in defense of the rights of the states and of constitutional government," it reads in bold letters. "Fortune denied their success but they achieved imperishable fame."

litical values such as populism and isolationism — including an aversion to foreign military adventures, treaties and trade agreements — endure across generations.

The member of Congress for a rural district may be a Democrat in one era, a Republican in another. But he is likely to be a white male with a traditional family and a tendency to value the past.

Rural Volatility

Country values, which tend to emphasize self-reliance and social conservatism, often work to the political advantage of Republicans. But that can be offset, at least in some rural areas, by a sense of unease with the economic status quo. Rural areas "lag behind the

cities in income and tend toward populism, left and right," says Albert J. Menendez, the author of several books on religion and politics.

Anger can spill out in different ways. Along U.S. 522 in southern Pennsylvania is a small red barn. On the side in neat white letters is written "Hungry — Eat Your Jap Car," and "Guns — Yes! Billary — Hell No!"

In this corner of rural America, gun clubs, veterans' organizations and evangelical churches abound. "There's a higher percentage of religious orthodoxy in rural America," says Menendez. "It's a little more conservative, a little more intense." It provides, he adds, "a sense of belonging."

But a sense of unease is also palpable,

not just on the side of the Pennsylvania barn but also in the local newspaper, the Fulton County News. On the front page of one recent issue were stories on the disappearance of family farms in the county, layoffs at the county's major manufacturing plant (which produces construction machinery), and the plight of the county's library system, which relies on donations and private fund-raising efforts for one-third of its budget.

In these ways, Fulton County is rural America writ small. Family farms, once the backbone of an agrarian economy, are giving way to agribusiness. Only a handful of congressional districts, all clustered in the Midwest, have as many as one resident in 10 actually living on a farm. Small towns increasingly need a

Prisons on the Range

Moving westward across the Plains, both the states and their counties tend to get larger. With a land area in excess of 4,500 square miles, California's Lassen County is almost as big as the entire state of Connecticut. But with less than 30,000 residents, its population is less than 1 percent as large.

Lassen County is tucked away in northeast California between the Sierra Mountains and the Nevada desert. It looks like an "old Western" movie in a lot of places, says Dave Moller, the news editor of the Lassen County Times. "There are still literally cowboys out on the range who gather the cattle. It's very wide open spaces."

Ranching and timber have long been the cornerstones of the Lassen County economy, but the federal government controls most of the land and its restrictive timber policy has forced the county to look elsewhere to maintain its economic stability.

The county's salvation has been a plethora of government jobs. It houses the northeast California headquarters of the Forestry Service, Bureau of Land Management and the state forestry department. But the biggest government employers are the two state prisons near the county seat of Susanville. They have roughly 4,000 inmates and 1,000 workers apiece. The newer prison, built in the 1990s, is a high-level facility. "I understand," says

> The prisons and the influx of workers and service jobs has changed the complexion of Susanville, the county seat.

Moller, "that O.J. Simpson would have been sent there" if he had not been acquitted of murder charges in 1996.

The prisons and the influx of workers and service jobs has changed the complexion of Susanville. Long a sleepy country town, "we're (now) more hustle and bustle," says Jim Chapman, the acting chairman of the Lassen County board of supervisors.

The county has also become increasingly Republican. Bob Dole be at President Clinton in Lassen by nearly 20 percentage points in 1996. Yet even when Lassen was Democratic at its core, notes Chapman, it was still conservative. "Democrats around here are more Jeffersonian in nature," he says.

Voters of both parties also tend to be a bit rebellious. When secessionist fever was spreading across rural northern California earlier this decade, Lassen County was in the forefront. Voters approved two secessionist measures that were on the county ballot in June 1992. One would have created a 51st state out of the northern part of the state; another would have joined counties in northern California and eastern Oregon into a new state called "Jefferson." Later that year, Perot's independent candidacy drew nearly 30 percent of the presidential vote in Lassen County.

"Agrarian self-reliance is our theme and that crosses party lines," says Chapman.

---

light industry or two to supply jobs, but their ability to attract them often depends on the adequacy of basic services — roads, schools, health care — that are uneven across rural America.

According to a recent study by Beale and Kenneth M. Johnson, a sociologist at Loyola University in Chicago, more than half the nation's roughly 2,300 rural counties (those without an urban center of 50,000 or more) lost population in the 1980s, but three-quarters of them showed population gains from 1990 to 1996. The major gainers have been counties with retirement or recreational facilities or those such as Clarke in Virginia that are within proximity of a major population center.

Among the recreation-retirement counties recording gains is Baxter, which gained population in both the 1980s and 1990s. According to the 1990 census, nearly 30 percent of the county population was aged 65 or older — more than double the national average.

Baxter has lured not only retiring Arkansans content to live out their days in their home state, but an influx from Kansas City, St. Louis and other major metropolitan areas.

Baxter is one of the locales benefiting from the same population growth that several investors attempted to serve with the Whitewater real estate development deal in the 1980s that involved Clinton and first lady Hillary Rodham Clinton, then the residents of the Arkansas governor's mansion.

What Lies Ahead

The political effects of a burgeoning rural America are difficult to gauge. For example, population growth based on retirees will have unpredictable political effects depending on which political concerns — Medicare, tax levels, property rights —may be motivating older voters in the future.

Adding to the uncertainty is the lack of a guarantee that the rural rebound will continue. "We could still have reversals," Beale says. The seven-year phaseout of farm subsidies instituted by the 1996 farm bill is a major uncertainty. "What happens when there is a large corn crop or a large wheat crop and nobody to buy it?" asks Beale. Moreover, economic conditions are better these days in major urban areas than early in the decade, when much of the recent movement to rural America took place.

Yet, he adds, population centers have grown so large and congested that "a number of people are fed up with the pace and stress of metro living. Under any type of average economic conditions," says Beale, "we'll have more people moving out of metro areas for non-[metro] areas than are moving in."

And this trend is apt to be encouraged in the computer age by the increasing ability of people to live where they want to, not where they have to. There are even a lot of farmers now who are on the Internet, says Ohio's Green. "There's more diversity out there [in rural America] than we have seen in the past."

All of this means the country cousin may be a growing force in the future. The trends are not likely to have much impact on the Electoral College any time soon. But new growth can sustain the vitality of rural America and preserve its political influence and aspirations — even as the agrarian myths of the past fade into memory. ■

Re-Election Prospects Brighten For 'Year of Woman' Senators

Not long ago, the historic "Year of the Woman" Senate Class of 1992 was facing extinction in its re-election year of 1998. But more recent developments suggest that most or even all the women who won that year may be back for the 106th Congress.

If they are, their return will almost surely frustrate Republican hopes for a 60-seat "filibuster-proof" majority in the chamber in 1999.

The 1992 Senate winners included four new women Democrats — Patty Murray of Washington, Carol Moseley-Braun of Illinois, and Dianne Feinstein and Barbara Boxer of California — in addition to Barbara A. Mikulski, D-Md., who was re-elected that year.

As the current election cycle began, all except Mikulski appeared likely to be leaving Washington after 1998. Murray, Moseley-Braun and Boxer have all seen their re-election poll numbers fall below 50 percent, a red warning sign for incumbents.

Feinstein, who served out an unexpired term in the 103rd Congress, won a full six-year term in 1994. But early in 1997 many West Coast observers expected her to give up the Senate next year for the California governorship.

In recent weeks, however, Feinstein's reluctance to mount a campaign has signaled that she may stay where she is. And although Democratic prospects of recapturing the Senate majority remain remote, Feinstein no longer looks likely to be the sole female survivor of her freshman class.

Murray, Moseley-Braun and Boxer have all shown surprising strength and, just as important, good fortune.

In the best news for any of the three so far, Moseley-Braun escaped a challenge from two-term Illinois Gov. Jim Edgar, the popular centrist Republican whom she had trailed in trial-heat polls by as much as 25 percentage points. Edgar, who has a history of heart trouble, said Aug. 20 that he would retire rather than run for either the Senate or a third term in Springfield.

That left Illinois Republicans without a top-tier challenger, at least temporarily. And in that, they mirror the predicament of their counterparts in Washington and California.

Moseley-Braun

Edgar

Murray

Smith

This all makes for unpleasant news for Republican strategists, who had seen the three women's seats as their best opportunities for defeating Democratic incumbents. Those three seats, combined with three Democratic vacancies in Ohio, Kentucky and Arkansas, were the heart of the GOP's strategy for expanding its 55-45 Senate majority.

In addition to these six seats, Republicans have had high hopes for upsets in Nevada, Wisconsin and South Carolina. Democratic leaders have all but conceded that the GOP is likely to gain at least a couple of seats in this cycle.

But the early odds have narrowed some, largely because key candidates have demurred. Edgar's decision echoed that of his neighbor, Gov. Tommy G. Thompson of Wisconsin. And in South Carolina, former Gov. Carroll A. Campbell Jr. has remained non-committal.

At the same time, Republicans admit they will have trouble defending their own open seat (Indiana) against a hard-charging run by Democratic former Gov. Evan Bayh. New York Republican Sen. Alfonse M. D'Amato consistently

polls behind a likely challenger, former Rep. Geraldine A. Ferraro (1979-85), as he prepares to seek a fourth term.

A woman challenger may also be in the future for three-term Republican Sen. Arlen Specter of Pennsylvania. Specter almost lost in 1992 to political neophyte Lynn Yeakel. On Aug. 25, former state official and state Democratic Chairwoman Linda Rhodes said she planned to take on Specter in 1998. Rhodes is a former state secretary of aging.

Republicans are also concerned about first-term Sen. Lauch Faircloth in North Carolina and party-switcher Ben Nighthorse Campbell of Colorado, who could be weakened by a primary challenge.

The Illinois Search

Moseley-Braun still tops the list of vulnerable senators, not least because she only recently retired the last of her nagging campaign debt from 1992.

Propelled by a wave of voter resentment over the Senate's handling of the Supreme Court confirmation hearings of Clarence Thomas, Moseley-Braun dispatched an incumbent Democrat in 1992 and became the first African-American woman elected to the chamber.

But her early missteps in office, her controversial 1996 trip to meet with Nigerian dictator Sani Abacha and her relationship with a former senior campaign staffer who faced allegations of sexual harassment have combined to diminish her icon status.

Edgar might have beaten her easily, but his exit leaves Republicans scrambling for an alternative. Edgar quickly gave his blessing to state Attorney General Jim Ryan, who will announce his plans Sept. 22. But Ryan, too, faces questions about his health. He was diagnosed with non-Hodgkin's lymphoma in 1996, but says he is in remission.

Illinois Republicans have not won a Senate election since 1978, but they have dominated other statewide offices with moderate nominees such as Edgar and James R. Thompson, who was governor from 1977 to 1991.

The GOP's Senate nominees have tended to be more ideologically conservative, including Rich Williamson, who

CQ Weekly Report Aug. 30, 1997

lost to Moseley-Braun in 1992, and state Sen. Al Salvi, who lost to Sen. Richard J. Durbin in 1996.

The only Republican to announce against Moseley-Braun so far is state Sen. Peter Fitzgerald. A wealthy lawyer with a background in banking, Fitzgerald, like Salvi, could use personal wealth to finance a conservative campaign on taxes and social issues.

Either Fitzgerald or Salvi might allow Moseley-Braun, an underrated campaigner, to solidify the multi-ethnic coalition that carried her in 1992.

The West Coast

Boxer, an outspoken liberal, has looked particularly vulnerable at times during her first term. She had been elected with less than a majority despite a big year for Democrats in her state, and Republicans have been licking their chops ever since — assuming they would have a stronger candidate than the conservative commentator Boxer defeated in 1992.

Yet the cost of a statewide campaign in California and the uncertainty of the new open primary format has truncated the GOP field. The new "jungle primary," created by a 1996 ballot initiative now under challenge in federal court, will list all candidates on one ballot. The top finishers from each party will proceed to the November ballot.

California sends the largest number of Republicans to the House of any state, yet all 23 of them have declined to challenge Boxer. Some Republicans talk of a celebrity savior such as actor Tom Selleck. But while waiting on Selleck's decision, most on the GOP side are focusing on the three announced candidates: San Diego Mayor Susan Golding, state Treasurer Matt Fong and businessman Darrell Issa.

Issa, who made an estimated $200 million selling car alarms, has already spent $2 million on a radio campaign that calls Boxer "one of the worst senators in California history." Issa is running to the right of the field. Golding is a clear supporter of abortion rights, while Fong supports them with restrictions.

Golding, who hopes to do well in the new open primary, has reached out to independents and even to Democrats.

Fong, meanwhile, hopes to appeal to the state's ever-swelling population of minorities, and both he and Golding hope to lure back suburban Republican voters, primarily women, whose defection helped Boxer in 1992.

Preliminary polls indicate Boxer, a formidable fundraiser, would lead all comers in the jungle primary and outpace any of her declared rivals in the general election as well.

Murray, the self-styled "mom in tennis shoes" of 1992, also has dodged a political bullet or two. GOP Reps. Jennifer Dunn and Rick White, both popular in their Puget Sound districts, have declined to run. Rep. George Nethercutt, who hails from the less-populous eastern third of the state, may yet run.

Rep. Linda Smith has announced against Murray, but Smith has alienated national Republican officials with her maverick ways and populist style — including her fierce opposition to political action committee (PAC) money. She refuses PAC money herself and has proposed legislation outlawing it altogether.

National Republican Senatorial Committee Chairman Mitch McConnell, R-Ky., a defender of the current fundraising system, has not only refused to campaign for Smith; he refuses to meet with her.

Pierre County Executive Doug Sutherland has announced himself as an alternative to Smith. But Smith has her own statewide network (she piloted two successful ballot initiatives before coming to Congress) and will be favored for the nomination unless Nethercutt or another late starter enters.

Colorado and Arkansas

Colorado Rep. Scott McInnis has done nothing to dampen speculation that he might challenge Campbell in their state's GOP primary. McInnis has raised more than $800,000 and talks openly about his preferred Democratic opponent (Rep. David E. Skaggs).

McInnis' ambitions have become apparent enough to set off preliminary scrambling among prospective successors in the Western Slope's 3rd District.

Several hopefuls in Arkansas may seek to succeed retiring Democratic Sen. Dale Bumpers, with former Rep. Blanche Lambert Lincoln and state Rep. Scott Ferguson formally announced on the Democratic side.

Only one Republican, state Sen. Fay Boozman, has declared. He gained a boost Aug. 21 with the endorsement of Republican Sen. Tim Hutchinson, a longtime personal friend.

Among the other potential GOP candidates is a newly minted Republican, Lu Hardin. Now the state director of higher education, Hardin ran for the Democratic nomination for the Senate in 1996, losing to state Attorney General Winston Bryant (who lost in November to Hutchinson). Hardin switched to the GOP on Aug. 20. ∎

Amid Cries for Reform, Parties And Politicians Pack Coffers

Reports show some fundraising in non-election year breaks records set in election years; Clinton expresses pride in money efforts

It was a week that could make campaign finance reformers want to tear their hair out.

On Aug. 5, in the middle of a non-election year when campaign finance investigations have raised a popular and bipartisan cry for reform, new data from the fundraising front showed that political parties and individual members of Congress are filling their coffers at a clip that in some cases broke records set in election years.

On Aug. 6, President Clinton, who has repeatedly called for tough reform legislation, said at a White House press conference that he was "proud" of his role in raising exactly the kind of "soft money" contributions that reformers most want to kill. "I plead guilty to that," the president said. *(Weekly Report, p. 1934)*

Then, in a televised slip of the tongue, the president added insult to injury by misstating the name of the favorite bill of most reformers — the one he himself has said he supports.

To top it off, on Aug. 7, Clinton visited two fundraising dinners to help garner $650,000 in soft money for the Democratic Party — money accepted in unlimited, unregulated contributions.

As some legislators gird for their last chance to overhaul campaign finance laws before the 1998 election year, the system they want to change is running at a furious rate, throwing off huge amounts of money at a time when the next federal elections are more than a year away.

For some, all this is proof that current campaign fundraising laws are desperately in need of an overhaul. "It just shows a system completely out of con-

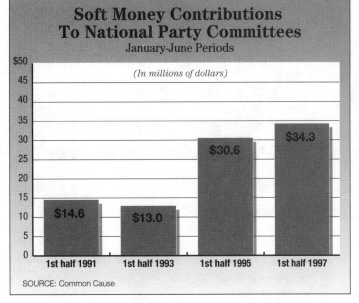

Soft Money Contributions To National Party Committees
January-June Periods

(In millions of dollars)

$14.6 — 1st half 1991
$13.0 — 1st half 1993
$30.6 — 1st half 1995
$34.3 — 1st half 1997

SOURCE: Common Cause

trol," said Ann McBride, president of Common Cause, a lead advocate of reform. The events of the week "show the absolute fundamental need to just flatly end this system."

But for proponents of the current system — or for those whose reform ideas would loosen rather than tighten the current restrictions — there was nothing inherently ominous in the week's developments. These advocates regard soft money donations as the exercise of free speech and the right of any American to participate in the political process.

"What is the problem?" asked Edward H. Crane III, president of the Cato Institute, who favors lifting limits on contributions as long as the source of all funding is fully disclosed.

"An open, dynamic political system requires lots of money," he said. "If the money is disclosed, all you have is money as a proxy for information."

If eternal vigilance is the price of liberty, he added, borrowing a phrase often attributed to Thomas Jefferson, "you should be able to spend whatever

the hell you want to protect those liberties."

The two sides are set to lock horns when Congress returns in September. Advocates of tightened campaign finance laws have threatened to slow or stop most business in the House and Senate unless they get votes on reform legislation.

Since even ardent reformers are wary of changing laws in the middle of an election year, the September-October period when Congress is in town is viewed as the last window for moving legislation before 1999.

Advocates of tight new restrictions will likely point to events of the week of Aug. 4 as proof that something needs to be done.

On Aug. 5, a study by Common Cause showed that Republicans and Democrats raised record amounts of controversial soft money in the first six months of this year.

The $34.3 million the two parties took in was more than twice the $13 million they raised in 1993 in the first six months after the last presidential election year. It was also more than the $30.6 million they raised during the first six months of last year, when both parties were pushing hard to maximize the funds available for the November 1996 elections.

Unlike the highly regulated and strictly limited "hard" money donations ($1,000 per individual per election, $5,000 per political action committee), soft money is unregulated and limited only by the generosity of the donor.

Individuals, businesses, law firms, labor unions and trade groups commonly give contributions of $25,000 to $50,000 to as much as $100,000 or more, records show. During the first six months of 1997, the largest soft money contribution was a pair of $500,000 donations to the Republican National Committee (RNC) by Amway President Richard DeVos and his wife.

While hard money donations to individual candidates can go straight into campaign work, soft money can go only to parties or organizations and must be used, technically, only for party-building efforts such as voter registration or get-out-the vote drives. Critics say both parties routinely abuse that by funneling the money into thinly veiled campaign activities.

Common Cause figures showed that Republican Party committees raised more than twice as much as their Democratic counterparts, with the RNC and three other GOP committees pulling in $23.1 million in the first six months of the year as compared with $11.1 million for the Democratic National Committee (DNC) and two other Democratic political committees.

On Aug. 6, President Clinton defended his own role in raising such money for Democrats, despite his calls for legislation to end the practice. As long as Republicans raise such money, and raise more of it than Democrats, he said, Democrats will raise it too.

"I'm proud of it," he said at a White House press conference. "I don't believe in unilateral disarmament . . . we have to raise enough to be competitive."

Clinton went on to renew his demand for Congress to pass campaign finance reform legislation, but he bobbled the name of the most prominent bill. "I am supporting Kennedy-Kassebaum," he said, referring to a 1996 health-care measure, rather than the McCain-Feingold campaign finance reform proposal (S 25), sponsored by Sens. John McCain, R-Ariz., and Russell D. Feingold, D-Wis.

McCain-Feingold is the chief vehicle for those who want a much tighter campaign finance system. It would ban soft money and set voluntary money-raising limits for candidates, rewarding those who complied with free TV air time.

"He couldn't even get the name of the bill right," said Ellen Miller, executive director of the group Public Campaign and a lead proponent of strict campaign finance reform.

"Sure, we all stumble from time to

time," she said. But she insisted that "this was a major gaffe" that revealed that Clinton's heart is not in the effort to limit such donations.

Meanwhile, dollar counts were emerging from the Federal Election Commission (FEC), where campaigns had to file reports in July detailing results for the first six months of the year. These reports showed that individual

Richard A. Gephardt, D-Mo., both prospective presidential candidates in 2000, placed second and third among House fundraisers, with $1.8 million and $1.4 million, respectively.

Leadership status has traditionally been a big help in fundraising; indeed, two other top GOP House leaders, Majority Leader Dick Armey of Texas and Majority Whip Tom DeLay, also of Texas, placed tenth and ninth respectively.

The top 10 Senate fundraisers included eight who are up for re-election next year, most of whom raised $1 million or more apiece in anticipation of statewide contests that can routinely cost several million dollars.

But the Senate's lead fundraiser in the first half of 1997 was Kay Bailey Hutchison, R-Texas, who does not face the voters again until 2000. She raised nearly $2 million. And holding down the No. 8 spot among top-dollar Senate fundraisers was John Kerry, D-Mass., who was just re-elected and does not have to run again until 2002. He raised more than $800,000.

Advocates of tighter campaign restrictions have promised guerrilla war on the floors of the House and Senate to force leaders to schedule votes this fall.

In the Senate, the sponsors of the McCain-Feingold bill threatened to slow or stall measures other than appropriations bills until they got a vote on their bill in that chamber. Meanwhile, a group of 24 House members has warned that it will attack anything that moves on the House floor unless leaders of that chamber schedule debate and votes on campaign finance.

"We strongly believe that this deliberate delay of campaign finance reform is no longer tolerable," said Rep. George Miller, D-Calif., and 23 other Democratic House members in a letter to Speaker Gingrich July 23.

"We will do everything in our power . . . to force consideration of this issue, even at the expense of consideration of other matters. All members should be prepared to arrive to work early and stay late, because regular order is intolerable while this most important issue remains absent from the calendar. Delay is death for campaign finance reform." ∎

Top Money Raisers

Here are the top incumbent fundraisers in the House and Senate during the first six months of 1997, according to an analysis by the Center for Responsive Politics. The Center based its study on Federal Election Commission records that showed campaign funds raised from Jan. 1 through June 30, 1997.

HOUSE

Charles E. Schumer, D-N.Y.	$1,834,530
Newt Gingrich, R-Ga.	1,818,548
Richard A. Gephardt, D-Mo.	1,439,861
Joseph P. Kennedy II, D-Mass.	1,041,944
Ciro D. Rodriguez, D-Texas	506,919
Jerry Weller, R-Ill.	497,417
Bud Shuster, R-Pa.	473,933
Nita M. Lowey, D-N.Y.	448,739
Tom DeLay, R-Texas	420,838
Dick Armey, R-Texas	415,070

SENATE

Kay Bailey Hutchison, R-Texas	$1,965,110
Arlen Specter, R-Pa.	1,729,949
Richard C. Shelby, R-Ala.	1,544,591
Bob Graham, D-Fla.	1,172,722
Christopher S. Bond, R-Mo.	1,151,063
Christopher J. Dodd, D-Conn.	1,128,148
Carol Moseley-Braun, D-Ill.	1,095,057
John Kerry, D-Mass.	816,581
Ron Wyden, D-Ore.	804,716
Lauch Faircloth, R-N.C.	797,816

candidates are raising hard money at prodigious rates in this non-election year. (Box, this page)

An analysis of the FEC data by the Center for Responsive Politics showed that four House members and seven senators already had raised more than $1 million each during the first half of 1997, while dozens more raised hundreds of thousands of dollars apiece.

Top House fundraisers included Rep. Charles E. Schumer, D-N.Y., who raised $1.8 million in preparation for a possible Senate race against incumbent Sen. Alfonse M. D'Amato, R-N.Y.

House Speaker Newt Gingrich, R-Ga., and House Minority Leader

Labor's Clout May Be Fleeting Despite Fast-Track Victory

Faction appears stronger than it has in years, but a closer look demonstrates it is hardly the Charles Atlas of politics

A venerable rally song of the labor movement asked: "Which side are you on?" House Democrats offered their answer this month by refusing to follow President Clinton's lead on fast track trade negotiating authority. They did not care what the president said, they were sticking with the unions.

"If the labor unions had not been so dominant in the Democratic Party, we would have won fast track," said House Speaker Newt Gingrich, R-Ga., who fought for fast track but had reason to take satisfaction in its defeat.

In fact, many Republicans could scarcely contain their pleasure at scoring a political three-pointer. In their view, the vote depicted House Democrats as opposed to free trade, Clinton as too weak to command his troops and the whole party as beholden to — if not indistinguishable from — the labor bosses.

For the moment at least, labor looked stronger than at any time since it muscled Walter F. Mondale to the Democratic presidential nomination in 1984. It looms large once again because it can raise money and mobilize fieldworkers at a time when precious few other constituencies in the Democratic Party can.

"In terms of organizations that are out there for working families, labor's basically it," said freshman Rep. Tom Allen, D-Maine.

That was why, in the aftermath of the fast-track fiasco, publications such as The Wall Street Journal leaped to label the Democrats "America's Labor Party." But labor's new strength may prove more apparent than real, and more elusive than lasting.

The Justice Department is already looking into the financial relationship between the Teamsters and the Democratic National Committee (DNC), and other unions may be scrutinized next.

Labor's resurgence, marked by increased AFL-CIO spending for candi-

The AFL-CIO opted for a more aggressive leadership style under John J. Sweeney, who announced to great fanfare that his union would spend upward of $35 million on the 1996 elections.

dates in 1996 and by a successful strike against United Parcel Service in 1997, has increased pressure to restrain union use of membership dues for politics. Limits will be considered by legislatures or ballot initiatives in at least a dozen states in 1998.

If labor suddenly finds itself with a higher and more powerful profile, it may find reason to regret it.

At the same time, the unions' momentary status as the party's fundraising engine is likely to prove a historical aberration. In the greater scheme of things, labor's financial clout has in fact declined as the number of dues-paying members has dropped from postwar highs. Only about one worker in seven now belongs to a union.

And that is only one reason that labor, despite its recent muscle-flexing, is far from being the Charles Atlas of politics.

"Organized labor is an important force in American society, but it is just one of many forces in American society, and likewise in the Democratic Party," Allen said.

Moreover, unions have not succeeded in supplanting other interests within the contemporary Democratic coalition.

"On every issue that labor is concerned with, from labor law reform to health care, the Democrats just aren't there," said Nelson Lichtenstein, a University of Virginia labor historian. "It's not just the Clinton wing, it's everybody."

If labor could push Democrats on fast track, Lichtenstein suggested, it was because labor had the wind at its back. Polls indicated a lack of popular demand for the initiative, and "environmentalists and a number of other groups also have reservations about the fast-track authority," said William G. Mayer, a visiting professor of political science at Harvard University.

"There's no major Democratic constituency group that's on the other side of the question," Mayer said. "For civil rights groups and women, it's not as though any of them have any great reason to be committed to free trade."

Money Matters

Labor has become the most important single contributor to the coffers of House Democratic candidates: Unions contributed nearly half — 48 percent — of the money House Democrats raised from political action committees (PACs) in 1996. Democrats in tightly contested races raised an even greater share of their PAC money from unions.

With the DNC carrying a debt of more than $15 million in the fall of 1997, labor unions were able to make the most significant contributions to Democratic candidates in off-year elections such as the New Jersey gubernatorial race.

But the Democrats' failure to win any of those contests showed how far labor and its money fall short of their

Gephardt: Fast Track to Spotlight

President Clinton's failure to win fast-track trade negotiating authority was not just a lift for the man who led the opposition, House Minority Leader Richard A. Gephardt, D-Mo., it was a new lease on what has already been a long political life.

Gephardt showed he could hold a position in the House against the combined onslaught of the majority leadership and the presidency. He also established himself more than ever as the favorite presidential aspirant of organized labor, which is once again the party's most conspicuous power center.

Perhaps most satisfying of all, Gephardt emerged the clear winner in a showdown with Vice President Al Gore, who had lobbied for the losing side. As these two men are the most obviously committed Democratic presidential candidates for the year 2000, it was a round that Gephardt the underdog needed badly to win.

It can be said that Gore took nowhere near as conspicuous a part in the fast-track fight as he had in the battle for the North American Free Trade Agreement in 1993. But what was important was that this time the photos and the videotape showed Gephardt smiling and triumphant instead of grim and resigned.

New York Times columnist William Safire went so far as to say the fast-track fight meant Gore was no longer the true party favorite for 2000, having ceded that honor to Gephardt, the unions' fair-haired boy.

This reversal came at a paticularly bad time for Gore. The focus of the White House campaign finance investigations has shifted in recent months from the man at the top to his lieutenants — including Gore and Interior Secretary Bruce Babbitt.

As a result, polls have shown the vice president slipping far more in the public's affections than the president he serves. While Clinton has climbed above 60 percent approval in many polls, Gore has fallen below 50 percent.

Gore, left, and Gephardt, shown in 1970s photographs, came to Congress as members of the Class of 1976.

And while he still ranks far above Gephardt when pollsters ask Democrats to name their next presidential nominee, the all-important aura of inevitability has weakened. It will be no surprise to see Gephardt narrow the gap when the next set of preference-for-president polls arrive.

Gore and Gephardt came to Congress together as members of the Class of 1976. Gore was seven years younger and less experienced. But as the son of Demcratic Sen. Albert Gore Sr., (House, 1939-44, 1945-53, Senate 1953-71), he had been born and raised in the capital, prepping for Harvard at prestigious St. Alban's.

In those days, Gore was the more consistent vote for labor. In their first three terms, Gore's average annual vote score from the AFL-CIO was nearly 82. Gephardt's was just 74.

In his fourth term, however, Gephardt raised his AFL-CIO rating above 90 in both sessions. He has rarely been below 90 since, while scoring a perfect 100 six times.

The two ambitious classmates clashed as rivals for president in 1988. Gephardt focused on the early Iowa caucuses; Gore, by then Tennessee's junior senator, skipped Iowa for the "Super Tuesday" contests in the South. Gephardt won in Iowa, but gained no momentum for later events. Gore did well on Super Tuesday, but faded when the show moved north.

Both decided to sit out the 1992 presidential campaign — convinced that President George Bush could not be beaten. That made them rivals for the vice presidential spot when Bill Clinton began to look like a winner.

Gephardt might have brought Clinton more of an urban and a Northern feel, as well as closer ties to labor. But Gore got the nod, partly on personal chemistry. Ever since, Gephardt has had to balance a general loyalty to Clinton with the prospect of renewing his rivalry with Gore. Watch for that balance to tilt as the millennium approaches.

purported strength.

Support from business-related PACs and individuals beggars labor spending on elections. The ratio has risen to 9-to-1 so far in the 1998 cycle, according to a Center for Responsive Politics analysis of Federal Election Commission reports. So-called soft money contributions (which go to parties rather than to individual candidates) tip the scale even further, with business beating labor in total reported contributions by 11-to-1.

But Republicans are always swift to note that unions provide essential ground support for Democrats, staffing phone banks, providing leaflets, and turning out the vote. The value of such unreported, in-kind contributions may have reached into the hundreds of millions, according to Leo Troy, an economist at Rutgers University.

Aggressive get-out-the-vote efforts in New Jersey, particularly by the AFL-CIO and the Communication Workers of America, helped raise the union household turnout rate from just 24 percent in 1993 to 33 percent in 1997. (*Weekly Report, p. 2784*)

"When one of theirs needs help, labor's in there early and they're in there big," said Steven F. Stockmeyer, a lobbyist with the National Association of Business Political Action Committees. "It's very hard for Democrats to find those kinds of resources elsewhere."

The key element in this capability is the money that unions can raise by appropriating part of their membership dues for political purposes. Although a recent Supreme Court decision said workers could have their money back if they protested such use, in practice few workers seek the rebate.

That is why Republicans have so ardently pursued amendments to campaign laws to stop unions from spending money from dues on campaigns — and why Democrats have adamantly opposed any such idea.

Historical Roots

Complaints about Democrats being captives of unions have been a familiar GOP theme since at least the New Deal, when the Democratic expansion of the federal government coincided with labor's greatest period of success in unionizing industrial workers.

During the 1944 presidential campaign, for instance, Republicans enjoyed taunting President Franklin D. Roosevelt that in selecting his running mate (Harry S Truman) he first had to "clear it with Sidney." The reference was to Sidney Hillman, head of the old Congress of Industrial Organizations' (CIO) political action committee, which donated $7 million, or 20 percent of the total collected by the Democratic campaign fund that year.

At times during its history, organized labor has appeared nearly to rule the Democratic roost. When he became president himself, Truman made the Taft-Hartley law, which had been enacted over his veto by a Republican Congress, into one of his main campaign themes in 1948. (Along with imposing other limitations on union activity, Taft-Hartley allowed states to ban closed shops by passing "right to work" laws.)

In its heyday, organized labor enjoyed a slew of legislative triumphs, from the creation of the National Labor Relations Board in 1935 to enactment of Medicare in 1965. But in recent years its agenda has stalled, except where its issues enjoyed broader support (enough to attract some Republican votes), with the 1996 minimum wage increase being one example. *(1996 Almanac, p. 7-3)*

In 1960, organized labor was already in decline, but 24 percent of American workers still belonged to unions. By 1995, union membership had fallen below 15 percent, and unions covered just 10 percent of the non-governmental work force.

Labor's ranks within the Democratic Party have plummeted too. Nearly one-third (32 percent) of self-identified Democrats in 1960 were union members; by 1992, the figure was just 17 percent.

Rather than watching legislation blocking permanent replacement of striking workers enter into law, for instance, labor has struck a defensive posture in trying to block such GOP initiatives as allowing employers to offer compensatory time off in place of overtime pay.

"Are you going to call it 'Big Labor'

when it's down to 5 percent of the work force?" asked Lichtenstein.

Despite its dwindling numbers, labor has remained a force in Democratic politics. During debate on the North American Free Trade Agreement in 1993, Clinton complained loudly about House Democrats who he felt were caving in to pressure from labor unions opposed to the pact.

"I think frankly [it's] the vociferous, organized opposition of most of the unions telling these members in private they'll never give them any money again, they'll get them opponents in the primary, you know, the real roughshod, muscle-bound tactics," Clinton said.

The folk image of union heavies applying muscle may endure, but there was little evident punishment from labor against those who crossed the line

---

"Congressional Democrats are groping for something that will allow them to break out of the president's playbook, which is only playing defense."

— Ruy A. Teixeira,
Economic Policy Institute

---

in support of NAFTA. Unions were unable to deny a single incumbent renomination in the 1994 primaries.

"Labor found little to cheer about during the last two years on the Hill," declared The Washington Post in a September 1994 headline.

With the Republican takeover of Congress and Clinton's consequent embrace of a centrist agenda — eventually pursuing such traditionally Republican grails as a balanced budget and an overhaul of welfare — labor appeared to have lost its voice, along with much of its membership.

"Considering how the Democratic Party has marched to the right, for the labor movement to still have any power is amazing," said Dana Frank, an associate professor of American Studies at the University of California, Santa Cruz, who has written about unions and international trade.

Labor, like a yo-yo in slow motion, began to bounce back up in 1995. The AFL-CIO opted for a more aggressive leadership style under John J. Sweeney, who announced to great fanfare that his union would spend more than $35 million on the 1996 elections.

Labor held its nose in support of Clinton and other Democrats who ran centrist campaigns in 1996, believing along with other Democratic constituencies that blocking a GOP monopoly on federal power was paramount.

"I think what happened in 1996 was that almost all of the factions in the Democratic Party could at least agree that they thought the Republican Congress was too extreme, and that sort of united the various wings," said Mayer, author of the 1996 book "The Divided Democrats."

But although unions gave at least $45 million in direct contributions to House Democratic candidates in 1995-96, only 13 of the 32 Republican incumbents the AFL-CIO targeted went down to defeat.

To ensure its threats on fast track had renewed heft after NAFTA, the AFL-CIO ran, as a kind of warning shot, TV and radio ads in 19 swing districts in April that criticized lawmakers for supporting tax breaks, "including one that actually rewards corporations for moving jobs overseas." Seven of the districts where the ads ran were held by Democrats.

House Democrats felt little loyalty to Clinton on the fast-track vote because they believe their political future is separate from his. Clinton did comparatively little to help them in 1996, and incumbent Democrats often ran ahead of him in their districts. *(Weekly Report, p. 441)*

Incumbents' Mandate?

Clinton's success in maintaining peace and prosperity might prove a boon to incumbents of both parties in 1998, helping to stanch predictable Democratic midterm losses. But even minor losses would leave House Democrats in the minority.

"We love the status quo!" crowed Rep. Bill Paxon, R-N.Y., in reference to the GOP's majority control of Congress and most governorships.

That compels congressional Democrats to find ways to re-create their majority outside Clinton's essentially defensive strategy of co-opting Republican themes and working with the GOP Congress for shared success.

"Congressional Democrats are groping for something that will allow them to break out of the president's playbook, which is only playing defense. It keeps them where they are, but that's not good enough if you don't like being in the minority," said Ruy A. Teixeira, an elections analyst at the labor-backed Economic Policy Institute.

"I think they're groping for something that will not just shore up the base but galvanize swing voters in their direction," Teixeira said. ∎

Cities: Decidedly Democratic, Declining in Population

Urban centers more central than ever to Democrats'
prospects in national and statewide campaigns

The train ride from Washington to New York takes only about three hours to provide a quick introduction to the state of urban America. Between the center of national government and the center of the nation's financial activity one finds a variety of cities large and small.

With their gleaming downtown skyscrapers, larger cities such as Baltimore and Philadelphia express the energy that befits centers of culture and commerce. But none of the cities along the heavily traveled Northeast Corridor can hide the unsightly backdrop of urban America — deserted factories, run-down housing and that sense of wholesale abandonment summed up as urban blight.

As such, this mix of cities offers a representative slice of urban America today — declining in population, but probably more decidedly Democratic in presidential and congressional voting than at any time since Franklin D. Roosevelt made the cities the core of the party's coalition. Of 67 urban congressional districts across the country, 61 were carried by President Clinton in 1996 and 58 elected Democrats to Congress. (Congressional Quarterly defines an urban district as having at least 60 percent of its population living within the central city of a metropolitan area.)

White flight to the suburbs has meant a greater voice for urban minorities, who have long tended to vote overwhelmingly Democratic. Yet at the same time, urban voters are not leaving all their eggs in the Democratic basket, as evidenced in recent years by the election of Republican mayors in New York, Los Angeles and a host of smaller

CQ Weekly Report July 12, 1997

MARILYN GATES-DAVIS

cities. *(Story, p. 38)*

In short, while cities are losing clout in terms of sheer numbers, they are far from being political backwaters. They have been the cornerstone of the two Democratic presidential victories in the 1990s, and the party's near monopoly on urban House seats (58 of 67) is what keeps it within striking distance of regaining a House majority.

Yet less than one out of every six districts across the country is urban, a proportion certain to decline further in reapportionment and redistricting after 2000. That means that Democrats need to also have a strong presence in another sector of the electorate if their huge advantage in the cities is to make a difference.

Clinton found such a niche with his breakthrough in the suburbs in the presidential elections of 1992 and 1996. But congressional Democrats have

shown little vote-getting appeal of late beyond city limits. While they control more than 85 percent of the urban House seats in the 105th Congress, they hold only 40 percent of those that are suburban, rural or mixed. *(Weekly Report, p. 1209, 1221)*

In terms of population, cities hit their apogee around 1950. The census that year found that 56 percent of the population lived in metropolitan areas, 33 percent in central cities and 23 percent nearby in what would be regarded as the suburban portion. The census in 1990 showed the metropolitan population up to 77 percent, a surge composed entirely of growth in the suburbs, which had doubled in size to 46 percent of the national population. The urban share was down slightly to 31 percent.

The nearly static urban proportion of the population represents the countervailing effects of two competing trends: sharp population losses since 1950 in most of the older cities of the Frost Belt, largely offset by dramatic population growth since midcentury in most of the newer urban centers of the Sun Belt.

In 1950, nine of the 10 largest cities lay in a swath extending from Boston to St. Louis, with Los Angeles the lone Sun Belt city to make the Top 10. Now, only four of the 10 are in the Frost Belt and six are in the Sun Belt. And there are now more urban congressional districts in the Sun Belt states of the South and West (37) than in the Frost Belt states of the Northeast and Midwest (30).

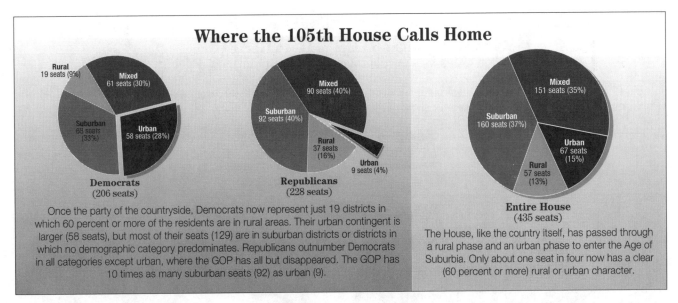

Where the 105th House Calls Home

Democrats
(206 seats)

- Rural 19 seats (9%)
- Mixed 61 seats (30%)
- Suburban 68 seats (33%)
- Urban 58 seats (28%)

Republicans
(228 seats)

- Mixed 90 seats (40%)
- Suburban 92 seats (40%)
- Rural 37 seats (16%)
- Urban 9 seats (4%)

Entire House
(435 seats)

- Mixed 151 seats (35%)
- Suburban 160 seats (37%)
- Urban 67 seats (15%)
- Rural 57 seats (13%)

Once the party of the countryside, Democrats now represent just 19 districts in which 60 percent or more of the residents are in rural areas. Their urban contingent is larger (58 seats), but most of their seats (129) are in suburban districts or districts in which no demographic category predominates. Republicans outnumber Democrats in all categories except urban, where the GOP has all but disappeared. The GOP has 10 times as many suburban seats (92) as urban (9).

The House, like the country itself, has passed through a rural phase and an urban phase to enter the Age of Suburbia. Only about one seat in four now has a clear (60 percent or more) rural or urban character.

Several factors contributed to the turnaround. Many of the cities of the South and West swelled with the military spending of World War II and the Cold War. And they have been sustained since by favorable business climates that Frost Belt cities have had trouble matching.

Urban population numbers also bloomed across the Sun Belt in the last half century as cities legally annexed adjacent land, incorporating high-growth suburban territory within their city limits. It was nearly impossible to accomplish this in the older, more settled metropolitan areas where outlying communities had long been separately incorporated and highly vigilant about city encroachment.

The size of Houston jumped from 160 square miles in 1950 to 556 square miles in 1980, according to Columbia University political scientist Kenneth T. Jackson in his book, "The Crabgrass Frontier." In the same 30-year period, the area of Jacksonville, Fla., mushroomed from 30 square miles to 841 square miles (which approaches the total land mass of Rhode Island).

Many of the Sun Belt cities have been free to grow and prosper in recent decades, unburdened by the transition away from a manufacturing economy that weighed down their Frost Belt counterparts. That transition has been debilitating for even the most economically diverse cities in the Northeast and Midwest. Chicago and Philadelphia have each lost roughly one-quarter of their population since 1950. Cleveland and Detroit have lost nearly one-half, and the once-prominent city of St. Louis has lost more than half of its population since midcentury.

Actually, St. Louis, Boston and Buffalo, N.Y., had more people in 1900 than in the mid-1990s, and the populations of Pittsburgh, Cincinnati and Newark, N.J., are roughly the same as they were at the turn of the century. *(Urban population changes, chart p. 37)*

Yet in presidential voting, the Democrats have managed to make more out of less. Their increasing domination of the Northern urban vote is all the more remarkable considering that the last three Democratic presidents (Clinton, Jimmy Carter and Lyndon B. Johnson) have all been sons of the small-town South.

A case in point is Chicago, where the

"Cities are more and more like Indian wards in the old days."

—Richard Wade, CUNY professor

---

number of votes cast for president in 1996 was less than half the number cast in 1952 (down from more than 1.8 million to less than 900,000), yet the plurality for Clinton was more than three times as large as it was that year for Illinois' native son Adlai E. Stevenson (up from about 160,000 to nearly 560,000).

The changing demographic mix had a lot to do with the improved Democratic showing. As whites left Chicago, the minority proportion of the city's population rose steadily. Chicago was less than 15 percent black in 1950; four decades later, it was nearly 40 percent black, and 20 percent of the population was Hispanic.

And Chicago is hardly unique. A more variegated racial mix has been a component of urban change in recent decades in both the Frost and Sun belts. New York, for instance, which was less than 10 percent black in 1950 was nearly 30 percent black in 1990 and 24 percent Hispanic. Detroit, which was 16 percent black in 1950 was more than three-quarters black at the last census. Los Angeles, which was 17 percent Hispanic in 1970 had grown to 40 percent Hispanic two decades later (the black population, at 14 percent, had fallen about 4 percentage points over the same period).

Nationally, minorities made up more than 40 percent of the population of central cities in 1990. And the urban slice of the electorate also tends to be disproportionately poorer than other sectors and more dependent on government help that the Democrats have traditionally been more willing to offer.

According to a study by David C. Huckabee of the Congressional Research Service in 1993, only nine of the 100 most affluent congressional districts in median family income were urban. Most of the urban districts were in the bottom half in terms of income.

But demographics alone do not account for the increased Democratic nature of the urban vote. Republicans had a lot to do with it as well, reinforcing the effects of population shifts with their own strategic decisions. When they moved rightward in the 1960s on social issues, shedding the "party of Lincoln" sobriquet to become the party of the suburbs and the South, they essentially conceded the cities in national races to the Democrats.

Consequently, the cities have be-

The 'Urban States' of America

Central cities as a percentage of state populations

Percentages reflect the share of each state's population that lived in central cities at the time of the 1990 census. Totals are based on the tabulated census count, which has undergone minor corrections since then.

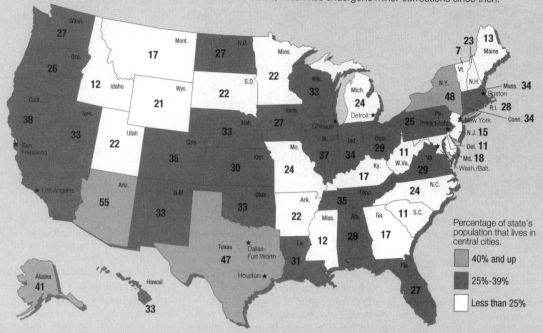

Percentage of state's population that lives in central cities.

40% and up
25%–39%
Less than 25%

★ Designates metropolitan area (central city and suburbs) with population of 4 million or more (1994 Census Bureau estimates).

The United States may have become a suburban nation in demographic terms, but poets and scholars still write paeans to the cities. "Each city has a peculiar location and spirit," wrote Kenneth T. Jackson two decades ago.

"Unlike the mass-produced suburbs, no intelligent observer could mistake Baltimore for Chicago, Minneapolis for Milwaukee, Los Angeles for Houston, or Portland for Memphis. The old downtown can give metropolitan residents, including suburbanites, a sense of place, a sense of uniqueness, and a sense of belonging."

Still, while the cities remain a bedrock of continuity in the American psyche, they too are changing.

According to the 1990 census, most city dwellers are in the most populous states, led by California (with 11.5 million people living in central cities), New York (8.7 million) and Texas (8 million).

Yet when urban population is computed as a share of a state's total population, the list changes dramatically. Topping the list is Arizona, where the last census showed that 55 percent of the population lived in the central cities (led by Phoenix and Tucson). Next came New York (48 percent urban), Texas (47 percent) and Alaska (41 percent).

At first glance, the list is stunningly counterintuititive. But it makes more sense when one considers three factors. The first is the burst of growth in the South and West in the postwar era. Equally important is the success that newer cities have had incorporating metropolitan growth within their legal boundaries. It is not too much of an exaggeration to say Arizonans live in Phoenix, Tucson or the desert — Alaskans in Anchorage or the tundra. The suburbs are relatively small in both states.

The third factor in these percentages of urban population is the decline of central cities in the industrial Frost Belt. Giant Northern states such as Pennsylvania, Ohio, Michigan and Illinois have seen much of their urban population move, either to the suburbs or out of state. The nation's largest city, New York, is the only major Frost Belt city that has not seen a precipitous population decline since 1950.

As a result, the newer Sun Belt cities of the South and West now have more representation in Congress than do the older cities of the North and Midwest. The West now boasts more urban House seats (21) than any other region.

In categorizing congressional districts, CQ uses a 60 percent standard. For instance, an urban district is one in which at least 60 percent of the population lives within the central city of a defined metropolitan area. A suburban district is one in which at least 60 percent of the population lives within a metropolitan area but outside a central city, while a rural district is one in which at least 60 percent of the population lives outside a metropolitan area (and outside towns of 25,000 or more). Where none of the categories accounts for 60 percent, the district is designated as mixed.

By this method, New York still has a dozen congressional seats, but Chicago is down to five, Philadelphia to three, Detroit to two and Boston and Baltimore to one each. Once-powerful Frost Belt cities such as St. Louis and Cleveland no longer have a seat they can truly call their own. Democratic Reps. Richard A. Gephardt and William L. Clay still call St. Louis home, but most of their constituents do not. So too in Ohio, where neither of the two Cleveland-area seats encompasses enough of the city to be considered urban.

come more helpful than ever to Democratic candidates for the White House — an importance that was evident in the 1996 presidential voting.

The nation's three largest cities (New York, Los Angeles and Chicago) constitute just 5 percent of the national population and even a smaller percentage of the national turnout. But they provided more than 25 percent of Clinton's nationwide margin of victory: 2.1 million of the 8.2 million votes by which Clinton carried the popular vote.

If one adds in Clinton's pluralities in Philadelphia and Detroit, the cumulative margin he collected just in these five cities represents nearly one-third of his national victory margin. *(Chart, this page)*

Historical Departure

This degree of domination is a far cry from the beginning of the century, when Republicans were widely viewed as the city's champions against a Democratic Party still closely associated with the rural South. Democrats did not seriously compete for urban America's presidential vote until 1928, when they nominated Alfred E. Smith (a product of New York's Lower East Side).

They completed their political takeover of the cities in the following decade, during the Depression, when FDR's New Dealers designed many of their programs to help working-class urban voters.

Republicans, though, were able to remain fairly competitive in urban voting into the early 1960s. They were still numerous in many city neighborhoods, and the party had some appeal among blacks because it maintained its historic commitment to civil rights. But the GOP lost much of its remaining urban base in 1964 ,when it nominated conservative Arizona Sen. Barry M. Goldwater over New York Gov. Nelson A. Rockefeller and moved decidedly rightward on social issues.

Now, the GOP's conservative mainstream is widely viewed as "pretty anti-urban, anti-social spending, anti-mass transit and anti-infrastructure spending," says Margaret M. Weir, a senior fellow in government studies at the Brookings Institution. To many city voters, "Republicans stand for shrunken government."

The GOP made a modest bid to regain an urban toehold in 1996, when they ran former Housing and Urban Development Secretary Jack F. Kemp as their vice presidential candidate. Kemp made well-publicized campaign forays into heavily black Harlem, south-central Los Angeles and Southside Chicago. Yet, the Republican presidential

Urban Population: Sun Belt Rises; Frost Belt Melts

Mention the word "city" and many people think first of New York or Chicago. But according to 1994 population estimates from the Census Bureau, six of the 10 largest cities in the United States are now in the Sun Belt. New York and Chicago are still in first and third place, respectively. But like most cities across the Frost Belt, each has lost population since 1950, about the time that many cities in the Northeast and Midwest saw their population peak. Meanwhile, most of the major Sun Belt cities have grown dramatically since mid-century, with the population often doubling or tripling or more.

In the chart below, each city's current population rank is noted at left.

Frost Belt Cities	1950	1994	Change, 1950-1994	
1) New York	7,891,957	7,333,253	− 558,704	(- 7.1%)
3) Chicago	3,620,962	2,731,743	− 889,219	(-24.6%)
5) Philadelphia	2,071,605	1,524,249	− 547,356	(-26.4%)
10) Detroit	1,849,568	992,038	− 857,530	(-46.4%)
Sun Belt Cities				
2) Los Angeles	1,970,358	3,448,613	+ 1,478,255	(+75.0%)
4) Houston	596,163	1,702,086	+ 1,105,923	(+185.5%)
6) San Diego	334,387	1,151,977	+ 817,590	(+244.5%)
7) Phoenix	106,818	1,048,949	+ 942,131	(+882.0%)
8) Dallas	434,462	1,022,830	+ 588,368	(+135.4%)
9) San Antonio	408,442	998,905	+ 590,463	(+144.6%)

Northern City Margins
Turnouts Down, Democratic Margins Up

Since Franklin D. Roosevelt's New Deal in the 1930s, major urban centers (especially those in the industrial Frost Belt) have been major players in the Democratic coalition. But at no time has urban America been more decidedly Democratic in its presidential voting than it is now.

While fewer people vote in industrial-state urban centers now than at mid-century, Democratic pluralities in many of these cities have increased dramatically. The cities have largely lost their Republican base, while those who remain and those who move in tend to be Democrats.

The chart below compares electoral data from the presidential election of 1952 with that of 1996 in a selected group of seven cities. The data are based on official results from both elections.

	Votes Cast (thousands)		City's Percentage of State Vote		Democratic Margin (thousands)	
	1952	1996	1952	1996	1952	1996
New York	3,411	1,961	48%	31%	359	1,173
Chicago	1,842	869	41	20	161	559
Philadelphia	959	533	21	12	160	328
Detroit	813	299	29	8	170	261
Boston	357	170	15	7	69	92
Baltimore	350	183	39	10	12	117
Milwaukee	307	208	19	9	9	88

SOURCE: America Votes

Can the GOP Come Back in the City?

Urban America remains reliably Democratic in voting for president and Congress. But a growing sense of social disintegration in the cities has led to some dramatic changes in the political order at the local level — changes that could presage a return to two-party voting in the metropolitan core.

During the last decade, four of the nation's largest cities — New York, Los Angeles, Chicago and Philadelphia — had black mayors. Now, none of them do. Part of that is due to demographics. None of the four is majority black. But there also seems to have been a change in voter attitude in the cities, where race-based politics is seen as a frill when viewed against the long-standing backdrop of urban decay.

"Because of economic conditions, there are far more moderate politicians on the [urban] scene, black and white," says University of Maryland political scientist Ronald Walters.

REUTERS

New York City Mayor Rudolph Giuliani, left, endorsed Democratic Gov. Mario M. Cuomo for re-election in 1994.

All four cities now have white mayors who campaigned on the need for government efficiency and law-and-order. In New York and Los Angeles, they are Republicans who have proved popular in spite of the strongly Democratic terrain. Rudolph W. Giuliani was elected mayor of New York in 1993 and is heavily favored to win re-election this fall. Richard Riordan, elected mayor of Los Angeles in 1993, easily won a second term this spring.

Other GOP mayors have also been elected in the face of Democratic majorities. Among them are popular Susan Golding in San Diego and Bret Schundler, who won re-election this spring in Jersey City, N.J., a short ferry ride from Ellis Island and the Statue of Liberty. Conservative Republicans are particularly proud of Schundler, who has run on an unabashed platform of free market capitalism in a city where whites are a minority.

But big-city Republicans are more often somewhat removed from the GOP mainstream, and their triumphs are not universally applauded within the party. Giuliani and Riordan hold their party at arm's length and present themselves as clean, efficient agents of change. Riordan endorsed Democrat Dianne Feinstein for re-election to the Senate in 1994. That same fall, Giuliani was conspicuously backing Democratic Gov. Mario M. Cuomo's unsuccessful re-election bid in New York.

"If [Giuliani] were in Congress, I suspect he would be in the left wing of the Democratic Party," says David A. Bositis, senior political analyst at the Joint Center for Political and Economic Studies.

The electoral success of the Republican mayors has been due less to "their political ideology than being linked to an agenda for change," says Rep. Earl Blumenauer, a Democrat who represents Portland, Ore.

Urban issues are not party issues by nature, Blumenauer says. "Local officials dealing with police and parks and people's backyards . . . can't afford to be gratuitously partisan."

Still, the willingness of voters in several big cities to back Republicans of any stripe for a major office is noteworthy and could be an early sign that the era of knee-jerk Democratic voting in the cities is coming to an end.

One reason to think so is that the urban political machines that once routinely delivered votes for Democratic candidates are a thing of the past. Civil service reforms have reduced patronage in city halls and modern election methods have made it harder to manufacture votes.

Just as important, however, is the Democrats' own loss of interest in the cities and their problems. No one ever thought Clinton would be another FDR, yet many urban advocates have found his support of budget austerity and the 1996 welfare overhaul a bitter disappointment. "Clinton has been pretty indifferent to the cities," says Bositis.

On June 23, at the annual meeting of the U.S. Conference of Mayors, Clinton announced a seven-point plan that included incentives for employers to hire welfare recipients and for police officers to buy homes in the city.

Frank Shafroth, director of policy and federal relations for the National League of Cities, characterized the list as recycling programs Clinton had proposed before. "The solutions are barely going to touch the surface," he said.

While the White House calls the new programs the most ambitious in 20 years, no one speaks of returning to the grand scale of "urban renewal" of the 1950s, the Great Society of the 1960s or even Richard M. Nixon's revenue-sharing plans of the 1970s.

Those eras of expansive federal involvement seem remote. The trends of the 1980s and 1990s have returned authority and responsibility to state and local governments. That trend corresponds with some city voters' new willingness to judge individual GOP candidates on their own terms.

City-savvy Republicans have shown they can win when they unite and turn out white voters. Where GOP politics are inclusive enough to appeal to middle-class minorities as well, their urban growth potential may be considerable. The more that Democrats emulate Clinton, wooing the suburbs while taking the cities largely for granted, the more opportunity the GOP may find downtown.

Lee Miringoff, director of the Marist Institute for Public Opinion in Poughkeepsie, N.Y., concludes that just as the suburbs are becoming less uniformly Republican, the cities are becoming less uniformly Democratic. In 2000 and beyond, both demographic categories could be coming into play in degrees not seen for generations.

From GOP to Democratic: Urban U.S. Over 20th Century

In the early 1900s, Democrats were still identified with the rural South and much of urban America voted Republican. But that began to change as increasing numbers of city dwellers, arriving from Europe or from rural America, were organized politically by the Democratic Party. In 1928, the shift got its symbol when the Democratic presidential nomination went to a son of urban America, Alfred E. Smith (from New York's Lower East Side). The transformation of cities into Democratic strongholds was cemented in the following decade by the Depression and by Franklin D. Roosevelt's New Deal, which directed much of its federal largess to the cities.

The chart below highlights results in a regional sampling of cities from five separate presidential elections over the course of the 20th century.

The elections featured are 1920, the first in which women were allowed to vote; 1928, when the Democrats ran Smith; 1936, when FDR won a landslide re-election victory based largely on his party's newfound urban appeal; 1960, when Democrat John F. Kennedy (a Boston Catholic) fashioned a narrow victory based largely on the strength of urban votes; and the 1996 election.

The chart indicates the party of the presidential winner in each of the five elections, with "R" for Republican and "D" for Democratic. The percentage represents the Democratic share of the city's total vote in that particular election.

	1920	1928	1936	1960	1996
New York	R 27%	D 60%	D 73%	D 63%	D 77%
Philadelphia	R 22%	R 40%	D 61%	D 68%	D 77%
Baltimore	R 39%	R 48%	D 68%	D 64%	D 79%
New Orleans	D 65%	D 80%	D 91%	D 50%	D 76%
St. Louis	R 38%	D 52%	D 66%	D 67%	D 75%
Denver	R 33%	R 36%	D 65%	D 50%	D 62%
San Francisco	R 22%	D 49%	D 74%	D 58%	D 72%

vote was even lower in many cities in 1996 than it had been in 1992.

In fact, Clinton wound up with a bigger share of the vote in cities such as New York, Philadelphia, Baltimore and St. Louis than FDR had in his landslide re-election win of 1936. That year, the cities were just another flower in FDR's garden, as he garnered more than 60 percent overall. Clinton, on the other hand, drew less than 50 percent overall — making his urban share all the more important. *(Chart, this page)*

A Steep Hill

The cities have tended to have more impact on presidential elections than on congressional elections. Urban residents have rarely enjoyed clout on Capitol Hill commensurate with their numbers.

Through much of the century, cities were gerrymandered out of seats by rural-dominated state legislatures. By the time the Supreme Court finally made one-man, one-vote the law of the land in the 1960s, the cities were already past their heyday.

Even in the years when Democrats were in control of Congress, power often rested with a conservative coalition of Republicans and Southern Democrats

who were hardly sympathetic to urban interests. Vestiges of that alliance remain today. "This is now a suburban country with a suburban government," says Richard Wade, a professor of urban history at the City University of New York. "Cities are more and more like Indian wards in the old days."

Today, urban House members have become a minority party within a minority party. Even though virtually all of them are Democrats, they constitute less than 30 percent of the House Democratic Caucus. And on critical votes that expose fault lines within the party, the city members often find themselves on the losing side. *(A Demographic Look at the House, pie charts p. 35)*

Welfare Test

On the July 1996 vote on the controversial plan to dismantle the federal welfare program, 64 percent of non-urban Democrats voted in favor, 87 percent of urban Democrats voted against. The result was a 98-98 split among House Democrats on the conference report, although overwhelming Republican support for welfare reform ensured the bill's easy passage.

Similarly, on this May's vote to adopt the fiscal 1998 budget resolution, which

included significant cuts in spending and taxes, 72 percent of non-urban Democrats voted in favor, 55 percent of urban Democrats voted against. Again with hefty Republican support, the measure passed.

On both votes, the majority of urban Democrats were joined by House Minority Leader Richard A. Gephardt, a former St. Louis alderman whose roots are in urban politics but represents a district that is predominantly suburban.

Former Mayors

And there are others on Capitol Hill like Gephardt, who do not have districts that CQ classifies as urban but come from a background in city politics. Among those in the House who have served as mayors are Republicans Sonny Bono of California (Palm Springs), E. Clay Shaw Jr. of Florida (Fort Lauderdale), Sue Myrick of North Carolina (Charlotte) and Kay Granger of Texas (Fort Worth), as well as Democrats Scotty Baesler of Kentucky (Lexington), Richard E. Neal of Massachusetts (Springfield), Tom Allen of Maine (Portland), Dennis J. Kucinich of Ohio (Cleveland) and Tom Sawyer of Ohio (Akron).

Former mayors in the Senate include Republicans Dirk Kempthorne of Idaho

A Tale of Two Bay Cities

Boston and San Diego, built on natural harbors at opposite extremes of the country, symbolize the divergence of fortune for the regions of postwar America.

Boston is a quintessential Frost Belt urban center. Rich in history (it was founded in 1630), culture and commerce, it has nonetheless seen its population fall dramatically in the 20th century. In fact, Boston had a larger population at the turn of the century than it has now, and it no longer ranks among the 20 largest cities in the nation.

San Diego, by contrast, was scarcely more than a village at the turn of this century, with about 17,000 residents. But it now has well over 1 million inhabitants (more than twice as many as Boston), making it the sixth most populous city in the country. West of the Mississippi, only Houston and Los Angeles have more people.

The two cities also have contrasting political histories. Since the days before the American Revolution, which was itself something of a local product, Boston has been a focus of the nation's political life. It was a hotbed of abolitionism in the years before the Civil War.

But through most of the 20th century, Boston, and by extension Massachusetts, have been Democratic bastions. With the exception of the Eisenhower and Reagan landslides, the state has voted Democratic in every presidential election since 1928. In 1972, it was the only state in the Union to do so.

Since 1960, two Democrats from the Boston area have become Speaker of the House, John W. McCormack and Thomas P. O'Neill Jr., and for generations the city has been home base for the Kennedy family. Most of Boston now lies within one congressional district that is represented by Joseph P. Kennedy II.

President Clinton carried Boston with 74 percent of the vote in 1996, better than native-son Michael S. Dukakis did

JAMES BLANK/SAN DIEGO CONVENTION AND VISITORS BUREAU

San Diego played host to the 1996 Republican National Convention.

during his presidential run in 1988, and nearly as well as John F. Kennedy did in sweeping his hometown in 1960.

But demographically, at least, Boston is not the same city it was then. The black share of the population has risen from less than 10 percent in 1960 to more than one-quarter in 1990, with nearly 11 percent of the city Hispanic.

In the process, Boston has gone through many of the same social upheavals as other major Frost Belt cities. Tensions over court-ordered school busing ran so high in the 1970s that former Alabama Gov. George C. Wallace actually carried the city in the 1976 Democratic presidential primary.

Navy Town

San Diego's growth was greatly accelerated with World War II and the struggle against Japan. Since then, and especially since the Vietnam War, the Navy has made San Diego its primary base on the Pacific (it is now home port for half the ships in the Pacific fleet).

The population of San Diego tripled from 1950 to 1990 and so did its area — from less than 100 square miles to more than 300. Counting the pensions paid to the vast numbers of retired service personnel, the area now has the highest military payroll in the nation.

Like other Sun Belt cities that serve as points of entry from Latin America, San Diego has a growing Hispanic population. Still, it is two-thirds white, and though Clinton carried the city in the 1996 presidential election, San Diego has a Republican pedigree in keeping with its military history.

The city has a Republican mayor (Susan Golding). Three of the four districts that include portions of the city have Republican congressmen. And a Republican former mayor, Pete Wilson, is now governor of California. In 1996, San Diego played host to the Republican national convention.

(Boise), Richard G. Lugar of Indiana (Indianapolis) and James M. Inhofe of Oklahoma (Tulsa), and Democrat Dianne Feinstein of California (San Francisco). And a host of current members of Congress have served on city councils, from Democratic Rep. John Lewis of Georgia (Atlanta) to Republican Sen. Jesse Helms of North Carolina (Raleigh).

But the present number of House Republicans who actually represent urban districts are no more than a corporal's guard. Most are newer members who swim comfortably in the party's conservative mainstream. A half dozen of them

represent Sun Belt constituencies in cities such as Tulsa, Okla.; Albuquerque, N.M.; Phoenix, Ariz.; and San Diego. Only three have urban Frost Belt seats: Jon Christensen of Nebraska (Omaha), Deborah Pryce of Ohio (Columbus) and Susan Molinari of New York's Staten Island, who recently announced that she would resign in August to take a job as a CBS anchorwoman.

Molinari has been a member of the House Republican leadership as conference vice chairman, but her departure means that the urban power brokers that remain will be on the Democratic side, at

best composing the underpinnings of a government in exile. Charles B. Rangel of New York is the ranking Democrat on the House Ways and Means Committee, as is Henry B. Gonzalez of Texas on Banking and Financial Services, John Conyers Jr. of Michigan on Judiciary, and California Democrats Henry A. Waxman on Government Reform and Oversight, Ronald V. Dellums on National Security and Howard L. Berman on Standards of Official Conduct. Like most other urban House Democrats, they represent safe districts that have enabled them to accrue seniority.

Yet for urban issues to advance in the current environment, Democratic Rep. Earl Blumenauer of Oregon, figures they must be presented in a broader (metropolitan) context that can draw support beyond city lines. Blumenauer, who represents Portland, suggests that issues such as land use, affordable housing, non-highway transportation spending and historic preservation all be discussed under the broader theme of "livability."

"We're in this together," says Blumenauer.

Republican Rep. Thomas M. Davis III, who represents an affluent district in the Northern Virginia suburbs, tends to agree. "On issues like crime, development, taxes, that's why people leave the city," he says. "That puts pressure on the suburbs as the cities disintegrate. You would like to see a better balance."

Local, Federal Split

Republicans have been able to break the Democratic hegemony in a number of cities at the mayoral level. But in races for federal office, says Republican Rep. Myrick, herself a former mayor of Charlotte, "the attitude yet (in the cities) is that we have to have federal money" and the Democrats speak best to that.

But, adds Myrick, "I think eventually that will change because there is no more money."

Democrats counter that there would be plenty of money for cities if it were not for the Republican majority's preference for defense spending and tax cuts. And on this argument, the Republicans are likely to continue to lose much of the urban core constituency in federal elections.

In national politics, says University of Maryland political scientist Ronald Walters, Republicans "are not pro-city. They're pro-suburban, and I think people in the cities instinctively understand that." Even though urban voters may not enthusiastically support Clinton and the direction of the Democrats in Congress, he adds: "People are trapped in the structure of choice." ∎

REAPPORTIONMENT

Statistics Stir the Passions Of Parties' Boosters

Proposed census methodology could alter demographics and apportionment of congressional seats

When President Clinton vetoed a supplemental disaster relief bill June 9 in part over a Republican attempt to ban a census method, many observers wondered at the GOP's adamance about a relatively arcane matter.

On its surface, the process of counting the nation's population is the obsession of statisticians and enumerators, a dry task not normally associated with aid to flood victims such as those this year in North Dakota and Minnesota.

Yet at the heart of the drama over the disaster relief bill was whether the Census Bureau should be barred from using statistical sampling techniques for the 2000 census, which the bureau says are needed to avoid the undercounts that tarnished the last decennial census.

Despite the technical nature of the issue, the way the census is done in 2000 does have enormous political consequences, affecting the apportionment of congressional seats and the distribution of federal dollars.

Census Bureau officials still plan to try to count as many individuals as possible in 2000. But they insist that it is impossible to tally every person in so massive a nation, and they want to use sampling to help determine information about those households that cannot be contacted through traditional methods.

Supporters of the sampling technique say it will decrease the cost of the census, increase accuracy and help reduce the endemic undercounts, which have been most acute among minorities.

CQ Weekly Report June 21, 1997

DOUGLAS GRAHAM

Reps. Tom Sawyer, D-Ohio, Christopher Shays, R-Conn., and Xavier Becerra, D-Calif., express their support for statistical sampling at a news conference June 4.

"Every time there has been an innovation in the census, people have been concerned about it because the census has been used for dividing up the pie, whether it's the political pie or the money pie," said Census Bureau Director Martha Farnsworth Riche.

But opponents of sampling, including GOP leaders in the House and Senate, argue that using statistical sampling will not yield a census as accurate as a head count and is unconstitutional.

The opponents of sampling say they are not backing down, despite being rebuffed by Clinton's veto of the fiscal 1997 supplemental spending bill over its provision to bar the use of sampling for the

purpose of apportioning seats in the House, as well as an issue related to government shutdowns.

Clinton then signed a version of the bill (HR 1871 — PL 105-18) on June 12 that included a much softer provision requiring the Commerce Department, which oversees the Census Bureau, to report to Congress on the details of its proposed methodology for conducting the 2000 census. *(Supplemental bill, Weekly Report, p. 1362)*

Still, there are signs the fight may flare when Congress takes up the fiscal 1998 Commerce, Justice and State spending bill, which provides funds for the Census Bureau.

"The Census Bureau is on notice that this Congress believes they're pursuing a risky scheme of statistical guessing, not accurate counting," said Dennis Hastert, R-Ill., chairman of the House Government Reform and Oversight subcommittee with jurisdiction over the issue and the GOP's point man. "This Congress doesn't want to be on board when the 2000 census goes over the cliff."

Meanwhile, sampling is not the only controversy surrounding the 2000 census. Groups representing individuals of mixed races and others are asking for a "multiracial" category on the 2000 census form in addition to the racial categories used in the last census: white, black, Asian or Pacific Islander, American Indian or Alaskan Native, and other.

Sampling Showdown

Both sides of the sampling debate claim that their opponents are maneuvering for political advantage.

Sampling supporters say the GOP opposition is worried that if sampling increases the minority count, Republicans could lose House seats. This is because most members of minority groups, blacks and Hispanics in particular, who go to the polls generally favor Democrats.

Opponents of sampling counter that the procedure would open the census to political tampering, saying the procedure could be used to skew the numbers to the advantage of one party.

The task of counting the nation's population often has been plagued by political controversy since its inception in the late 1790s.

The last census, in 1990, was no exception. It was the most expensive census in history, yet still failed to count 1.6 percent of the population (roughly 4 million people), according to Census Bureau estimates. It also sparked a controversy that dragged into 1996, when the Supreme Court settled the issue. *(1996 Weekly Report, p. 822)*

The dispute centered on the decision in 1991 by Bush administration Commerce Secretary Robert A. Mosbacher not to adjust the 1990 census, despite a post-enumeration survey using sampling that revealed an undercount that was greatest among minorities.

(Minority individuals are more often missed because of such factors as higher rates of multiple-family living arrangements, changes of residence and homelessness among minority groups than for the overall population.)

Among those who urged Mosbacher to adjust the count was Newt Gingrich, R-Ga., who at the time was House minority whip. However, Gingrich, now House Speaker, has joined other GOP congressional decision-makers in opposing the use of statistical sampling in the 2000 census.

Mosbacher's decision not to adjust the census sparked outrage from civil rights groups and others, and a court challenge by jurisdictions such as the cities of New York and Los Angeles.

The plaintiffs in the *Department of Commerce v. City of New York et al.* claimed that those individuals who were missed were denied their constitutional right to equal representation under the law. However, the Supreme Court ruled in March 1996 that Mosbacher's decision was "well within the constitutional bounds of discretion over the conduct of the census provided to the federal government."

Hoping to avoid the mayhem that plagued the 1990 census, the Census Bureau has been moving forward with plans to use statistical sampling in the 2000 census. These plans are based in part on the recommendations of two National Research Council study panels. One concluded in 1995 that, in a country the size of the modern United States, "it is fruitless to continue trying to count every last person with traditional census methods of physical enumeration."

Charles L. Schultze, a senior fellow emeritus at the Brookings Institution, said, "It's one of the few cases where

you can both save money and get higher quality." Schultze chaired one of the National Research Council panels that has endorsed sampling.

The bureau will begin mailing out census forms in mid-March 2000. After about four weeks, the bureau plans to begin contacting a selected sample of households that have not responded to try to reach at least a 90 percent response rate in each of the census tracts (which contain about 4,000 people). For example, if after the fourth week it has received responses from only 60 percent of the households in a tract, the bureau will attempt to contact three of the four remaining households in that tract.

Once it reaches at least 90 percent, the bureau will use responses from all respondents to produce population estimates for the final 10 percent of housing units that have not responded.

The bureau will then conduct a second separate sample of 750,000 households nationwide to double-check the quality of its work. Bureau officials say this second sample will ferret out errors, refine the sampling process and help eliminate the undercount.

The bureau's plan to use sampling has won the support of Barbara E. Bryant, who served as Census Bureau director under President George Bush and who recommended adjusting the 1990 census but was overruled. Other supporters include the American Statistical Association, the U.S. Conference of Mayors, minority group advocates such as the Leadership Conference on Civil Rights, and many Democratic members of Congress.

"Banning sampling from the year 2000 census is a tidy way of making sure millions of Americans, mostly minorities and poor people, are not counted," said Rep. Carolyn B. Maloney, D-N.Y.

While the drive to ban sampling has been largely identified with Republicans, some GOP lawmakers support the use of sampling, including Sen. John McCain of Arizona and Rep. Christopher Shays of Connecticut.

If the bureau is prevented by Congress from using sampling, Riche estimated the 2000 undercount might be about 1.9 percent. She also said that the bureau probably would need an additional $675 million to $800 million to conduct the census as accurately as possible without doing sampling, on top of the $4 billion it is already expected to spend.

While some GOP estimates of the cost differ from those of the bureau, Republican leaders have promised to provide the additional money.

"I speak for the leadership, the resources will be there," Hastert said.

Active Opposition

Hastert says the benefits of paying for a census without sampling include avoiding additional costs that might result if a census with sampling was overturned by the Supreme Court — not an unlikely event, they say, because the Constitution requires an "actual enumeration."

"Nothing less than the U.S. Constitution says that every American shall be actually enumerated," said Rep. Harold Rogers, R-Ky., who chairs the House Appropriations subcommittee with jurisdiction over the Census Bureau. "It does not say guess, estimate, pontificate, manipulate."

In his veto message on the supplemental spending bill, Clinton noted that the Justice Department under his administration, as well as under Presidents Jimmy Carter and Bush, issued opinions concluding that the Constitution does not forbid sampling.

But critics also have other reasons to oppose sampling, not the least of which is a belief that sampling will diminish the accuracy of the census.

Opponents highlight the Census Bureau's revelation that if Mosbacher had chosen to adjust the 1990 census, Pennsylvania might mistakenly have lost a House seat to Arizona.

The initial results of the post-enumeration survey indicated that Pennsylvania would lose a seat to Arizona and

Wisconsin would lose a seat to California. Census Bureau officials later revealed that there was a computer mistake in the original survey and that the only likely shift would have been from Wisconsin to California.

While some opponents agree that sampling may improve the national count, they argue that it will be less accurate at the census block level (the smallest of the survey's population subdivisions). They complain that the bureau has not provided enough information about the potential error rate for sampling at this level.

Clark H. Bensen, an independent data analyst who has done redistricting work for Republicans, says his analysis of the bureau's 1995 test using sampling showed that the error rate varied greatly from block to block.

However, the National Research Council, in a June 10 report on the bureau's 1995 test, found that "using block-level data, sampling should have, at worst, a neutral effect on congressional redistricting, and it should yield more accurate redistricting when blocks are aggregated into meaningful legal political units."

On the undercounting of minorities, opponents of sampling say the bureau could reduce the problem by stepping up its community outreach and promotional activities and updating addresses — which the bureau is, in fact, doing now.

"I'm given pause that the medicine could be worse than the disease," said Peter Skerry, a visiting fellow at the centrist Brookings Institution and a political scientist at Claremont McKenna College in Claremont, Calif.

Political Factors

While some GOP leaders say they are not jockeying for party advantage, others are more blunt in assessing the consequences: Republican National Committee Chairman Jim Nicholson has said, based on an internal report that the GOP has not released, that Republicans could lose as many as 25 House seats if statistical sampling is used in the 2000 census.

Others strongly dispute this figure, noting that there are many steps in the process of redistricting. The biggest lies with state legislatures, which in most states have authority to draw redistricting plans, and governors, who in most states have veto power. Many legislatures are controlled by the GOP, and 32 of the 50 governors are Republicans.

"There is no basis [for concerns] that there will be a large number of seats shifting to the Democrats," said Jeffrey

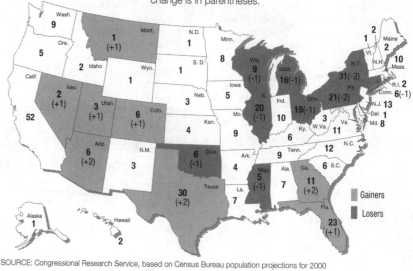

Reapportionment Projections for 2000

The map shows the current number of seats for each state in the House of Representatives, and highlights those states projected in January by the Congressional Research Service to gain or lose House seats following the 2000 census. The potential seat change is in parentheses.

SOURCE: Congressional Research Service, based on Census Bureau population projections for 2000

M. Wice, a lawyer who has worked with Democrats on redistricting issues.

Nonetheless, the stakes are high because, as after every census, there will be winners and losers.

A Congressional Research Service study released in January offered a glimpse of which states might benefit from reapportionment following the 2000 census. The study, based on the Census Bureau's July 1996 population projections for the year 2000, projected that 11 seats would likely shift hands. (Map, this page)

A longstanding pattern would continue, with some fast-growing Sunbelt and Western states picking up House seats and some Northern industrial states losing ground. The biggest winners would be Texas, Arizona and Georgia, which would each gain two seats. New York and Pennsylvania each would lose two seats.

Other Sticking Points

While the sampling issue has grabbed most of the attention, the issue of whether to include a "multiracial" category on census forms also is simmering.

The White House Office of Management and Budget (OMB), which under the 1980 Paperwork Reduction Act is required to scrutinize all federal questionnaires to ensure they do not place an extraordinary burden on the public, is expected to issue a public notice in July of its recommendations on the issue.

Supporters of the "multiracial" op-

tion say it will provide a more accurate portrait of the nation's population and will help break down racial barriers.

"The government is forcing multiracial children and adults to choose between one of their parents" when signifying their race on the census form, said Susan Graham, president of Project RACE, a group that has been lobbying for the creation of a multiracial category on the census form.

However, some African-Americans and others worry that the option might have a negative effect on other groups of minorities. The NAACP has said a multiracial category might ultimately dilute "the benefits to which minority group members are entitled under civil rights laws and under the Constitution," testified Harold McDougall, the organization's Washington, D.C., office director, before a House subcommittee in May.

The Census Bureau released results of a sample test in May using various questions that showed adding a multiracial category had little effect on the numbers of people who identified themselves as white, black or American Indian. Statistically significant changes were reported in the Alaska Native and Asian and Pacific Islander categories.

Graham said she does not expect the OMB will rule in her group's favor. If that is the case, she said her group plans to pursue the issue in Congress. Rep. Tom Petri, R-Wis., has introduced a bill (HR 830) requiring a "multiracial" or "multiethnic" census category. ■

Politics and Marketing Merge In Parties' Bid for Relevance

As traditional loyalty fades and the voter becomes a consumer, parties struggle to redefine themselves and their 'products'

It could have been a sales and marketing meeting for a large corporation. And, in a sense, it was.

Two months after the November 1996 election, Speaker Newt Gingrich, R-Ga., was telling a meeting of the Republican National Committee (RNC) that the party was like a soft drink that only needed the right marketing to reach its maximum market share.

Gingrich's text that day was the annual report of Coca-Cola, the global soft drink giant that has its headquarters in Atlanta, near Gingrich's suburban home.

"The symbol of their annual report last year was infinity," Gingrich said, hinting at how high one's goals can get. Making the point more directly, the annual report said that the average human being consumes 48 ounces of liquid a day, and that "only" two of those ounces were currently Coca-Cola.

Some might consider this a satisfying degree of product penetration on a planetary basis. But not Coke; and apparently not Gingrich, either.

The Speaker's point was that a good sales force is never sated, and that Republicans had to sell a whole lot more of their philosophy and their candidates before they could claim any bonuses.

Gingrich may not be one of those "go for the gold" motivational speakers who are paid to pump up sales personnel. But such a pitch was just what the RNC wanted and expected. At the close of the 20th century, marketing technique and party politics are close to being one and the same.

Democrats are less likely to use the language of the corporate boardroom to express themselves, but they face a nearly identical market challenge.

The major parties are no longer reli-

CQ Weekly Report Aug. 16, 1997

able voter organizers (as evidenced by the poor turnout in recent years) or candidate recruiters. Both parties still act as conduits carrying ideas between elected officials and the people, but neither now controls who will run or what those who run will say.

"They have simply become one of a number of organizations relevant to candidates," says Jeff Fishel, an emeritus professor of government at American University in Washington.

In fact, the parties may be said to exist now primarily as brand names that individual candidates choose to apply to themselves as a shortcut to identification in the marketplace. Aside from managing their respective brands, the parties' main value in recent years has been as repositories for campaign cash. "Now their major role is the distribution of money," says Garrison Nelson, a professor of poitical science at the University of Vermont.

The parties have become "basically what you might call holding companies," says Walter Dean Burnham, a political science professor at the University of Texas. "They organize cash and spread it around."

Federal laws closely restrict the raising and spending of money by individual candidates. In any given primary or general election, a candidate may not take more than $1,000 from an individual or $5,000 from a political action committee. But the parties may accept unlimited "soft money" donations as long as the funds go for loosely defined "party building" activities.

Both parties need a measure of quality control — making sure that their candidates' messages are consistent with the party's national message — but both must also worry about product identity, about making sure they are not just marketing one interchangeable "cola" against another.

Both parties have deep internal disagreements as to how to accomplish these goals at a time when less than half the electorate is sufficiently motivated to vote in a presidential election and party identification is weak by historical standards.

Some believe the answer lies in effective governing through compromise, as in the recent budget deal between President Clinton and the Republican majorities in Congress.

Others, in both parties, prefer a constant warfare of contrasts, as in a sales campaign designed to supplant an established product with a new one.

Either way, whichever emphasis a party chooses will be judged by its success as a market strategy, with voters playing the role of consumers.

Much has been made of the parties' diminished role in recent years, and the subject will be revisited if new campaign finance laws eventually restrain their role in political fundraising.

One measure of erosion has come in voter identification. In 1960, the Gallup Organization found 47 percent of poll respondents identified themselves as Democrats, 30 percent as Republicans and just 23 percent as independents or members of other parties.

In the 1990s, those numbers have converged. Polling by the Pew Research Center for the People and the Press over a 54-month period ending in June has found an average of 33 percent of the respondents calling themselves Democrats, 29 percent Republicans and 33 percent independents (with a handful naming other specific parties).

But if a plurality of the electorate now prefers neither party, the disaffected show no sign of coalescing around an alternative. Ross Perot's challenge to the two-party system in 1992 received 19 percent of the popular vote for president, the most for a third-choice candidate since 1912. But in 1996, despite polls that found 60 percent of the nation wanting a third party, Perot's return bid received less than half as many votes as his first.

Since then, Perot's fledgling Reform Party has suffered a schism so severe that rival factions are planning competing conventions on different dates in different cities.

But that is only part of the reason most scholars and political professionals remain convinced the two-party system will be around for some time to come.

"It would take something cataclysmic to eliminate one or the other of the major parties from their role of significance," says Fishel.

At the same time, Fishel and others say, the role of the parties has changed and will continue to change.

"They lost the monopoly they had, particularly on candidate recruitment and finance. That certainly does not mean they're going out of business, just that they have to compete with other groups," says Fishel.

The difficulty of establishing party hegemony in the traditional sense is apparent in states where individual politicians have achieved great success that does not translate into broader popularity for their party (what marketers call "sharing brand equity").

Two such politicians are Republican Gov. Tommy G. Thompson of Wisconsin and Democratic Gov. Howard Dean of Vermont. Each has won three terms in office, and neither will attract more

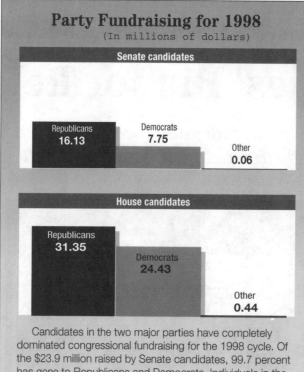

Party Fundraising for 1998
(In millions of dollars)

Senate candidates

Republicans
16.13

Democrats
7.75

Other
0.06

House candidates

Republicans
31.35

Democrats
24.43

Other
0.44

Candidates in the two major parties have completely dominated congressional fundraising for the 1998 cycle. Of the $23.9 million raised by Senate candidates, 99.7 percent has gone to Republicans and Democrats. Individuals in the two parties have also raised 99.2 percent of the $56.2 million given to House candidates so far.

SOURCE: Center for Responsive Politics, based on Federal Election Commission data

than token opposition in seeking a fourth term in 1998.

Thompson has thrived in Wisconsin by focusing on jobs, welfare and schools. But despite his own phenomenal popularity, his state has voted Democratic for president three times during his governorship, and the congressional delegation now has two Democratic senators and a 5-4 Democratic tilt in the House.

Dean has survived a Clinton-like experience, having proposed an extensive revision of the health care system in his first term and been rebuffed. He has run since on a low-tax, business-friendly platform and an image of centrism. Yet he is seen more as a beneficiary than as a cause of the state's departure from its Republican moorings.

Dean worries that his party will veer off its current centrist course and begin pushing policies the voters will not buy. That was what concerned him when he spoke to about 250 college Democrats shoehorned into a conference room in a Washington hotel in July.

"I think there will be a struggle in the year 2000 over the direction the Democratic Party is going," Dean said. "If it goes to the left, we'll be dead."

For his part, Thompson is convinced

the GOP has what the voters want but falls short in the selling. He is happy to claim credit for the strong economy, the end of welfare "as we know it," and the enactment of a balanced-budget agreement and a tax cut.

Yet Thompson frets. The Democrats are winning "the propaganda wars," he says, running with a ball they found "on our football field."

Even if the GOP were getting all the laurels it might want, Thompson recognizes that political achievements have a short shelf life.

"What you've done for people yesterday doesn't get you many votes," he glumly admits.

Restive Republicans

A common theme in GOP conversations of late has been the party's failure to "get credit" for its achievements.

"The Republican Party is probably doing the best it's done in years overall," says Stephen W. Roberts, Iowa's Republican national committeeman. "[But] at a time when we should be flying high, our [public] perceptions and our public relations are clearly not as good as Clinton's."

The more importance one attaches to the recent budget deal and tax cut, or to the enactment of other key "Contract With America" promises, the more one has to wonder what the GOP will do for an encore.

"I don't know what the fall agenda is going to be," conceded RNC Chairman Jim Nicholson on July 15, two days before the party's summer meeting in Cleveland.

So pronounced was this feeling at the Cleveland meeting that Michigan's popular Republican Gov. John Engler, another favorite for re-election in 1998, called for a party summit. To loud applause, Engler said it was time top party officials and elected leaders got the GOP looking ahead, instead of engaging in what he called excessive "hand-wringing."

Republican expectations, if not quite at Coca-Cola levels, are nonetheless at historic highs. They already have more governorships than at any time since the New Deal and their first back-to-back congressional majorities since the 1920s. *(Chart, p. 49)*

For GOP, Roaring '20s Ended With a Whimper

The politics of the 1920s, the last decade in which Republicans dominated Congress, were as contradictory as the times. A fast-forward age of flappers, speak-easies and daring exploration, the Roaring 20s were tempered by nostalgia for a less complicated America thought to have existed before World War I.

Harding　　**Coolidge**　　**Hoover**

New technologies were speeding communication. Radio reordered home life. Automobiles were suddenly everywhere. Yet religious revivals were also common, and liberal trends at all levels of education and intellectual life were challenged by powerful defenders of tradition. This yearning for the future and the past at once was reflected in the internal dissension that preoccupied the nation's two major parties.

Republicans sustained a majority in both chambers from 1919 to 1931 (and in the Senate until 1933). They also won all three presidential elections held in the 1920s by landslides. But it was not a decade of unbroken success: Democrats made a big comeback in the off-year congressional voting of 1922 and managed a modest gain in 1926. The GOP was also plagued by factionalism: A small, reform-minded group of Progressives was strong enough to hamper such basic functions as electing a Speaker.

The pursuit of a Republican agenda in Washington was also hobbled by weaknesses in the White House. The brief administration of Warren G. Harding was fraught with scandal, culminating in the Teapot Dome investigation (named for the site of naval oil reserves transferred to private hands in exchange for bribes). Harding died of a heart attack in 1923 and his successor, Calvin Coolidge, was known more for his vetoes then for any legislative program of his own.

The Democrats, meanwhile, were stymied by their own infighting and by post-war disillusionment that soured many voters on the party of wartime President Woodrow Wilson. The low point came at the party's embarrassing 1924 national convention in New York, where the presidential nomination contest remained deadlocked for 102 ballots. The eventual winner was John W. Davis of West Virginia, a compromise choice from far down the bench who got less than 29 percent against Coolidge in November.

The Democrats fared better in the congressional election that year, losing only 24 seats in the House and three in the Senate. "When it comes to electing Governors, Senators, Congressmen, Mayors and the like, the Democrats are very much stronger than they are in Presidential elections," noted journalist Walter Lippmann during this period. "They are a party which is much stronger in its parts than as a whole."

One of these parts was embodied in 1928 by Alfred E. Smith, the next Democratic candidate for president and the first Catholic nominated by either party. Smith, of German and Irish ancestry, captured the imagination of the "New Immigrants" who had in many cases supported Republicans. But he lost most everything else to Republican Herbert Hoover — including half the South, where anti-Catholic sentiment offset the historic aversion to the party of Lincoln.

With all their economic and political prosperity, Republicans scarcely noticed that they were beginning to slip among women, who were exercising their recently acquired right to vote. As more women voted, many diverged from the Republican leanings of their fathers or husbands.

Comes the Crash

The stock market crash of 1929, followed by a Republican high-tariff bill and deepening global Depression made Hoover seem inept and insensitive. Hoover believed deeply in the laissez-faire philosophy Harding had popularized as a "return to normalcy" scarcely a decade earlier. But when Republicans promised in the early 1930s that "prosperity" was "just around the corner," the voters turned to the Democrats.

By the midterm congressional election of 1930 the Republican margin was whittled to two in the House and one in the Senate. But several Republicans had died in that year, necessitating an unusual number of special elections before the start of the 72nd Congress in 1931. The Democrats gained four seats in these elections, putting them back in control of the House.

The Republicans' fate was sealed in 1932 when Democrat Franklin D. Roosevelt was elected president, with strong majorities in both chambers that would continue to expand until the GOP was reduced to double digits in the House and to just 17 seats in the Senate.

Apart from the Revolution and the Civil War, no other transformation in American politics has been as sudden, as comprehensive or as lasting.

Yet they feel short-changed, in part because they feel the recent shifts in American politics should be benefiting them even more.

To be sure, the party has cashed in on regional realignment, particularly in the South, which was once so Democratic that it gave that party a head start of about a dozen governorships and two dozen Senate seats, not to mention about 100 seats in the House.

In the 1994 election, the GOP achieved its first majority of Southern governorships, first majority of Southern Senate seats and first majority of Southern House seats since Reconstruction. And the party has widened its margin in all three categories since.

Of nearly equal importance to GOP strength in Congress has been the party's domination of the Mountain West.

Republicans hold every House seat in the Rocky Mountain states except three districts in Denver and Boulder, Colo., and Tucson, Ariz. That adds up to only 22 House seats (including Alaska). But in the Senate, where even the emptiest states are entitled to two representatives, GOP dominance in the region gives them 14 senators.

Driving the Republican success in the West has been the region's long-standing resentment of federal authority over land and natural resources. The salience of this issue in the 1980s and 1990s has all but closed the regional market to Democrats. Democrats pay lip service to the idea of regaining some of the ground the party has lost in the South, but even top party officials speak of the Mountain West as a lost cause, at least for now.

"I don't see a real reversal happening," said Floyd Ciruli, a Democratic pollster in Colorado and a former state party chairman. said.

Ideological Realignment?

The changing issue mix in the Mountain West bespeaks a greater change in American politics, with much of the citizenry losing whatever faith it had in the federal government's ability to make a positive difference in their lives.

It is this ideological realignment that Republicans expect will bring the political consumers to them in droves.

That this has not yet happened may be a tribute to the Democrats' willingness to reposition themselves in the market, finding other ideas to sell rather than pushing major new domestic programs.

"I think the Republicans, with their zeal, don't all recognize the need to be pragmatic, especially when they have a very narrow margin" in Congress, said William F. Connelly Jr., a political scientist at Washington and Lee University in Lexington, Va. "I think they have in fact provided an opening for an adroit Democratic politician to steal the center."

Many Republicans in Congress, particularly younger House members, contest this view. They blame their frustration on poor public relations in their confrontations with a slick president.

"The only thing we did badly was our public relations — it wasn't our policy," said Republican Rep. Matt Salmon of Arizona. "Our problem is in our ability to communicate our message and to communicate our strategy."

The Republicans, however, may be facing strains unlike any since their era of dominance ended with the Depression of the 1930s.

Once the fiscal issues of deficits, taxes and spending are off the table, what will provide the new cement to hold the party together?

"You have a situation where you have a majority still trying to define itself now

that it's accomplished as much of its 1994 agenda as it can at this time," said Burnham of Texas. "Basic to the Republicans is limiting the federal government — but once they've accomplished that they undercut their own message and will want to play defense a lot."

Few Republicans are likely to accept

"The only thing we did badly was our public relations — it wasn't our policy."

— Rep. Matt Salmon, R-Ariz.

that prescription or be happy relying strictly on incumbency for success. But a danger for the party is that its various factions, no longer marching side by side under the proud banners of tax cutting and budget balancing, will now pursue their own agendas.

The Republican majority rests on a three-legged stool of fiscal conservatism, social conservatism (most dominant in the party's rising Southern wing) and distrust of federal intrusion on private property rights.

Fiscal conservatives have long been the senior partner, and it is doubtful that a Republican Party preoccupied with social issues will be able to expand outside the South and the Mountain West.

"I think the Republicans, as they begin to succeed on some of their economic goals, begin to confront a dilemma because the next natural goal to pursue is their social agenda, such as abortion," said Oregon State University political scientist Bill Lunch.

"Those ideas are more controversial; they divide the electorate differently. All these proposals would be a big advantage for Republicans in the South but work against them in the Northeast and the West Coast."

Nonetheless, it is clear that social issues have been the fuel for the party's growth in recent years, in its regional power centers and beyond.

Sen. Tim Hutchinson, R-Ark., a Southern Baptist minister, expresses impatience at Lunch's implication. Hutchinson says he shares his party's concerns about federal spending and other fiscal matters, but describes social issues as his "roots" and "pri-

mary motivation."

Hutchinson said he is pleased with the highlighting of issues such as a particular abortion technique its opponents call "partial birth" abortion and, to a lesser extent, religious matters such as prayer in public schools.

These are the issues that play well in the South, Hutchinson said, and have earned Republicans their majority in Congress.

"You have to look at where the party's growing and where its future is. In the Northeast, it's pretty bleak," Hutchinson said. "It would be kind of foolish for the party to abandon that which gives us strength and our majority to please an area where the Republican message isn't playing as well."

Hutchinson was then quick to joke that he wasn't running for president, and was thus free to look at the map a little bit differently. Dominating the markets of the South and West may be enough to ensure Republican strength in Congress. Looking to the White House presents a different problem.

How the Republicans deal with their national marketing image could, in turn, affect their domination of regional markets. For example, some Western Republicans worry that the national party might abandon them on certain bedrock resource issues.

Boise State University political scientist John Freemuth says opinion leaders in his region have an eye on environmentalist Republicans in the House.

"There are plenty of Republicans, Newt Gingrich included, who are trying to position the party in a pro-environment way that makes some Republicans out here nervous," Freemuth said.

Democrats' Dilemma

Democrats have watched the Republicans' internal squabbles with satisfaction, in no small part because of their own identity crisis.

Having suffered dramatic losses below the presidential level since 1992, Democrats are trying to set aside their many differences so as to appeal to the broad middle of the electorate. In so doing, they are finding themselves talking about issues such as taxes and crime that they had long conceded to the GOP.

"We're playing in the center of a field that for a few years we'd given to them," said a senior White House official. "We're not going to give them those issues anymore."

In 1992, the party found the keys to the White House by offering a national ticket with two 40-something politicians from the South who called themselves "New Democrats." Both had been associated with the Democratic Leadership Council (DLC), a centrist alternative to the Democratic National Committee born in the ashes of the party's 49-state debacle in 1984.

So much emphasis was given to this "new generation" campaign theme in 1992 that Marlin Fitzwater, spokesman for President George Bush, came back with an advertising slogan from Coke. In a half-serious aside to White House reporters, Fitzwater said "the Democrats have the Pepsi boys, we have the Real Thing."

Calling a product new is among the oldest advertising gimmicks extant. But it worked for Clinton just as it had worked for others, including the New Nixon, the New South and even the New Deal.

The theme always carried an implicit criticism of "old Democrats," who were understood to stand for big government programs. But in 1996, Clinton widened the separation even further, offering himself openly as a third-way option to both the Gingrich House and to the traditional Democratic politics that had controlled the House before Gingrich.

Thus, for Democrats other than Clinton, holding the White House in 1996 was a relief, but not a vindication. The failure to recapture either chamber of Congress will mean a long winter of discontent for Democratic legislators, many of whom came to Capitol Hill with no thought of ever living in the minority.

The choice that confronts the party as a whole and its individual candidates is now much like the choice confronting Republicans: Do we stress our ability to govern or our differences with those who are governing?

As Clinton has blurred the once-sharp lines between the parties in signal areas such as taxes, welfare, crime, foreign policy and defense spending, the key question for Democrats has become whether to stay in the center.

"We're all New Democrats now," said House Minority Leader Richard A. Gephardt, D-Mo., in September 1996. But while Gephardt has a history of association with the DLC that is as old as Clinton's and Gore's, his current role in the House pulls him back toward the party's traditional power base among the poor, racial minorities and union activists (particularly from public employee unions).

That was apparent in Gephardt's high-profile opposition to the Clinton

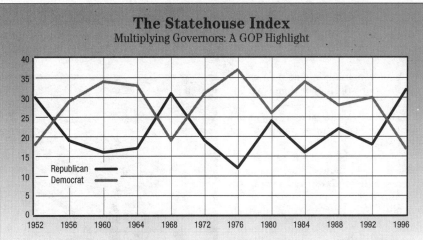

The Statehouse Index
Multiplying Governors: A GOP Highlight

Democrats held a majority of the nation's governorships for decades (with brief interruptions) after the New Deal. They did so building on domination of the statehouses in the South. The GOP reversed the ratio, both in the South and nationally, beginning in 1994.

MARILYN GATES-DAVIS

White House on trade issues, on the 1996 welfare overhaul and to the balanced-budget agreement of 1997.

Democrats in the House have a particularly tricky time finding a national market for their ideas. Not having the institutional power of a Senate minority, they are orphaned by divided government, left out in the cold when the president of their own party needs to negotiate with the House majority. No one was angrier about Clinton's 1995 decision to pursue a balanced budget than House Democrats.

"The Democrats have great difficulty," said Burnham, "especially because a Democratic president is warming up to the Republicans on things that are disagreeable to liberals."

Having It Both Ways

House Democrats typically defend their position by denying the necessity of choosing between the needs of one voter-consumer and those of another.

"I think the Democratic Party will lose if it tries to target voters simply on the basis of their own personal need," said Rep. Sam Gejdenson, D-Conn., who argued that the party has to appeal to a sense of fairness on the part of more affluent voters. "I think it's a foolish notion that you would give up the government as something that tries to help those who need the help."

At times, this side of the Democratic impulse prevails. Clinton negotiated with Republicans and they hoped he would let them write the tax-cut package, but in the end he insisted on extending the family tax credit to people with no income tax liability — over GOP objections.

Overlapping the issue of persuading

the poor to vote is the question of how Democrats get minorities to vote in higher numbers. Democrats have near locks on the most prominent racial groups — Jews, blacks, and even Hispanics, who were tilting toward the GOP in the 1980s but voted overwhelmingly for Clinton, particularly in 1996. These groups are even more threatened by some of the Republican agenda — affirmative action, English only restrictions, immigration policy — than suburbanites wary of the religious right.

Although minorities are by definition a smaller part of the populace, their tendency to vote en bloc, combined with the gender gap voting of women, gives the Democrats a solid base in any election. But it is a less than reliable vote in that its turnout rate fluctuates, depending on the issues, candidates and circumstances.

But minorities will continue to grow as a portion of the population, particularly in California (where Democrat Cruz Bustamante became the first Hispanic Speaker of the state Assembly this year).

That is why Republicans are constantly talking about the need to attract minority voters. Republicans are concerned about Clinton's ability to carry some of "their" states, such as Arizona.

"The fate of the GOP in the Southwest rests on our ability to regain traction with the Hispanic community," said Sen. John McCain, R-Ariz. The party's image is not helped, McCain said, by the perception that Republicans are opposed to legal immigration. "I can not overstate the seriousness of the problem," he added.

A Clash of Partisan and Family Loyalties

Blood may be thicker than water — but is it thicker than party affiliation?

Marjorie McKeithen, a 31-year-old Baton Rouge attorney, plans to find out. The daughter of Louisiana's Republican secretary of state and granddaughter of a Democratic former governor, she is planning to seek the Democratic nomination in 1998 against Republican Rep. Richard H. Baker in Louisiana's 6th District.

Baker will be difficult to dislodge. But the effort should make for an interesting test of the cross-currents that complicate party politics these days in the Deep South.

McKeithen does begin with some name recognition. Her grandfather, John J. McKeithen, was Louisiana's governor from 1964 to 1972 and remains well known in the state. (He had heart bypass surgery in July.)

But the historical base of the clan lay in the northeastern corner of the state — far from the Baton Rouge area where Marjorie McKeithen is striving to make her mark.

Compounding the younger McKeithen's difficulties is her father's queasiness about endorsing her. Fox McKeithen, who switched parties in the 1980s, has become an important Republican fundraiser and campaigner. Now Louisiana's secretary of state, he has also been mentioned as a prospective gubernatorial candidate and worries that his daughter's campaign may interfere with his own 1999 re-election bid.

Fox McKeithen's move to the GOP was symbolic of the party's growth in the Bayou State and throughout the South, once considered off-limits to the "party of Lincoln."

Still famous for his imitation of Earl K. Long (a former governor flamboyant enough to have provided Paul Newman with a movie role), Fox McKeithen's defection from populist Democratic ranks represented a cultural shift. It signified

MCKEITHEN FAMILY PHOTO

Democrat Marjorie McKeithen and grandfather John McKeithen, Louisiana's former governor.

that Louisiana's Republican Party was growing out of its button-down, country club image.

Considered a racial moderate in his day, Gov. "Big John" McKeithen had helped avert the conflagrations that swept other states during the time of desegregation. He is probably best remembered as the champion of the New Orleans Superdome, built in downtown New Orleans over the objections of rural interests. A dynamic speaker of the old school, he also played well on television, concluding each commercial with a successful catch phrase, "Won'tcha hep me?"

His career was cut short in 1972 when he ran unsuccessfully for the Senate as an independent. Since then, Louisiana has been increasingly friendly to the GOP. The current governor, Mike Foster, is the third Republican to hold the office since McKeithen left it.

The ground continues to shift, and it continues to pose dilemmas for the McKeithens. The young McKeithen describes herself as a "fiscal conservative" and a "traditional southern Democrat," but she will rely heavily on black support in her race against Baker.

State party officials say that women candidates will attract extra interest following the 1996 election of Democratic Sen. Mary L. Landrieu.

The 6th District grew marginally more Democratic in 1994, and President Clinton's received a plurality of its vote in 1996 (at the same time Baker was collecting 69 percent of the vote in winning his sixth term).

Democrats hope that Marjorie McKeithen's choice signals the party's reviving health in Louisiana. They are happy, in fact, just to have a candidate: Two incumbent Republican House members from Louisiana were re-elected without opposition in 1996.

"Obviously, minorities are fast becoming majorities," said Rep. Maxine Waters, D-Calif. "That's the direction of the country. The Democratic Party enjoys a strong working base, and that's going to get bigger."

A Chance for Rebirth?

If immigration and racial voting patterns make future alignments unpredictable, so too does the changing matrix of campaign finance laws.

If "soft money" is eliminated by future reforms, the parties may see their roles reduced further. Or they may see a rebirth of their old utility as needs arise.

"To abolish soft money is just to channel funds into less reportable channels, and, the odds are, less constructive channels," said Larry J. Sabato, a University of Virginia government professor and co-author of a 1996 book about campaign finance malfeasance.

If the fundraising function is removed, it is possible that the political system will find it necessary to reinvent the parties — finding in them once again what Sabato called the "organizing entities of democracy" that could "force compromise and encourage cohesion."

"If there's any lesson of history about the two major parties in American politics," says Fishel of American University, "it is that they're incredible adaptive survivors." ∎

DOUGLAS GRAHAM

Rep. Howard Coble, R-N.C., is among the Hill's dwindling ranks of smokers.

Tobacco Industry Courts the Hill With Compromise, Conciliation

Big Tobacco will move to center stage on Capitol Hill in 1998, embarking on a tailored strategy to end the "Great War" over smoking.

As tobacco pushes for congressional approval of a landmark legal settlement that is favorable for the industry, it has taken a series of steps to win support.

It has converted former enemies like state attorneys general and the American Medical Association into allies.

It has curried favor with influential members of Congress by making campaign contributions.

And it has assembled a powerful lobbying army to win what the industry hopes will be a last decisive battle.

"This is an industry that wants to come in from the cold," says Scott Williams, an industry spokesman in Washington. "There is a new group of executives who don't want to be pariahs of the corporate world."

The tobacco industry portrays the deal as a framework to reduce the nation's smoking habit and pay its share of the devastating consequences.

But anti-smoking advocates say the industry is up to its old tricks, looking to

CQ Weekly Report Nov. 8, 1997

cut corners now that it has succeeded for the first time in winning a settlement that gives it the promise of legal immunity.

"Big Tobacco has got its greatest wish," says Stanton A. Glantz, a medical professor at the University of California at San Francisco and one of the industry's biggest critics. "It has moved resolution of the tobacco issue into the one place in the universe where it has the most power — Congress. And it has a Republican Congress that it believes will be favorable to its interests."

The pact exacts a high price of $368.5 billon over 25 years from the tobacco industry to compensate the states for care of persons disabled by smoking, antismoking programs and children's health insurance. But it also carries a huge payoff for the industry: immunity from classaction lawsuits and punitive damages for past misconduct, and an annual cap on damages paid in any single year.

And while the tobacco industry has many loyal allies in Congress — including a number of members themselves who are smokers — it is by no means certain that lawmakers can be convinced to overlook growing objections from smoking foes who say the settlement does not impose a

TOBACCO POLITICS

Tobacco PAC Contributions

A recent study by the Center for Responsive Politics found tobacco contributions ranked eighth among major industries for soft money donations in the 1996 election cycle.

Studies by the center and Michael Begay, a professor of health policy management at the University of Massachusetts at Amherst, show the tobacco industry put most of its weight behind Republicans in the 1996 election cycle.

Begay found contributions were distributed in roughly equal shares to candidates of both parties until the Republicans gained control of Congress in 1994. Three charts from his study, at right, show the pattern of contributions by tobacco political action committees from 1976 to 1996.

The center found Republican candidates got more tobacco contributions than Democratic candidates by a 3-1 ratio in the 1996 election cycle. And for the same cycle, it found Republican Party committees got more soft money donations from Big Tobacco than their Democratic counterparts by a ratio of better than 5-1.

The tobacco industry did not ignore Democrats in the 1996 election. The center's list of top recipients of PAC contributions in the 1996 election cycle includes several Democrats from tobacco-growing states such as Sen. Wendell H. Ford and Rep. Scotty Baesler, both of Kentucky, and Rep. Bart Gordon, of Tennessee.

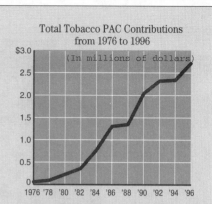

Total Tobacco PAC Contributions from 1976 to 1996
(In millions of dollars)

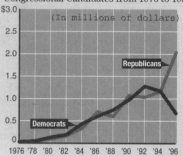

Tobacco PAC Contributions to Congressional Candidates from 1976 to 1996
(In millions of dollars)

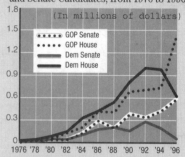

Tobacco PAC Contributions to House and Senate Candidates, from 1976 to 1996
(In millions of dollars)

Tobacco Industry Money

1979-1994	Total	Democrats	Republicans
PACs	$10,679,669	$5,515,110	$5,164,559

1995-96	Total	Democrats	Republicans
PACs	2,768,519	667,098	2,101,421
Soft money	6,833,271	1,064,680	5,768,591
Total	9,601,790	1,731,778	7,870,012

1997*	Total	Democrats	Republicans
PACs	595,721	179,621	416,100
Soft money	1,942,881	323,472	1,619,409
Total	2,538,602	503,093	2,035,509

* First half of 1997

SOURCE: Center for Responsive Politics

SOURCE: Michael Begay

Top Senate Recipients of Tobacco PAC Contributions, 1996 Election Cycle

Rank	Senator	Amount
1	Wendell H. Ford (D-Ky.)	$63,998
2	Jesse Helms (R-N.C.)	57,250
3	Lauch Faircloth (R-N.C.)	52,250
4	Mitch McConnell (R-Ky.)	47,200
5	Fred Thompson (R-Tenn.)	47,000
6	Kay Bailey Hutchison (R-Texas)	44,923
7	John W. Warner (R-Va.)	39,150
8	Mike DeWine (R-Ohio)	32,000
	Christopher S. Bond (R-Mo.)	32,000
9	Conrad Burns (R-Mont.)	31,500
10	Kent Conrad (D-N.D.)	31,000

Top House Recipients of Tobacco PAC Contributions, 1996 Election Cycle

Rank	House member	Amount
1	Thomas J. Bliley Jr. (R-Va.)	$34,675
2	Edward Whitfield (R-Ky.)	33,600
3	Charlie Norwood (R-Ga.)	33,500
4	Bart Gordon (D-Tenn.)	33,350
5	Scotty Baesler (D-Ky.)	31,550
6	Newt Gingrich (R-Ga.)	30,500
7	Ron Lewis (R-Ky.)	25,500
8	Walter B. Jones Jr. (R-N.C.)	25,100
9	Vic Fazio (D-Calif.)	25,000
10	Tom DeLay (R-Texas)	23,500

MARILYN GATES-DAVIS

sufficient penalty on the industry and falls short of protecting the public health.

As a result, the tobacco industry has acted to dramatically beef up what has historically been one of the most powerful lobbying operations in American politics. A review of lobbying reports for the first half of 1997 by Congressional Quarterly shows that the industry has added new players and a new look in Washington as it promotes its cause.

The reports show the industry spent $15.7 million on lobbying, including hefty fees for two new, superstar law firms:

● $4.7 million to Verner, Liipfert, Bernhard McPherson and

for Sen. Jesse Helms, R-N.C.

In addition, Lance Morgan, a Washington veteran, was hired to be the industry's chief spokesman for the issue. Morgan, who has worked for Sen. Daniel Patrick Moynihan, D-N.Y., had no previous ties to the tobacco industry.

Although these lobbyists have kept a low profile to date, it will not last for long. "Pro-settlement forces are massed just over the horizon, and they're waiting to go into action," said Leon G. Billings, a Maryland legislator and longtime anti-smoking advocate.

Critics say the industry has been trying to buy credibility

Tobacco Industry's Spending On Lobbying in 1996 and 1st Half of 1997
(In millions of dollars)

Companies	1996	1997	Total
Philip Morris Cos.	$19.58	$7.0	$26.58
Tobacco Institute	3.32	1.46	4.78
RJR Nabisco Inc.	1.64	2.04	3.68
Smokeless Tobacco Council	1.50	.67	2.17
Brown & Williamson Tobacco Corp.	.58	1.72	2.3
Loews Corp.	.14	1.24	1.38
U.S. Tobacco Inc.	NA	1.38	1.38
Other	.18	.15	.33
Total	$26.94	$15.66	$42.60

SOURCE: Congressional Quarterly and Center for Responsive Politics; based on lobbying reports filed with Congress

Fees Paid by Tobacco Industry To Outside Lobbyists in 1st Half of 1997
(In millions of dollars)

Companies	1997
Verner, Liipfert, Bernhard, McPherson & Hand	$4.7
Barbour Griffiths Rogers	.8
Hecht, Spencer & Assocs.	.32
Patton Boggs	.26
Winburn, Jenkins & Wheat	.24
Oldaker, Ryan, Phillips & Utrecht	.22
Baker, Donelson, Bearman & Caldwell*	NA
Other	1.4
Total	$7.94

* Just hired, not reported.

SOURCE: Congressional Quarterly and Center for Responsive Politics, based on lobbying reports filed with Congress

Hand, where former Senate Majority Leaders George J. Mitchell, D-Maine, and Bob Dole, R-Kan., and former Texas Democratic Gov. Ann W. Richards all work.

● $800,000 to the firm of former Republican National Committee Chairman Haley Barbour, who helped elect dozens of GOP lawmakers.

The industry also hired Republican Howard H. Baker Jr. just before the end of the reporting period in June to help enhance its influence on Capitol Hill. Baker, a former Senate majority leader and Washington rainmaker, is married to former GOP Sen. Nancy Landon Kassebaum of Kansas. Baker recently resigned as chairman of the board at the Mayo Clinic in Minnesota because he is working for tobacco.

The pace of spending by the industry is roughly on par with 1996, when it earmarked $26.9 million on lobbying Congress, according to the Center for Responsive Politics. Records show the industry increased spending on outside lobbying firms in the first half of 1997 to $7.9 million, more than the $5.6 million it spent in all of 1996 for similar services.

Besides Barbour, Baker and Mitchell, other former members of Congress in the lineup include Democratic Sen. Walter D. Huddleston of Kentucky, a tobacco company lobbyist, and several former House members: Republican Stan E. Parris of Virginia and Democrats James V. Stanton of Ohio, Ed Jenkins of Georgia and Alan Wheat of Missouri.

The industry's outside lobbyists also include former aides with ties to leading lawmakers on Capitol Hill. Among them: Edward W. Gillespie, former policy and communications director for Republican House Majority Leader Dick Armey of Texas, and Darryl Nirenberg, former chief of staff

by hiring prominent new lobbyists and developing allegiances from anti-smoking groups with the promise of future support for anti-smoking campaigns.

Meanwhile, anti-smoking advocates have been moving to assemble their own campaign to defeat the settlement. For example, Minnesota Attorney General Hubert Humphrey III, a critic of the settlement, has hired the lobbying firm of two former House members, Thomas J. Downey, a Democrat from New York, and Rod Chandler, a Republican from Washington, to help fight it.

A lobbying team led by two former Senate majority leaders has considerable sway on Capitol Hill, where former members roam freely on behalf of private clients. But as if to gild the lily, the industry has also continued its tradition as a generous political donor.

The Center for Responsive Politics, a nonprofit group that monitors campaign spending, found that the industry's political action committees (PACs) gave soft-money donations of $1.6 million to Republicans and $323,472 to Democrats in the first half of 1997. Soft money is contributed to political parties, not individual candidates. There is no limit on the amount that can be contributed.

It also found that the industry gave $595,721 to campaigns of members of Congress in the first half of 1997. The biggest recipients were Lauch Faircloth, R-N.C., $20,000; and Jim Bunning, R-Ky., $16,000. They represent two big tobacco-producing states.

A new study by Michael E. Begay, a professor of health policy and management at the University of Massachusetts at Amherst, said the industry retooled its campaign finance strategy after the 1994 election, sharply leaning toward Republican candidates in the 1996 election, changing its poli-

Costly Mix of Soldiers and Cigarettes . . .

Among the many enduring images from World War II, some of the most compelling involve cigarettes and smoking. Those famous photographs of FDR flashing his irrepressible grin, a cigarette-holder clenched in his teeth. Bill Mauldin's unforgettable cartoons of war-weary soldiers, cigarettes dangling from their lips.

From World War II through Vietnam, cigarettes were as integral to life in wartime as C-rations and combat boots. "I remember in Vietnam they gave us all two cigarettes with our rations," said Pennsylvania Democratic Rep. John P. Murtha, a Marine veteran.

But the Pentagon, whose troops once lived by the motto "smoke 'em if you got 'em," is now trying to kick tobacco. The Defense Department's long-term goal is to reduce tobacco use by military personnel from its current level of 32 percent to 20 percent by the year 2000.

To achieve that goal, the Pentagon launched a controversial initiative in November 1996 to raise prices of tobacco products in commissaries, the military's taxpayer-subsidized supermarkets.

Regional commissary prices vary widely, but the new policy resulted in a significant increase in the price of a carton of cigarettes. In many areas, the cost of a carton of name-brand cigarettes such as Marlboro went up by about $4, from $11 to $15, according to defense officials. That is still about $2 less than major supermarket chains such as Safeway charge for a carton, because tobacco products sold at commissaries are exempt from state and local taxes.

It is too early to tell whether the price rise will cause soldiers and sailors to quit smoking. But it has already resulted in a dramatic decline in sales of cigarettes by commissaries. In the past fiscal year, those sales went down by 42 percent, according to the Pentagon. Sales fell by $87 million, from $454 million to $367 million.

Buy It in Bulk

For decades, the Pentagon has been in the business of discounting tobacco. And until the new policy went into effect, business was booming, both in commissaries and military exchanges, which are the equivalent of a general retail chain such as Wal-Mart.

Tobacco products at some commissaries were sold at a 76 percent discount compared with nearby commercial outlets. Military personnel, their dependents and retirees who smoked would often buy cigarettes in bulk.

At Fort McCoy, in Wisconsin, sales of tobacco products accounted for 49 percent of the commissary's retail business in fiscal 1995. At Virginia's Fort Monroe, tobacco sales accounted for 38 percent of the commissary's retail sales in fiscal year 1995.

But with the administration taking a harder line against smoking, and defense officials growing anxious over the rising medical tab for smoking-related illnesses, the Pentagon's generous cigarette subsidies became unsustainable.

"You can't subsidize a product whose use causes you to turn around and subsidize health care for the use of that product. It's illogical," said Stephen J. Rossetti Jr., who directs the Pentagon office that devised the new policy.

A report released in December 1996 by the Pentagon's Inspector General underscored the diminishing economic returns from tobacco sales. In fiscal 1995, commissaries and exchanges generated sales of $747 million; at the same time, health care and "lost productivity costs" attributed to tobacco use totaled $930 million.

Still, the new policy spawned sharp protests on Capitol Hill. Members of a House National Security subcommittee panel complained that the Pentagon had failed to adequately consult Congress before cutting the cigarette subsidies. Perhaps not coincidentally, the panel is dominated by members who have received political contributions from tobacco interests and represent tobacco-rich states.

GOP Rep. Saxby Chambliss, whose south-central Georgia district is home to a Brown and Williamson tobacco plant, was angry that the Pentagon had scrapped a longstanding formula under which commissaries were required to set prices for items at only 5 percent above wholesale. Under the new policy, tobacco products are sold at a higher price set by military exchanges, which are not directly subsidized.

"The lower commissary prices are a benefit, set by law, to members of the military community," said Christopher Cox, an aide to Chambliss. If the Pentagon takes subsidies

cy for the previous 20 years of giving evenly to candidates of both parties.

Begay links the shift to favor Republicans to tobacco control efforts by the Clinton administration, including the push by the Food and Drug Administration (FDA) to gain authority to regulate nicotine, and the classification of environmental tobacco smoke as a carcinogen by the Environmental Protection Agency. But Begay said the most important factor was probably the Republicans' historical pro-business reputation.

But two industry sources suggest the shift may also reflect a reaction to another event, on April 14, 1994, when seven tobacco company industry executives were called to testify in a hearing before Democratic Rep. Henry A. Waxman of California, in a House Commerce subcommittee.

The executives, who had long relied on lobbyists to be their representatives in Washington, were required to step into the glare of media scrutiny themselves. They testified under oath that they did not believe nicotine to be addictive, a view for which the industry has since come under attack by regulators and the Clinton administration.

Waxman himself now realizes the impact of his actions. "It was a turning point in terms of how people viewed the tobacco industry," he says. "It presented a human face that was not attractive." Waxman says the shift in tobacco industry campaign spending was simply an attempt to "buy the Republican Party."

Much of the preparation by the tobacco industry for the upcoming congressional battle began long before any legislation implementing the agreement was even offered in Congress.

Sen. John McCain, R-Ariz., unveiled what is expected to be the industry's tobacco-control bill on Nov. 5 because it virtually mirrors the terms of the $368.5 billion settlement over 25 years. It calls for diverting $28.5 billion of the settlement money to aid tobacco farmers who would be hurt if con-

...Has Pentagon Saying No to Tradition

"Just gimme a coupla aspirin. I already got a Purple Heart."

ed the sensitivity of Pentagon policies toward tobacco and smoking on Capitol Hill.

For all the furor stirred by the Pentagon's new policy, the fact remains that commissaries and exchanges are still able to undercut convenience stores in pricing tobacco because military outlets do not charge state and local taxes.

That means every day, young soldiers are walking into exchanges and commissaries and buying cigarettes at artificially low prices. In Southern states, most of which have comparatively low tobacco taxes, the difference might amount to only 25 cents a pack, but it is a discount nonetheless.

Local Losses

For local governments, the military's tax exemption on tobacco products means lost revenues. A new report by the Congressional Budget Office estimates that those entities forgo as much as $146 million annually in tax revenues as a result of the exemption.

But after the flap over the change in commissary pricing, the Pentagon is not likely to come up with any sweeping new anti-smoking measures, such as eliminating the remaining price differential or banning sales of tobacco products altogether.

In many quarters, there is a widespread belief that a soldier or sailor on duty defending the nation should be permitted to smoke as long as cigarettes are legal. In addition, cutting off tobacco sales on military bases — or raising prices further — would likely drive smokers off base to buy their cigarettes.

The Pentagon's most recent policy pronouncement on tobacco had nothing to do with its campaign to restrict smoking. Rather, it concerned the campaign by the Defense Department — after a half-century of giving away cigarettes and subsidizing their sale — to become the first federal agency to gain a share of the proposed $368.5 billion settlement with tobacco companies, which Congress will soon consider.

"We, like states and other entities in the United States, are trying to see if it's possible to get some reimbursement for the additional costs of caring for smoking-related illnesses," said Pentagon spokesman Ken Bacon.

away for tobacco, Cox said, it could do the same for soda and sugar, other products deemed harmful to health.

Chambliss and other members of the panel were so angry that they attached a provision to the defense authorization bill (HR 1119) that would have effectively stripped Rossetti's office of its authority over commissary and related issues, transferring responsibility to the Pentagon's comptroller.

The effort failed when a House-Senate conference committee dropped the provision. But the episode demonstrat-

sumption of tobacco dropped.

The legislation also earmarks money to cover the cost of anti-smoking programs and care for sick smokers. It would accept more restrictions on advertising and impose penalties of up to $2 billion a year for failing to hit targets to reduce teen smoking.

But it ignores tougher measures recommended by President Clinton and lawmakers who want a $1.50 increase in the price of a pack of cigarettes and a bigger role for the Food and Drug Administration in regulating tobacco.

Strange Bedfellows

According to interviews with industry lobbyists and insiders, the tobacco industry began laying the groundwork in Washington to build support for the settlement talks late last year.

The first key addition was the Verner Liipfert firm, which

as lead lobbying firm for the industry supplants a role once played by the Tobacco Institute. The firm focused on building support for settlement talks, including an effort to draw in key anti-smoking advocates such as Matthew Myers, executive vice president and general counsel of the two-year-old National Center for Tobacco-Free Kids.

Three months before the June settlement, Mitchell invited Myers of Tobacco-Free Kids to meet with Berl Bernhard, chairman of Mitchell's law firm, Verner Liipfert. "We've been retained by the tobacco companies," Mitchell told Myers.

"They've spoken to people at the White House. They've said they are prepared to make fundamental change in how they do business. Would you be willing to hear out one of my partners?" Mitchell asked. Myers was skeptical, having heard pleas before about a change of heart by the industry, but he accepted.

When Bernhard showed up at Myers' office, he made a straightforward presentation about the possibility of negotia-

TOBACCO POLITICS

No Sanctuary in the Capitol

You know it will be a busy day on the House floor when you see it — a partially smoked cigar resting on a marble fireplace ledge in the Speaker's lobby just off the floor of the House.

The cigar belongs to Sherwood Boehlert, R-N.Y., who keeps it there to enjoy as he waits between votes in the chamber.

Such overt signs of tobacco use in Congress are increasingly rare. Boehlert is a member of perhaps the most rapidly declining club in Congress: members who smoke.

As Congress takes up the $368.5 billion tobacco agreement, one element of the tobacco companies' clout in dealing with Congress is the weakest it has ever been.

The companies still dole out large political donations, and most tobacco-state members feel the need to defend the crop upon which their local economies depend, but tobacco interests cannot necessarily rely on support from powerful members of Congress who smoke.

Smoking has long been associated with power; tales of deals cut in smoke-filled back rooms abound. And Capitol Hill once reflected that, with many members lighting up at will — during committee meetings, for example.

Sen. Orrin G. Hatch, R-Utah, a passionate anti-smoking crusader and a key player in congressional consideration of the tobacco settlement, says that when he chaired the Labor and Human Resources Committee in the early 1980s, ranking Democrat Edward M. Kennedy, D-Mass., "used to smoke cigars and blow smoke in my direction" until he realized that Hatch would not be provoked. Ironically, Hatch and Kennedy this year teamed up to push an unsuccessful tax increase of 43 cents a pack in cigarettes to pay for a child health proposal. Kennedy still smokes an occasional cigar.

House Agriculture Committee Chairman Bob Smith, R-Ore., who was a chain smoker for 40 years until giving up cigarettes more than a year ago, remembers large groups of members smoking behind the brass railing at the back of the House chamber. "We all used to gather and it used to be loaded" with members, he says. "Now there's only two or three."

Harold Rogers, R-Ky., now smokes cigars, but he remembers that when he first came to Congress in 1980, he smoked a pipe everywhere.

"When I came here in 1980, I smoked a pipe. I smoked at every Energy and Commerce subcommittee and full committee meeting I was in, and no one paid any attention. That's a no-no now."

Another sign of the decline of the smokers' caucus is the need for members of the leadership and their aides to leave closed meetings to have a cigarette. Reporters staking out meetings on the budget in the 104th Congress, for example, knew they could rely on House Speaker Newt Gingrich's former spokesman, Tony Blankley, or Republican Conference Chairman John A. Boehner of Ohio to slip out for a smoke — and sometimes dispense details on how the meeting was progressing.

The members who do smoke are sensitive about it. Several members declined to speak about smoking on the record for this story.

Boehlert attributes this skittishness on the part of his fellow members to the change in perception of what smoking says about a person. "So many of us started because we thought it was macho," he says. "No longer do I associate it with strength. I associate it with weakness."

James V. Hansen, R-Utah, co-chairman of the anti-tobacco caucus in the House, says that of the remaining smokers in Congress, "most of them are trying to give it up."

This shift in attitude has changed where and when members smoke in the Capitol complex. The Senate has barred smoking on its floor since 1913, though the chamber still sports spittoons.

The House, in the rules which govern "decorum" on the floor, such as the requirement that men wear coats and ties, began limiting smoking to certain areas on the chamber floor in 1986, and in 1990 banned smoking on the floor entirely. In 1995, that ban was explicitly extended to the area behind the brass railing, though a standing ashtray remains on the floor, and members can still be seen smoking there on occasion.

Each member of Congress determines the smoking policy in his or her office, and each committee makes its own rules. Few panels ban the practice, largely because smokers, sensitive to their declining clout, no longer try to smoke at meetings.

But those changes are not enough for Earl Blumenauer, D-Ore. He has sponsored a resolution (H Res 247) that would ban smoking in and around the House chamber, including the two parties' cloakrooms, the Speaker's lobby and the Rayburn room, just off the House floor. The ornate Speaker's lobby, which is lined with the portraits of former Speakers, is the one place members do light up regularly and with impunity.

Blumenauer says it is time for the House to catch up with the rest of America in terms of smoking regulations in the workplace. "We have 16-year-old volunteer pages" who are exposed to smoke, he says, making it hard to persuade them not to start. He says many members have told him they are "sick about how we treat our employees and the face we present to the public."

And, he says, the need to crack down on smoking is even more important now with the tobacco settlement in question. "What sort of credibility do we have if we can't do what the rest of America has managed to do in terms of dealing with tobacco in the workplace?" he asks.

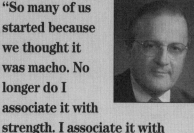

"So many of us started because we thought it was macho. No longer do I associate it with strength. I associate it with weakness."

—Rep. Sherwood Boehlert, R-N.Y.

tions between state attorneys general and tobacco companies to resolve the states' claims to recover health care costs.

Myers said he didn't decide to attend the negotiations as an observer until after an April 1 meeting with Mississippi Attorney General Mike Moore and his friend Richard Scruggs, a lawyer who is the brother-in-law of Senate Majority Leader Trent Lott, R-Miss., and another tobacco lobbyist, J. Phil Carlton, a former North Carolina Supreme Court judge hired to be the industry's contact with the White House.

Myers says he decided to join the discussions after talking with Moore on April 2. And Myers was in the room in a Washington suburban hotel in Crystal City, Va., the next day, when Steven F. Goldstone, chairman of RJR Nabisco, and Geoffrey C. Bible, chairman of Philip Morris, sat down to begin negotiations.

In Myers, tobacco industry gained an influential voice who could work with the attorneys general to attract anti-smoking advocates such as former American Medical Association President Dr. Lonnie Bristow to the talks. Myers' center has not endorsed the settlement, but has hired former Minnesota Rep. Vin Weber as a lobbyist to push for a broad tobacco bill.

Other traditional anti-tobacco groups have also joined the industry side, leaving the opponents of smoking divided for the first time.

Bristow says the split emerged in a meeting of public health groups last April and has persisted. "Some groups were interested in the progress in the talks. Others were vociferously opposed and didn't want to lower themselves," he said.

The American Lung Association calls the deal a "bailout" for an industry with "a dismal record of lies and bad faith." But some of tobacco's toughest enemies, including Bristow, are cautiously backing the deal — at least as a starting point — to reduce tobacco's advertising allure and to pay health costs.

The AMA, the American Cancer Society and the American Heart Association, among others, have formed a coalition called ENACT — Effective National Action to Control Tobacco — to push comprehensive tobacco-control legislation.

The groups lined up with President Clinton — who didn't endorse the settlement — to call for changes in the deal. Clinton said Sept 17 that he wanted full regulatory authority over tobacco for the FDA and stiffer penalties if companies miss targets to cut teen smoking.

The AMA called for strengthening the agreement. "Since the announcement of the tobacco settlement, almost 300,000 children have taken their first puff," said Dr. Randolph Smoak Jr., AMA vice chairman. Each day we delay action on a national tobacco control policy, we risk not one life but thousands."

Despite the prestige that the tobacco industry has brought to bear on this effort, attacks on the tobacco settlement continue unabated--even snaring the industry's new lobbyists.

Last month, longtime tobacco gadfly John F. Banzhaf III, a George Washington University law professor, led a campaign to push Baker from his job as chairman of the board of trustees of the prestigious Mayo Clinic in Minnesota.

Banzhaf said that Baker's new role as a tobacco lobbyist "dishonors the memory" of his late wife, Joy, who died in 1993 after an 11-year battle with lung cancer. Baker resigned from

SCOTT J. FERRELL

Drivers pass a Kool cigarette billboard on U.S. 29 south of Gainesville, Va.

the clinic's board in a letter dated Oct. 23. He said he didn't see a conflict but wanted to avoid problems, and believed a legislative resolution of tobacco issues was in the "national best interest."

There is no doubt that tobacco's new array of lobbying strength, while impressive, was born of necessity. Mark Eaton, managing director of the Burley and Dark Leaf Tobacco Association, a growers' group, observed: "On the Hill, some of the friends of tobacco outside 'tobaccoland' have dried up. The industry may have felt a need to hire some new firms with new contacts to extend their reach to other members [of Congress] from outside tobacco country." ∎

Internet Sites for Information On Tobacco Issues

Tobacco BBS (Bulletin Board System). Information on smoking, news stories and links to other sites.
  http://www.tobacco.org

Centers for Disease Control and Prevention. Health and tobacco information and links to other groups.
  http://www.cdc.gov/nccdphp/osh/tobacco.htm

RJR Nabisco Inc. Company information and news.
  http://www.rjrnabisco.com

National Center for Tobacco-Free Kids. Information about reducing smoking, news stories and links to other sites.
  http://www.tobaccofreekids.org

Tobacco Control Resource Center and The Tobacco Products Liability Project. Details of tobacco lawsuits and links to other sites.
  http://www.tobacco.neu.edu

SOURCE: Congressional Quarterly

HOME BUILDERS LOBBY

Property Rights Advocates Climb the Hill to Success

After tasting failure in 104th, home builders come back with a narrower bill and a lobbying blitz to win their case in the House

Lobbyists for the nation's home builders were ready for the final push. They stood guard by the steep marble steps outside the House chamber. They staked out the dimly lit tunnels under the Capitol to buttonhole members racing from their offices to the House floor.

Fifteen lobbyists wanted to deliver one last message to House members: Support legislation (HR 1534) that would give property owners greater access to federal courts and new clout with local zoning boards.

The House clearly found the home builders' case persuasive, easily passing HR 1534, 248-178, on Oct. 22 despite opposition from environmental groups; some moderate Republicans; and governors, mayors and federal judges.

Passage of the bill culminated months of behind-the-scenes maneuvering and a well-orchestrated stealth campaign by the 190,000-member National Association of Home Builders, chief organizer of the lobbying effort.

It is a classic tale of Washington influence and how a single association responsible for $295,250 in campaign contributions in the first six months of 1997 and $57,500 in soft money contributions to both political parties mobilized support with a small army of lobbyists and some last-minute hardball from Western lawmakers.

The bill is aimed at providing property owners and business developers a new legal tool to get their way with local zoning and planning commissions.

Proponents of the bill complain that zoning boards unjustly delay building projects. HR 1534 would seek to correct this problem by allowing builders to seek a speedy hearing in federal court, bypassing a time consuming state court appeals process federal courts insist upon.

But a hastily assembled opposition

CQ Weekly Report Oct. 25, 1997

of local officials, governors and environmental groups complain that the measure would be used by developers as a legal club to bludgeon zoning commissions into submission. They envision developers plunking down unwanted projects in residential neighborhoods, including oversized Wal Marts and seedy adult bookstores.

Brushing aside such concerns, the home builders said the bill provided a big opportunity to increase their visibility on the Hill and to translate the association's network of developers and property owners into a formidable force in Washington.

"We put everything we had into it," said Jerry M. Howard, the home builders association's senior staff vice president for governmental affairs, noting that his team was so well-positioned before the vote that it was "awfully hard to get by us."

Howard was one of those lobbying at the Capitol: "I'm like [World War II Gen.] Omar Bradley. I get down there with the troops."

Examples of the home builders' work abound. Early drafts of the property rights bill were written by Linowes and Blocher, a Silver Spring, Md., law firm retained by the association. Local home builders contacted members and flew to Washington to make their case.

"They worked the grass roots very hard," observed W.J. "Billy" Tauzin, R-La., a supporter of the bill.

Lobbyists were assigned specific states and stayed in touch with staff aides and members for six months before the vote. They worked closely with the Republican leadership, which shared its whip counts and put the bill on the legislative fast track.

According to Howard, the association (abiding by Senate and House rules on gifts) offered staffers tickets to Orioles baseball games and some attended. The Senate allows gifts of up to $50,

while the House bans gifts outright. If House staffers attended, they reimbursed the builders for the cost of the tickets, Howard said.

All this work was done out of the limelight, catching the opposition off guard. The association eschewed flashy news conferences. Elton Gallegly, R-Calif., the bill's top sponsor, quietly signed up hundreds of cosponsors.

Of course, the victory could be short-lived. The Clinton administration is threatening a veto, and Senate Majority Leader Trent Lott, R-Miss., said he is unsure if the bill will be scheduled for floor consideration before adjournment. Even if the bill were considered, it would probably face a filibuster.

Plotting a New Strategy

In surveying the political landscape, the home builders and their allies acknowledged that new approaches were needed after property rights bills were killed in the 104th Congress.

In the last Congress, bills, including one sponsored by then-Senate Majority Leader Bob Dole, R-Kan., were aimed at compensating owners for government actions that diminish property values. *(1996 Almanac, p. 3-3)*

Under the Fifth Amendment, the government is barred from "taking" property without just compensation, such as fair market value.

Property rights advocates contend that federal regulators flout this protection when they impose money-losing restrictions on property owners, but offer no compensation to make up for the losses.

But environmentalists prevailed in the 104th Congress using the counter argument that requiring greater compensation would tie agencies in knots. Many fiscal conservatives worried the approach would bankrupt agencies with costly compensation claims.

This year, the home builders abandoned the compensation tack, focusing instead on a narrower procedural question.

They first began developing the bill at the office of Linowes and Blocher. John J. Delaney, a partner with the firm, said he was an author of the early drafts.

Any provisions dealing directly with compensation were dropped. Instead, HR 1534 zeroed in on providing property owners more power to get their proposals addressed by local zoning boards.

"We've learned from past experiences," said Tauzin. "You take the victories you can win. It's called incrementalism."

Under current law, developers must first exhaust appeals to planning agency decisions in state courts and be denied compensation before a federal court will hear a Fifth Amendment takings claim.

That process can stretch on for years, forcing average homeowners and developers into legal limbo. It also offers little incentive for planning boards to act expeditiously on building requests. And those boards can keep developers at bay by turning down proposals and asking for endless revisions to building plans, proponents argue.

"It turns into a process of gamesmanship," said Nancie G. Marzulla, president and chief legal counsel of Defenders of Property Rights. "The process, particularly at the local zoning level, can go on for years and years and cost thousands of dollars."

To address the situation, HR 1534 would give property owners the option of taking their case directly to a federal court after filing at least two appeals to a planning board decision.

At least one of the appeals would have to be to an elected body, such as a city council, if available in the locality. Other appeals could be filed to the planning board or other agency with jurisdiction over planning decisions.

"The bill before us simply assures plaintiffs with a Fifth Amendment takings claim that a meaningful federal option exists," said Howard Coble, R-N.C.

The Opposition

The opponents, including many Democrats and some Republicans, said the bill amounted to little more than a naked power grab by developers and

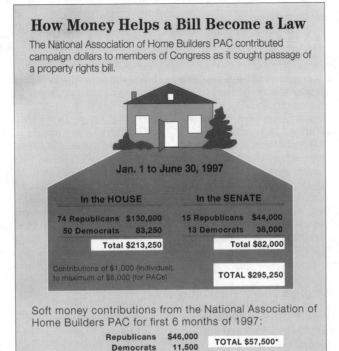

How Money Helps a Bill Become a Law

The National Association of Home Builders PAC contributed campaign dollars to members of Congress as it sought passage of a property rights bill.

Jan. 1 to June 30, 1997

In the HOUSE		In the SENATE	
74 Republicans	$130,000	15 Republicans	$44,000
50 Democrats	83,250	13 Democrats	38,000
Total $213,250		**Total $82,000**	

Contributions of $1,000 (individual), to maximum of $5,000 (for PACs)

TOTAL $295,250

Soft money contributions from the National Association of Home Builders PAC for first 6 months of 1997:

Republicans	$46,000	**TOTAL $57,500***
Democrats	11,500	

*Contributions to National Republican Congressional Committee, Republican National Committee, Democratic Congressional Campaign Committee, National Republican Senatorial Committee.

SOURCE: Center for Responsive Politics

their Washington representatives.

They said the bill would upset a delicate balance between developers and average citizens and give wealthy property owners a legal stick with which to thrash local governments into submission.

For example, Glenn P. Sugameli, an attorney with the National Wildlife Federation, said many small governments would not have the financial resources to defend a federal court case and would easily be pressured.

"I think it would destroy the balance of power between large developers and small to medium-size localities," he said. "This would give them a big legal club to get what they want at the expense of . . . the public."

That argument was echoed by the National Governors' Association, National League of Cities and U.S. Conference of Mayors. In an Oct. 21 letter to members of Congress, they went on record against the bill.

"By pre-empting the traditional system for resolving community zoning and land-use disputes, this bill would undermine authorities that are appropriately the province of state and local governments and create a new unfunded mandate on state and local taxpayers," the associations said.

Many of the opponents, particularly

Republicans, said they found it particularly ironic that the Republican backers of the bill were proposing a federal solution to an inherently local problem.

"I have lived under the rule that all politics is local," said Marge Roukema, R-N.J. "And there is nothing more local than private property and local zoning questions."

Republicans have argued strenuously for turning more power over to states and localities, but Coble and other supporters of HR 1534 countered that the developers' problems were so acute that a federal response was warranted.

"There comes a time when you have to make exceptions to the rule, and this may be one of them," he said.

House Republican moderates fell short in their effort to alter the bill. An amendment by Sherwood Boehlert of New York that would have deleted the provisions on appealing local zoning decisions was defeated, 178-242.

Boehlert offered a simple explanation for the defeat: "The home builders flexed their muscle."

How To Win in Politics

The builders emerged victorious largely because they wielded the kind of grass-roots influence that counts most with members of Congress.

Many in the opposition said the home builders used their influence to pressure members into supporting a bill that few members fully understood.

Boehlert and other opponents said the bill was sold as a narrow procedural change, when in fact it would shake up local zoning matters.

"It's strictly a procedural bill," said Delaney of Linowes and Blocher.

Republican Nancy L. Johnson of Connecticut, for example, was an initial cosponsor of the bill who later withdrew her support. She said she was initially sympathetic to the home builders.

"The reason the bill got so far is that the home builders do have a problem," she said. "And most of us have seen it."

Johnson conceded, however, that she backed the bill at first to give it some momentum, but that she "did not understand clearly the degree to

An Eye for an 'Aye' in the House

Long-festering tensions between Western and Eastern House Republicans erupted into war the week of Oct. 20 over land development, grazing and railroads.

Western House Republicans have long been frustrated with Eastern Republicans, who often ally themselves with environmental groups to defeat legislation important to Western constituents. On the property rights bill (HR 1534), Westerners weren't about to broker opposition.

So, to keep the troops in line, they issued a blunt warning to their Eastern colleagues: Pass HR 1534 or the Westerners would work to defeat a bill (HR 2247) to reauthorize Amtrak, the national passenger railroad network. The bill, which was next on the floor schedule Oct. 22 after property rights, is a priority for many Easterners, whose constituents ride the rails every day. *(Weekly Report, p. 2594)*

Republican George P. Radanovich of California, who confirmed that the message was sent to Eastern members, including New York Republican Jack Quinn, said Westerners were frustrated that Eastern Republicans too often defeat bills important to the West. The Westerners said HR 1534 would provide landowners new rights to challenge unjust local planning decisions in federal courts.

"I think we basically let them know that there were certain issues important to the Northeast that we weren't going to support unless we got some support for some of our Western issues," said Radanovich.

Some moderate Republicans, including Sherwood Boehlert, R-N.Y., argued that the bill was an intrusion in local land use planning and would benefit developers at the expense of average citizens.

Boehlert offered a substitute amendment, rejected 178-242, that would have deleted a key provision to allow landowners to get their federal court cases on the fast track.

It is unclear just how many votes on the property rights bill were swayed by the Western threat. Quinn, who voted in favor of the bill, said the threat did not sway his vote.

The bill, passed Oct. 22 by a vote of 248-178, was opposed by 147 Democrats and 30 Republicans, 16 from the Northeast and 10 from the Midwest.

As it turned out, a handful of Westerners still worked to defeat the Amtrak bill Oct. 24, but not over the property rights bill. Instead, they were seeking revenge for Boehlert's opposition to legislation that would revise grazing policy on federal lands. (HR 2493) *(Weekly Report, pp. 2308, 2594)*

A Simmering Conflict

The face-off over the property rights bill is only the latest chapter in the conflict. It first boiled over during consideration May 7 of legislation to ease provisions of the Endangered Species Act for flood control projects. *(Weekly Report, p. 1126)*

Boehlert angered Western colleagues when he prevailed with an amendment to gut the bill. That gave bill proponents little choice but to pull it. Westerners have been looking for payback ever since.

And on HR 1534, the Westerners wanted to make sure that history would not repeat itself.

"Our approach to this problem is going to be both carrot and a stick," said Radanovich of Eastern Republican defections. "The stick may be we're just not going to be there for them on issues of importance."

which it compromised local zoning boards."

It was clear that many members were under pressure from the home builders and the GOP leadership to support the bill. The home builders are active in many congressional districts and often command the ear of members.

"They're grassroots guys," said Fred Upton, R-Mich. "They are very hard-working activists."

Other pressure was brought to bear

Johnson

by Western Republican proponents of property rights. They threatened to bolt from supporting the Amtrak reauthorization bill, considered on the floor after HR 1534, if the property rights bill went down. *(Weekly Report, p. 2594)*

The legislation still faces a steep climb. In an Oct. 21, statement of administration policy, the White House issued strong opposition and a veto threat.

The statement contended that HR 1534 "would shift authority over state and local land use issues to federal courts, creating a threat of expensive litigation that would favor the wealthy developer over the common homeowner."

Opponents of the bill noted that the margin of victory fell well short of a two-thirds veto-proof majority. In the Senate, the bill does have some strong proponents, including Lott and Judiciary Committee Chairman Orrin G. Hatch, R-Utah.

But the measure would likely face stiff opposition and a filibuster from Democrats. Patrick J. Leahy of Vermont, the ranking Democrat on Judiciary, is a strong opponent.

But at least for now, the home builders see the House victory as making their mark in Washington, and they will consider their options in the Senate.

"I think you're going to see [the home builders] be a lot more active across the board," said Howard.

Hill Foes of New Clean Air Rules Unite Behind Moratorium Bill

Bipartisan opposition hopes business interests will drum up enough support to override a possible veto by Clinton

Congressional opponents of stringent new clean air regulations have united behind a bill to block them, and they are hoping business interests affected by the rules can gin up enough support to beat back an expected presidential veto.

As the administration officially announced the final version of the clean air standards July 16, opponents said they would push a bill (HR 1984) to impose a four-year moratorium on the standards and call for more scientific studies.

James M. Inhofe, R-Okla., chairman of the Senate Environment and Public Works subcommittee on clean air issues, said the plan is to provide businesses and other opponents of the rules time over the August congressional recess to generate support for HR 1984. The legislation would be marked up in September.

Thomas J. Bliley Jr., R-Va., chairman of the House Commerce Committee, concurred. But he warned that while he has the votes in committee to approve HR 1984, he would hesitate to proceed unless assured of enough support on the floor to beat a veto. "We expect [the rules' opponents] to work hard between now and Labor Day to get us support in the House," Bliley said.

HR 1984 is backed by a broad bipartisan House coalition. Among its supporters are Commerce Committee ranking Democrat John D. Dingell of Michigan, moderate Republican Fred Upton of Michigan and GOP conservative David M. McIntosh of Indiana.

CQ Weekly Report July 19, 1997

EPA Administrator Carol M. Browner and Vice President Al Gore at a news conference at the White House on July 16.

They are coordinating their efforts with a well-financed coalition of industry executives, local elected officials, some governors and labor groups that say the regulations would be harmful economically.

Their strategy was developed in the weeks after the Clinton administration's June 25 endorsement of the standards for ozone and tiny airborne particles. *(Background, Weekly Report, p. 1512)*

But the opposition faces an uphill battle. There appears to be little doubt that President Clinton would veto a bill to defer the new standards, for which implementing legislation is still to be written. Supporters of the regulations expressed confidence that the opponents in the House would fall short of the two-thirds vote to override such a veto.

"I don't think they are going to be able to get that," said Henry A. Waxman, D-Calif., a senior member of the House Commerce Committee.

There are other substantial obstacles. Environment and Public Works Committee Chairman John H. Chafee, R-R.I, said he is reluctant to endorse legislation, putting him at odds with subcommittee Chairman Inhofe. Proponents of the regulations are threatening a filibuster.

Trump Card?

The proponents, led by environmentalists, their liberal allies in Congress, and other lawmakers from regions that would benefit from the rules, say the scientific evidence and the politics of the issue are on their side.

The new rules tighten the existing standard for ozone, a main component of smog, and create for the first time a standard for tiny airborne particles produced by sources such as coal-fired power plants and diesel engines. *(Details of new standards, box, p. 62)*

The proponents say the debate is about protecting health, particularly that of children and the elderly.

They are circulating a study showing a link between tiny particles and an increase in cases of sudden infant death syndrome. They insist that the new rules would reduce health risks for asthmatic children.

Dingell and other opponents counter that the Clean Air Act is working well as is. They say the new regulations are based on flimsy science and that the Environmental Protection Agency (EPA), which developed the rules, would impose millions of dollars in compliance costs with no appreciable benefits.

"The choice here is not between clean air and dirty air," said Dingell. "It is a choice between clean air and jobs."

Highlights of the Revised Rules

The clean air regulations announced at a White House ceremony July 16 by Environmental Protection Agency (EPA) Administrator Carol M. Browner would tighten federal limits on ozone, a major component of smog, and for the first time regulate microscopic particles that compose soot.

The ozone standard would be 0.08 parts per million measured over eight hours, instead of the existing standard of 0.12 parts per million measured over one hour. Particles as small as 2.5 microns in diameter would be regulated; the smallest particles regulated under existing rules are 10 microns. (*Politics of the regulations, p. 61*)

Browner said the regulations are aimed at utilities and smokestack industries. She said that each year the standards would prevent about 15,000 premature deaths, 350,000 asthma attacks and 1 million cases of significantly decreased lung function in children.

The agency would require pollution controls for ozone beginning in 2004 and for particulate matter in 2005. Regions would not be cited for non-compliance until 2007 for ozone and 2008 for particulate matter.

According to EPA literature, implementation of the rules would have four features:

● Communities and businesses with strategies in place to meet current ozone standards would proceed as planned and would not have to change course to meet the revised air quality standards.

● Industry emissions would be reduced through use of a market-based system of pollution "allowances," which could be granted to utilities that limit soot and smog emissions. This regional "trading plan" for emissions mirrors that employed in 1990 legislation to reduce acid rain. Because utilities could sell or trade their allowances, they would be encouraged to clean up more than required and recover their cost by selling valuable credits to utilities that wanted to expand.

● Regions that worked collectively and were able to reduce soot and smog using this market-based approach would be labeled "transitional" areas and would not be cited for non-compliance.

● EPA would complete another full scientific review of the health effects of fine particulates before any "non-attainment" designations would be made or local pollution controls required. The agency would take five years to gather and analyze the data and then allow three more years for areas out of compliance to submit plans on how they would meet the new standard.

The regulations differ in two ways from the revisions EPA proposed in November:

● For ozone, communities would be cited for non-compliance after four violations instead of three. "This should provide greater stability in the standard for businesses and communities by requiring more bad air days before an area is found to be out of attainment," says EPA literature.

● Concentrations of fine particles in a 24-hour period could not exceed 65 micrograms per cubic meter, rather than 50 micrograms, "in order to provide maximum flexibility for local areas and sources," EPA says.

At a July 16 news conference, Dingell said that HR 1984, sponsored by Upton and Rick Boucher, D-Va., would strike a balance between environmental protection and economic growth.

Caution Signs

With the political stakes high, many in the opposition are cautious. House Majority Whip Tom DeLay, R-Texas, an outspoken critic of EPA, said that to avoid being tarred as opposed to environmental protection, Republicans would not proceed without significant Democratic support.

In fact, moderate Republicans from New England and the mid-Atlantic regions are among the strongest supporters of the rules, while Boucher and other Democrats from coal and industrial states line up against Clinton.

To Republican supporters of the rules, such as Sen. Alfonse M. D'Amato, the issue is about safeguarding his home state of New York from pollution from plants in the Midwest. For Democratic opponents such as Rep. Ron Klink, the battle is over protecting jobs in his industrial western Pennsylvania district.

"It's good to have a lot of Democrats out there leading us," said DeLay. "It offsets our greenie Republicans."

Boucher said these splits explain Bliley's reluctance to move forward without enough votes to prevail. "Why fight a fight that can't be won?" Boucher said. "There will be a political price to be paid by all people on all sides of the equation."

Another challenge for the rules' opponents is navigating the shoals at the Senate Environment and Public Works Committee. The Republicans have a two-seat majority and cannot afford defections, particularly given strong support for the rules among committee Democrats.

Chafee is not the only committee Republican who has not embraced legislation to block the rules. Robert C. Smith, R-N.H., also said he has not signed on to HR 1984, noting that environmental officials in his state support the regulations.

He said he would favor a proposal that reduces migrating industrial pollution but does not impose overly stringent requirements on his state. "Let's apply the standards where the sources are causing the problem," said Smith.

Smith said that given Chafee's position on the issue, the committee would probably reach an accommodation on the regulations. "I think it's got compromise written all over it," he said.

Participants in the clean air fight also have to weigh its effect on another of the year's big environmental issues.

The administration is engaged in international negotiations expected to conclude by year's end in Kyoto, Japan, on an agreement to reduce emissions from automobiles and other industrial sources that are believed to cause global warming.

Congressional action would most likely be required to implement an agreement, either through legislation or Senate ratification of a new global climate change treaty. A bitter fight on clean air could deter the administration from taking an equally hard line in talks on climate change, which divides along similar political lines as clean air. ■

Government Institutions

The seven articles of this section provide insight into the workings of the major institutions of American government: Congress, the presidency, the judiciary, and the bureaucracy.

Partisanship, often criticized as an impediment to "good government," is in fact an important and defining characteristic of American politics. Partisan politics is a reflection of fundamental differences of opinion among the American people over the direction of government policies. On occasion, however, the two major parties are able to work together—whether for reasons of strategy, tactics, or philosophy—toward a common goal. In July 1997 Congress passed budget and tax cut legislation with broad bipartisan support. But by the end of the first session of the 105th Congress in November, partisanship had reappeared to slow some pieces of legislation and scuttle others.

Party alignment is only one of many "cleavages"—or fault lines—running through Congress. These other cleavages, too, are a product of the different interests and perspectives of the American people: urban versus rural versus suburban; coastal versus interior; industrial versus agricultural; and Western versus Eastern. This last cleavage is the topic of the second article in this section of the *Guide*.

President Bill Clinton ended the 1997 legislative session with a stinging defeat. He was unable to rally his own party in support of trade legislation. Does that defeat presage weakened presidential leadership in the 1998 session? CQ editors analyze the president's strengths and weaknesses entering the new year—a midterm election year.

Few topics have engendered as much partisan bickering as investigations into alleged executive branch abuses of power and the law. The 1978 statute allowing for the creation of independent counsels was long supported by Democrats when used against Republican presidents. Now the tables have turned, which raises the question: Can investigations ever truly be "nonpolitical"?

In the next selection, CQ editors review recent Supreme Court decisions that have served to limit the authority of Congress. The Constitution, as we noted in the Foundations section, is highly elastic. Although the Tenth Amendment limits Congress to those powers specifically enumerated in the Constitution, over time the purview of Congress has expanded and contracted.

The final two selections concern the bureaucracy. In theory, Congress legislates, and the bureaucracy administers. In truth, however, the bureaucracy makes many political decisions. Sometimes, this is due to the inability of Congress to pass timely legislation, as reflected in the first of the two articles. More often, however, Congress legislates the broad outlines of an issue and leaves the bureaucracy to fill in the details. In the case of telecommunications reform, Congress is unhappy with the way in which the Federal Communications Commission has implemented the legislation.

Partisanship Returns To Hill, Limiting Legislative Output

After Congress forged a momentous, bipartisan agreement in July to balance the budget and cut taxes, some political experts wondered what was left for Republicans and Democrats to fight about.

Quite a lot, as it turned out.

As the first session of the 105th Congress ground to a close Nov. 13, weary lawmakers were just happy to get out of town. Amid partisan disputes over abortion and campaign finance, and a bitter Democratic family feud over trade, the bonhomie and bipartisanship surrounding the budget deal became a hazy summer memory.

That ballyhooed accomplishment was overshadowed by the huge stack of bills that Congress failed to send to the president. Among those measures were the popular six-year reauthorization of the nation's highway and mass transit programs (HR 2516, S 1173); legislation to revamp the Internal Revenue Service (HR 2676); a major rewrite of the Endangered Species Act (S 1180); and the highly controversial proposal to revise the post-Watergate campaign finance laws (S 25). (*Weekly Report*, p. 2838)

There were a number of reasons why these bills fell off the table. Some, such as the campaign finance bill, were the object of fierce political warfare between Republicans and Democrats. Others, such as the IRS bill, could have been enacted, but GOP leaders decided to hold them until next year, in part to maximize their political impact.

Zero for Three

It was clear that the session's final days were most painful for President Clinton, who saw three of his major foreign policy initiatives go down in less than a week.

The president's desperate bid to win congressional approval of legislation (HR

SCOTT J. FERRELL

Gingrich talks with White House a few hours before adjournment Nov. 13.

2621) renewing his fast-track authority to negotiate trade deals ran into a brick wall of opposition erected by his fellow Democrats in the House.

A nettlesome dispute over abortion cost Clinton two other key priorities — a plan to pay off back debts to the United Nations and a proposed $3.5 billion commitment to help underwrite an International Monetary Fund (IMF) program to deal with global financial crises.

But it was not just Clinton's proposals that got buried. The cherished plans of Senate Foreign Relations Committee Chairman Jesse Helms, R-N.C., to reorganize the State Department and revamp the United Nations (HR 1757) were stalled by the same imbroglio over abortion.

Senate Majority Leader Trent Lott, R-Miss., badly wanted to move the six-year, $145 billion highway bill, which had wide bipartisan support. But that legislation was held hostage by Democrats to force a vote on a campaign finance bill. In the end, neither measure ever came to a vote in the Senate.

Lott has vowed to bring back the highway bill as soon as Congress reconvenes in January. Prospects for the bill are good. Now that Clinton has dropped his opposition to legislation aimed at reining in the power of the IRS, that proposal stands a good

chance of becoming law as well.

But with the 1998 election season rapidly approaching, the atmosphere will hardly be conducive for issues that stoke political or ideological passions, such as a revised fast-track proposal or a campaign finance law overhaul.

"If you thought this was a partisan year, just wait," said Vermont Democratic Sen. Patrick J. Leahy.

Happy Trails

After it became clear over the weekend of Nov. 8-9 that Clinton had fallen short in his bid to gain fast track, Republican leaders pulled the bill at his request. At that point, there was little remaining drama and intrigue in the endgame maneuvering.

After the usual string of late nights, too many dinners of take-out pizza and exhausting closed-door negotiations, lawmakers were itching to depart. On the last day of the session, Lott admiringly recalled a remark made by former President Dwight D. Eisenhower. "There are many problems in Washington," Lott quoted Ike as saying. "One of [them] is we have too long been away from home."

Within hours, Lott got his wish. The Senate departed first, adjourning at 7:55 p.m. The House, which struggled to clear a $31.8 billion bill funding the Departments of Commerce, Justice and State and the federal judiciary (HR 2267), followed suit at 10:44.

It was the earliest end of a first session of Congress since 1965, but it could not have some soon enough for some wags in the House Republican cloakroom. On their tape announcing the floor schedule for Nov. 14, the day after adjournment, the cloakroom played a scratchy tape of the old Roy Rogers theme, "Happy Trails to You."

What Congress Did

Aside from the budget package, Republicans and Democrats disagreed

CQ Weekly Report Nov. 15, 1997

over what ranked at the top of the list of first-session accomplishments.

Democrats pointed to Senate approval in April of the chemical weapons treaty (S Res 75), a key national security priority of Clinton's. But the treaty was bitterly opposed by conservatives, and was not highlighted in GOP leaders' post-adjournment news conferences. *(Weekly Report, p. 973)*

House Speaker Newt Gingrich, R-Ga., named the unfinished IRS bill (passed by the House, pending in the Senate) and a measure (S 830) to overhaul the Food and Drug Administration's regulatory procedures as Congress' next-best achievements.

In the session's last days, several more modest bills flowed down the legislative sluice. In one of its final actions, Congress cleared legislation (S 738) aimed at rescuing Amtrak, the nation's passenger rail service, from bankruptcy.

But those bills, which Clinton was expected to sign, are hardly the stuff of a rich legislative legacy. The limited output this year was reflected in the post-adjournment wrap-ups of Republicans, who repeatedly emphasized the importance of the budget deal.

House Appropriations Committee Chairman Robert L. Livingston, R-La., felt the need to remind reporters that this was the first year since Republicans took control of Congress in 1995 that all 13 annual appropriations bills were enacted separately, rather than as pieces of year-end omnibus bills.

But passing all of the nuts-and-bolts spending bills, even weeks after the new fiscal year began on Oct. 1, took a Herculean effort and six continuing resolutions. Conservative Republicans in the House sought to use the spending bills to advance several causes: to block Clinton's plans to begin voluntary school testing and use a new "sampling" technique for the census, and to push forward with their own proposal for school vouchers.

On those three issues, the two sides essentially fought to a draw. Clinton had to delay his testing plan, while the school vouchers were scuttled by the Senate.

As for the census, the president can go forward with his plan to use statistical sampling, which is a technique aimed at ensuring the poor and minorities are not undercounted. But Republicans, who sharply oppose sampling, can challenge the constitutionality of the procedure in court on an expedited basis.

The split-the-difference approach won grudging acceptance from both sides. "On testing we scored a touchdown, on the census we moved the ball," said an aide to Rep. Tom Coburn, R-Okla., who was involved in the negotiations on all three issues.

But when it came to the battle over abortion that stalled the $13 billion foreign operations bill (HR 2159) — as well

DOUGLAS GRAHAM

Gephardt, left, and Bonior hold a Nov. 13 news conference to discuss Congress' future goals.

as the measures to fund the U.N. and IMF — everyone walked away a loser.

In recent years, the foreign operations bill has repeatedly been blocked by the efforts of House anti-abortion activists to attach a rider barring family planning groups from using their own money to perform or lobby for abortions overseas.

This year, the anti-abortion lawmakers, led by Rep. Christopher H. Smith, R-N.J., figured they had a new point of leverage in Clinton's bid to gain passage for fast track. Give ground on overseas abortions, Smith and the others informed the administration, and you can pick up as many as a dozen votes, perhaps enough to get over the top.

Clinton, widely criticized for his willingness to abandon long-held positions, hung tough in opposing the abortion restrictions. Afterward, the president said that, if the abortion dispute had somehow been resolved, he would have been able to garner a majority for fast track, although Republicans cast doubt on that assertion.

But the demise of fast track did not end the saga of the Mexico City abortion restrictions, so called because they were unveiled at an international conference held at that city in 1984.

When the final version of the foreign operations bill came to a vote in the House and Senate, the administration

put a major push on for the funding for the United Nations and IMF.

Secretary of State Madeleine K. Albright and Treasury Secretary Robert E. Rubin delivered a blunt message to congressional leaders: Failure to clear the back debts to the United Nations could harm efforts to cobble together a new international coalition against Iraqi leader Saddam Hussein. And failure to come through with $3.5 billion for the IMF might undermine that institution's ability to calm jittery Asian financial markets.

Both arguments struck a chord with senior Republicans, who are worried about the growing tensions with Iraq and economic instability in Asia. But Smith and his anti-abortion allies renewed demands that the foreign policy matters be linked to their proposal to impose a modified version of the Mexico City restrictions.

Spin Patrol

The administration balked, which was not surprising since the president had days earlier refused to give ground in the abortion confrontation when fast track was hanging in the balance.

That left Gingrich and other GOP leaders with a dilemma. They could cross Smith and risk incurring the wrath of a substantial bloc of conservative Republicans, or stiff the administration. They opted for the latter course, triggering outraged protests from the White House and congressional Democrats.

But Gingrich tried to fix the blame squarely on the administration, which he said merely needed to demonstrate greater flexibility on the abortion curbs to secure its two key international funding objectives.

In their broader judgments of the first session, Gingrich and other congressional leaders fell into predictable partisan patterns. The Speaker pronounced the session "very productive," with the budget agreement ranking as the most important accomplishment.

Senate Minority Leader Tom Daschle, D-S.D., by contrast, said the budget deal was one of Congress' only meaningful achievements. Daschle chose to highlight the ability of Senate Democrats to use procedural maneuvers to block the GOP's agenda.

In what could be a preview of election-year confrontations to come, Daschle said the unity of Democrats made it relatively easy to mount the 41 votes needed to sustain filibusters. "It keeps getting easier," he said. ∎

CONGRESS

Westerners Adjust Their Sights And Take Home Some Wins

By reaching out to Easterners and moderating their goals, lawmakers push through bills on federal grazing and landowner power

Western lawmakers may be getting wise to environmental politics.

They pushed through a handful of bills in the House this fall to revise federal grazing policy, give landowners new legal clout and curb presidential power to protect environmentally sensitive federal lands.

The measures reflect a new-found moderation on the part of Republicans who live west of the Mississippi River and who often vote together in a bloc. They are building coalitions with some Eastern colleagues, getting the support of the leadership and, when necessary, playing hardball.

"Two years ago we assumed as a new majority that it would be easy to solve some of these problems," said Richard W. Pombo, R-Calif. This year, "legislation is definitely more targeted, a lot simpler, and we're doing a lot more groundwork than we were doing."

That represents a turnabout. The Westerners were roughed up in the last Congress by critics who said they were out to gut environmental protections. They were seen as such pariahs that they could not build coalitions or get major bills signed into law, let alone passed by the House.

Since then, they've regrouped. They've abandoned efforts to enact sweeping legislation, focusing instead on narrower bills and incremental change. No more are they trying to usher in a new direction in environmental policy all at once.

House Agriculture Chairman Bob Smith, R-Ore., said many Western Republicans realize that they overreached and assumed that members would automatically embrace their agenda.

Now, the Westerners are more astute in packaging their bills, doing the

CQ Weekly Report Nov. 15, 1997

FILE PHOTO

Eastern and Western legislators worked out a compromise on grazing policy.

spadework to educate members and running their own whip operation. Some of their successes:

● Giving property owners greater access to federal courts and new clout with local zoning boards. HR 1534 passed, 248-178, on Oct. 22. (*Weekly Report, p. 2591*)

● Revising grazing policy on federal lands and increasing the grazing fee from $1.35 to $1.84 per animal unit month, or the acreage needed to feed a cow and her calf for a month. HR 2493 passed, 242-182, on Oct. 30. (*Weekly Report, p. 2676*)

● Curbing presidential authority, granted under the 1906 Antiquities Law, to set aside federal tracts vulnerable to environmental threats. HR 1127 passed, 229-197, on Oct. 7. (*Weekly Report, p. 2481*)

Tensions still run high between Eastern Republicans, who often vote against the Westerners on environmental grounds, and the Westerners, who resent them for it. But differences have not stood in the way.

"There's a kind of recognition that this party has to reach out East and West," said Smith.

The Westerners are benefiting from stronger backing from the leadership, which, in the wake of the aborted summer coup against House Speaker Newt Gingrich, R-Ga., needs to shore up its support in the party. The Western caucus makes up about a third of the GOP Conference and contains some of its most outspoken members.

During the defeat in May of a bill favored by Westerners that would have eased requirements of the 1973 Endangered Species Act for flood control projects, the leadership offered little support, declining to engage its vote counting operation. In contrast, the leadership actively worked to pass Smith's grazing bill the week of Oct. 27. (*Weekly Report, p. 1126*)

"People are starting to see that the Westerners have some rights, that we're not asking for ridiculous things, but things of moderation," said James V. Hansen, R-Utah, a senior member of the House Resources Committee.

Of course, the Western bills must still pass muster in the Senate, where they face an uphill climb. Even if the bills were to overcome Senate opposition, the Clinton administration is threatening to veto all of them. (*Box, p. 67*)

In addition, environmental groups argue that the bills, all of which they oppose, will come back to haunt Republicans in the midterm elections, particularly among suburban swing voters.

"I think there will be consequences," said Gregory S. Wetstone, the legislative director for the Natural Resources Defense Council, an environmental group. "The message will get out. I think members are going to be sorry."

A New Direction

The Westerners have not changed their stripes. They are still fighting hard

Hard Times Ahead in Senate

The Western lands bills passed by the House this fall face a rough road in the Senate next year.

Energy and Natural Resources Committee Chairman Frank H. Murkowski, R-Alaska, said the bills would probably have to move in the opening months of 1998. Otherwise, the bills would probably be overwhelmed by election-year politics or pushed off the usually packed end-of-session schedule in the Senate. One possibility is to wrap many of the proposals into a single proposal, Murkowski said.

● **Grazing policy.** Passed by the House on Oct. 30, a bill (HR 2493) to revise federal grazing policy could face opposition from deficit hawks and allies of some environmental groups. But Larry E. Craig, R-Idaho, a senior member of Energy and Natural Resources, said supporters of revamping administration policy would probably unite behind the House bill. Under HR 2493, grazing fees would increase to $1.84 per animal unit month, from $1.35. Many opponents of the bill favor a much bigger increase. Dale Bumpers of Arkansas, the senior Democrat on Energy and Natural Resources, is likely to lead the charge against the bill on the Senate floor, and a filibuster could doom it. The White House is threatening a veto.

● **Property rights.** Judiciary Committee Chairman Orrin G.

Bumpers

Hatch, R-Utah, said he hopes to move forward next year on legislation that would provide property owners new rights. He said any Senate bill would probably be modeled on HR 1534, which passed the House on Oct. 22. That bill would give property owners greater access to federal courts and new clout with local zoning boards. *(Weekly Report, p. 2591)*

The effort is strongly supported by the Senate leadership. But it is already facing a headwind from Democrats. A filibuster appears likely, and a veto is threatened.

● **Antiquities Law.** Utah's senators and many other Westerners have advocated legislation along the lines of HR 1127. The bill, passed 229-197 on Oct. 7, would curb presidential authority, granted under the 1906 Antiquities Law, to set aside federal tracts vulnerable to environmental threats. President Clinton angered many in the West by setting aside 1.7 million acres in Utah as the Grand Staircase-Escalante National Monument in 1996. Any effort to amend the Antiquities Act, which Clinton used to make the designation, faces resistance from the White House and from allies of environmental groups in both parties. *(Weekly Report, p. 2481)*

● **Biosphere reserve.** The House on Oct. 8 passed a bill (HR 901) to sharply curtail U.S. participation in United Nations-sponsored programs known as World Heritage sites and biosphere reserves. The measure is not given much chance, because of opposition from the White House and a likely filibuster threat. *(Weekly Report, p. 2484)*

---

against land managers and environmental groups that try to restrict activities on federal land.

They continue to favor the rights of property owners and protection of commercial uses of public land, and they champion such causes as federal funding for building logging roads in national forests. But they are trying to portray their efforts as moderate and friendly to the environment. They don't want to leave themselves open to attacks from Democrats and environmental groups for being "extremists," as they did in the 104th Congress.

"We've come to the conclusion that our policies provided for greater environmental protection," said George P. Radanovich, R-Calif., who has taken a leading role on Western issues. "So our strategy has changed. The challenge has been how do we 'outgreen' the greens."

At the same time, Radanovich said, the Westerners are pushing more incremental legislation. On the grazing bill, Smith worked closely with an Easterner, Sherwood Boehlert, R-N.Y., a leading voice on environmental issues, to craft a compromise that proved decisive in getting the bill through the House.

In the end, the bill was far narrower than a grazing bill considered in the 104th that would have overturned Clinton administration rules for grazing on public land. *(1996 Almanac, p. 4-14)*

Boehlert gave Smith high marks, saying he is a big factor in Westerners' success this year. "People ask, 'How come you guys worked this out?'" said Boehlert. "I say, 'That's easy, we're both adults.'"

By working with the Westerners, Boehlert has helped bridge differences in the party, but he has also laid himself and other moderates from the Northeast open to attack from environmental groups.

James C. Greenwood, R-Pa., said he wonders if some Eastern legislators are putting themselves at risk. He observed that since the loss on the flood control bill in the spring, the Westerners have chalked up nothing but victories.

Westerners see their clout only increasing, as population is drained from the Northeast and flows West. Westerners stand to gain seats in redistricting after the 2000 census.

But Republicans must also protect their dwindling numbers of Northeasterners, as well as moderates, if they are to build a stronger majority in the House.

"At this point in the process, I think the Northeastern moderates have more to lose than Westerners," said Greenwood.

Coalition Building

The success of the Westerners, even modest victories, will continue to depend on coalition building. And tensions continued to run high. For example, Radanovich and other Westerners harbor resentment toward Boehlert. They say he works too closely with environmental groups and Democrats.

On Oct. 5, about 25 Westerners and Easterners met to discuss their differences. One suggestion that resulted was that both sides join forces in an environmental caucus to vet legislation before it gets to the floor.

But the Westerners do not want Boehlert to represent the Easterners, and so far no other strong candidate has appeared.

"As far as we're concerned, if there is a group effort to build consensus in the party, Sherry is off the table," said Radanovich.

Boehlert responded: "Doesn't bother me. Anything we can do to lighten the load, I applaud." ■

The 'Comeback Kid': Down but Not Out

Despite 'fast track' defeat, Clinton still has leverage to press his second-term agenda

When the sputtering about the death of his presidency has subsided, after every newspaper columnist has written his political obituary and when the last of the Sunday talk-show hosts leaves the graveside of President Clinton's second term, that should be about the time Clinton miraculously resurrects himself. Again.

After all, this is the president who lost his economic stimulus plan in 1993, at a time when his party controlled both houses of Congress, and then, the following year, lost his battle with the legislative branch to overhaul the nation's health care system. Both initiatives were centerpieces of his first term, and both were important to helping him build his legacy as president. Each was arguably more politically significant than a bill to give the president "fast track" trade negotiating authority. *(Stimulus plan, 1993 Almanac, p. 706; health care overhaul, 1994 Almanac, p. 319)*

Clinton asked congressional leaders to pull the fast-track bill (HR 2621) on Nov. 10 rather than risk what may have been a humiliating defeat. While an overwhelming majority of House Republicans were prepared to vote with him, the president could rally only a fifth of House Democrats, which was interpreted as a serious, and in some circles fatal, repudiation of the president by his own party. Former top Clinton aide George Stephanopoulos was among the chorus of political analysts that quickly declared the president a lame duck and his legislative agenda dead. *(Weekly Report, p. 2828)*

But Clinton's survivability quotient leaves every reason to believe that the "Comeback Kid" will find a way to recover. Throughout his presidency, Clinton has shown a wily ability to piece together legislative majorities when he needs them. "This is a tactical presidency," said Donald Kettl, director of

REUTERS

Controversial alliances with Gingrich, shown here walking behind Clinton at the January inauguration, gave the president legislative successes he could repeat in 1998.

the LaFollette Institute of Public Policy at the University of Wisconsin-Madison. "Clinton creates a new bipartisan coalition every time he needs something done."

Perhaps the surest sign that news of his political death is exaggerated was the reaction of the people who have the most to gain from a moribund Democratic president — the Republican leaders of Congress. Despite their rhetoric about the president's dismal showing on the trade legislation, neither House Speaker Newt Gingrich, R-Ga., nor Senate Majority Leader Trent Lott, R-Miss., are counting Clinton out next year, especially during the first half when both sides have their greatest opportunities for accomplishing a few things before partisan gridlock sets in during the fall campaign season.

Gingrich for one said he does not expect to be dealing with a lame-duck president next year, and he invoked one of his characteristic historical allusions as evidence.

"In August 1864, the general assumption was that [President Abraham] Lincoln would be decisively defeated, and there was serious talk about replacing him on the ticket. In September, Atlanta fell. Lincoln was re-elected by a fairly wide margin," Gingrich said in an interview Nov. 13 as Congress was about to adjourn.

"Lame ducks last until the next newspaper comes out," he said. "This guy is creative, strong-willed, energetic and charming. We just have to figure out what his angle of recovery is."

A Necessary Evil

Presidential scholars view Clinton's willingness to do business with the opposition as a necessary evil for a modern president in an era of divided government. In buoyant economic times and in the absence of a galvanizing crisis either at home or abroad, the American public expects only modest, don't-rock-the-boat policies from its chief executive, not big

CQ Weekly Report Nov. 15, 1997

Great Society-style initiatives.

"Governing from the middle, if it works for Bill Clinton and [British Prime Minister] Tony Blair, is the kind of thing that executives of democracies everywhere will be watching," said political scientist Kettl. He predicted that centrist politics will also dominate the presidential campaign in 2000.

Mix-and-Match Majorities

Veterans of past battles between Clinton and Congress expect that he will again next year employ a strategy of mix-and-match majorities to get what he wants, relying more on Republican moderates, Senate Democratic centrists and other philosophical kin than on liberal House Democrats. He has used the strategy with some success since Republicans took control of Congress in 1994, and especially since the wrenching budget showdown and government shutdowns of 1995 and 1996, when both he and GOP leaders began to look for common ground somewhere between the extremes of unbridled conservatism and liberalism.

The fact that this strategy failed so spectacularly on fast track does not strike congressional veterans as proof that it will never work again.

"The trade issue is kind of a special issue that probably is not very reflective of where the cooperation or lack of cooperation is going to emerge in the future," said former Republican House member Robert S. Walker of Pennsylvania (1977-97), a Gingrich adviser. "I think there are a number of areas where the president and Congress can find cooperation."

Walker cited such works-in-progress as a regulatory reform bill to cut red tape for business and industry and possible bipartisan discussions about what to do with a budget surplus.

An analysis of the legislative debacles of other presidents shows that Clinton's showing on fast track was weak but not likely fatal. Clinton's probable fast-track vote count — an estimated 43 out of 205 Democrats were willing to stick with him — was low by historical standards but hardly the worst of any recent president. Ronald Reagan is remembered, incorrectly, as unfailingly popular with his own party members in Congress, but he in fact holds the modern record for abysmally low party support on a major vote, according to a Congressional Quarterly vote analysis.

During the first year of his second term, which, coincidentally is just where Clinton is now, Reagan won the support of only 8 percent of House Republicans on a major tax vote. By contrast, Clinton appeared to have won the support of 21 percent of his party on the trade initiative before the vote was called off.

That 1985 vote was on a rule that would have allowed floor debate on a measure to overhaul the tax code, which was then Reagan's top domestic priority. Then, as now, members of the president's party complained that they had been ignored by the White House, which was working with the House's Democratic majority to craft the tax bill. *(1985 Almanac, p. 11-C)*

Clinton's Strengths

Several factors conspire to keep Clinton in the legislative game next year. The powers that control either end of Pennsylvania Avenue are highly motivated to get work done: The president's paramount concern is his legacy, and the GOP majority that controls both houses of Congress wants most to complete a legislative record for incumbents to run on.

For Clinton's part, he will be attempting to put the finishing touches on a centrist and incrementalist program begun in the wake of his most devastating legislative defeat, the rejection of his health care initiative early in his first term.

The health care plan was seen as too complex, too bureaucratic and too much a product of big-government mentality. It was rejected in 1994 by Democrats and Republicans alike, and did not get crucial support from key committee chairmen.

"That was in many ways his Vietnam," Kettl said. "It cast a shadow across his administration and it was a mistake he was determined not to repeat. Since then, he has insisted on coming up with things that can win, with bipartisan coalitions."

The health care debacle is blamed in part for the electorate's decision to finally finish off a trend that began in the mid-1970s, when Democrats began losing seats in Congress. Voters took control of Congress away from the Democrats in 1994 and gave it to the Republicans.

Since then, Clinton's legislative coalitions have relied heavily on Republicans. And in a perverse twist, he has used strong GOP votes to win on the post-health care initiatives that will mark his place in history: an overhaul of New Deal welfare programs, a balanced federal budget for the first time since the Vietnam era, a tax cut for the middle class and the opening of America's trading borders with Mexico and Canada under the North American Free Trade Agreement.

At the same time he was building bridges to Republicans, Clinton was distancing himself from the left wing of his own party. He severed many of his remaining ties to liberals for good last year, when he declared that he and House Democrats should go their separate ways in their re-election campaigns, a public renouncement with real sting. "Bill Clinton is a guy particularly lacking in party loyalty," said George Edwards III, director of the Center for Presidential Studies at Texas A&M University.

But Clinton was playing practical politics, acknowledging that he and the core of the House Democratic Party have grown steadily further apart. Factors such as the demise of traditional Southern Democrats, the advent of gerrymandered districts that concentrate urban and black voters, and a growing, disproportionate reliance on labor union money have produced a House Democratic minority substantially more liberal than its Senate counterpart.

Rep. James P. Moran, D-Va., who supported fast track, said, "Democrats in the Senate, all of whom have to represent entire states, are listening to Clinton's leadership."

In the House, the kind of traditional Democratic interests that geared up to stop fast track, such as environmental groups and big labor, still have a lot of influence. The fast-track debate brought out "old-time Democratic politics," said Moran. "It's constituency group politics. It's protectionism. It's part of a herd mentality."

No doubt House Democrats will continue to try to nudge Clinton their way on issues next year, while Republicans will pick fights from the right to try to draw distinctions between themselves and the Democrats in an election year.

Al From, president of the centrist Democratic Leadership Council, said that Gingrich faces the same problem with conservatives in the House that Clinton does with liberals. "Gingrich is in big trouble today because he has a bunch of people who are just as crazy in the right in his party," he said.

When it suits their purposes, House Democrats still dutifully line up behind their president. Half the caucus supported him on the compromise welfare bill in the last Congress and three-fourths of them backed the balanced-budget deal this year.

Also, some practical considerations will keep Clinton and the Democratic left at least loosely bound together for the midterm election of November 1998.

Even some of the most liberal and supposedly alienated

Democrats do not mind having the president visit their districts to help raise money. "He actually becomes more important as the year goes on because people will be counting on him," said a senior House Democratic aide.

There's Always Next Year

The president's supporters say that the near disaster on trade will have long faded when Congress returns to a busy pre-election season in late January or early February.

"Every time you lose, you lose a measure of your influence," said Howard Paster, chairman of the Hill & Knowlton public relations firm and formerly Clinton's chief congressional strategist. "And every time you win, you build it back up. It's an ebb and flow.

"Clearly, losing fast track at the end of this session is a downer," Paster added. "But it does not mean in the remaining 38 months of this presidency he won't have other votes when [House Democrats] are with him."

Clinton is helped by job approval percentage ratings that have been holding steady in the mid-50s. "The public opinion polls show a very high level of support for the president, and he seems to be where most of the people in the country want him to be," Kettl said.

Between now and the start of the 1998 campaigns, Clinton will be bartering with Gingrich and Lott to get a few things he wants in exchange for letting them have a few things they want.

For instance, if the economy keeps booming, the two sides could find themselves dickering over what to do with the first budget surplus since 1969 — spend it, cut taxes or use it to begin paying down the national debt. That is a prime example of how the year might well be spent, not in pursuit of grand new initiatives, but in tinkering with those that Clinton already is counting on to round out his legacy.

House Majority Leader Dick Armey, R-Texas, in a recent interview, laid out a crowded if modest agenda for the second half of the Congress. "We have plenty of work out there to do," he said. "Now, there's nothing that is going to make the national bestsellers list, but there is work to do in this Congress."

Among other things, he predicted renewed efforts on a product liability bill, which would limit businesses' exposure to suits over faulty products; on charter school legislation, which would give parents and teachers more control over some schools; and on an overhaul of superfund, the federal fund used for major environmental cleanups.

Another item on the holdover agenda is resumption of work on a six-year, multibillion-dollar highway bill that bogged down this year in disputes over the total level of funding for the bill and over an unrelated dispute with Democrats over campaign finance reform legislation.

Also high on the list will be a proposed rewrite of the law protecting endangered species and work on a proposed settlement between the tobacco industry and state attorneys general. Republicans also intend to finish work in the Senate on legislation restructuring the Internal Revenue Service. The House passed the legislation Nov. 5. (Weekly Report, p. 2755)

Modest, Incremental, Possible

For his part, Clinton has indicated that he intends to pursue legislation to curb the power of managed care organizations while giving more rights to patients — modest compared with his 1994 health care initiative, but typical of his more incremental approach. On the foreign policy front, he may take another stab at fast-track legislation, which even his own aides admit was the victim of a late-starting and poorly organized lobbying effort in the House. Also on the president's list is the issue of expanding the North Atlantic Treaty Organization to formerly communist countries.

Despite his rocky relations in the House, Clinton, in anticipation of his State of the Union address Jan. 27, is working with both House and Senate Democrats to try to arrive at a common agenda for 1998.

Much of next year could be dominated by Republican-inspired debate over overhauling the tax code. But few expect that or other major initiatives to be completed. "Sweeping entitlement reform or a massive tax overhaul are going to be awfully tough," Paster said. "It's tough in divided government, and things like that tend not to be second-term initiatives anyway."

The highlight of the past legislative year provides a blueprint for how the president and Congress could work together in 1998. After the political war over the budget in 1995 and 1996, Clinton, Gingrich and Lott arrived at a compromise balanced-budget plan that, in the end, pleased no one completely but achieved the objectives of both sides.

The president, who campaigned in 1992 on a pledge to end deficit spending, was able to redeem a policy he backed away from after Republicans mauled his first effort in 1993 over tax increases. And Republicans were able to deliver on promises to balance the budget and cut taxes, which helped propel them to power in 1994.

The trick is to find issues that offer each side a plausible win, without forcing them to compromise too far on party-defining principles. A booming economy helped make it much easier for both sides to reach a balanced budget, cut taxes and provide extra spending for key programs.

"If you look at five years of the Clinton presidency, he has passed most of the legislation he has tried to pass," Paster said. "He wins most of his battles. Nobody wins everything." ∎

THE JUDICIARY

Independent Counsel Law Draws a Fickle Audience

Detractors become defenders as power shifts sides, but questions remain about effectiveness and cost of the 1978 statute

Not long ago, Sen. Orrin G. Hatch, R-Utah, and former Watergate special prosecutor Archibald Cox took diametrically opposing positions on the 1978 law creating "independent counsels."

Hatch hated it because it spawned a seemingly endless stream of investigations of the Reagan administration. Cox was an unabashed supporter. As a Democrat and a victim of President Richard M. Nixon's "Saturday Night Massacre," he saw it as the only way to keep politics out of the investigation of high officials.

Then the White House changed from Republican to Democrat, and Congress changed the other way. As the accused became the accuser, some deep-seated philosophies flew out the window.

"I've changed my viewpoint," said Hatch, chairman of the Senate Judiciary Committee. "Before, I would just as soon repeal the independent counsel statute. Now I see there is reason to have it."

Cox still supports the law, but with less enthusiasm and with major changes. "It contains more evils than benefits," said Cox, now professor emeritus at Harvard University Law School. He said the law has lost the public's confidence and has politicized a process it was supposed to clean up.

"That's one of the great tragedies," he said. "The whole idea was to remove it from politics."

Perhaps no one knows more about the politicization of the independent counsel statute than Attorney General Janet Reno, who has appointed at least a half-dozen of them. She is reviewing

CQ Weekly Report Nov. 15, 1997

BETTMANN UPI PHOTO

Kenneth W. Starr, independent counsel for Whitewater, has come under attack among Democrats for an investigation that appears to have no boundaries.

allegations that could lead to the appointment of an independent counsel to investigate whether political donations improperly influenced Interior Secretary Bruce Babbitt's decision to reject an Indian casino project in Wisconsin. And she must decide by Dec. 2 whether to seek independent counsels to investigate the campaign finance practices of President Clinton and Vice President Al Gore, as well as personal finance issues involving former Energy Secretary Hazel R. O'Leary. Reno also could extend her "preliminary investigation" on any of them for another 60 days. Clin-

ton and Gore gave separate interviews Nov. 11 to Justice Department officials also probing whether either man broke the law by making fundraising calls from the White House.

While making her decision, Reno has found the controversial law puts her in a classic no-win political bind. If she decides against an independent counsel, Republicans will say she caved in to demands from the Clinton White House. But if she calls for an independent investigation, Democrats will say she was swayed by a highly effective GOP campaign to pressure her. *(Weekly Report, p. 2529)*

Over the years, Congress has blown hot and cold over the value of the independent counsel statute, which was inspired by the Watergate scandal and has been deployed 18 times. At a cost of millions of dollars, these investigations have seldom led to the conviction of top officials. *(Weekly Report, p. 2848)*

Defenders say the statute is the only way prosecutors can avoid a real or perceived conflict of interest. Independent counsels, appointed in a two-step process by the attorney general and a presumably independent panel of judges, are deliberately outside the chain of command of those they investigate.

Critics on the left see Reno's current plight as evidence the process of appointing an independent counsel has, itself, become too political. Critics on the right deride the law as an affront to the Founding Fathers' concept of three distinct branches of government, with checks and balances. Independent counsels occupy a place somewhere between the executive and judicial

COMPLEX AND OFTEN CONFUSING WAYS...

☞ IN THEORY

the independent counsel statute works as follows:

Someone suggests that a high official has committed a serious crime. The attorney general conducts a 30-day "threshold inquiry" to see whether the allegations are "specific and credible." If they are, he or she starts a 90-day preliminary investigation that includes the "threshold" period. It triggers the appointment of an independent counsel if he or she concludes that there are "reasonable grounds to believe that further investigation is warranted." A three-judge panel then names an inde-pendent counsel, who conducts an investigation free from any conflict of interest.

30-day threshold inquiry

90-day preliminary investigation

☞ IN REALITY

the statute is more complex.

In about 90 percent of the cases, the original allegations are based on stories that appear in newspapers and magazines. Current Attorney General Janet Reno has said she does not believe such clippings alone necessarily merit starting an investigation. On Oct. 3 she wrote a dismissive letter to House Judiciary Committee Republicans, saying their accusations that President Clinton and Vice President Al Gore may have committed crimes during fundraising seemed to add up to little more than clippings. Nonetheless, news clippings

are hard to dismiss. They are specific and generally credible, if not always accurate.

Similarly, the people making the accusation are often hard to dismiss for lack of credibility, says former Attorney General William P. Barr. About the only way to do that, he says, is if a letter comes in "written by someone who says that the head of the CIA requires them to wear a colander on their hat to avoid getting rays, or something like that."

Once the charges are found to be specific and credible, the attorney general begins a 90-day preliminary investigation. At this point, the movement toward appointing an independent counsel gains momentum.

90-day preliminary investigation

60-day extension

At the end of 90 days — with an optional 60-day extension — the attorney general, to avoid appointing an independent counsel, has to conclude that there are no grounds for further investigation. That is difficult. She has to reach this conclusion based on her limited probe. During the 90 days she may not empanel a grand jury, issue subpoenas, plea bargain or grant immunity.

She may not rule out an independent counsel simply because the accused lacked criminal intent. In white-collar crime, intent is often what separates a minor infraction from a major crime — for example, a bookkeeping error from tax evasion. Nevertheless, since 1987, attorneys general have not been allowed to consider intent.

She does, however, have a significant escape valve added in 1983: She can base a decision not to appoint a counsel on grounds that the crime in question has not traditionally been prosecuted by the Justice Department. This could come into play when she determines whether to seek a counsel to investigate Clinton and Gore for fundraising on federal property — a violation never prosecuted by the Justice Department.

Three-Judge Panel

Once the decision is made to appoint a counsel, the matter is referred to a three-judge panel. Currently, the panel is chaired by David B. Sentelle, an appellate court judge in the District of Columbia Circuit. Two other appellate judges, John D. Butzner Jr. of the 4th Circuit and Peter T. Fay of the 11th Circuit, fill out the panel.

Over the years, most judges on this panel have been Republicans, or at least appointed to the bench by a Republican president. The panel is selected by the Chief Justice of the United States, who has been a Republican since the independent counsel statute was enacted in 1978.

Sentelle is often criticized by Democrats, particularly for his selection of Kenneth W. Starr to investigate the Whitewater land deals. Starr replaced Robert B. Fiske Jr., a special prosecutor appointed by Reno during the two-year period in which the independent counsel statute lapsed. Starr, a solicitor general in the Bush administration, has close ties to several GOP operatives, including former presidential candidate Pat Robertson.

Sentelle's political leanings also are clear. He is a former Republican Party chairman in Mecklenburg County, N.C., who named his daughter "Reagan" after the president who put him on the federal bench. He came under fire in 1994 when, shortly before appointing Starr, he had lunch with Sen. Lauch Faircloth, R-N.C., who wanted to get rid of Fiske.

To choose an independent counsel, Sentelle and his colleagues consult a "talent book" they have put together from memory, services such as Lexis-Nexis (which tracks legal cases) and outside recommendations. The person must be willing to work for $55 an hour — not much for an attorney. Many counsels insist on keeping their other clients during the investigation.

Another limitation is that the panel

... TO APPOINT INDEPENDENT COUNSELS

cannot choose people whose firms have a connection to the case. This proved difficult in 1990 in selecting someone to investigate corruption charges at the Department of Housing and Urban Development. HUD is a never-ending source of litigation, and firms throughout the country have had a piece of it.

Like the judges, the majority of counsels have been Republicans — if their affiliation could be identified. Current panel members say they prefer to choose people from the opposite party as the president, who is now a Democrat. Sentelle says he particularly likes former solicitors general.

Once panel members have a counsel in mind, they ask the person pointed questions about his or her political contributions. They do not mind some activism. In favoring people from the opposite party as the administration, they are encouraging people that have a party affiliation. Still, they say they do not want to appoint someone who has contributed to a presidential candidate.

"We would not necessarily disqualify [a] person for making the contribution to his congressman," Butzner said at a conference at the meeting of the 4th Circuit, last June. "But if the contribution was to the president or the candidates for president . . . we will not accept that person."

No Limits
Counsel is free to pursue "related matters"

Once appointed, the independent counsel has virtually no limitations. When the attorney general makes the recommendation, she files an application proposing the subject of the investigation. But the counsel is free to pursue related matters.

This has come into play in the Whitewater investigation, which has strayed from the original Arkansas land deals that gave it its name. Starr spent

three years, among other things, determining that former Deputy White House Counsel Vincent W. Foster Jr.'s death was a suicide. In at least one case, the Clinton Justice Department tried to block the expansion of the counsel jurisdiction but was rebuffed by the panel.

The attorney general has virtually no control over the counsel. All she can do is remove him or her for flagrant violations of the law. The three-judge panel likewise can do little. Congress and the Supreme Court, in its 1988 ruling in *Morrison v. Olson*, have made clear that they do not want a three-judge panel running a mini-executive branch of government.

The result is that the independent counsel has virtual free rein over the course of the investigation. "We have no way to say 'You're spending too much; you're not spending it on the right things,'" Butzner said.

Legal Fees

The judicial panel comes back into play as the counsel's work nears completion. First come legal fees. Since 1983, the statute has provided market-rate legal fees for people who are targets of counsel investigations and not indicted.

The close of an investigation normally sets off intense haggling between the three judges and attorneys for those under investigation. The reimbursement does not apply to witnesses, which creates complications because counsels have often upgraded and downgraded people's status between witness and subject. Sorting out which legal fees correspond to which status makes bookkeeping confusing.

The judges routinely challenge fee requests. In the case of Janet G. Mullins, who was alleged to have improperly rifled through presidential candidate Bill Clinton's passport file, the judges decided her attorneys had

aggressive in their defense. She got about half the $400,000 her lawyers had billed.

In other cases, the panel has docked funds for lawyers who hold news conferences or otherwise promote their client's cause with the media, which they consider an inappropriate activity. Reimbursement of legal fees may have an unintended consequence. The target only gets legal fees if not indicted, which shifts the balance of power toward prosecutors. The threat of indictment is a powerful weapon for obtaining a plea or getting testimony under any circumstances. But if the threat has immediate financial repercussions, it is even more powerful — even if both sides know the indictment has little chance of ending in a conviction.

After any indictments run their legal course, the counsel closes the investigation and submits a final report — a remarkably controversial part of the process. In the early days, counsels submitted succinct reports describing what they did and how much they spent.

But independent counsel Lawrence E. Walsh's report on the Iran-contra scandal ran more than 1,000 pages in three volumes. It contained classified material and grand jury testimony known only by Walsh. Numerous Reagan officials who had not been indicted came under heavy

End investigation
submit reports

criticism. The Bush administration tried to suppress it, but Sentelle released all but the classified portions to the public.

Walsh argues that such a report is necessary to ensure the public is getting an honest evaluation of any misdeeds by government officials. Others say the role of a prosecutor is to prosecute when appropriate, and not to prosecute when not appropriate.

Lawrence E. **Walsh**

branches, and generally are not accountable to either.

On a more practical level, the statute has been criticized for giving independent counsels unchecked power — an invitation to open-ended fishing expeditions that sometimes entangle the innocent and ruin reputations. The independent counsel is subject to little

LANNA HARRIS, THE ASSOCIATED PRESS

Oliver L. North, shown in 1987, was a top target of the Iran-contra investigation. His conviction was overturned.

oversight, has virtually unlimited resources and may be motivated principally by ambition. There is little accountability in terms of costs, scope or the way they conduct investigations.

The two examples of excess cited most often are Lawrence E. Walsh's Iran-contra investigation, which looked into whether the Reagan administration illegally diverted funds from weapons sales to Iran to support the Nicaraguan contras, and Kenneth W. Starr's Whitewater investigation, which is looking into Arkansas land deals involving the president and first lady.

Walsh's $48 million inquest used tactics that enraged Republicans. He indicted former Defense Secretary Caspar W. Weinberger on the eve of the 1992 election, a move that prosecutors often avoid. He met regularly with reporters, which many prosecutors also avoid. And his final report criticized numerous officials who were not indicted — another practice scorned by prosecutors.

Walsh, according to some critics, became a taxpayer-funded investigative journalist backed by the power to subpoena witnesses, empanel grand juries and threaten prosecution. His final report included selective grand jury testimony that furthered his arguments.

"It may be fair, it may not be fair," observed Theodore B. Olson, the target of a 1986 independent counsel probe. "But the person responding to this report has no way of knowing whether something has been taken out of context."

Likewise, Starr has come under attack among Democrats for an investigation that appears to have no boundaries. Originally appointed to investigate Arkansas land deals, Starr has expanded his investigation to Washington and to other matters. His critics say he is motivated by anti-Clinton zeal and by a desire to advance his ambitions to be appointed by the next GOP president to a seat on the Supreme Court.

Practices such as Starr's are highly unusual in the world of judicial prosecutions, observed Norman J. Ornstein, senior fellow at the American Enterprise Institute, a Washington think tank. Normally, prosecutors do not conduct open-ended investigations to see where they lead. They are limited by time, money and priorities. They accept plea agreements in many cases and charge ahead only in a select few. And they are always accountable either to the electorate, or to someone else who is.

"If you give unchecked state power to any human being, or group of human beings, you are unleashing a force that in many instances is destructive," Ornstein said. "You need the checks. It's a fundamental principle of the federalists. It's a fundamental principle of small-d democratic culture."

In his dissenting opinion in *Morrison v. Olson*, a 1988 case that upheld the constitutionality of independent counsels, Supreme Court Justice Antonin Scalia made a similar observation.

"How frightening it must be to have your own independent counsel and staff appointed, with nothing else to do but to investigate you until investigation is no longer worthwhile," he wrote.

Then there is the frequently asked question: What has the independent counsel law accomplished? Most of the convictions that have not been overturned involved minor players and people outside the government. None of them make a particularly compelling argument for the enormous expense of funding independent counsels.

Michael K. Deaver, deputy White House chief of staff under Reagan, is arguably the most important federal official to be convicted, and that was for committing perjury while under investigation for lobbying activities.

The top Iran-contra targets, national security aides Oliver L. North and John M. Poindexter, had their convictions overturned on appeal because they involved testimony they had given under immunity. The highest official ever to be indicted, Reagan Defense Secretary Weinberger, was pardoned by President Bush before his case went to trial.

Starr has won several convictions, including former Arkansas Gov. Jim Guy Tucker, former Clinton Associate Attorney General Webster Hubbell, and Clinton associates James B. and Susan McDougal, among others. But these people have little to do with the intended reach of the independent counsel statute: Except for Hubbell, none has ever worked for the executive branch of the federal government.

Ordeal

"It is not a pleasant experience, either in terms of time or emotionally," said Olson, who is a prime example of how the statute can ensnare relatively low-level aides on dubious charges.

Olson was an assistant attorney general in the Reagan administration, charged with violating the 1948 law that prohibits witnesses from misleading a government official. The question: whether Olson lied to Congress about the Reagan administration's alleged withholding of documents on a superfund toxic waste cleanup. The crime was alleged to have taken place in committee testimony, and in a legal memo he wrote to superiors on how to handle congressional requests for superfund documents.

Olson spent a year under suspicion, with a legal bill of $1.25 million, before independent counsel Alexia Morrison decided not to indict him. The court reimbursed him for $860,000 (and would have reimbursed nothing, had he been charged). He split the rest with his attorney.

Critics of the independent counsel statute argue Olson was forced to endure a legal nightmare, and could have been criminally prosecuted, because the Reagan administration and a Democratic Congress had different views on environmental policy.

The courts later ruled that the 1948 law did not even apply to interaction with Congress, which is political by nature. It was intended, the courts said, to punish people who gave false information to the FBI, the Internal Revenue Service or other non-political agencies.

Since the law's inception, independent counsels have been appointed to investigate people who were never considered its principal targets, on charges the laws' authors never envisioned. Indeed, the first two targets after enactment in 1978 were President Jimmy Carter's aides, Hamilton Jordan and Tim Kraft. Both were accused of using cocaine; neither was indicted. The Justice Department does not spend much time, under normal circumstances, on such allegations.

It is "extremely rare for the federal government to conduct a full-scale grand jury investigation to determine whether an individual used marijuana or cocaine on a specific occasion, particularly where the allegations are received well after the fact, are of dubious credibility and will not lead to seizure of any drugs," observed former Associate Attorney General Rudolph Giuliani, now mayor of New York.

Arguably the most inconsequential of the investigations was that of Janet G. Mullins and three State Department colleagues, who were accused of rifling through the passport file of presidential candidate Bill Clinton in 1992. They were never charged; the independent counsel decided it was not a crime.

"These people didn't do anything — anything! — wrong," says Olson, who later represented one of the four. "These people had been doing their jobs honorably."

Mullins' legal fees were about $400,000, and she recovered about half of that. Today a lobbyist for Ford Motor Co., she has nothing good to say about the statute. "It's flawed and so is the whole aura around it," she said. "It has now become a political weapon to pursue in the realm of criminal justice."

Independent counsel Joseph E. diGenova agreed. He not only declined to indict her, but he also issued a public apology. Now he is one of the statute's most consistent and virulent opponents. "This statute is absolute garbage," he said. "It was bad then, it's bad now. It ought to be repealed."

Too Political?

Supporters and opponents of the statute agree that over its 19 years it has become heavily politicized. Sen. Carl Levin, D-Mich., a key player in its 1982, 1987 and 1994 reauthorizations, cites the intense pressure on Reno — topped by threats of impeachment — to appoint an independent counsel Dec. 2.

"Politics, in the last couple of years has just swamped the statute," Levin said. "To tell an attorney general that impeachment proceedings will follow if she doesn't reach a certain conclusion is to undermine the statute."

Republicans point to 1980s cases when they, too, were under intense pressure to appoint a counsel. More recently they point to James Carville, the campaign operative who assisted Clinton in his 1992 victory. Carville has announced he would mount public campaigns to discredit Starr, and David B. Sentelle, the judge who appointed Starr.

The level of politics at play is reflected in the fact that few people in Washington have taken a consistent position on the statute through Republican and Democratic administrations. Hatch has changed his mind to support it, even though he has reservations about its constitutionality. His House counterpart, Judiciary Committee Chairman Henry J. Hyde, R-Ill., has been lukewarm. Now he, like Hatch, is applying pressure on Reno.

Olson, along with former Reagan Justice Department spokesman Terry Eastland, believes that the statute is bad and should be repealed. But before that happens they want it applied to the Clinton administration as vigorously as it was applied to Republicans. Eastland wrote a book, "Ethics, Politics and the Independent Counsel," opposing the statute. But now he writes Wall Street Journal columns encouraging Hatch and Hyde.

Olson may be the statute's most experienced opponent: After he was cleared, he became a private attorney representing other targets of investigation, including President Reagan. It was his challenge to the law that made it to the Supreme Court, which upheld the law in 1988, ruling that it did not usurp the president's power. *(1988 Almanac, p. 123)*

Today, Olson says the statute is the law of the land, and he wants it enforced. "You [Democrats] won," he said. "It's constitutional. We opposed reauthorization even into your administration and you insisted on having it. Now you must abide by this law."

Possible Solutions

Even supporters say major changes to the law are in order — to prevent minor players from getting caught up, to create more accountability and to get rid of some of the politics.

Some proposals offered by lawmakers and experts would limit the people "covered," which currently comprises the president, vice president, Cabinet members, senior White House staff members, Justice officials down to the rank of assistant attorney general, the CIA director and deputy director, the IRS commissioner, and the chairman and treasurer of presidential campaigns. The attorney general also may appoint a counsel for members of Congress or federal employees whose in-

REUTERS

Perhaps no one knows more about the politicization of the independent counsel statute than Attorney General Janet Reno.

vestigation could cause a conflict of interest for the Justice Department.

Also being floated are proposals to limit the scope of investigations to actions that took place while a covered official was in office or getting elected to office, or to limit a prosecutor's time or money.

Rep. Jay Dickey, R-Ark., has introduced a bill (HR 139) that would make the statute harder to trigger, more sharply define the independent counsel's focus and force independent counsels to apply for an extension if they are not finished in two years. Rep. John Conyers Jr., D-Mich., has a similar proposal (HR 117).

Another proposal, first floated in the 1970s by former Tennessee Sen. Howard H. Baker Jr. (1967-1985), and gaining credibility with both supporters and opponents of the statute, would create a permanent Office of the Independent Counsel within the Justice Department. It would be a non-political appointment, perhaps for a set term, not unlike the FBI director.

Those who support the concept of independent counsels say they are absolutely necessary in a few cases to ensure that high officials receive unbiased scrutiny.

Rep. Barney Frank, D-Mass., points to the Starr investigation. Frank believes Starr has gone overboard, but he says Starr does give the public a certain level of confidence. He cites Starr's recent conclusion, after three years of study, that former Deputy White House Counsel Vincent W. Foster Jr. took his own life. "The Starr appointment was bad," Frank says. "But he cleared up the Vince Foster situation. Only nuts now believe he was murdered."

Accordion Statute

Since 1978, the independent counsel statute has expanded and contracted depending on the circumstances, and politics, of the time.

After the Jordan and Kraft experiences, the statute's authors believed it was too easy to trigger an investigation. Accordingly, in their first reauthorization (PL 97-409) in 1982, they made some major changes. *(1982 Almanac, p. 386)*

They shortened the list of people to whom the statute applied. They gave the attorney general more discretion to consider the credibility of the accuser and the specificity of the charges. And they added a section that could affect whether Reno seeks a counsel to look into Clinton and Gore fundraising: In considering whether to call for an independent counsel, the attorney general was required to follow "the written or other established policies of the Department of Justice with respect to the conduct of criminal investigations." Clinton and Gore are accused of raising money on public property, an apparent violation of a 19th century statute known as the Pendleton Act. The Justice Department is not believed to have ever prosecuted anyone under this statute.

Also in 1982, Congress changed the name of the office from "special prosecutor" to independent counsel, and provided legal fees for those under investigation.

If Congress' intent in 1982 was to soften the statute, its mood had changed considerably by the time the statute was up for renewal again in 1987. By then, Democrats had retaken the Senate, giving them control of both

chambers — a legislative perch from which to square off against a Republican president. By then, too, the Iran-contra affair and other investigations had given Democrats, and some moderate Republicans, a new appreciation for the statute.

This time Congress checked the attorney general's autonomy. The new law (PL 100-191) denied the attorney general the authority to dismiss a case for lack of credibility or specificity after the first 30-day inquiry. The attorney

FILE PHOTO

Jay Dickey has introduced a bill (HR 139) that would make the statute harder to trigger, more sharply define the independent counsel's focus and force independent counsels to apply for an extension if they are not finished in two years.

general also was denied the power to dismiss a case because the accused lacked criminal intent. Authorizers gave the independent counsel expanded jurisdiction to prosecute crimes related to the original one. *(1987 Almanac, p. 363)*

The 1994 reauthorization (PL 103-270) brought about the least significant changes. It added members of Congress as possible targets of investigations, but at the discretion of the attorney general.

More interesting was that Congress allowed the statute to lapse for two years. At the outset, Republicans, still smarting from the Iran-contra investigation, were determined to let it expire. But as Clinton's Whitewater dealings

came into the public eye, they changed their minds. *(1994 Almanac, p. 295)*

What Congress Will Do

In late 1996 and early 1997, sentiment seemed to be turning against the independent counsel statute, at least in its current incarnation.

With pending investigations of Clinton, former Agriculture Secretary Mike Espy and former Housing Secretary Henry G. Cisneros, Democrats learned that they, too, could be targeted by independent counsels. Republicans were still upset about Iran-contra, and did not seem to be getting anywhere with Whitewater. Some speculated in the summer and fall of 1996 that Starr was waiting for the 1996 election to pass before indicting Hillary Clinton, if not the president. When this did not happen, the Whitewater probe faded into the background.

At the same time, several news organizations, including ABC News Nightline and Vanity Fair, focused on the statute's shortcomings. Conyers and Dickey introduced their bills and pushed for immediate consideration.

But the move to rein in independent counsels quickly faltered, first from a lingering reluctance to deal with the Dickey bill until Starr's investigation had wound down, and more recently when the Clinton and Gore fundraising practices emerged.

Now it seems the most likely time to change the statute will be in 1999, when it is up for renewal. Given that even supporters are pushing for changes, the law that emerges may be quite different from the current statute. Ultimately, however, changes may depend on the political landscape at the time. If Reno declines to call for independent counsels in December, Republicans may respond in 1999. And if a major investigation is under way then, the statute is likely to gain new life, as it did in 1987.

But without any scandals, the dynamics could be quite different. If both parties remember how their own presidents were investigated, and if both believe they will occupy the White House after the 2000 election, they would be motivated to tone down or eliminate the statute.

Most experts think restrictions are more likely than repeal. But if both Democrats and Republicans feel they have more to lose than to gain by renewal, the statute may be phased out. That would be fine with Mullins, who went through the Clinton passport probe. "The body count is high enough now that someone should say 'enough is enough,'" she says. ∎

Brady Decision Reflects Effort To Curb Congress' Authority

In 5-4 ruling, justices say lawmakers have no power to require local background checks on prospective handgun buyers

A deeply divided U.S. Supreme Court on June 27 struck down a major portion of the1993 Brady gun control law. Combined with other rulings this term and in recent years, the decision shows a high court making its most significant effort since the New Deal era to limit congressional powers.

The 5-4 ruling in the combined cases of *Mack v. United States* and *Printz v. United States* strikes down the portion of the Brady Act requiring local law enforcement officials to conduct background checks on prospective handgun purchasers. Congress had no authority to require such checks, the court concluded. The law's five-day waiting period for gun purchases will remain intact.

"The federal government may neither issue directives requiring the states to address particular problems, nor command the states' officers, or those of their political subdivision, to administer or enforce a federal regulatory program," Justice Antonin Scalia said in the majority opinion.

The ruling follows by two days that in *City of Boerne v. Flores*, in which the court struck down the 1993 Religious Freedom Restoration Act, also saying Congress had overstepped its powers. *(Weekly Report, p. 1526)*

In 1995, in *United States v. Lopez*, the court struck down a federal ban on guns near schools, a ruling that followed and drew on the court's 1992 ruling in *New York v. United States*, throwing out a federal requirement on state regulation of nuclear waste.

"Now we have a set of rulings showing the court wants to limit Congress to

KEN HEINEN

The Supreme Court justices, from left: Clarence Thomas, Antonin Scalia, Sandra Day O'Connor, Anthony M. Kennedy, David H. Souter, Stephen G. Breyer, John Paul Stevens, Chief Justice William H. Rehnquist and Ruth Bader Ginsburg.

its enumerated powers," said Cass Sunstein, law professor at the University of Chicago. "The court hasn't been in that business since the early New Deal."

Some conservatives were delighted with the trend toward restraining Congress' powers. "This is an imposition on state and local governments," Senate Judiciary Committee Chairman Orrin G. Hatch, R-Utah, said of the Brady Act.

The recent rulings have reinterpreted and narrowed the scope of certain parts of the Constitution previously viewed as giving Congress broad powers. The *Boerne* case significantly narrowed Congress' discretion under its 14th Amendment duty to implement equal protection laws. The *Brady*, *Lopez* and *New York* cases shift the balance of power from the federal government to the states. In *Lopez*, that balance is found in the legal conflict between the 10th Amendment, which limits Congress to those powers specifically enumerated in the Constitution, and the Interstate Commerce Clause, which gives Congress the broad and

vague power to regulate interstate commerce. In *Brady* and *New York*, the court relied on an "implied" limitation on federal authority inherent in the Constitution.

These rulings mean future Congresses will have to be much more careful in drafting legislation. Bills affecting many areas will have to be more closely tied to interstate commerce. Mandates on states will have to be cast as voluntary and perhaps linked to federal funding. Legislation creating new rights will be limited to redressing specific wrongs.

Officers 'Dragooned'

The court rejected the Brady background check, saying Congress had exceeded its authority and was essentially commandeering or "dragooning" local law enforcement officers. It is supposed to sunset when a national database for instant background checks is available for gun dealers to use in November 1998.

The majority opinion was based heavily on the *New York* case, as well as a reading of the Constitution, the Federalist Papers, and historical precedent.

"We held in *New York* that Congress cannot compel the States to enact or enforce a federal regulatory program," wrote Scalia, who was joined by Chief Justice William H. Rehnquist and Justices Sandra Day O'Connor, Anthony M. Kennedy and Clarence Thomas. "Today we hold that Congress cannot circumvent that prohibition by conscripting the State's officers directly."

In his dissent, Justice John Paul Stevens argued that the ruling amounted to a sweeping denial of the sovereignty of the national legislature. In the future, he said, Congress may have

Handgun Decision Excerpts

Excerpts from the Supreme Court's decision on the Brady Handgun Violence Prevention Act (PL 103-159) in the cases of Printz v. United States *and* Mack v. United States. *The majority opinion, written by Justice Antonin Scalia:*

"The Constitution . . . contemplates that a State's government will represent and remain accountable to its own citizens. . . . This separation of the two spheres is one of the Constitution's structural protections of liberty.

"We held in [a previous case] that Congress cannot compel the States to enact or enforce a federal regulatory program. Today we hold that Congress cannot circumvent that prohibition by conscripting the State's officers directly.

SCOTT J. FERRELL

Brady with Maryland Attorney General Joseph Curran.

"The Federal Government may neither issue directives requiring the States to address particular problems, nor command the States' officers, or those of their political subdivisions, to administer or enforce a federal regulatory program. It matters not whether policymaking is involved, and no case-by-case weighing of the burdens or benefits is necessary; such commands are fundamentally incompatible with our constitutional system of dual sovereignty."

From the concurring opinion written by Justice Sandra Day O'Connor:

"The Court appropriately refrains from deciding whether other purely ministerial reporting requirements imposed by Congress on state and local authorities pursuant to its Commerce Clause powers are similarly invalid. . . . The provisions invalidated here, however, which directly compel state officials to administer a federal regulatory program, utterly fail to adhere to the design and structure of our constitutional scheme."

From the dissenting opinion, written by Justice John Paul Stevens:

"When Congress exercises the powers delegated to it by the Constitution, it may impose affirmative obligations on executive and judicial officers of state and local governments as well as ordinary citizens.

"The provision of the Brady Act that crosses the Court's newly defined constitutional threshold is more comparable to a statute requiring local police officers to report the identity of missing children to the Crime Control Center of the Department of Justice than to an offensive federal command to a sovereign state.

"If Congress believes that such a statute will benefit the people of the Nation, and serve the interests of cooperative federalism better than an enlarged federal bureaucracy, we should respect both its policy judgment and its appraisal of its constitutional power."

trouble drawing on local support during emergencies such as wars, natural disasters or epidemics.

He doubted the wisdom of basing the ruling on the *New York* case, which was handed down by many of the same justices ruling in Brady. He also said the analysis of the Constitution and historical precedent was deeply flawed.

"Historical materials strongly suggest the founders intended to enhance the capacity of the federal government by empowering it — as a part of the new authority to make demands directly on individual citizens — to act through local officials," Stevens wrote, adding that the reasoning would "undermine most of our post-New Deal Commerce Clause jurisprudence."

Burdensome?

The Brady law (PL 103-159) was named after President Reagan's press secretary James S. Brady, who was injured by a handgun in the 1981 assassination attempt on the president. During the five-day waiting period local police are supposed to make "reasonable efforts" to verify that the prospective purchaser does not have a criminal background and is not an illegal immigrant, mentally incompetent, or otherwise disqualified from owning a gun. *(1993 Almanac, p. 300)*

Two sheriffs, Richard Mack of Graham County, Ariz., and Jay Printz of Ravalli County, Mont., brought suit against the background check, calling it burdensome. District courts in both states agreed, finding that Congress had exceeded its authority under the 10th Amendment.

These decisions, however, were reversed on appeal by the 9th Circuit.

Lawyers for Mack and Printz argued that the federal government was essentially forcing them to use limited resources to carry out a federal mandate.

The Justice Department argued that the background check was not comparable to the *New York* mandate because it did not require states to make laws. It said the background check was a routine, ministerial requirement of the type that had been upheld previously. The government argued that throwing out background checks could also call into question routine state-federal cooperation on such matters as sharing crime statistics.

Reacting to the court decision, President Clinton ordered his top law enforcement officials to remind local police agencies that they still may voluntarily make background checks.

Senate Majority Leader Trent Lott, R-Miss., said he would move to enact legislation to speed the implementation of the national database.

One irony is that the ruling could slow the purchase of handguns. The law says prospective buyers need not wait the entire five days once they have been cleared in a background check. If no one conducts the check, they would have to wait the five days.

Brady Act supporters minimized the ruling's practical effects. "I'm heartened that the rest of the law, especially the waiting period, survived intact," said Sen. Edward M. Kennedy, D-Mass.

The National Rifle Association, a longtime opponent of the Brady Act, hailed the decision. ∎

Paralyzed Congress on Sidelines In Financial Services Evolution

As industry infighting has stymied legislators, courts and regulators have stepped in to break down venerable Glass-Steagall barriers

©MARILYN GATES-DAVIS

If State Farm Insurance waited for Congress to dismantle longstanding restrictions on banking activities, it might find itself standing still until early next century.

Instead, the Illinois-based insurance giant is moving ahead with plans to open a chain of thrifts in Illinois, Missouri and Arizona. "We just view this as another way of serving our insurance customers," said Steve Witmer, spokesman for the State Farm Insurance Companies.

State Farm's use of a legal wrinkle that permits non-banking companies to obtain thrift charters is just one example of dramatic changes rocking the financial services industry. Americans are putting more money into investments such as mutual funds than into insured bank deposits; commercial giants such as General Electric are offering credit cards and brokerage services, and banks, eager to expand, are opening insurance agencies.

Further blurring the lines, moves such as the $9 billion consolidation of Travelers Group and Salomon Inc., announced Sept. 24, are creating giant brokerage and financial services companies.

These sweeping realignments are placing mounting pressure on Congress to revamp Depression-era laws that were intended to restrict banks, securities firms and insurers from entering each others' lines of business. "Financial modernization [legislation] should remove outdated restrictions that serve no useful purpose," Alan Greenspan, chairman of the Federal Reserve Board, testified at a May 22 congressional hearing. "The result would be a more ef-

CQ Weekly Report Sept. 27, 1997

ficient financial system providing better services to the public."

But lawmakers have failed since the early years of the Reagan administration to reach a consensus on an omnibus banking bill, and the 105th Congress appears to be facing another round of gridlock. *(1996 Almanac, p. 2-51; 1991 Almanac, p. 75; 1988 Almanac, p. 230; 1984 Almanac, p. 271)*

The latest setback occurred Sept. 18, when the House Commerce Committee postponed indefinitely a markup of a bill (HR 10) that would have lifted many of the industry restrictions. Although Chairman Thomas J. Bliley Jr., R-Va., originally hoped to take up the measure in early September, his committee remains deeply fractured over differences between the insurance and banking industries.

The postponement came three months after the House Banking and Fi-

nancial Services Committee approved HR 10 by a razor-thin, 28-26 margin, with Chairman Jim Leach, R-Iowa, vowing to oppose key provisions on the floor. *(Weekly Report, p. 1431)*

Still more discouraging for the bill's proponents, Senate Banking Committee Chairman Alfonse M. D'Amato, R-N.Y., and the committee's top Democrat, Paul S. Sarbanes of Maryland, have shown little interest in tackling the legislation and have yet to schedule a hearing on it. And the White House, reflecting policy disagreements within the administration, has been decidedly lukewarm about pressing the issue.

Regulators Move In

With Congress paralyzed by the fierce infighting between powerful financial lobbies, the role of setting rules for the fast-changing marketplace has fallen to unelected regulators and the courts. And on that battlefield, banks appear to have the upper hand, partly due to the legal clout of the Office of the Comptroller of the Currency (OCC), currently held by a banking ally, Eugene Ludwig. *(Story, p. 80)*

In fact, a series of regulatory and legal decisions over the last decade has expanded the reach of banks so much that the powerful banking lobby is somewhat ambivalent about the need for legal changes. But insurance and securities firms contend that they are finding it increasingly difficult to compete, and diversified financial firms want the power to buy banks. *(Story, p. 82)*

The maze of regulatory rulings has entangled the Comptroller of the Cur-

Champion for New Bank Powers

Few Americans have heard of Eugene Ludwig, but he is well-known in the Capitol as a powerful regulator willing to cross lawmakers in order to expand the reach of banks.

Ludwig, a banking and intellectual-property lawyer, was nominated by President Clinton to serve as the nation's 27th Comptroller of the Currency in 1993. The independent office of the Treasury Department supervises the lending and investing activities of more than 3,000 federally chartered commercial banks.

Ludwig brushed briefly with scandal in January when it was learned that he attended a Democratic National Committee-sponsored coffee at the White House prior to the 1996 election. Discussion focused on banking regulations, and the guests included top executives of the nation's largest banks, among them Hugh L. McColl of NationsBank Corp. and Thomas G. Labrecque of Chase Manhattan Bank. GOP lawmakers sharply criticized Ludwig's presence at the meeting, but the issue quieted down after Ludwig said his attendance was a mistake and that he did not know the bankers would be there.

But the comptroller is continuing to draw fire from both sides of the aisle over another issue: granting increased powers to banks at a time when Congress has been deadlocked over balancing the competing demands of the banking, insurance and securities industries.

Late last year, for example, Ludwig issued a ruling opening the door for banks to apply to set up subsidiaries that could engage in such financial activities as insurance, securities and real estate. Previously, only bank holding companies — not individual banks — could establish subsidiaries that could engage in various financial activities.

The comptroller has also pressed ahead with rulings by his predecessors giving banks power to sell insurance nationwide. And he has lobbied Congress to liberalize many banking laws, telling lawmakers in May: "We need a broad reconsideration of the legal framework in order to promote a robust competitive marketplace."

Ludwig

His rulings expanding the powers of banks have drawn unusually blunt attacks from leading lawmakers, who contend that Ludwig is exceeding his authority. "His area of aggression exceeds his area of expertise," said Rep. John D. Dingell, D-Mich. In a speech to bankers last year, House Banking Chairman Jim Leach, R-Iowa, said, "Having lost legislatively, the comptroller is in effect thumbing his nose at Congress and proceeding administratively."

But Ludwig insists that banks need more flexibility in order to maintain their competitiveness in a fast-changing marketplace. His rulings have stood up to court challenges, and he has won kudos from leading bankers, who say Ludwig is merely extending a string of earlier rulings by the Office of the Comptroller of the Currency dating to the mid-1980s.

Ludwig has won praise as well for consolidating and updating regulations, some of which had not been applied in decades. "He's also done some fabulous work that relates to the foundation of banking regulations," said Alfred M. Pollard, senior director for legislative affairs of The Bankers Roundtable, which represents major banks.

Bank powers aside, Ludwig is a strong proponent of the Community Reinvestment Act, which requires banks to make loans in low-income neighborhoods.

Even Ludwig's critics, such as insurance executives, give the comptroller high marks for integrity, contending that he was unfairly caught up in the White House coffee scandal. "While I may disagree with him, I believe he is an honest man," said Paul A. Equale, a lobbyist for the Independent Insurance Agents of America.

Ludwig briefly found himself in an awkward position over the 1993-94 New Year's weekend when Clinton asked him for advice regarding the White House handling of the Whitewater controversy. Ludwig declined, although he told The Wall Street Journal: "I must say I was torn."

Ludwig's five-year term expires in 1998; it is not clear whether he will serve a second. He has been mentioned as a possible candidate for the Federal Reserve Board.

rency, the Federal Reserve Board, the Securities and Exchange Commission, state insurance commissioners and federal judges. Industry lawyers battle over whether certain products, such as annuities or lines of credit, ought to be defined as banking or insurance or something else, and whether they should be regulated by a particular state or federal office.

"Every new ruling has a way of exposing fresh inequities and creating new uncertainties," former Federal Reserve Board Chairman Paul A. Volcker told a congressional panel in May. "In the absence of clear and up-to-date congressional mandates, there is seemingly

endless squabbling in the courts."

Veteran lawmakers of both parties view financial modernization as a high priority, saying America needs to revamp its laws in order to keep pace with worldwide market changes.

"Congress wants to preserve our right to write laws, which frankly has been overshadowed by the OCC and other regulators," said John A. Boehner, R-Ohio, chairman of the House GOP Conference. "If we don't modernize our financial services industry, America's ability to compete in the world is going to be severely undermined."

The stakes for consumers could hardly be greater. Treasury Secretary

Robert E. Rubin estimates that partially deregulating the industry could save Americans as much as $15 billion out of the nearly $300 billion they spend yearly on brokerage, insurance and banking services.

On the other side, some consumer advocates warn that the legislation could lead to a dangerous consolidation of the financial industry, eventually driving fees higher and squeezing credit.

That the determination of Boehner and other leading lawmakers has failed to pry loose the bill is a testament to the power of the feuding financial lobbies. Congressional leaders of both parties, like players on a minor college football team facing the conference champs, have been reduced to conceding that all they can do is to try their hardest.

"More remains to be done," House Majority Leader Dick Armey, R-Texas, and other leaders said in a terse Sept. 18 statement announcing the Commerce Committee postponement. "We will redouble our efforts."

Collapsing Walls

The law that Armey and others would revamp is the Glass-Steagall Act of 1933, a durable measure written in an era when Americans stood in soup lines and the word "plastic" referred to polymer research — not credit cards.

The act set up barriers between the banking, insurance and securities industries, largely preventing affiliations between the different financial sectors. The goal of Depression-era lawmakers was to stabilize the banking sector in the wake of some 4,000 bank failures and curb possible abuses of bank securities activities.

But the once-solid walls separating different types of financial institutions are now collapsing.

Much of the change has been driven by technological advances. Thanks to innovations such as automated teller machines (ATMs), telephone banking and computer transactions, consumers can conduct their financial business at electronic speed, breaking down international investment borders as well as the boundaries between different types of financial institutions.

In addition, companies are offering hybrid products that do not easily fit into the old definitions of banking, such as mutual funds with check-writing options or savings accounts that resemble insurance annuities.

"Revolutionary improvements in technology and escalating competition are redefining the financial services business," William T. McConnell, president-elect of the American Bankers Association, said at a May House Banking Committee hearing. "The lines between different types of financial service firms have been blurred beyond recognition."

While spurring a general boom in the industry, the changes have also left some securities firms and smaller banks in difficult straits, and they have forced other institutions to dramatical-

ly revamp their services.

In some respects, the increased competition has set back banks because Americans have moved their money from traditional deposits into other accounts that produce more earnings, such as mutual funds. The market share of financial assets held by banks and thrifts plummeted from almost 60 percent in 1977 to 28 percent this year, according to the American Bankers Association.

That loss of money has implications

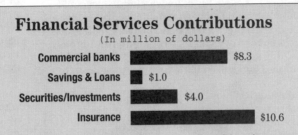

Financial Services Contributions
(In million of dollars)

Commercial banks	$8.3
Savings & Loans	$1.0
Securities/Investments	$4.0
Insurance	$10.6

In addition to competing for customers, financial services companies compete for political influence. The chart shows the amount of political action committee (PAC) money contributed by different types of financial service companies during the 1995-96 campaign cycle.

But these numbers tell less than half the story. Candidates on average get close to 60 percent of their contributions from the financial services industry through individuals, rather than PACs, with the securities industry in particular relying on individual contributors, according to the nonpartisan Center for Responsive Politics.

The center is still compiling data on individual contributors. When the final numbers are tallied, they may reveal that the securities industry contributed as much as insurers.

SOURCE: Center for Responsive Politics

not just for the banks' bottom line, but also for customers who rely on loans — especially in rural areas.

"We're not creating new wealth in North Dakota fast enough," said Terry Jorde, president of the Towner County State Bank in Cando, N.D., which lends primarily to farmers. "We've seen a great outflow of money."

Expanding Business

Rather than sitting idly on the sidelines while their assets dribble away, banks — especially the larger ones— have expanded into other areas.

Bank of America, for example, operates a subsidiary that deals largely in the underwriting and distribution of corporate debt and fixed-income securities. It operates another subsidiary that handles various lines of insurance, including credit, life, property and casualty.

Banks would like to be able to expand further, gaining the legal authority from Congress for virtually unlimited fi-

nancial dealings through their subsidiaries rather than facing various regulatory caps. But even their limited ventures into insurance and securities would not have been possible without a series of regulatory rulings over the last decade.

In 1986, the OCC issued a letter allowing nationwide sales of insurance by banks. One year later, the Federal Reserve Board issued the first of a series of opinions that would allow bank holding companies to set up subsidiaries to sell securities.

These and other rulings, coupled with a 1994 law enabling banks to set up branch offices nationwide (PL 103-328), have helped banks post double-digit profits for many areas of their business. (*Interstate banking, 1994 Almanac, p. 93*)

But the bank expansion has raised alarms in other quarters.

Consumer groups warn that bank customers are being pressured into buying risky financial products offered by a subsidiary in order to get a loan. They also say consumers may be misled into thinking products offered by a bank holding company subsidiary are covered by the Federal Deposit Insurance Corp., the independent agency that insures bank deposits up to $100,000.

"Consumers have already experienced problems with bank sales activities and, as bank powers expand, can expect more deceptive and misleading practices," said Mary Griffin, the insurance counsel with Consumers Union, the publisher of Consumer Reports.

Securities and insurance executives charge that banks are enjoying an unfair competitive advantage because they are subject primarily to bank regulators, rather than state insurance commissioners and the Securities and Exchange Commission. They also say the government rules have become dangerously unbalanced, with both domestic and overseas banks having the power to acquire other financial businesses even though insurance and securities firms cannot acquire banks.

Among the major takeovers this year is the acquisition of the nation's oldest securities firm, Alex. Brown & Sons, by the parent company of Bankers Trust, and the acquisition of another securities firm, Dillon Read & Co., by Swiss Bank Corp.

A Decade of Key Rulings

With Congress deadlocked over banking legislation, regulators and judges have stepped into the breach with a series of decisions expanding the reach of banks — sometimes over the objections of insurers and securities firms. Here is a summary of major regulatory and court decisions issued in recent years that affect the banking industry:

1986: The Office of the Comptroller of the Currency issued a letter permitting banks to sell insurance nationwide. The comptroller based the decision on a provision of the National Bank Act of 1916 that authorized national banks located in towns of 5,000 or fewer residents to sell insurance.

However, the 1916 provision does not explicitly state whether banks could sell insurance outside those small towns and had been the subject of considerable debate. For years before the comptroller's letter, national banks had been restricted to selling insurance in small towns and surrounding rural areas where insurance might not be readily available.

1987: The Federal Reserve Board authorized bank holding companies to engage in limited securities activities. It allowed bank holding companies' subsidiaries to derive up to 5 percent of their gross revenue from underwriting and dealing in various securities, such as commercial paper and municipal revenue bonds.

The ruling was based on section 20 of the Glass-Steagall Act of 1933, which states that no bank can be affiliated with an organization "engaged principally" in activities that are generally off-limits to banks, such as securities underwriting.

1989: The Fed expanded the activities of so-called section 20 subsidiaries, allowing them to derive up to 10 percent of their revenues from securities underwriting. Large bank holding companies were permitted to engage in longer-term corporate debt securities.

1991: The Fed authorized foreign banks to underwrite securities in the United States directly through subsidiaries, instead of through the subsidiary of a holding company as required of domestic banks.

1993: Upholding the interpretation of the Comptroller of the Currency, a Circuit Court judge in Washington, D.C., ruled in a case brought by the Independent Insurance Agents of America that banks can indeed sell insurance from towns of 5,000 or fewer residents. The insurance agents decided against appealing the case to the Supreme Court, but the issue continued to spawn various legal and regulatory disputes.

1995: Amid debate over whether certain products should be defined as insurance or banking, the Supreme Court ruled that annuities are a banking product and may be sold by banks. The court stated that "annuities . . . are functionally similar to other investments that banks typically sell."

Insurers had contended that annuities involve the pooling of risk, and therefore should be regulated as insurance products.

1996: In a landmark decision in March, the Supreme Court ruled that banks can sell insurance from offices in small towns, even in states that have laws prohibiting such sales. The ruling overrode a Florida law barring affiliations between banks and insurance agents. *(1996 Almanac, p. 2-51)*

1996: On Dec. 15, the Fed issued a series of rulings greatly expanding the ability of bank holding companies to underwrite securities. It increased the amount of gross revenue that a bank subsidiary could derive from securities activities from 10 to 25 percent. It also eased "prudential limitations," or firewalls, between bank holding companies and their bank and securities subsidiaries, allowing bank directors, officers or employees to serve on the board of the securities subsidiary, so long as they do not constitute the majority.

The rulings cleared the way for bank holding companies to acquire major securities firms in a series of takeovers this year.

Securities lobbyists say it is imperative for Congress to allow their companies to expand by acquiring banks, or America's premier position in the world of investment banking will be imperiled. "You're a sitting duck right now — they can come in and buy you," said Bruce Thompson, director of government relations for Merrill Lynch & Co.

But non-banking companies are striking back by making inroads into banking services.

State Farm, for example, is just one of several major insurance companies preparing to open up savings banks. Merrill Lynch and other securities companies offer a plethora of financial services that compete with banks, including credit cards and checking accounts.

Roiling the waters, commercial companies are entering the financial arena with gusto. The largest finance company in the country, according to the American Bankers Association, is a subsidiary of General Electric that offers consumer and commercial loans, credit card services, insurance, a group of mutual funds and securities services.

This array of new services has left regulators scrambling to apply the law to the realities of the marketplace — or even just categorize the products.

But rather than settling the issue, each new regulation seems to stir up more uncertainties.

"Unfortunately, in some instances, important safeguards are being weakened and the playing field is uneven," said Volcker. "Legislation is overdue."

Congressional Deadlock

There may be no greater advocate of financial legislation in Congress than Leach, the House Banking Committee chairman. He presided patiently over a four-day June markup of HR 10, carefully outlined his views on many of the dozens of amendments, calmly accepted setbacks on a series of votes and repeatedly pleaded with members to approve a measure.

Even so, he ended up with such a contentious product that banks, thrifts and consumer groups opposed it, and Leach himself said he might vote against it on the floor.

Undaunted, the Commerce Committee mobilized for a September markup. GOP leaders spoke of combining elements of the Banking and Commerce committee products in time for a showdown vote on the House floor this fall.

Then reality hit.

To put together a financial bill, the committee faced the task of assembling a nearly impossible jigsaw puzzle of competing interests. Their choices included:

• Whether to bow to the powerful insurance lobby and allow state officials to regulate the insurance products of national banks, or to continue to give such oversight to a federal regulator.

• Whether to allow banking and commercial companies to acquire each other, thereby risking the opposition of many banks. Securities and insurance firms tend to favor such a provision because they would not have to divest their commercial holdings in order to obtain a bank.

• Whether to step up regulations of newer bank products, as favored by consumer advocates and insurers, or pare back regulations in order to win the support of banks.

Making the politics more combustible, lobbyists for several of the industries threatened to use their considerable clout to wage all-out war against the measure unless they got their way.

"We're thrust in the middle of this holy war," said Michael G. Oxley, R-Ohio, chairman of the Commerce Committee's Finance and Hazardous Materials Subcommittee. "I'd rather be fishing — even if I don't catch anything."

Trying to cobble together enough support for passage, Oxley and Bliley fashioned a bill that tilted toward the banking position on many of the regulatory positions. However, they also alienated bank lobbyists by proposing to reduce the regulatory profile of the Comptroller of the Currency, dropped the provisions that would have allowed for a partial mixing of banking and commerce, and produced a regulatory proposal for financial holding companies that drew the opposition of most of the affected industries.

The draft bill drew withering fire from the insurance lobby even before it was circulated during the week of Sept. 15. "If the bill is offered as described, we will invoke all our resources to oppose the bill," stated a Sept. 12 letter to committee members from the Independent Insurance Agents of America and the National Association of Life Underwriters.

Taking up the insurers' cause, the committee's senior Democrat, John D. Dingell of Michigan, prepared an amendment that would empower state insurance commissioners to define and regulate bank insurance products. He appeared to have the support of roughly half the committee.

Compounding the committee's problems, many in the banking industry opposed the bill due to the regulatory changes. Securities lobbyists, although more supportive, outlined considerable concerns about the prospect of banking regulators overseeing financial holding companies, as well as the loss of provisions mixing banking and commerce.

GOP leaders decided on Sept. 18 to postpone the markup indefinitely. But they left open the prospect that the bill would still be considered this year, saying in a brief statement, "We . . . reaffirm our commitment to passage of legislation this Congress."

"Congress should not allow yet another opportunity to act in the national interest slip away."

— House Banking Committee Chairman
Jim Leach, R-Iowa

With key Republican constituencies girding for war, the bill had simply become too hot to handle. "The controversy was going to rage," said a veteran financial lobbyist. "It was too hot to throw it out on the floor and have people at each other's throats."

A Dakotan's View

And what if the deadlock continues?

That would be just fine with North Dakota's Jorde. Even though larger financial companies and top government officials say the laws should be updated, Jorde and many other community bankers contend that many of the current restrictions are necessary to prevent a dangerous consolidation of economic power.

Jorde points to her own bank as an example. Chartered 30 years ago by residents of the tiny town of Cando (population: 1,600) who wanted their own financial institution, the 12-employee bank is tightly bound to the local economy. It will assign a loan officer to spend days studying the financial health of a single farm, Jorde says.

But in a world without Glass-Steagall, where impersonal "one-stop shopping" financial firms would handle banking, insurance and brokerage operations, many folks in rural America would lose access to credit, she says.

"They [the companies] will basically deploy their assets and their revenue to the parts of the country where the return on equity is the highest and the levels of risk are the lowest," she said. "There are higher levels of risk in rural communities. . . . I think it would be devastating. Loans are what run the community."

Some community activists raise similar concerns. They fear that lifting financial restrictions would allow banks to neglect low-income neighborhoods, and to focus their resources instead on wealthy areas to increase their profits.

"The case for passing radical new legislation at this time is far from compelling," said Allen J. Fishbein, general counsel of the Center for Community Change in Washington, D.C., a nonprofit organization that provides assistance to low-income neighborhoods. "It will reinforce the trend, already prevalent, toward the de-linking of banks from local communities, thereby further de-emphasizing the needs of underserved communities and households."

But many financial executives and regulators say the door is already open to financial consolidation, and Congress can best serve consumers by clarifying the rules of the game.

Unless the government acts, for example, consumers could be facing a second, separately regulated banking system created by numerous companies applying for thrift charters, banking lobbyists contend. "You've got a totally parallel banking system that will obviously, over time, attract a great number of the deposits from the current banking system because it's less regulated," said Edward Yingling, executive director of government relations for the American Bankers Association.

Yingling and other bank officials want to eliminate the thrift charter — a position fiercely resisted by the thrift industry and just one more issue for lawmakers to resolve in HR 10.

Lawmakers had taken a step in that direction in 1996, when they passed legislation (PL 104-208) that will merge the Bank Insurance Fund with the Savings Association Insurance Fund in 1999 — but only if thrifts are phased out by then. *(1996 Almanac, p. 2-43)*

Despite the obstacles, Leach thinks Congress needs to keep at it. In a seven-page letter to House Speaker Newt Gingrich, R-Ga., on Sept. 19, the chairman contended that the issues are too important to ignore, even if the bill leads to fierce fighting on the floor.

"The goal of the Congress . . . should be to enact legislation which is in the public interest and which provides balance among all affected parties — criteria which may also cause angst for everybody," Leach wrote. "Congress should not allow yet another opportunity to act in the national interest slip away." ∎

THE BUREAUCRACY

New FCC Panel Members Face Pressure Over '96 Overhaul

Lawmakers criticize pace of implementation and raise concerns about court challenges, consolidation and rising cable rates

When Congress passed the telecommunications act in February 1996, lawmakers gave to the Federal Communications Commission much of the power to implement their plan for opening up all sectors of the industry to competition.

But more than a year and a half after its implementation, some lawmakers have questioned whether the commission has botched the job.

Key rules the commission has issued to accomplish the act's intent have been challenged in court. Concerns have been raised about the slow development of competition, especially in the local telephone market; an increasing trend toward consolidation in the telecommunications industry; and the dramatic rise of cable TV rates.

For the FCC, concern over implementation of the act comes as the commission has a full menu of other diverse items on its plate, including the applications of foreign companies to enter the U.S. long-distance market and approving the television ratings systems developed by the broadcast industry.

It is under these circumstances that four new commissioners — including a new chairman — will take their places on the five-member commission. The only holdover is Susan Ness, who occupies one of the FCC's three Democratic seats.

FCC General Counsel William E. Kennard has been nominated to succeed FCC Chairman Reed Hundt, who announced in May that he was stepping down. If confirmed, Kennard will be the first black to head the commission.

The other nominees include Gloria Tristani, a member of the New Mexico

CQ Weekly Report Oct. 4, 1997

DOUGLAS GRAHAM

Dorgan speaks during the Oct. 1 hearing on FCC nominations.

commission that regulates state utilities and granddaughter of former Sen. Dennis Chavez, D-N.M., (House 1931-35, Senate 1935-1962) who will take over the second Democratic slot.

Michael K. Powell, chief of staff in the Justice Department's antitrust division and son of the retired head of the Joint Chiefs of Staff Gen. Colin L. Powell, and Harold W. Furchtgott-Roth, the chief economist on the House Commerce Committee, have been appointed to the two Republican seats.

The Senate Commerce Committee, which held confirmation hearings Sept. 30 and Oct. 1 for the four nominees, is expected to vote on their nominations Oct. 8. Given the plethora of issues awaiting the new commissioners, who occupy full-time positions that pay at least $115,000 a year, Senate Commerce Committee Chairman John McCain, R-Ariz., is pushing for speedy confirmation by the Senate.

"The challenges are enormous," said Gene Kimmelman, co-director of the Washington office of the Consumers Union advocacy group, of the work awaiting the new commissioners. "The

fundamental situation is that the industry vastly over-promised . . . what their competitive desires were to cross into each other's markets and Congress bought that. . . . Now you find rates going up and the industry backtracking" on its promises.

While Kimmelman may take a dim view on the state of the telecommunications act, others say that the new commissioners face a host of complex issues — and their moves will continue to be monitored closely on Capitol Hill.

All four nominees already have indicated that ensuring competition will be one of their chief goals. "Ultimately, the best way to keep rates low is through competition," Kennard told lawmakers. "If confirmed, I intend to ask the hardworking FCC staff to roll up their sleeves once again and mount a new offensive for competition."

Yet there appears to be little appetite in Congress for reopening the telecommunications act in any significant way. "Nobody is willing to say, 'Let's open it up,' " said Sen. Conrad Burns, R-Mont., who added that Congress needs to give the law more time to work.

New Opportunity

For Congress, the four vacancies presented lawmakers with a unique opportunity to influence the agency's direction.

Some members of Congress and observers say there is no doubt that Congress has more closely watched than ever before who will occupy the seats at the commission than they ever have in the past. "We vested a great deal of authority in the FCC," said Rep. Michael G. Oxley, R-Ohio. "It's natural to follow the power."

A Senate Commerce Committee aide added that given the unprecedented turnover on the commission and the "simmering frustration" over how the telecommunications act has been implemented, there is little surprise that many members have placed more emphasis on these particular nominees.

As a result, there was intense jockeying over who would be nominated to fill the four slots.

McCain was aggressive in pushing Powell's nomination. He opposed Rachelle B. Chong's renomination to a Republican seat on the commission, paving the way for Powell to be nominated after Senate Majority Leader Trent Lott, R-Miss., offered up Furchtgott-Roth's name for the first GOP slot.

Sen. Ernest F. Hollings of South Carolina, the ranking Democrat on the Commerce Committee, lost his effort to install Ralph B. Everett, his former staff member on the Commerce Committee, as the new FCC chairman. Everett also was being pushed by the Congressional Black Caucus.

Instead, the White House chose Kennard, who had already been nominated for a Democratic seat on the commission. By choosing Kennard for the chairman's slot, the White House was able to accommodate the demands of rural-state lawmakers who wanted someone sympathetic to the concerns of rural residents for the second Democratic seat, which led to the appointment of New Mexico's Tristani. Tristani has experience at the state level in dealing with communications issues.

State of Competition

For many members of Congress, the most pressing issue facing the commission is continued implementation of the telecommunications act (PL 104-104), which with its enactment in 1996 swept away 62 years of telecommunications policy. *(1996 Almanac, p. 3-43)*

The act's supporters promised consumers more choices at lower prices as various telecommunications companies moved into one another's markets. Lawmakers envisioned cable companies offering telephone services, local phone companies moving into the long-distance market and long-distance companies expanding to offer local phone service.

So far, many of the promises made by the act's supporters have not come to fruition, and some members of Congress are asking why.

"The law has not lived up to the rhetoric that accompanied its passage," McCain, who voted against the legislation because he did not think it went far enough in deregulating the telecommunications industry, told Kennard after

the nominee said he believed the FCC had done a good job of implementing the act.

McCain has said that while many of the problems that have emerged are inherent to the act itself, the FCC has exacerbated the problem by interpreting the law "in the most bureaucratic fashion."

Some blame the commission for failing to implement the act as Congress instructed.

DOUGLAS GRAHAM
Kennard testifies at the hearing.

"The commission made some serious errors in reaching beyond the statute's mandate," said Rep. Rick Boucher, D-Va.

Local Market

Rep. W.J. "Billy" Tauzin, R-La., chairman of the Commerce telecommunications subcommittee, said "my first wish is that they would simply read the bill we passed. If they follow it . . . we can begin the process that the bill promises in terms of competition."

Others blame the local telephone companies for blocking competition while at the same time complaining about the FCC's refusal so far to allow any of the Bell companies to enter the long-distance telephone market.

"It is important for the new FCC to continue to remain tough on companies that want the best of both worlds, that is to retain monopolies in their own market places while competing in other areas of telecommunications," said Rep. Edward J. Markey, D-Mass.

Many lawmakers and even outgoing Chairman Hundt have expressed frustration about the slow pace of competition in the local telephone market. All the nominees echoed this concern. "The act is working but not particularly well, particularly in bringing competition to [local] markets," Powell said.

While praising the act as generally sound, Kennard, who has been responsible for defending the FCC's rules against litigation, said that speeding up the development of competition in the local telephone market was one of his top priorities. Noting it took a dozen years for full competition to develop in the long distance market, he said "I think all of us who are involved in working on implementing the '96 act would be disappointed if it took a dozen years to bring competition to local telephone."

Several of the FCC's key decisions aimed at opening the local telephone markets to competition have been challenged in court. Most notable among these was the interconnection order that set out the conditions and rates under which few competitors could enter the local telephone market.

Local telephone companies, which challenged the order in court, argued that the FCC rules would put their competitors at an advantage because they would force the incumbent phone companies to offer their networks at "bargain basement prices," according to William P. Barr, GTE Corp.'s executive vice president and general counsel. In July, the 8th U.S. Circuit Court of Appeals, based in St. Louis, struck down major parts of the commission's interconnection order, saying that the FCC did not have the authority to set the rates competitors must pay to the incumbent local phone companies to use their networks.

Last month, local telephone companies and state regulators, in separate moves, went to court again to stop the FCC from requiring local phone companies to open their networks using the agency's pricing system. They argued that the FCC is trying to go around the appellate court's decision by requiring telephone companies to use the pricing mechanism, which the court said it did not have the authority to set, as one of the conditions for gaining entry into the long-distance market.

Long-distance companies such as AT&T and MCI are pointing fingers at the local phone companies, saying they are trying through litigation to block the development of true competition. "Breaking up a monopoly has been hard to do," said Jonathan B. Sallet, MCI's chief policy counsel.

The local telephone companies have shot back, saying that long distance companies are only interested in the lucrative business market and are not serious about providing local residential service. At the same time, the

Baby Bells complain that the FCC has established hurdles beyond what the telecommunications act required for their entry into the long-distance market.

Sen. Wendell H. Ford, D-Ky., raised the issue with the FCC nominees, saying it appears that the commission keeps "moving the goal posts" on the Bells. Kennard and the other nominees agreed that in order for competition to grow, it is "vitally important" for the commission to be clear about what the standards are for entry into the long-distance market.

The Senate Judiciary Antitrust Subcommittee has held one hearing Sept. 17 on the state of competition in the local phone market. McCain also plans to hold hearings in the Commerce Committee on the issue most likely next year. A Commerce Committee aide said McCain might consider making minor adjustments to the legislation next year if need be.

Sen. Herb Kohl, D-Wis., has introduced legislation (S 1188) that would consolidate all the court challenges to the FCC's rules under the jurisdiction of the District of Columbia federal court and court of appeals.

Pressure Is On

For now, Congress appears content to step up pressure on the FCC to use the power within its means to fix the problems that have slowed the development of competition.

For example, some have suggested that on the pricing issue, the FCC work closer with the states to establish an acceptable rate mechanism for opening local markets to competitors.

During the confirmation hearings, many senators from rural states expressed concern that changes to the way universal service is funded will result in an increase in local telephone rates in rural areas. Universal service is intended to provide comparable telecommunications services to every community at affordable prices.

"I wouldn't in a million years vote for a telecommunications act that I felt was going to impose a substantial increased price burden on those who live in smaller towns in this country or in rural areas of this country," said Sen. Byron L. Dorgan, D-N.D.

Kennard said the commission is determining what the funding mechanism should be for providing universal service, but acknowledged that "one of the greatest challenges of the new commission . . . will be to resolve this issue."

Another area of concern is the rise in cable rates, which according to out-going Chairman Hundt, have risen in recent years faster than the rate of inflation, as well as the pace of viable competitors to cable companies.

Consumers Union and the Consumer Federation of America filed a petition Sept. 23 asking the FCC to freeze cable rates and overhaul its mechanisms for determining what are fair rates. Hundt has said the rate increases appear to be primarily due to such factors as the addition of new channels and increasing costs of new programming.

Kennard said in written testimony

"Nobody is willing to say, 'Let's open [the act] up.' "

— Sen. Conrad Burns, R-Mont.

---

that the FCC would be "vigilant" about monitoring changes in cable TV rates and would "adjust its regulations as necessary to protect consumers."

But under the act, all cable rate regulation is set to expire by March 1999. Some lawmakers and consumer groups are concerned that without sufficient competition by then in the cable market, rates will continue to rise. Direct broadcast satellite companies have attempted to make the biggest run at cable but are still hampered by their inability to easily provide local broadcast signals.

Kennard said Congress made it clear that "sufficient competition should exist to replace regulation." He said the FCC would monitor the competitive trends in the cable market to ensure that goal has been met before rate regulation expires.

Boucher and others have suggested that the FCC establish a low-priced first-tier cable selection, which would include local broadcast stations, and would enable competitors to more easily compete with cable to provide expanded programming in a second tier.

Meanwhile, underlying all the griping about the development of competition is concern over the mergers that have taken place among telecommunications companies since the passage of the act.

For example, Bell companies have moved aggressively on this front, with mergers announced between SBC Communications Inc. and Pacific Telesis, and more recently between Bell Atlantic and NYNEX. In the long-distance market, MCI is likely to be gobbled up either by British Telecommunications PLC or WorldCom Inc.

Pressure on the Peacock

Even though Congress has placed control over many telecommunications issues in the hands of the FCC, it has by no means surrendered.

The recent controversy over television ratings is one example where lawmakers managed to impose their will even before the commission had a chance to act.

The telecommunications act required that new television sets include "v-chip" technology, which would allow parents to block objectionable programs. Broadcasters agreed to develop a voluntary ratings system that would be used in conjunction with the v-chip. The act requires that the ratings system be approved by the FCC.

Even before the commission had ruled on the system that was put in place at the beginning of the year, most broadcasters gave in to pressure from advocacy groups and members of Congress this summer and agreed to revise the voluntary age-based ratings system, similar to the one used for motion pictures, to include more information about the content of programs. The new ratings system, which went into effect Oct. 1, will now include the letters S, V, L or D to indicate whether a program contains sex, violence, coarse language or suggestive dialogue. (Background, Weekly Report, p. 2014)

All the major networks agreed to use the system except NBC. McCain has stepped up pressure on the network to agree to use the new ratings system by threatening to move legislation (S 363) that would require the network to adopt the new guidelines or restrict violent programming to hours when children are least likely to be watching.

He also appears to be looking to the new FCC members to take steps to force NBC to sign on to the new ratings system. In response to a question by McCain, Powell, Furchtgott-Roth and Tristani said they would be open to reviewing whether a network had agreed to use the new ratings system as part of the license renewal process for broadcasters. Kennard said he would consider the situation in the context of evaluating the new ratings system.

So far, NBC is not budging. The network says it is concerned that the real goal of some of the new systems' supporters is censorship. NBC says it will continue using the original age-based ratings system and include on-screen advisories for some programs. ∎

Politics and Public Policy

The term *public policy making* refers to actions the government takes to confront issues on the public agenda and the method by which a decision to act is reached. The work of government—Congress, the presidency, the bureaucracy, the judiciary—and the people who run it is to make and implement the policy decision.

But which issues are addressed? How does an issue get on the public agenda? The policy agenda evolves as new problems are recognized and old problems reach a critical mass. Many issues brew for years or even decades before a consensus is reached to act, and then devising and implementing a plan of action may take many more years. To some extent, however, the government—Congress and the president in particular—can frame the agenda.

Resentment of the Internal Revenue Service has been a staple of American politics for as long as the IRS has existed. As the complexity of the revenue code increased, so too did public antipathy to paying taxes. In September 1997 the Senate Finance Committee elevated the issue to the public agenda, holding public hearings on the IRS as a prelude to legislative action.

Hazardous waste and nuclear waste are two issues that have been on the public agenda for decades. After much planning and study of the hazardous waste issue, Congress created the "Superfund" in 1979, but the enormity of the problem and legal entanglements have kept the issue alive for nearly two decades. The issue of nuclear waste has been on the agenda for almost as long, in large part because no consensus has ever been achieved on the long-term disposal of spent fuel and contaminated equipment.

After issues have been identified and legislative remedies have been passed and implemented, the success of the remedy is evaluated. Welfare reform is a comparatively recent topic on the public agenda; it is too early to pass final judgment on the reforms that have been implemented. Although the early returns are positive, the long-term prognosis is in doubt.

The final two selections in the *Guide to Current American Government* concern American trade policy and women in the military. The former issue, in a broad sense, is as old as the American Republic. The founders of the nation debated free trade versus protectionism, which is the crux of the fast-track negotiating power sought by President Clinton. Women serving in the military is an issue of more recent vintage. Women were integrated into the military in the 1940s, but limitations on their service were slow to fall.

IRS HEARINGS

Congress and Country Fired Up After Hearings on IRS Abuses

Fresh wave of taxpayer resentment and calls for tax code overhauls heighten hopes for change but also concern over 'IRS bashing'

Congressional hearings into alleged abuses by the Internal Revenue Service were not four days old, but already the furor was sweeping across the nation.

In Oklahoma City, a wrecker shop owner who had allegedly attacked two collection officers with gasoline last June went on local television Sept. 29 to vow that he would not plead guilty as expected, declaring instead that now is the time to fight the agency.

In Newport News, Va., Michael E. Mares, chief of the tax committee for the American Institute of Certified Public Accountants, was hearing of taxpayers who had decided to renege on their commitments to repay back taxes and instead claim harassment at the hands of the IRS.

In Fargo, N.D., Barbara Bennett, an IRS taxpayer service specialist, had to deal with two walk-in complaints of harassment and mistreatment by an agent in her office, an "unusual" occurrence, she said.

In the Milwaukee IRS office, calls claiming persistent, long-term problems with tax collectors were skyrocketing, said Ted Reis, a district office spokesman.

By Oct. 1, well over 2,000 calls, e-mails and faxes had flooded into the Senate Finance Committee.

"There has been quite a change in attitude out there among the taxpayers," sighed Quinton Bland, an IRS revenue officer in Oklahoma City.

Three days of Senate Finance Committee hearings Sept. 23-25 have touched a nerve, sparking a firestorm of protest against an agency that Americans love to hate. The hearings featured a retired New York priest describing how IRS

CQ Weekly Report Oct. 4, 1997

agents harassed him for eight months over an alleged $18,000 debt but refused to show him a tax return; a Bakersfield, Calif., woman who cried while laying out a 17-year battle over a tax bill owed by someone with a name similar to that of her optometrist husband; and IRS revenue agent Jennifer Long, who testified about "egregious tactics" used "to extract unfairly assessed taxes, literally ruining families, lives and businesses, all unnecessarily and sometimes illegally."

On the last day, acting IRS Commissioner Michael P. Dolan offered a blanket apology and promised rapid reforms.

"Those hearings were really rather historic," proclaimed Rep. W.J. "Billy" Tauzin, R-La. "You actually got an apology from the IRS. When was the last time that happened?"

Amazed by the reaction, GOP leaders want to harness that anger not only to overhaul the IRS but to scrap the entire federal tax code.

"Hopefully, by April 15, we can form

a consensus around a major, decisive tax reform . . . that would move us to a much simpler system, a more honest system, and a fairer system," declared House Speaker Newt Gingrich, R-Ga.

It is a tall order, but the Republicans believe they cannot lose. If they succeed, they will have left a startling mark on the economic, political and social landscape. Their struggle to make that mark may have given them the political issue that will carry them all the way to the 2000 elections.

What is good for the GOP, however, may prove bad for the Treasury. IRS bashing may soon raise a serious new question: How far can Congress go before a climate of contempt for the IRS begins to undermine a collection system that is historically based on voluntary compliance?

"The IRS cannot survive two more years of this kind of bashing," said Robert Tobias, president of the National Treasury Employees Union and an advocate of administrative reform.

The hearings focused on a handful of egregious violations, not "what's actually going on out there," said Pamela F. Olson, vice chairman of committee operations for the American Bar Association's section on taxation and a witness at one of the House Ways and Means Committee hearings. "I was rather dismayed at what happened last week. . . . It got out of hand."

Tax experts worry that such public displays could embolden tax protesters and scofflaws, who will dare the IRS to come after them with the expectation that a besieged agency will either lay off or be too overwhelmed to care.

"This is only going to hurt the honest taxpayer, because they're going to have to pay more if other people are cheating," said a resentful Quinton Bland. "But as long as we have the current regime [in Congress], we're going to have IRS bashing. They don't have the communists or Russia to kick around anymore, so what's the next best thing?"

Ripe for Reform?

The organizers of last month's IRS hearings, both in the Senate Finance Committee and the House Ways and Means Committee, readily concede that they were trying to lay the groundwork both for an IRS overhaul and a future tax bill. Indeed, House Republicans had been advised by influential GOP pollster Frank Luntz to move on to tax and IRS issues after the balanced-budget agreement was reached.

"America is ripe for fundamental tax reform, and no one will weep for the IRS agents, tax attorneys and CPAs who might be put out of work," Luntz wrote in a recent memo to the GOP conference.

But even GOP leadership aides prone to bravado said they have been taken aback by the hearings' results. Months of hearings on campaign finance abuses have failed to capture the public's imagination. Yet three days of horror stories by ordinary taxpayers have gained extraordinary traction, throwing the IRS, the Department of Treasury and even the White House on the defensive.

After days of standing firm against proposals to expand outside control of the IRS, the administration is ready to propose an independent citizens' review board — with 33 local panels spread across the country — to handle complaints from aggrieved taxpayers.

The testimony resonated because Republicans were able to find witnesses both inside and outside the IRS to attest to intentional harassment of middle-income taxpayers.

Never mind that most audits land on the affluent, said William Gale, a senior fellow in economic studies at the Brookings Institution. Middle-income earners pay almost all their taxes through paycheck withholding, giving them little opportunity to evade the tax collector. Audits generally hit taxpayers with large estates and capital gains. Besides, Gale said, the IRS goes after the rich for the same reason robbers go after banks: That's where the money is.

"Republicans have made tax enforcement into a lower-class issue," Gale said. "It's politically brilliant. Whether it's true . . . is doubtful."

"I simply don't believe IRS agents target lower-income people for audits, because it would be a monumental waste of time for everybody," said Don-

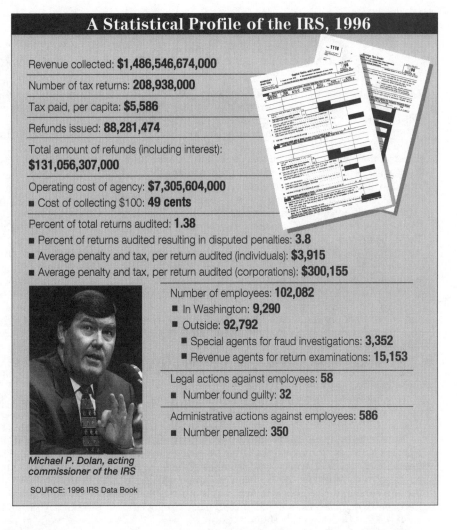

A Statistical Profile of the IRS, 1996

Revenue collected: **$1,486,546,674,000**

Number of tax returns: **208,938,000**

Tax paid, per capita: **$5,586**

Refunds issued: **88,281,474**

Total amount of refunds (including interest): **$131,056,307,000**

Operating cost of agency: **$7,305,604,000**
- Cost of collecting $100: **49 cents**

Percent of total returns audited: **1.38**
- Percent of returns audited resulting in disputed penalties: **3.8**
- Average penalty and tax, per return audited (individuals): **$3,915**
- Average penalty and tax, per return audited (corporations): **$300,155**

Number of employees: **102,082**
- In Washington: **9,290**
- Outside: **92,792**
  - Special agents for fraud investigations: **3,352**
  - Revenue agents for return examinations: **15,153**

Legal actions against employees: **58**
- Number found guilty: **32**

Administrative actions against employees: **586**
- Number penalized: **350**

Michael P. Dolan, acting commissioner of the IRS

SOURCE: 1996 IRS Data Book

ald Kettl, director of the La Follette Institute of Public Affairs at the University of Wisconsin.

Centerpiece Issue

The GOP is moving quickly. Bill Archer, R-Texas, chairman of the Ways and Means Committee, vows that the House will pass a bill to overhaul IRS operations this year over the administration's objections. On Oct. 10, Majority Leader Dick Armey, R-Texas, will launch a "Scrap the Code" tour of the country, debating Tauzin on the merits of replacing the progressive income tax with either a flat tax or a national sales tax. And dozens of bills to revise, reform, or abolish the IRS and the tax code have blossomed in recent days. *(Bills, p. 92)*

"The GOP has decided taxes and tax reform are their issue, and they're going to ride it as far as it can go," said Kettl, who has been studying the recent IRS reform efforts. "They're not going to leave it to Steve Forbes in 2000. They're going to use it as a centerpiece for 1998."

The first part of this ambitious agen-

da is already teed up. The Ways and Means Committee plans to act soon on a broad and bipartisan bill (HR 2292) that would enact the recommendations of the National Commission on Restructuring the IRS. The commission, chaired by Sen. Bob Kerrey, D-Neb., and Rep. Rob Portman, R-Ohio, issued a 190-page report June 25, recommending the first sweeping changes to IRS governance and management since 1952. The bill would:

● Create a joint congressional oversight committee.

● Establish an independent board of directors, modeled after private-sector corporate boards, with the power to direct long-term strategy at the IRS; hire and fire senior leadership, including the IRS commissioner; and review IRS budgets. The seven-member, presidentially appointed board would include the secretary or deputy secretary of the Treasury, an IRS union representative, and five "high-stature, nonpartisan professionals" from the private sector.

● Grant new powers and greater flexi-

GOP's Motives for Taking on IRS . . .

The anti-IRS crusade has awakened passions in the Republican Party not felt since the days of the "Contract With America." The tax man as oppressor is a notion that is as American as tea steeping in Boston Harbor, and it is as Republican an issue as they come. For the first time in months, the majority party has succeeded in reconnecting itself with populist resentment about the burdens of taxation and large government bureaucracies.

There is yet another compelling reason why the IRS bashing on Capitol Hill has brought the GOP back to life. Since they came to power in the elections of 1994, many Republicans have become convinced that the Clinton administration has used the agency and its audit powers against its political adversaries, including several prominent conservative organizations.

One of the party's most visible leaders, House Speaker Newt Gingrich, R-Ga., has more than a passing interest in the outcome of one audit. The agency has been looking into a group of unusual tax-exempt organizations Gingrich was associated with before he became Speaker.

Going after the IRS, taking with them every taxpayer who has feared the knock of a revenue agent at the door, gives Republicans a chance for sweet vengeance.

"I think there is a feeling that this administration has used the IRS against its political enemies," said former Rep. Robert S. Walker, R-Pa., an informal adviser to Gingrich.

Now that they have got the public's attention, Republicans are hoping to turn the debate from the agency's weaknesses to the tax code itself — and more importantly, to the question of whether the GOP's vision of a diminished role for government in the lives of Americans is a better fit for the country in the 21st century than are the activist government policies of the century about to expire.

"The IRS is a beautiful issue for Republicans because so much is wrapped into it, and so many people understand it," said Grover G. Norquist, president of Americans for Tax Reform, an anti-tax group allied with the GOP. "We did the budget, and now we're back to drawing the distinctions between the parties."

A 'Motherhood Issue'

The attack on the IRS could help move the party out of its Contract phase and into the preparatory stages for the 1998 midterm elections. Republicans hope to use the debate over overhauling the agency to soften the electorate for a discussion about sweeping changes in the tax code that are at the heart of current GOP philosophy.

"Taxes are a motherhood issue for Republicans," said Washington and Lee University political scientist William F. Connelly, who has written extensively about the congressional GOP. "But the key thing is, the role of government is central to the tug of war between Democrats and the Republican majority over the long haul. Just bashing the IRS is not enough. Radically altering the tax code is a way of addressing the larger issue of the role of government."

Republicans have yet to agree among themselves what their alternative will be, but they share a common loathing of the present eye-glazingly complex tax code based on progressive tax rates. GOP options range from a flat tax, which would apply a single rate to all taxpayers, to a national sales tax applied to the purchases of goods and some services.

At this stage, it matters not that Republicans disagree, say party leaders. They were badly in need of a compass, and they finally may have found one.

Having completed a balanced-budget deal with the White House, they had, after more than two years, closed the book on the most important item of the policy agenda that helped propel them into the majority. Since the August recess, Republicans had been adrift, without much of an agenda beyond the routine work of passing appropriations bills. Plus, Gingrich, the leader who brought them to power, seemed permanently stuck in a cycle of low poll ratings, ethical questions, attempted coups and erratic attentiveness to the business of the House.

Though Republicans had been trying for months to focus attention on the IRS and their ideas for refashioning both the agency and the tax code, the issue did not catch fire until a round of recent Senate Finance Committee hearings in which everyday people, including a retired Catholic priest, testified to their suffering at the hands of IRS bullies.

"As opposed to what was going on with the Thompson hearings, that was great television: ordinary citizens listing the horrors visited upon them," said Rich Galen, a GOP media strategist and Gingrich adviser, contrasting the Finance hearings with the hearings into campaign finance abuses led by Sen. Fred Thompson, R-Tenn.

Gingrich seized on the public's interest in the issue, which was made all the neater by the forced silence of top IRS officials, who because of privacy laws were prohibited from directly answering taxpayers' allegations at the hearings. In a letter to President Clinton on Sept. 30, Gingrich wrote: "For five years, the administration officials in charge of the IRS have fiddled while the agency burned the hopes and dreams of thousands of innocent taxpayers."

But more dear to Gingrich and other Republican leaders than the broad appeal of criticism of the IRS is the opportunity presented by the tax code issue. They believe that that, more than anything else they have come up with lately, has the potential to energize voters for 1998. In a non-presidential year, when success belongs to the party that can get its true believers to the polls, diehard Republican activists who have been unhappy with the compromises made in the budget deal with Clinton may be eager to return to the fold.

Democrats on the Run

Clinton put up a stoic defense of hardworking and honest IRS employees — most of the evidence brought out at the hearings was anecdotal — and acting IRS Commissioner Michael P. Dolan apologized for the agency's sporadic abuses. But Democrats nonetheless were on the run.

Norquist said gleefully that Clinton must have taken "a stupid pill" when he decided to stick up for the IRS. He noted that most Americans never come into direct contact with big government agencies like the Environmental Protection Agency or the Occupational Safety and Health Ad-

... Are Both Personal and Political

ministration, but the vast majority file tax returns every year.

Congressional Democrats decided it was best to start talking about reforming the agency.

Charles B. Rangel of New York, the ranking Democrat on the House Ways and Means Committee, called the IRS "a politically potent, explosive issue" and said of the agency's response: "I don't think saying you're sorry is enough." He vowed to work for legislation this fall.

Likewise, House Minority Leader Richard A. Gephardt, D-Mo., in an unusually warm letter to Gingrich on Oct. 1, pledged his "full cooperation in bringing forward legislation this year to reform the management problems at the Internal Revenue Service."

Leaders Gird for Battle

The IRS has frequently been a handy target for Capitol Hill, but veterans of those earlier wars are taken aback by the intensity of this round. "In the past, you really didn't have the congressional leadership engaged in the battle, even during the Watergate period," said Don Alexander, a former IRS commissioner under Presidents Richard M. Nixon and Gerald R. Ford. "The attack was being led by people much further down the totem pole."

For Republicans, this political battle is also personal.

Earlier this year, Ways and Means Chairman Bill Archer, R-Texas, and Senate Finance Chairman William V. Roth Jr., R-Del., assigned the Joint Committee on Taxation to look into allegations that conservative groups were being unfairly targeted for IRS audits. The investigation is still under way, according to a top committee aide.

Among the organizations that said they have been targeted are the National Rifle Association, Citizens Against Government Waste and the National Center for Public Policy Research. The NCPPR said it got audited in 1995, shortly after the organization waged an aggressive campaign opposing Clinton's proposed health care overhaul in 1993 and 1994.

The IRS also has about 50 ongoing investigations of tax-exempt groups, that keep their special status by forswearing any overt political activity.

In one embarrassing case for Republicans, the agency early this year denied tax-exempt status to former GOP

Chairman Haley Barbour's National Policy Forum, judging it to be too partisan. Barbour had been running the now-defunct organization since 1993, claiming it had tax-exempt status. (During the Thompson hearings, questions have been raised about $1.6 million transferred from the forum to the Republican National Committee to help repay a loan during the 1994 election.) *(Weekly Report, p. 1112)*

Barbour's friend Gingrich also has a personal stake in the outcome of an IRS audit. The House ethics investigation that this year resulted in the Speaker admitting violations of House rules and being reprimanded by the House opened the door for an agency investigation of several tax-exempt organizations Gingrich was involved in for several years leading to the 1994 takeover of Congress.

Three tax-exempt foundations affiliated with Gingrich have been contacted by federal investigators. The ethics case raised questions about whether the groups were financing political activity, but the Committee on Standards of Official Conduct could not reach a conclusion on that issue. *(Weekly Report, p. 476)*

"SOME QUESTIONS FOR NEWT GINGRICH," blared the headline on a recent news release from the Democratic National Committee. "Given that the IRS is investigating your improper use of tax-exempt groups for political purposes, do you think it's appropriate for you to criticize and threaten the IRS?"

Slings and Arrows

Republican pollster Frank Luntz suggested "talking points" on the IRS to members of the House GOP Conference. Among them:

● "America is ripe for fundamental tax reform, and no one will weep for the IRS agents, tax attorneys and CPAs who might be put out of work."

● "One of the lessons of 1994 that still applies today is that bold is better. The complete and utter destruction of the income tax system as we know it will convince Americans the GOP is really serious about returning government to the people."

● "Most voters would rather have their purse or wallet stolen than be audited by the IRS. That's correct. Half of all Americans would rather be mugged than face an audit by this mysterious and hated . . . institution."

● "Bill Clinton and the Democrats used Medicare to drive a wedge between us and the electorate. The IRS can do the same for us against the Democrats."

Gingrich adviser Galen noted that the Speaker had been advocating reform of the agency long before the ethics case. Indeed, in his 1995 book "To Renew America," Gingrich described the public's "sense of rage at the Internal Revenue Service's attitude."

Former IRS commissioners said the intense pressure on the agency from the congressional leadership could have the effect of slowing down some IRS investigations. And a top IRS official who spoke only on background said, "We try not to involve our front-line employees in these types of things so we can insulate them from outside influence. But they read the paper like everyone else."

"I think it is not helpful," said Shirley D. Peterson, an IRS commissioner under President George Bush who is now president of Hood College in Frederick, Md. "The IRS has a tough enough job when it's given the right resources and just allowed to do its work. There's no way accusations like that can fail to affect the morale of employees."

Overhauling the IRS

This is a partial list of bills pending before Congress that would overhaul the Internal Revenue Service and tax collections:

● **IRS Restructuring and Reform Act of 1997 (S 1096, HR 2292):** Sponsored by Sen. Bob Kerrey, D-Neb., and Rep. Rob Portman, R-Ohio, this legislation would implement the findings of the congressional National Commission on Restructuring the Internal Revenue Service. The bills would establish an outside governing board to oversee the IRS, curb additions to the tax code and streamline the tax filing system.

● **IRS Improvement Act of 1997 (HR 2428, S 1174):** Drafted by the Clinton administration and sponsored by Rep. Charles B. Rangel, D-N.Y., and Sen. Daniel Patrick Moynihan, D-N.Y., these bills are largely identical to the Kerrey-Portman legislation, granting increased authority to the IRS commissioner over personnel matters and encouraging electronic filing of tax returns. But there is one key difference: the composition of a new IRS management board. Where Kerrey-Portman would turn oversight over to a board largely comprising outsiders from the private sector, the administration bill confines membership almost completely to government officials, chiefly from the Treasury Department.

● **Freedom and Fairness Restoration Act (HR 1040, S 1040):** Sponsored by House Majority Leader Dick Armey, R-Texas, and Sen. Richard C. Shelby, R-Ala., these bills would abolish the progressive income tax and replace it with a flat tax. The rate would be set at 20 percent of wages and pensions, then fall to 17 percent in 1999.

● **S 593:** Sponsored by Sen. Arlen Specter, R-Pa., this bill would scrap the progressive income tax in favor of a modified flat tax of 20 percent with limited deductions for charitable contributions and interest payments on home mortgages. Specter would also permit "personal allowances" for taxpayers and their dependents.

● **National Voter Opportunity to Inform Congress Effectively on a Flat Tax and a Cap on Tax Increases Act (HR 2057):** Sponsored by Rep. Peter Hoekstra, R-Mich., this bill would authorize a national advisory referendum on a flat income tax. The bill would also establish a one-time national vote on tax increases in 1998.

● **National Retail Sales Tax Act (HR 2001):** Sponsored by Rep. Dan Schaefer, R-Colo., this bill would abolish the IRS and replace the federal income tax with a 15 percent national sales tax.

● **S Res 16, H Res 111:** Sponsored by Sen. Richard G. Lugar, R-Ind., and Rep. Joel Hefley, R-Colo., these resolutions would express the sense of the Senate and the House that the federal income tax should be replaced with a national sales tax.

● **Tax Code Termination Act (HR 2490, S 1225):** Sponsored by Rep. Steve Largent, R-Okla., and Sen. Tim Hutchinson, R-Ark., these bills would scrap the entire federal tax code by Dec. 31, 2001, forcing a complete rewrite of U.S. tax law.

● **HR 2462:** Sponsored by House Budget Committee Chairman John R. Kasich, R-Ohio, this bill would eliminate the so-called marriage penalty, in which some married couples filing jointly pay higher taxes than they would if they filed separate returns.

● **Taxpayer Dividend Act (HR 2496, S 800):** Sponsored by House GOP Conference Chairman John A. Boehner of Ohio, and Sen. Spencer Abraham, R-Mich., these bills would designate an expected $135 billion in surplus revenues for tax cuts through 2002. The expected revenues are above any amount originally projected by the balanced-budget agreement.

● **Taxpayer Confidentiality Act (HR 2563):** Sponsored by House GOP Conference Vice Chairman Jennifer Dunn of Washington, and Rep. John Tanner, D-Tenn., this bill would limit IRS summons authority and its ability to request information not directly pertinent to a tax return.

bility for managers over personnel issues.

● Establish new training programs for employees.

● Create new incentives and marketing efforts to encourage greater electronic filing of tax returns, which would save processing costs. (Almost 15 million returns were filed electronically in 1996, but that was just 7 percent of the 209 million returns filed.)

● Place new controls on Congress to prevent members from further complicating the tax code.

The House legislation, sponsored by Portman and Rep. Benjamin L. Cardin, D-Md., and a companion bill (S 1096) sponsored by Kerrey in the Senate are almost identical to legislation (HR 2428, S 1174) drafted by the Clinton administration and sponsored by Charles B. Rangel of New York, the ranking Democrat on House Ways and Means, and Daniel Patrick Moynihan of New York, the ranking Democrat on the Senate Finance Committee.

But there is one major difference: Where the Kerrey-Portman governance board would be dominated by the private sector, the administration's would be composed almost exclusively of officials from the IRS and Treasury.

Treasury Secretary Robert E. Rubin has taken a hard line against the Kerrey-Portman language, saying a private-sector board would invariably lead to conflicts of interest and tax policy skewed to the benefit of big business.

"This is a case of a private board being given public authority over the fundamental conduct of American tax policy," agreed Kettl, who has studied the Kerrey-Portman plan for the Brookings Institution. "It crosses any conceivable demarcation between the public and private sector."

To bill proponents, Rubin's opposition boils down to a turf battle over tax policy and a reluctance to let the IRS slip out of Treasury's purview. The Kerrey-Portman legislation explicitly says that the Treasury Department would retain full authority over tax policy and that board appointments would be subject to conflict-of-interest laws. A management board of Treasury Department and IRS officials would be nothing more than the status quo, Kerrey said.

"We've been talking by each other," Kerrey said of his negotiations with the White House. "And they're not talking about our bill."

But bill proponents have taken heart in the war of words over the management board. "By focusing on this one provision, they have in effect acquiesced to the rest of the provisions," Portman said.

Grand Old Plans

Clearly though, GOP leadership has far bigger things in mind. Both Gingrich and Armey said repeatedly the week of Sept. 29 that as long as the IRS had to administer a tax code as complex as the current version, true reform would be impossible. Armey called the tax code "an abomination to the human spirit" and "an embarrassment to human intellect."

Of course, the GOP's recent tax law (PL 105-34) only made matters worse, with 315 additional pages of bewildering deductions, credits and other provisions. Some tax specialists said the 1997 tax law will make it that much more difficult to simplify the code in the future, because it creates new beneficiaries, such as couples with children and families with college-age dependents. But Republicans insist the more complex the code gets, the more pressure there will be to scrap it.

"This has put us back on the right track," Tauzin said. "The party needs a big idea, and if you want a really big idea, one that really captivates the people, what could be better?"

Politically, Tauzin's logic is unassailable. Legislatively, the GOP has an uphill battle. Gingrich said he would like a tax overhaul moving in Congress next year. Archer said 1999 would be more likely. But Portman and Tauzin say it will never happen with Clinton in the White House.

Administration's Defense

The president has said repeatedly that no flat tax rate or national sales tax rate would raise enough revenue without being so high that it would fall of its own weight. And he has supported the IRS's attempts at internal reform, as well as its record of collections.

In 1996, the agency collected nearly $1.5 trillion from 209 million tax returns. Of those returns, just 1.4 percent were audited, and of the audited returns, only 3.8 percent resulted in penalties. Dolan told reporters Sept. 30 that 435 times over the past three years, IRS employees were disciplined for some form of taxpayer mistreatment. At least four managers have been suspended since last month's Senate hearings.

"We have had a commitment to change and a commitment to building the Internal Revenue Service that the American people deserve," Rubin said. "And we have accomplished a great deal."

Archer fired back, saying that the White House's response to the Septem-

ber hearings made Clinton "part of the problem instead of part of the solution."

The legislative stalemate is not all Clinton's fault. Republicans are divided into two adamant camps: One, led by Armey, backs a flat tax of 20 percent, falling to 17 percent in 1999. The other, led by Archer, favors a 15 percent national sales tax with no income tax.

Both proposals have big problems.

Gale said a true flat tax with no exemptions would have to be set at 21 percent to raise the $1.5 trillion in revenues needed to operate the federal government. If tax writers had to grandfather in long-term business invest-

---

> "The party needs a big idea, and if you want a really big idea, one that really captivates the people, what could be better?"
>
> —Rep. W. J. "Billy" Tauzin, R-La.

---

ments made with the understanding that their interest could be depreciated, the tax rate would go to 23 percent.

Offering businesses that exemption would raise a clamor from homeowners, who would contend that they purchased their homes expecting a mortgage deduction. With that, the rate climbs to 24.4 percent.

Businesses now deduct the cost of their employees' health insurance policies from their tax bill. Without the exemption, Gale said estimates show the number of uninsured Americans would climb by as much as 14 million. To prevent that and keep the health insurance deduction, the rate would move to 26.5 percent. The politically powerful nonprofit sector will try to retain a deduction for charitable contributions, raising the rate to 27 percent.

To head off charges that the flat tax is a sop to the rich, the GOP would have to retain the earned-income tax credit: 27.5 percent. Large, high-tax states would insist on maintaining the deduction for state and local taxes: 29 percent. Businesses would push to maintain their huge deductions for payroll taxes: 31.9 percent.

"Fundamental tax reform is characterized by congressional leaders as a win for everybody. In fact, it is not. It would require tremendous discipline on the part of Congress," Gale said. Judging from the complexity of the 1997 tax bill, members might not be up to that.

Sales Tax: No Cakewalk

The consumption tax has even more fundamental problems. An evenly applied sales tax is inherently regressive, falling hardest on the people who must spend the largest share of their income on the fundamentals such as food and clothing. To avoid that charge, Tauzin has devised a national sales tax with complexities that make it hard even for him to explain. Taxpayers would receive a large enough monthly credit on their paychecks to raise them above the poverty line. In effect, Tauzin said, no one below the poverty line would pay taxes. His proposal would also not tax resale and wholesale transactions, interest on debt, exports or educational expenses.

"When you get right down to the nut of it, I don't see any real radical revision [of the tax code] coming," said Mortimer M. Caplin, IRS commissioner under President John F. Kennedy and a longtime Washington tax attorney. "The flat tax, the national sales tax — these are all just slogans."

Such skepticism has led some Democrats to dismiss the crusade as GOP posturing, especially since this year's tax law is one of the most complex ever enacted. If the GOP wanted to simplify the tax code, Congress could close loopholes, broaden the tax base and still retain a progressive income tax.

"They put problems on top of existing problems, and now they come back and say they want to privatize the IRS and they're going to sunset it, and on top of that, they're going to flat-tax/consumption-tax it," Rangel grumbled. "Now if that's not enough to get them through the next election, I don't know what is."

For their part, the political infighting in Washington has left IRS workers beyond the Beltway feeling battered and scared, conceded Reis, the Milwaukee IRS spokesman.

"I think good will come of all this. It usually does when the dust settles," says Fargo's Barbara Bennett, gamely looking for a bright side. "But we're going to have to take the bad with the good, and I'm sure we're going to lose some good people out of this."

But the reformers have no plans to let up when the momentum is in their favor.

"I have been hearing from people saying, 'You know, these hearings could really do some damage,' " Kerrey conceded. "Well, it's our job to exercise oversight, and we're not going to wait every 21 years or so just because people tell us we might be undermining the agency." ∎

Congress Prepares New Assault On Troubled Superfund Sites

House and Senate leaders say talks have been positive,
but Georgia site underlines unresolved issues

TIFTON, Ga. — Grace Garner sits in her dimly lit living room and talks of the Marzone Inc. pesticide plant across the street from the timeworn house where she has lived for 33 years.

The plant was once a valued employer and neighbor. Back then, Garner said, she paid little notice to the odor from the plant or the yellow dust that coated everything in sight.

"If I had my doors open, there were times when the odor was so strong we could hardly eat," she said. "But I didn't think nothing about it."

Now the plant is seldom out of her mind, as she wonders whether 30 years of industrial pollution caused her uterine cancer, heart attack and arthritis. She acknowledges that there are no health studies to prove a link, but Garner, 68, said she worries nevertheless — about her four children and the health of her neighbors in this south Georgia city of 14,000 between Macon and Valdosta.

Since 1989, the closed Marzone plant has been a federal superfund site, part of the 16-year-old program to clean up the nation's worst hazardous waste dumps. Eight years later, the two-acre site is still littered with toxic chemicals. A mountainous pile of contaminated soil awaits removal.

"Sometimes, I want to take my young 'uns and get out of here," Garner said, reflecting on the 50 years she has lived in the community and the money she has sunk into her home. "But we can't just up and leave what we got."

Garner's frustrations with the superfund program are shared by members of Congress, businesses and environmentalists alike. For nearly five years, Congress has tried and failed to revamp a program dogged by inefficiencies, costly snail's-pace cleanups, endless lit-

CQ Weekly Report June 28, 1997

SUZANNE ZODA, ENVIROCOMM

Cleanup workers sample soil at the Marzone site.

igation and round after round of partisan sniping.

Now, lawmakers are at a crucial point in the effort to revise the law in the 105th Congress. In the coming months, they will try again to reach a consensus. There are some signs of progress. House and Senate leaders have placed superfund at the top of their priority lists, and differences on key issues have been narrowed.

But time is slipping away. Not only has the authorization lapsed, but the taxes that help finance superfund expired at the end of 1995.

Recent election years have not been kind to superfund legislation, miring it in partisanship. That means Republicans must plan to advance legislation by this fall. And to do that, they must still bridge differences on issues that have sunk bills in the past.

Most Republicans favor more sweeping changes to cleanup standards and reduced liability for businesses than do Democrats. The Environmental Protection Agency (EPA) has tried on its own to improve management of the program, but Republicans say there is no substitute for a comprehensive bill.

"I think EPA is attempting to change the program," said K.C. Tominovich, who works on superfund for the National Federation of Independent Business. "But EPA has gone about as far as it is going to go without comprehensive legislation."

Talk of revised legislation may mean little to Grace Garner, but she shares a basic goal with many in Congress: She wants the site cleaned up quickly and safely. The story of Tifton and the history of the superfund program prove that the goal is easier to state than to achieve.

A Toxic Legacy

At the core of the superfund program is a basic question: How best to clean up the nation's worst toxic waste dumps? In Congress, as in Tifton, the question is not easily answered.

The reason: The stakes are high for nearly everyone involved. Environmentalists, business leaders, community residents and federal regulators are trying to solve environmental problems that were decades in the making — and that create a combustible mix of emotions and financial worries.

The law puts businesses and insurance companies on the hook for millions of dollars in cleanup costs. Community residents fear the health effects of toxic waste dumps in their back yards, while others fight to avoid be-

The Limits of the Law

TIFTON, Ga. — For Allen Davis and many residents in this community 180 miles south of Atlanta, the Marzone Inc. pesticide plant was a place where you could get a well-paying job and avoid the back-breaking and less lucrative alternatives of picking cotton or sorting peanuts.

Today, many in Tifton say they are only starting to understand what it means to have lived or worked near potentially cancer-causing chemicals — and the limits of the superfund law in responding to related health problems.

Congress created superfund to address the most urgent threats, present and future, to public health.

The law ordered the Agency for Toxic Substances and Disease Registry, administered by the Department of Health and Human Services, to conduct studies and assess health hazards.

But the law does relatively little else about the consequences of decades of exposure to hazardous substances. Critics say such community health problems are rarely given sufficient attention, but officials running the program say that is not their primary role.

"The law is not there to address the health effects that people have already experienced," said Annie M. Godfrey, the Environmental Protection Agency's Tifton project manager. "I think it's confusing sometimes to the community about what we can and cannot do."

Davis sat on his front porch accompanied by about a half-dozen former plant employees and other residents. It was an impromptu neighborhood meeting near the Marzone plant site, once owned by the Chevron Chemical Co.

The residents painted a picture of a community devas-

The Marzone superfund site is in the small south-central Georgia city of Tifton. Its population is largely working class: The 1990 census showed 29 percent of its workers engaged in manufacturing, construction, transportation or agriculture.

tated by health problems.

There are no comprehensive studies to support their claims or link their problems to the Marzone site. Chevron officials deny any connection.

But residents talk of friends felled by cancer, children with developmental disorders and an overwhelming sense of living with the tragic consequences of industial pollution.

"Back during the time this plant was there, it was done in the name of creating jobs," said Davis. "The people who lived there, it was a way of life for them. The man told you he paid you good money. They paid to kill you is the way I see it."

Larry Bryant has spent much of his life in South Tifton. His father worked at a plant near Marzone and died of stomach cancer at age 61. The 42-year-old Bryant walks with a cane and is battling stomach cancer as well.

Nearby is Lovett D. Brantley, 64. Brantley worked in the plant in the 1950s, he said, mixing chemicals, hauling trash and "doing a little bit of everything." By modern standards, the workers wore little protective gear. They used small respirators, but their skin was left exposed.

"We were always told don't eat it," said Brantley of the powdery chemicals he and his co-workers mixed in the plant. "If you don't eat it, it won't hurt you. We'd get so covered by it, you couldn't tell people's color."

Davis says that the health problems of communities are often overlooked in Washington. Indeed, such problems are not even close to the front burner in the latest round of congressional talks on revamping superfund.

"We don't have the money to fight Congress," said Davis.

coming burial grounds for wastes dredged up from superfund sites. The EPA is under assault from all sides.

The very nature of the program and the players involved make the problem difficult. A look at Tifton's Marzone site explains why.

The plant opened in 1950; Chevron Chemical Co. operated it for two decades. Workers mixed powder and liquid chemicals to make pesticides for use on nearby agricultural fields, handling compounds such as DDT (later banned in 1973 because of health concerns), toxaphene and chlordane.

Over the years, many of the chemicals penetrated the soil, presumably the result of accidental spills or on-site dis-

posal. As with many other toxic waste sites, responsibility for waste-tainted areas was complicated by changes in ownership. In 1970, Chevron sold the Tifton plant, which changed hands several times after that. One of the owners was the Marzone Chemical Co., which bought the property in 1980.

Long countenanced as the inevitable byproduct of industrial progress, toxic waste sites soon came to be seen as intolerable threats to public health. In the 1970s, the nation experienced high-profile environmental disasters, most notably the 1977 discovery in Niagara Falls, N.Y., that the Love Canal residential subdivision had been built atop a former chemical dump. The

public clamored for action. *(Timeline, p. 98)*

In 1980, Congress responded by enacting the superfund law. It was founded on a basic financial principle: that those responsible for toxic-waste pollution, not the government, should pay for cleanup, and that companies would have to pay to clean up pollution they generated before enactment, even if they broke no environmental laws at the time of disposal. *(1980 Almanac, p. 584)*

Congress had changed the rules of the game and, like many other businesses large and small, Chevron was now responsible for paying millions of dollars in cleanup costs. For chemical companies such as Chevron and the communi-

PHOTO COURTESY OF CH2M HILL

At the Marzone waste site, above, controversy led EPA to abandon use of a thermal desorption unit. The agency now is considering hauling the waste to a landfill. Left, EPA's Godfrey gives information to Martha Crosby, who lives near the Marzone site.

SUZANNE ZODA, ENVIROCOMM

ties where superfund sites are located, the law keeps adding up to the same unsettling reality: The past continues to haunt them.

Cleaning Up Tifton

All but shut down since 1983, the empty Marzone plant looks like an archaeological dig. The two-acre site is surrounded by a neighborhood of modest red brick homes and neatly trimmed lawns. Contaminated soil has been removed and placed at one end of the site in a giant pile, covered with a black tarp.

One local resident, who Chevron officials say declined an offer to move, lives next door. Chickens run freely within yards of the waste site, while horses graze in an adjacent field. Residents report that children often play close to the site and in a nearby creek.

The Marzone plant was officially listed as a superfund site in August 1989 and is one of 1,208 sites now included in the program. EPA officials say chemicals from the site threaten groundwater, and they worry about the risks of exposure to contaminated soil.

It was up to Annie M. Godfrey, EPA's Atlanta-based project manager, to formulate a cleanup plan. She tried to strike a balance between competing factors, including community opinions, cost considerations and bureaucratic prerogatives.

When Congress wrote the superfund law, it charged EPA with carrying out cleanups that would permanently get rid of pollution where practical. In Tifton, the agency initially chose a $4.8 million remedy in 1994 that would use a machine called a low temperature ther-

mal desorption unit. The unit is designed to cook soil at high temperatures much like a double boiler until the chemicals turn into gas, which is then captured elsewhere in the machine. Once the soil at Tifton was cleaned by the machine, it was to be placed back on the site.

EPA chose the machine in part because it offered a permanent solution, whereas the alternative of shipping contaminated soil to a landfill did not.

But problems mounted. Additional soil tests found elevated levels of dioxin, widely regarded by scientists as a possible cause of cancer and other illnesses, on some parts of the site. That spurred Tifton residents to question whether air emissions from the heating process would be harmful and to ask for an investigation by a separate federal agency, the Department of Health and Human Services' Agency for Toxic Substance and Disease Registry (ATSDR).

The agency flagged problems with the machine, including whether controls were in place to guard against harmful air emissions. They recommended some changes, such as installing a monitor to test for hydrocarbons. ATSDR officials say they did not consider their requests out of the ordinary.

But Chevron and the EPA balked. They said what the agency wanted done was impractical and would increase the cost of the project. The soil cleansing unit had already been set up, and Chevron was incurring $10,000 a day in "standby" costs as the two agencies locked horns.

"We felt like the [machine] selected would already meet all the federal agency health and safety requirements," said G. Michael Marcy, a Chevron spokesman. "No technology was available to meet the [toxic substance agency's] demand without additional research and years of delay."

EPA chose to abandon the cleanup method and proposed that the waste instead be sent to a landfill, an alternative it had originally rejected. It made a final decision on June 18, choosing the landfill option.

Godfrey said she demonstrated flexibility and was mindful both of costs and the need for a cleanup method that was more than adequate to protect human health.

"It became obvious to me that it was going to skew the cost so much that we needed to take a different direction," she said. "I wanted to get the site cleaned up. I saw that this situation could drag on or

The Key Outstanding Issues

Lawmakers need to resolve a number of issues if they hope to move a comprehensive superfund overhaul. The following four issues are at the crux of the debate:

● **Liability:** Efforts to enact superfund legislation in the 104th Congress foundered largely over disagreements about who should pay for cleanups. Republicans and some Democrats favored repealing, on fairness grounds, a provision in current law that can hold a company liable for cleanup of waste it dumped legally before superfund was enacted in 1980. But these members backed away from full repeal after conceding that they could not find the money to pay for full repeal and facing strong opposition from most congressional Democrats and the Clinton administration.

With this major battle over retroactive liability behind them, congressional negotiators in both parties say the broad outlines of a deal could be in reach. "I think we're much closer than people realize," said Michael G. Oxley, R-Ohio, chairman of the House Commerce subcommittee with jurisdiction over superfund.

For example, there is broad agreement that small businesses that generate office and household trash often are dragged unfairly into cleanups and should be taken out of the liability net. Still, a big challenge will be bridging differences between conservative House Republicans, such as Ways and Means Committee Chairman Bill Archer, R-Texas, who favor broad liability repeal, and Democrats and environmentalists wary of going too far and letting "polluters off the hook."

● **Cleanups:** Critics within industry say the law mandates overly stringent cleanups that result in too few health benefits for the money. They favor mandating remedies that are both protective of public health and cost-effective.

The Senate Republican superfund bill (S 8) would eliminate a provision in current law that requires the Environmental Protection Agency (EPA) to pursue cleanups that offer permanent remedies, which critics say can add millions of dollars to the cost. Supporters of S 8 say it aims to provide EPA with greater flexibility to consider factors such as costs, human health protection and the long-term effectiveness of the treatment.

Some Democrats and many environmentalists say the law already provides significant flexibility and worry that easing standards would lead to less thorough cleanups, putting communities at risk. They fear that EPA would

Archer

contain pollution rather than eliminate it, and they want to ensure meaningful treatment of the most polluted areas at superfund sites.

● **Taxes:** The superfund program is funded through a mix of general revenues and appropriations from the program's trust fund: The program's fiscal 1997 appropriation was $1.4 billion.

In the past, the trust fund, better known as the "superfund," was fed by taxes, amounting to about $1.7 billion annually, on the raw materials used to make chemicals and on foreign and domestic petroleum products, as well as a broad-based environmental tax on large companies. But these taxes expired at the end of 1995.

The Clinton administration and some Senate Republicans favor reauthorizing the taxes right away. But Archer and other key House Republicans oppose renewing the taxes without comprehensive superfund legislation and have blocked any attempt to push the taxes through separately.

According to the latest figures from the Congressional Budget Office, there is enough money in the trust fund to pay for the program through 2000. The EPA estimates that by the end of fiscal 1997, the fund would have an unobligated balance of $2.5 billion.

● **Resource Damages:** One issue becoming more prominent this year is the damage caused by hazardous waste sites to natural resources such as rivers that may require billions of dollars to remedy. Robert C. Smith, R-N.H., chairman of the Senate Environment and Public Works subcommittee on superfund, said the issue will probably be the most difficult one to agree on.

Businesses, municipalities and other potential targets of claims of natural resource damage are taking notice: They fear being required to pay for waste site cleanups, only to face more costs for damage to nearby natural resources.

S 8 would limit the damages that could be recovered, including some of the costs unrelated to site restoration. But senators from states where natural resource damages are issues — such as Max Baucus of Montana, the ranking Democrat on the Environment and Public Works Committee — oppose pushing the limits too far. The Clinton administration opposes the provisions in S 8, saying they could stand in the way of cleanups.

---

we could propose a remedy."

Even so, the decision affects only a part of the operation, and cleanup of the remainder of the site awaits further action years down the road.

The Backlash

To many of the residents and the environmental groups who have monitored the situation in Tifton, Marzone raises questions about EPA's willingness to satisfy big corporate polluters while shortchanging cleanups and communities.

Joel S. Hirschhorn, a technical adviser to the Tifton community group People Working for People, said he has detected a trend across the country toward less expensive cleanups, and he is worried that, in the name of cost containment, EPA may be embracing less-than-adequate solutions.

Hirschhorn observed that industry critics often attack the superfund law as inflexible, arguing that it requires cleanups more stringent than necessary. But he said Tifton demonstrates that the law provides leeway to embrace lower-cost, industry-friendly options.

The relative costs of cleanup methods — $1.5 million for sending the waste to a landfill, much lower than the cost of using the heating unit — was a major factor. EPA explained its decision this way: "Although this remedy may not reduce toxicity by treatment, this negative aspect is balanced with the ease of implementability and the cost effectiveness."

Moreover, changing the regulators' minds could have been prohibitively expensive. Chevron contractors say that making the changes requested by the toxic substances agency to the desorption machine would have added perhaps $1.5 million to the cost of the cleanup alone, on top of the base price of $4.8 million.

That bottom-line logic did not sway community activists. "If you say low-thermal desorption is the best method for cleanup, why not make the necessary changes?" asked Shirley Jordan, executive director of People Working for People. "EPA is supposed to be there to protect the community, but it seems like they are at war with us."

Also upsetting to community activists is that much of the waste is scheduled to be shipped out of Tifton to a landfill in another community.

Not only that, but the bulk of the waste is legally classified as "non-hazardous," meaning the waste will be shipped to an industrial landfill, rather than as "hazardous," which would make the waste far more expensive to handle.

Godfrey explained that "hazardous" and "non-hazardous" are defined by the federal Resource Conservation and Recovery Act. She said the waste is far safer in the controlled surroundings of a landfill than at the Tifton site.

But many in the community say EPA was merely using a legal loophole to save Chevron millions of dollars.

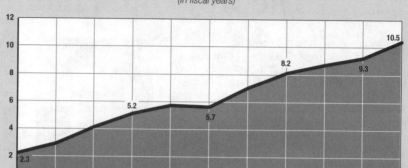

Average Time for Completion of Cleanups at Sites
(In fiscal years)

The General Accounting Office, for a report issued in March, studied the number of years it took to complete cleanups of superfund toxic waste sites owned by private interests, then produced averages by the year in which each project was completed.

As the chart above shows, the average life span of these superfund projects more than quadrupled over 10 years, from 2.3 years for projects completed in 1986 to 10.5 years for projects completed in 1996.

Source: General Accounting Office

"Just a few years ago, they were the ones who were saying it was too hazardous to haul off," said local resident Lovett D. Brantley. Added resident Terry Clark, "If it's not hazardous, why move it at all?"

The Business Perspective

While neighbors of toxic waste sites allege inequities, in Washington it is businesses that complain of unfairness. To them, superfund remains a seedbed for litigation and subjects businesses to costly and unnecessary bureaucratic mandates.

The critics point to a March 1997 General Accounting Office report on the pace of cleanups. It concluded that the time required to complete cleanups increased from 2.3 years in 1986 to 10.5

years in 1996. *(Chart, this page)*

The administration argues that the increase is due to the increasingly complex nature of superfund cleanups. And EPA Administrator Carol M. Browner repeatedly has pointed to the administration's efforts to "reinvent" the program through administrative changes. But the industry critics say the changes, though steps in the right direction, have been applied unevenly and lack the force of law.

"To say that they haven't been important is foolish," said Michael W. Steinberg, a partner with law firm Morgan, Lewis and Bockius, which prepared a report on the changes for the Chemical Manufacturers Association. "But to say the program has been permanently transformed would be equally inaccurate."

Digging Out

In the 20 years since the Love Canal disaster, Congress has struggled to find the best way to clean up toxic waste sites.

Toxic Legacy: Investigators discover that the Love Canal residential subdivision in Niagara Falls, N.Y., had been built atop a chemical dump site. Chemicals

leaking from discarded drums are found to be poisoning residents. Public attention turns to the threat posed by wastes from decades of industrial production, as dozens of other chemical wastelands are discovered throughout the nation.

. . . .

1980
Congress Responds. In response to revelations at Love Canal and other toxic dumps, President Jimmy Carter signs the Comprehensive Environmental Response, Compensation and Liability Act (PL 96-510) that Congress cleared during a lame-

duck session. The law creates a pool of cleanup money known as superfund, and charges the Environmental Protection Agency with identifying sites around the nation that are contaminated with hazardous waste and most in need of cleanup. The law gives the government authority, once the sites are identified, to make a single individual or business that dumped waste at the site pay for the cleanup.

1982
Problems Begin. Anne M. Gorsuch, administrator of the Environmental Protection Agency who later married and took the last name Burford, is voted in contempt of Congress for refusing to turn over documents, sought by two House panels, on hazardous waste sites included in the superfund program. Environmentalists and congressional critics charge the administration of President Ronald Reagan is attempting to gut the program. The House Energy and Commerce Committee reports a "dramatic decline" in enforcement of the cleanup law.

For example, a big complaint of business is that superfund liability can compel a single large and profitable corporation to cover all the cost of cleaning up a site if other polluters at the site cannot afford to pay their share. At Tifton, EPA tapped Chevron as just such a deep pocket.

EPA now has a program to pick up part of the costs of polluters who cannot afford to pay, thus relieving some businesses of what is commonly known as the "orphan share." But Steinberg notes that this assistance excludes many sites with large orphan shares. "Most parties at most sites are not seeing the administrative reforms kick in," he said of the changes overall.

The Clinton administration's actions on superfund also draw fire from environmental groups, although for different reasons. Lois Gibbs, executive director of Citizens Clearinghouse for Hazardous Waste Inc., an environmental group, said the administration has done little. Ironically, she said, some of its efforts to respond to communities, such as appointing ombudsmen in all 10 EPA regions, have added a layer of bureaucracy that makes it difficult to reach the front office in Washington.

"I don't see EPA responding to citizens' concerns," she said. "All of the new stuff is feel-good stuff. Tifton isn't any better now than when I went out to visit it four years ago."

Congress at Bat

Can Congress break the logjam? The only answer is maybe. But given the recent history of legislation on the program, even this amounts to a ray of optimism. In recent months, House and Senate leaders have engaged in

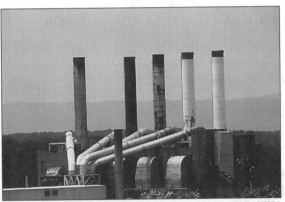

The Avtex textile plant in Front Royal, Va., was shut down by EPA in the late 1980s because toxic waste was being dumped into the Shenandoah River.

SCOTT J. FERRELL

discussions that all sides say have been positive.

In the 104th Congress, Democrats used superfund and other issues to tar the GOP's environmental record. And as Republicans in the House and Senate work to move a bill in the next few months, they will be looking for bipartisan support.

"We can't pass something on a partisan basis because the other guy on the end of [Pennsylvania] Avenue has the veto pen," said Michael G. Oxley, R-Ohio, chairman of the House Commerce subcommittee with jurisdiction over superfund. "That's just a fact of life. We have to deal with that. There is a growing sense that we need to work on a bipartisan basis."

While consensus on the major issues is by no means assured, the sides do not appear as dug into the ideological trenches of the past. "This has been a cooperative effort from the beginning," said Senate Environment and Public Works Committee Chairman John H. Chafee, R-R.I.

Republicans, for example, are no

longer insisting on a full repeal of retroactive liability, which can compel a company to pay to clean up of waste legally deposited before superfund's enactment. Republican and some Democratic critics had long contended it was unfair to punish someone for activities that were legal at the time.

Another positive sign for possible compromise, say key Republicans, is the budget agreement, which calls for renewing taxes for the cleanup trust fund that expired in 1995 and increasing funding for the program — but, they say, only if overhaul legislation is enacted.

That, says House Commerce Committee Chairman Thomas J. Bliley Jr., R-Va., could put necessary pressure on the negotiations. "The election is over," Bliley said, remarking on the prospects for legislation. "We have the strongest budget resolution on this subject since I've been here."

However, the White House disputes the GOP interpretation that the budget deal on superfund is contingent on comprehensive legislation.

What seems clear is that the time for action is near or never for the 105th Congress. Republican Robert C. Smith of New Hampshire, chairman of the Senate Environment and Public Works subcommittee on superfund, said that getting a superfund bill through in an election year would be next to impossible, as both sides will be jockeying for partisan advantage.

But whatever course they take, the people of Tifton will worry about future generations. "I'm concerned about these young people growing up around here," said Garner. "I'd like to have the site cleaned up as soon as possible." ∎

1983
Resignations. Burford and superfund program Director Rita M. Lavelle are accused of politically manipulating superfund cleanups. Allegations include withholding a grant to clean up the Stringfellow Acid Pits in California to avoid boosting the re-election campaign of Democratic Gov. Edmund G. "Jerry" Brown Jr. Lavelle is fired Feb. 7 and in 1984 is sentenced to a six-month jail term and fined $10,000 on counts of perjury and obstructing a congressional probe. Under fire from Congress, Burford resigns her post on March 9.

1986
A New Response. Responding to pressure from Congress, Reagan agrees to sign into law a revision of the program. It is reauthorized for five years and given $8.5 billion, a fivefold funding increase. Along with the money come strict standards the EPA is instructed to follow, including the mandate to begin work at 375 sites within the next five years. But ensuing years bring a series of delays and litigation.

1994
Democrats Fall Short. With relatively few sites repaired, a broad consensus develops among environmentalists, business interests and insurers that the program is broken and a legislative fix is needed. Yet despite winning bipartisan approval from five committees and the Clinton administration, overhaul legislation dies in the final weeks of the 103rd Congress — the victim of divisions over proposed taxes, new cleanup standards and wages paid by federal contractors.

1995
Republican Takeover. Republicans take control of both chambers of Congress, and unsuccessfully push a proposal to repeal the superfund program's "retroactive liability" provision, which can hold a company responsible for paying to clean up wastes dumped before superfund's enactment. Republican supporters of the repeal maintain it is unfair to reach back in time and compel a company to clean up waste that was deposited legally. Democrats counter that the proposal would "let polluters off the hook."

MARILYN GATES-DAVIS

NUCLEAR WASTE

Nuclear Waste Bill Produces Its Own Heated Reactions

Legislation to consolidate hodgepodge of sites into one prompts protests, questions about safety, costs and the role of government

While Congress has struggled for years over where to store nuclear waste, about 30,000 metric tons of highly radioactive spent materials are sitting in temporary sites around the country waiting for a home.

The issue has pitted environmentalists against industry.

It has ignited conflicts between Western lawmakers who don't want their states to be radioactive repositories against East Coast lawmakers whose districts are dotted with temporary sites.

And it is costing utility customers millions of dollars every year.

Most of the sites are at 74 nuclear power plants. Many are near towns and populated areas. Others are alongside rivers, lakes and saltwater beaches.

At the Palisades Nuclear Power Plant on Lake Michigan, for example, 13 130-ton canisters filled with highly radioactive spent fuel sit on a pad. The plant is 40 miles west of Kalamazoo, a town of 81,000 people.

The site is just one in a patchwork of temporary disposal sites in 35 states for the nation's commercial nuclear waste.

Congress has studied, debated and fretted for years over where to store the nation's commercial nuclear waste that has accumulated over the past 40 years.

A plan to consolidate the waste into a single, temporary site at Yucca Mountain in Nevada — already long delayed — is continuing to raise questions in Congress over such issues as safety and cost.

The problem has plagued utilities for

CQ Weekly Report Oct. 18, 1997

SCOTT J. FERRELL

Protesting HR 1270 at the Capitol on Sept. 24 are, from left, Dianne D'Arrigo of the Nuclear Information Resource Service, Harvey Wasserman of Greenpeace, and singers Jackson Browne and Bonnie Raitt. Behind them is a replica of a nuclear waste cask.

years, too. Some utilities are storing waste in air-cooled casks, which are kept on concrete pads or in bunkers. There are 10 such "cask" systems in the country. It has cost $12 million to $20 million to build each one, a bill that ratepayers are paying every time they turn on a light.

The Yucca Mountain Dispute

Congress envisioned in 1982 that spent fuel would be permanently buried starting in 1998. In 1987, it designated Yucca Mountain, 100 miles northwest of Las Vegas, as the provisional burial site. *(Almanac 1987, p. 307)*

But construction of the permanent crypt was slowed by questions about safety, by government studies of the site's vulnerability to heat, earthquakes and erosion — and by vehement opposition from Nevada's congressional delegation. Nuclear waste produced by de-

fense activities, consisting mainly of residue from the reprocessing of spent nuclear fuel, is also expected to be stored at Yucca Mountain.

The bill to establish the temporary dump (HR 1270) has run into problems of its own. The House will begin floor debate of the bill soon; a House vote will set up a showdown with President Clinton, who has vowed to veto an interim storage site until an Energy Department study is completed next year on the viability of the permanent site at Yucca Mountain.

A similar bill (S 104) cleared the Senate, 65-34, on April 15, two votes short of the number needed to override a veto. *(Weekly Report, p. 902)*

In the House, the Rules Committee will choose between two versions of the bill: one approved by the Commerce Committee on Sept. 18, and the other by the Resources Committee on Oct. 8. The Resources bill was sent to the floor with an unfavorable report, meaning the bill was not recommended for passage. *(Weekly Report, p. 2482)*

The Resources Committee's bill includes a faster startup date, in 2000 instead of 2002, and does not include such Commerce provisions as one specifying an oversight role for the Environmental Protection Agency.

The Commerce Committee bill is expected to emerge on the floor and win bipartisan support.

Supporters say a temporary government site is needed because the nuclear plants' customers — industry and individuals — are footing the bill for private storage, and paying fees to the government to dispose of the waste. They also

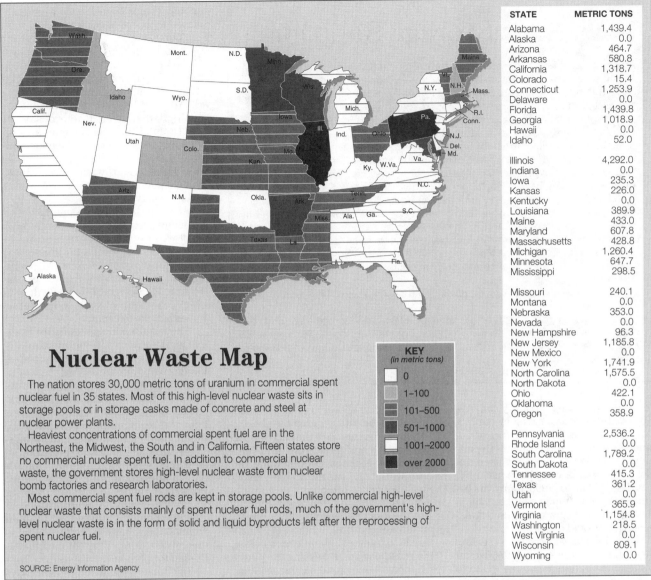

STATE	METRIC TONS
Alabama	1,439.4
Alaska	0.0
Arizona	464.7
Arkansas	580.8
California	1,318.7
Colorado	15.4
Connecticut	1,253.9
Delaware	0.0
Florida	1,439.8
Georgia	1,018.9
Hawaii	0.0
Idaho	52.0
Illinois	4,292.0
Indiana	0.0
Iowa	235.3
Kansas	226.0
Kentucky	0.0
Louisiana	389.9
Maine	433.0
Maryland	607.8
Massachusetts	428.8
Michigan	1,260.4
Minnesota	647.7
Mississippi	298.5
Missouri	240.1
Montana	0.0
Nebraska	353.0
Nevada	0.0
New Hampshire	96.3
New Jersey	1,185.8
New Mexico	0.0
New York	1,741.9
North Carolina	1,575.5
North Dakota	0.0
Ohio	422.1
Oklahoma	0.0
Oregon	358.9
Pennsylvania	2,536.2
Rhode Island	0.0
South Carolina	1,789.2
South Dakota	0.0
Tennessee	415.3
Texas	361.2
Utah	0.0
Vermont	365.9
Virginia	1,154.8
Washington	218.5
West Virginia	0.0
Wisconsin	809.1
Wyoming	0.0

Nuclear Waste Map

The nation stores 30,000 metric tons of uranium in commercial spent nuclear fuel in 35 states. Most of this high-level nuclear waste sits in storage pools or in storage casks made of concrete and steel at nuclear power plants.

Heaviest concentrations of commercial spent fuel are in the Northeast, the Midwest, the South and in California. Fifteen states store no commercial nuclear spent fuel. In addition to commercial nuclear waste, the government stores high-level nuclear waste from nuclear bomb factories and research laboratories.

Most commercial spent fuel rods are kept in storage pools. Unlike commercial high-level nuclear waste that consists mainly of spent nuclear fuel rods, much of the government's high-level nuclear waste is in the form of solid and liquid byproducts left after the reprocessing of spent nuclear fuel.

KEY
(in metric tons)

- 0
- 1–100
- 101–500
- 501–1000
- 1001–2000
- over 2000

SOURCE: Energy Information Agency

PATT CHISHOLM

say the bill will reduce the danger to residents and to the environment.

The unfavorable report by the Resources Committee, chaired by Republican Don Young of Alaska, served notice that Nevada, which is trying to fend off any nuclear waste repository, is not without allies. John Ensign, R-Nev., called HR 1270 a "war on the West," echoing a battle cry started in the 1980s, when Congress decided to build a burial site in the remote West rather than on the East or West coasts or in the Midwest, South or Northeast, where much nuclear power is generated

The search for a site began with the passage of the Nuclear Waste Policy Act of 1982. Five years later, Congress passed amendments to that act — then dubbed the "Screw Nevada Law" by

Sen. Harry Reid, D-Nev.— that designated Yucca Mountain as the permanent repository. The 1982 law required the Energy Department to dispose of the nuclear industry's waste by 1998 and required nuclear utilities to pay one-time fees for nuclear waste collected before 1983 and an ongoing fee set by the Energy Department at a tenth of a cent per kilowatt-hour.

Nuclear utilities have made a national temporary disposal site a priority. "There's been a very coordinated effort," said Steve Unglesbee, a spokesman for the industry's lobbying arm, the Nuclear Energy Institute.

Individual nuclear utilities are lobbying members of Congress from states where nuclear waste is stored now. And they have given campaign donations to

lawmakers, too.

A study by the Center for Responsive Politics found that the political action committees connected to the nuclear utility industry gave $935,347 in the first six months of 1997 to more than 270 House members and 35 senators. The study found the top recipients in the Senate included Frank H. Murkowski, R-Alaska, $26,583. He is the chairman of the Senate Energy and Natural Resources Committee and was chief sponsor of S 104. In the House, top recipients included two leading Commerce Committee members, John D. Dingell, of Michigan, the panel's ranking Democrat, $14,850; and Thomas J. Bliley Jr., R-Va., the panel's chairman, $13,000.

The industry also is taking its fight into court. Nuclear utilities and about

No Easy Storage Solution

The nation's first commercial reactor opened in Shippingport, Pa., in 1957, marking the beginning of the nuclear power industry in America.

And it set off a search, continuing today, for a way to dispose of a hazardous byproduct: highly radioactive spent fuel rods.

All commercial nuclear power plants in the United States use light-water reactors that are fueled by metal rods filled with ceramic pellets of enriched uranium. The uranium is bombarded with neutrons, causing atoms to split in a nuclear reaction that yields more neutrons and heat. Fuel rods last as long as four years, until byproducts accumulate that hinder the nuclear reaction. The reactor must then be shut down to remove the used rods.

Spent fuel rods generate intense heat and must be stored in pools of water for cooling. They must be handled remotely by workers because they emit dangerous levels of radiation. When the pools fill to capacity, some utilities transfer spent fuel rods into large air-cooled concrete and steel containers.

The Energy Department plans to complete a study next year on the viability of storing the spent fuel permanently in compacted volcanic ash at Yucca Mountain in Nevada.

Other nations are working on plans to bury spent fuel rods in granite, clay or salt caverns.

France and Great Britain reprocess spent fuel to produce uranium and plutonium and concentrated waste products. Private industry has not pursued reprocessing in the United States because of abundant uranium to make nuclear fuel.

30 states and state regulatory commissions last year won a ruling by the U.S. Court of Appeals for the District of Columbia Circuit that the Energy Department must begin accepting used nuclear fuel from power plants under the 1982 law on Jan. 31, 1998, four years before a temporary dump could be built in Nevada and 12 years before the permanent dump would open.

Jay Silberg, an attorney representing the states and utilities, says the federal government should move the waste to sites used for storing defense nuclear waste, including the Hanford nuclear reservation in Washington, the Idaho National Engineering Laboratory and a site near Aiken, S.C.

But environmental groups oppose the temporary nuclear waste dump, arguing that it would be cheaper and safer to keep the waste at the current sites until a permanent site is designated. The watchdog group Public Citizen says the industry has created a "phony crisis" over the issue.

A November 1996 study by the Nuclear Regulatory Commission (NRC) found a likelihood of one accident a year involving drainage of more than one foot from a storage pool at a nuclear plant. But it also found this was not likely to result in a serious threat to the public from fuel damage.

Supporters of the temporary Yucca Mountain dump have argued that spent fuel would be safer at a remote site.

The 40-foot depth of the current storage pools is designed to cover 12-foot-tall fuel assemblies, cooling them and containing the radiation they emit. Since pools are often outside containment buildings, some environmentalists fear the loss of enough water to uncover submerged fuel, which could be a threat to humans. When water is lost, the rods heat up, increasing the potential for a release of radioactive material.

The NRC report found there had been 14 partial drainages, ranging from just a few inches to more than 5 feet of water from storage pools over the last 12 years. For example, in December 1994, a 365-pound bolt fell into a storage pool at E.I. Hatch Nuclear Plant Unit 1, operated by Georgia Power Co. near Baxley, Ga. The bolt punctured a stainless steel liner, draining 2 inches of water from the pool.

The NRC found no serious consequences from any of the incidents.

Environmental Opposition

Most environmental groups oppose the temporary interim storage facility, citing a number of potential problems including risks in transporting the waste to Nevada. They call for continuing to keep spent fuel in pools under careful monitoring until they are cool enough to put in casks and eventually moved to a permanent facility.

Tom Cochran, a senior scientist for the Natural Resources Defense Council, said federal courts will likely make the Energy Department assume ownership and management of the waste.

"Yucca Mountain is the last hope for geologic disposal," Cochran said. "I don't think Congress is going to be up for spending another $6 billion to $8 billion to start from scratch on another site. There is a growing sense, I think, that Congress is going to step in . . . and force a solution," he said.

Forcing the Energy Department to act is precisely what supporters say HR 1270 will do. The department would move casks to Nevada for temporary, and eventually permanent, disposal. The bill would mandate that the permanent facility open in 2010 unless the Nuclear Regulatory Commission determines it is not acceptable.

The bill also would require the Energy Department to develop a nationwide rail and truck transportation system, including help for towns along the way to plan for potential emergencies. At the disposal site, it would limit radiation releases to a level that exposes the average local resident to no more than 100 millirems — or about one-third the level of background radiation received by an average person each year. The bill would authorize the Environmental Protection Agency to advise the NRC on whether that standard is adequate.

Critics charge that the bill is laden with too many benefits for the utility industry and would drain money that is needed for permanent disposal.

The Congressional Budget Office says the five-year, $3.1 billion cost of the nuclear waste program — including the $1.5 billion cost of interim storage — will be paid by $1.2 billion in utility fees paid by customers for spent fuel disposal and $1.9 billion in government spending for waste disposal related to research and the nuclear weapons complex.

In Michigan, Consumers Energy , operator of the Palisades plant, has begun looking at casks that could be used to transport waste to Nevada. In South Haven, a town of 6,000 residents six miles from the Palisades plant, local businessmen and residents say they want the casks moved.

"We'd rather not have it stored next to Lake Michigan. Most people feel that it needs to go somewhere. The federal government is supposed to take it," says Larry King, executive director of the South Haven Chamber of Commerce. ■

Long-Term Challenges Temper Cheers for Welfare Successes

Even supporters caution that a downturn in the economy or inadequate state efforts could hinder overhaul's progress

Welfare reform has gotten mostly rave reviews in the year since Congress and President Clinton rewrote the laws. The caseload is in a historic free fall. Welfare offices are abuzz with the need to quickly find jobs for recipients. Many states have extra federal money and are spending more for child care and caseworkers to get the job done.

At the same time, the red-hot rhetoric has cooled on both sides of the debate over the nation's grand experiment with its welfare system. Skeptics who predicted that the law would unleash new armies of the homeless have tempered their claims.

Yet despite the remarkably promising developments, it is much too soon to declare that welfare has been reformed. The program not only owes many of its early achievements to the sustained strength of the nation's economy, but many experts believe the unexpectedly good progress may in itself contain the seeds of future difficulties.

"We can't expect the results we had this year to continue," cautioned Rep. E. Clay Shaw Jr., R-Fla., Congress' most persistent advocate for overhauling welfare. "Many of the people getting off welfare now should have never been on welfare in the first place."

If last year's legislation is going to prove to be a durable solution, according to welfare administrators, lawmakers and other analysts, its success will depend largely on future developments. Still shaping the law's ultimate success are such basic questions as these:

CQ Weekly Report Oct. 25, 1997

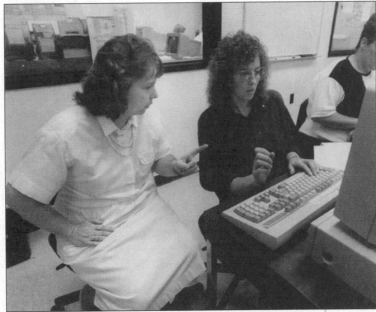
MO. DEPT. OF SOCIAL SERVICES: BOB HULSEY PHOTOGRAPHER
Missouri's FUTURES program prepares clients for self-sufficiency.

● **Can the current decline in the caseload be sustained?**

The true test of the current record three-year decline in the welfare rolls will come whenever the economy begins to sputter.

As Gov. Thomas R. Carper, D-Del., sees it, the influence of a robust economy on the early success of the welfare overhaul cannot be overstated.

"Whoever had the idea of launching welfare reform in the middle of one of the most prolonged economic recoveries in the country's history deserves a medal," Carper said.

Not only is the economy employing more people, but there also may now be more of a stigma attached to collecting welfare, encouraging recipients to leave the rolls and discouraging others from applying. No one knows how strong that stigma would be in a weaker economy.

● **Will newly hired former welfare**

recipients be able to remain in the work force?

Requiring welfare recipients to go to work is one thing. Making sure they get jobs — and keep them — is the tough part. This can involve counseling, job preparation, child care assistance, transportation and health care.

States' ability to provide these long-term investments and reorient their bureaucracies are keys to success. States can also try to take advantage of federal efforts to make low-income jobs more attractive than collecting welfare.

● **Can the states and the federal government continue to cooperate?**

The new law gives states extensive authority over their welfare programs. But they still rely on billions of dollars in federal aid.

The federal government imposes many requirements on states that want the money, from demanding that they place an increasing percentage of welfare recipients in the work force to requiring them to enforce child support laws. These federalism issues create constant tensions; how they are resolved will help shape the overall outcome.

The challenge is particularly daunting for state and local bureaucracies. They are responsible for taking a system that was largely devoted to determining eligibility and passing out checks, and transforming it into a massive job placement operation for many of the nation's poorest and least skilled

States Use Innovative Methods . . .

The 1996 welfare law transferred almost all authority over welfare programs to the states, stipulating that future federal aid would be partly based on each state's success in getting welfare recipients off the rolls and into jobs. Several states, eager to make sure they get federal assistance, have taken innovative steps to meet the work goals.

The welfare law (PL 104-193) required that by July 1, 1997, states had to convert their programs, formerly funded under Aid to Families with Dependent Children (AFDC), into block grant programs funded under Temporary Assistance to Needy Families (TANF). By Oct. 1, 1997, states were required to place 25 percent of families and 75 percent of two-parent families in work-related programs. *(1996 Almanac, p. 6-3)*

This is what three states are doing:

WISCONSIN

About a year ago, Andrew S. Bush wrote in the American Public Welfare Association's magazine that Wisconsin's new welfare program would "reorient the social safety net, basing assistance not on an entitlement but on parents' demonstrated efforts to secure their own support."

Bush, director of the Hudson Institute's Welfare Policy Center, still believes in the success of W-2, or "Wisconsin Works," a program he helped fine-tune in 1994. He said recently that Wisconsin "changed the whole tone of public discussion on welfare."

Wisconsin Works is built on the premise that all welfare recipients can be placed into one of four "work" categories: unsubsidized work and three types of subsidized work — trial jobs, community service and "transition." Republican Gov. Tommy G. Thompson, who campaigned for welfare reform when he first ran for governor in 1986, created the Department of Workforce Development to oversee the new program. It took effect in January 1997 and was to enroll all new applicants by Sept. 1. *(Thompson, p. 108)*

Under Wisconsin Works, applicants are assigned a financial and employment planner, a case manager who oversees job searches and employment and who determines an applicant's eligibility for state services such as child care, medical assistance, food stamps, loans and tax credits. The planner places the applicant in a job category.

The first category, unsubsidized work, is what all able-bodied welfare recipients are supposed to aim for. The employee earns wages paid by an employer, and the state may provide social services, such as child care, until the person is financially independent. Families can receive child care until their income rises to about $32,000 (200 percent of the federal poverty level).

If a suitable job cannot be found, the applicant may be placed in a subsidized work category called "trial jobs," which are similar to apprenticeships. The employer, aided by up to a $300-per-month state subsidy, trains a W-2 participant at minimum wage or more for up to six months. After that, the position is likely to become permanent.

Community service jobs are for those without the skills to get paid work. Participants receive a monthly check of $673 and spend up to 30 hours a week in a job and up to 10 hours a week in training and education programs. The job may be in a public library, in a school, or with a private employer.

The last category, called "W-2 transition," is for those who cannot work because of mental illness, drug addiction, or another disability. They receive $628 a month and spend up to 28 hours a week in skills training programs or work activities, and up to 12 hours a week in education or training.

Participants cannot spend more than two years in any category except unsubsidized employment, and no more than five years total in the three subsidized programs.

Wisconsin and other states have created support systems to help former AFDC recipients get jobs; the difficult part is keeping them employed. On Oct. 11, Gov. Thompson signed into law an incentive called the Employment Skills Advancement Program, which allows W-2 participants who have worked for at least nine months to get a high school equivalency degree, English-language training, or vocational skills.

FLORIDA

Three months before Congress cleared a welfare overhaul bill in August 1996, the Florida legislature enacted WAGES, or Work and Gain Economic Self-Sufficiency. The approach is no-nonsense: Find a job fast or lose benefits. It is built on a "strong, upfront expectation that people will go to work," says Don Winstead, project director for WAGES.

WAGES places a lifetime limit of four years on benefits, with no more than 24 months of benefits in five years. During a six-week orientation, applicants are warned that failure to find employment results in penalties, starting with suspension of benefits for 10 days.

citizens. Some states are better equipped for this task than others.

"A lot will depend on how the states implement it," said Wendell Primus, whose opposition to the legislation prompted him to resign as a top official in the Department of Health and Human Services (HHS). Primus, now director of income security at the Center on Budget and Policy Priorities, a liberal-oriented public policy research group, said the real test will be how they react in a recession.

● **What impact will these changes have on larger societal trends?**

The welfare law's most fervent advocates and detractors agree that the effort's long-term success should not be measured simply by how many people leave the welfare rolls or gain employment. The real test is its impact on the lives of poor people — whether it helps lift them out of poverty, discourages out-of-wedlock births, encourages the formation of two-parent households and invigorates low-income neighborhoods with a renewed reliance on work.

The legislation fulfilled Clinton's 1992 campaign pledge to "end welfare

. . . To Keep Federal Funds Flowing

During orientation, applicants look for work with minimal supervision. After that, those who are unsuccessful are assigned a case manager who helps with job searches and placements.

Statistics show that the welfare caseload is shrinking in Florida, although skeptics wonder whether it will continue to shrink when the economy turns sour. The Florida Department of Labor and Economic Security released numbers in September showing that more than 59,000 families out of 200,000 had left the welfare rolls since September 1996.

"We're driving under the influence of a good economy," said Jack Levine, executive director of the Florida Center for Children and Youth, an advocacy group based in Tallahassee. He said the numbers convey a "false sense of security" and do not take into account what might happen if a job shortage hits the booming tourism industry, which provides most entry-level jobs.

Winstead agreed that "a strong and growing economy is the best tool we've got," and that the state should plan for an inevitable dip. "Now is really sort of the best case scenario," he said. "If we can't do welfare reform in this economy, we're never going to be able to do it."

Even before WAGES, Florida had been innovative. In February 1994, it became one of the first states to place a time limit on benefits. A pilot project called the Family Transition Program began in the Pensacola (Escambia County) and Gainesville (Alachua County) areas, eventually expanding to six more counties.

Alachua's program is voluntary, while Escambia's is mandatory. Participants are limited to two years of benefits, with exceptions for people whose disabilities or lack of skills hinder them from getting entry-level jobs. The pilot program also allows aid recipients to accrue more savings while still qualifying for benefits.

MISSOURI

Under the state's version of the 1988 federal Job Opportunities and Basic Skills Training Program (JOBS), Missouri began enrolling families in "Self-Sufficiency Pacts" in the spring of 1995. The pacts, which are promises by welfare recipients to leave public assistance within two years, are continuing as part of Missouri's new temporary assistance program.

In exchange for the promise to leave welfare, the state guarantees child care, transportation and some work-related expenses. The pacts also allow families to save up to $5,000 and still get benefits, while other welfare households are cut off at $1,000.

Missouri also has garnered national attention through a demonstration project in Jackson County (Kansas City) that relies heavily on local business involvement, with subsidies for hiring welfare recipients.

Missouri's Department of Social Services still determines eligibility and benefits and sends out subsidy checks to employers, but a civic organization called the Local Investment Commission (LINC) monitors employers and manages welfare cases. LINC is the brainchild of Bert Berkley, a Kansas City envelope company owner who proposed the idea in 1991.

Participating businesses receive a supplement of $267 a month for each welfare recipient they hire, which  comes from funds that would have been used to pay welfare benefits. The employer must pay employees at least as much as they would have received on welfare.

The Jackson County project is similar to one put in place under a 1994 state welfare law sponsored by former Democratic Rep. Joe Maxwell, now a state senator. Maxwell plans to introduce legislation next year that would encourage more job creation and give welfare recipients more freedom to accrue assets.

If Missouri concentrates solely on federal welfare requirements, Maxwell said, "we're going to be like a little dog chasing its tail." Maxwell wants the state to involve more communities and businesses in long-term efforts to keep people working.

In the community-based effort in Kansas City, LINC seems to be making progress. According to Executive Director Gayle Hobbs, 1,342 people out of 2,089 have stayed off public assistance since LINC started placing them in jobs in 1995, and 747 have returned to welfare.

as we know it," though the Republican-led Congress gave him a much more conservative and sweeping document than anything he had envisioned. Welfare as it is now known will take years to fully shape.

Experiments Under Way

A welfare overhaul was already under way when Clinton signed the measure (PL 104-193) in a Rose Garden ceremony Aug. 22, 1996. Forty-three states were operating under waivers from federal law by the Clinton administration — a practice that started under President Ronald Reagan and then expanded — enabling them to experiment with new approaches.

They were motivated by increasing public pressure to change the welfare system from the proverbial handout to a hand up. But no experimentation could fully prepare anyone for the onslaught of the federal legislation, which swept away six decades of federal welfare policy. (1996 Almanac, p. 6-3)

The law directed that $16.4 billion in federal welfare funding be sent to states in predetermined lump sum payments, known as block grants. Doing

Welfare History

The nation's main welfare program was created during the New Deal, and kept expanding through the 1970s, even after President Richard M. Nixon called for moving people from welfare to work.

1935

The Social Security Act, signed by President Franklin D. Roosevelt, establishes Aid to Dependent Children (later renamed Aid to Families with Dependent Children, or AFDC), a federal safety net that provides money for children with absent or unemployed fathers.

1962

Changes in welfare policy increase federal reimbursements to the states for rehabilitative services from 50 percent to 75 percent of costs, encouraging states to expand services such as vocational training. For the first time, Congress promises to fund those services for potential welfare recipients in an effort to keep them off the rolls. *(1962 Almanac, p. 212)*

1964

Three years after President John F. Kennedy created a pilot food stamps program by excecutive order, Congress clears legislation (PL 88-525) making it permanent. The program allows families to purchase low-cost stamps redeemable for food at local grocery stores. *(1964 Almanac p.110)*

1967

Congress requires every state to institute a work-incentive, work-training program for AFDC recipients. *(1967 Almanac, p. 895)*

---

so ended the 61-year-old federal guarantee of providing welfare checks to all eligible low-income mothers and children. States were instead given almost complete control over eligibility and benefits.

Nevertheless, many federal mandates prevailed. Among them: that adults receiving welfare benefits are required to work within two years of receiving aid, and that adults are generally limited to five years of federally funded welfare aid regardless of whether a job is available.

The wide-ranging law also created new procedures to establish paternity and enforce child support orders, provided more child care funding, reduced food stamp benefits, imposed new restrictions on legal immigrants' ability to obtain federal aid, and made it harder for low-income disabled children to get federal cash assistance.

For reasons that go far beyond Congress' ability to legislate, the nation is experiencing an unprecedented three-year decline in its welfare rolls. As of June, there were about 10.5 million welfare recipients, a 26 percent drop from a peak in 1994. It is unclear how many of those former welfare recipients are now working. But there are encouraging signs, including a dramatic increase in the number of female heads of households — a profile fitting the vast majority of welfare recipients — employed in the civilian labor force. *(Trends, p. 109)*

The new law has helped this process through an infusion of federal funds. States receive a fixed amount of federal welfare funding based partly on how many welfare recipients they had earlier in the decade.

Because caseloads have plummeted over the past three years, states have gotten at least $1.5 billion more in federal funds so far than they might have gotten under the previous law.

What Happens to Welfare

States may have succeeded in reducing their welfare rolls, but some factors contributing to that success may not be sustainable. For one thing, the caseload was probably ripe for reduction: It held steady for nearly two decades, then increased beginning in 1989, around the time of a recession, to a peak five years later.

Other factors look promising. Imposing new responsibilities on welfare recipients may have encouraged many to leave the rolls. For several years now, states have accelerated their welfare-to-work efforts. These included

---

subsidizing jobs, conditioning welfare benefits on a recipient's willingness to perform community service, and forcing recipients to sign contracts requiring them to take more responsibility for their lives.

The new federal law ushered in an era of even tougher work requirements and limits on benefits. The time limits may loom in the distance, but they are already on the minds of recipients. "It's the threat of being required to work that motivates them to get off welfare, or equally important, not to enter welfare in the first place," said Robert Rector, a senior policy analyst at the conservative Heritage Foundation. He said many who leave the rolls have income from unreported jobs or are supported by friends or relatives.

The growing societal emphasis on work over welfare may have broader implications for how the program is perceived, said David Butler, associate director of operations at Manpower Demonstration Research Corporation, based in New York, which evaluates social programs for the disadvantaged. "Is this change in message stigmatizing welfare more than it has in the past," he said, "so that people who would have felt more comfortable applying for welfare are not applying?"

Gary Stangler, director of Missouri's Department of Social Services, referred to "a psychological change in the culture of welfare, that more people are becoming motivated to find work or training."

Even so, the hardest cases are yet to come. Many of those who remain on the rolls are more likely to face multiple obstacles to getting jobs. They may need a combination of child care, transportation assistance, special medical attention, mental health counseling or substance abuse treatment.

Arranging such services puts a premium on good casework and following through on what Lawrence M. Mead, a political science professor at New York University, calls "the new paternalism." It refers to the government setting standards for welfare recipients to help them become self-sufficient and penalizing those who fall short. Or as Mead puts it, to provide "help and hassle, the way parents do for their kids." Relatively few states do that effectively, he added.

More far-reaching changes are possible in the future. States have not rushed to reduce cash benefits or eligibility for the aid, but they could under federal law. They could also opt to contract out for more welfare services.

Staying Employed

The toughest part of welfare reform traditionally has not been getting jobs for recipients but helping them stay employed. Many welfare recipients cycle on and off the rolls, tumbling back to welfare when they suffer setbacks at work, lose their child care, experience health problems or have difficulty in their personal relationships.

The welfare system is "not set up to service that group," said Toby Herr, director of Chicago-based Project Match,

> "The gradual enrichment of government-provided benefits to low-wage workers has induced some people to leave the rolls."
>
> Gary Burtless
> Senior fellow, Brookings Institution

which tries to help welfare recipients with the barest job skills become more self-sufficient. "There's overwhelming evidence that people aren't going to leave welfare with only one job."

States' ability to follow through with welfare recipients after they enter the work force may help spell long-term success.

"If we pull out all the supports from people as soon as they step into employment, then they're going to fall back into the welfare rolls," said Don Winstead, welfare reform administrator at the Florida Department of Children and Families. "We've seen that in the past."

Welfare recipients who enter Florida's work force are told how to budget their resources to afford child care, how to continue receiving health insurance through Medicaid and how to receive advance payments of the earned-income tax credit, which aims to reduce or eliminate taxes for the working poor.

This is a conscious effort to take advantage of recent government enhancements in health insurance, tax breaks, child care and minimum wages for low-income workers. For instance, Illinois, Michigan and Washington state now provide child care assistance based strictly on income without regard to whether the person receives welfare.

"The gradual enrichment of government-provided benefits to low-wage workers has induced some people to leave the rolls," said Gary Burtless, a senior fellow at the Brookings Institution, a Washington think tank.

Missouri is not going to try to instruct its welfare caseworkers — who are still involved in determining eligibility for such services as food stamps and Medicaid — in the intricacies of welfare-to-work efforts, Stangler said. It is instead relying more on community groups, businesses and neighborhood organizations.

Experts say states would be well-advised to invest their windfall in welfare-to-work efforts, to help cushion themselves for when the economy worsens. One goal would be to give welfare recipients enough work experience to enhance their work prospects when jobs become scarce. Some places are trying to channel welfare recipients into those local industries that seem most recession-proof, said Elaine Ryan, director of governmental affairs at the American Public Welfare Association, which represents welfare administrators.

Federal-State Tensions

The overhaul legislation gave states vast control over their welfare programs, but the federal government is still heavily involved — in some cases, more than the states would like. For example, some states want relief from welfare mandates.

One is a requirement that at least 75 percent of two-parent families on welfare participate in specified work activities by Oct. 1, 1997. These two-parent families account for only about 7 percent of the welfare caseload. But about half the states have not complied with this work requirement, stirring up criticism about their welfare-to-work efforts.

"That's their fault," said Rep. James M. Talent, R-Mo., a prominent conservative voice on welfare policies. "If you have two adults at home and both of them are able-bodied, one of them should be working."

This requirement may be eased, either through legislation or regulation. "Anybody with any common sense knows you cannot take a new policy and turn it around overnight," said Eloise Anderson, director of California's Department of Social Services.

Two-parent families represent 18 percent of California's caseload, the nation's highest such percentage. Many of them are refugees with particular difficulties getting jobs, such as a

Thompson's Welfare Revolution

Thompson

When Republican Tommy G. Thompson first ran for governor of Wisconsin in 1986, he complained that the state's relatively generous welfare benefits made it a magnet for poor people. His solution: cut benefits, which he did.

Thompson won that election, and two more since, focusing some of his attention on the need to require welfare recipients to work. Now, after nearly 11 years governed by Thompson, Wisconsin is undeniably a welfare magnet — for experts and journalists seeking to better understand how the state has revolutionized its welfare system.

And Thompson, 55, has become one of the nation's preeminent voices on overhauling welfare. His message also has evolved. He now advocates bold changes instead of piecemeal reform.

"You have to be willing to scrap the whole system," he said in an interview. "It's sort of a mind-set. You can't tinker around. You have to have radical surgery to make it work."

Thompson said he invested the initial savings from cutting welfare benefits in training programs for recipients. His administration then devised ways to penalize welfare recipients who did not take steps toward self-sufficiency. The "Learnfare" program, for instance, reduced benefits to the families of school-aged children who did not regularly attend school.

After that, the state became even more ambitious. This year it essentially replaced its welfare system with one based on moving recipients into jobs. *(Story, p. 104)*

The keys to success, Thompson said, are requiring welfare recipients to work and providing them with the necessary health care, child care, training and transportation to make it happen.

These initiatives, combined with Wisconsin's economic prosperity, have helped cut its welfare caseload by more than half since 1993. Thompson said the reductions during his tenure have helped the state save $1 billion.

With fewer welfare recipients, the state spends more money per recipient — about $15,000 each, he said — to try to make them more employable.

Thompson said it is easier for states if they do "not require anyone to work, just send them a check and not require anything. But that's not compassion. That's apathy."

The hope is that when the economy worsens, welfare recipients who have work experience will have a better chance of finding employment.

Thompson, who can be stridently partisan, was known as "Dr. No" during his tenure as a state legislator, a reference to his constant criticism of Democratic initiatives. He has since learned to work more with Democrats. It was their dare to scrap the traditional welfare system that gave the state its final push for a new approach.

---

language barrier, Anderson said.

States are also looking to ease a requirement from the 1988 federal welfare law (PL 100-485) that their child support enforcement information be kept in a single, statewide computer system by Oct. 1, 1997. Seventeen states, including California, Michigan, Illinois, Ohio and Pennsylvania, have not yet complied. The penalty is especially steep — loss of the state's federal child support aid and perhaps some or all of its welfare block grant. A bipartisan bill may be introduced early next year to give HHS more discretion in imposing the penalty. *(1988 Almanac, p. 349)*

A higher-profile issue has been the administration's contention that welfare recipients who are required to work for their benefits should be protected by federal labor laws. That decision cheered labor leaders but irked some state officials, who say that they need discretion in handling what they consider to be training programs.

House Speaker Newt Gingrich, R-Ga., has vowed to exempt welfare recipients from these labor laws, saying that

opponents of this effort would "undermine and destroy welfare reform." Clinton successfully resisted the effort this summer in negotiations on the spending bill (HR 2015 – PL 105-33) aimed at balancing the federal budget. *(Labor laws, Weekly Report, pp. 2043, 1847)*

It is unclear just how important the exemptions are to states, because the strong economy has made it easier to place welfare recipients in jobs and generally has lessened the need for large-scale state-run work programs. States will probably ask for more flexibility — and more federal aid — whenever the economy skids.

Shaw, who chairs the House Ways and Means Subcommittee on Human Resources, predicted that Congress would be receptive to helping states during a recession. "We're not going to let people sleep on grates and go hungry," he said.

Better still, said Rep. Sander M. Levin of Michigan, the subcommittee's ranking Democrat, Congress ought to increase the $2 billion contingency fund that states can tap into when unemployment is high. "The best time to fix that is

in times of prosperity," he said.

However, no major changes to the law's core provisions are anticipated any time soon. At Clinton's request, this year's budget law authorized $3 billion to help states move welfare recipients into the work force, and softened some restrictions on aid to legal immigrants.

But Congress took no action to counteract reductions in food stamps or to reinstate an individual's entitlement to cash benefits. Even such vehement opponents of the welfare law as Sen. Paul Wellstone, D-Minn., and Rep. Charles B. Rangel of New York, Ways and Means' ranking Democrat, foresee little hope for restoring the entitlement.

The Lives of the Poor

Few people involved in trying to overhaul the welfare system believe that the caseload reduction, by itself, represents true reform.

"The real litmus test for welfare reform," Gov. Carper of Delaware said, "is does it prepare a person for work, to find a job, continue to work in that job or a better job, and is the family of that former welfare recipient better off be-

Welfare Trends

Analysts are compiling statistics and sifting through databases to track the impact of the welfare overhaul legislation. They start by looking at the welfare caseload. But they watch other information as well, including data on employment and poverty, and the rate of teenage and out-of-wedlock births.
Here are a few early indications from some of those databases:

Number of Recipients on Welfare Since 1960

(In millions of recipients)

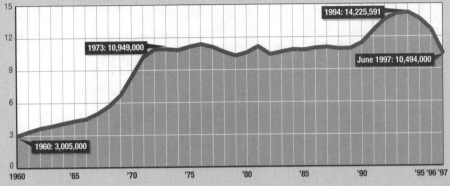

The nation is in an unprecedented three-year decline in its welfare rolls.

The number of recipients of Aid to Families with Dependent Children (AFDC) — the main cash welfare program until recently — was fairly steady from 1971 to 1989, when the total was 10.9 million. (A recession helped push the figure to nearly 11.4 million recipients in 1976, but then it abated.)

But the total ballooned by 30 percent over the five years ending in 1994, when 14.2 million people living in 5 million families received AFDC. Nearly one in seven children received welfare at that point. The weakened economy was blamed for swelling welfare rolls; so was a rise in out-of-wedlock births.

Welfare usage has fallen precipitously since then.

As of June, there were about 10.5 million welfare recipients in 3.8 million families as the nation made the transition from AFDC to its successor, Temporary Assistance for Needy Families. The number of welfare recipients had dropped by 3.7 million, or 26 percent, from its height in 1994. The caseload fell by 14 percent in the first 10 months after President Clinton signed the law (PL 104-193) on Aug. 22, 1996.

"Welfare reform is working far better than anyone had predicted it would," Clinton said Oct. 8. "It shows that we can accomplish great things when our policies promote work and reflect our values."

Clinton's Council of Economic Advisers indicated in May that more than 40 percent of the decline was attributable to economic growth, about 30 percent to state experiments with their welfare programs, and the rest to other policy initiatives such as enhancing tax credits for low-income workers.

SOURCE: HHS Administration for Children and Families

Female Heads of Household Who Work

(Annual average, in millions of women)

There has been a dramatic increase in the number of female heads-of-household — a profile that fits the vast majority of welfare recipients — employed in the civilian labor force.

There was an average of 413,000 more female heads of household working during the first nine months of this year than during a typical month in 1996. That far exceeds the previous average annual increase of 145,000 in such workers since 1987.

In September, 7.9 million female heads of household were working, an increase of 456,000 over September 1996.

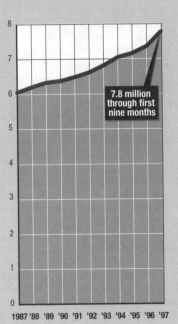

7.8 million through first nine months

SOURCE: Bureau of Labor Statistics

Trends in Teen Births

Teen Birth Rate Ages 15-19
(Births per 1,000 females)

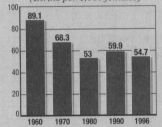

The teenage birth rate — a factor often linked with lengthy stays on the welfare rolls — has declined 12 percent since 1991. In 1996, there were 54.7 births per 1,000 females aged 15-19.

However, the percentage of those births to teenagers that were out-of-wedlock has remained at 76 percent for the past three years.

The Congressional Budget Office previously found that 77 percent of unmarried adolescent mothers become welfare recipients within five years of the birth of their first child. And many of them stay on welfare for a long time.

Overall, about 32 percent of all births in the United States are out-of-wedlock.

Percent of Teen Births Out-of-Wedlock

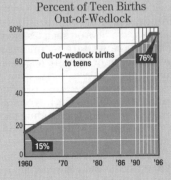

Out-of-wedlock births to teens

SOURCE: Child Trends, Inc.

MARILYN GATES-DAVIS

Welfare on the Web

Revolutionary changes in the nation's welfare system have coincided with a revolution in the way information is disseminated by computer. The result: An abundance of welfare-related data and analysis is now available through the World Wide Web. The following are useful web sites, selected both for the information they impart and for ease of use.

Research and analysis:

● **American Public Welfare Association.** Web site: *http://www.apwa.org* Organization of administrators involved in human services; the site includes links to each state's social service agency.

● **Center on Budget and Policy Priorities.** Web site: *http://www.cbpp.org* Analysis focusing on low- and moderate-income families.

● **HandsNet.** Web site: *http://www.handsnet.org* Network of human service organizations.

● **Heritage Foundation.** Web site: *http://www.heritage.org* Conservative-oriented analysis.

● **Hudson Institute.** Web site: *http://www.hudson.org* Technical assistance and analysis from a conservative-oriented group that helped design Wisconsin's innovative welfare system.

● **Manpower Demonstration Research Corporation.** Web site: *http://www.mdrc.org* Evaluation of welfare-to-work initiatives.

● **Institute for Women's Policy Research.** Focus is on the impact of welfare initiatives on women. Web site: *http://www.iwpr.org*

● **Urban Institute.** Web site: *http://www.urban.org* Useful especially for its project, "Assessing the New Federalism."

● **Welfare Information Network.** Web site: *http://www.welfareinfo.org* A foundation-funded welfare information clearinghouse to assist state- and community-based initiatives.

Government-related sites:

● **Census Bureau.** Web site: *http://www.census.gov/ hhes/ www/poverty.html* A source for poverty data.

● **Department of Health and Human Services — Administration for Children and Families.** Web site: *http://www.acf. dhhs.gov* The agency oversees federal programs for children and families. The site includes caseload information and a guide to welfare projects in the states.

● **National Association of Counties.** Web site: *http://www. naco.org* County-oriented viewpoint and information clearinghouse on the impact of the welfare law.

● **National Conference of State Legislatures.** Web site: *http://www.ncsl.org* State-oriented perspective on welfare reform and federal legislation.

● **National Governors' Association.** Web site: *http://www.nga.org* The governors' perspective on welfare initiatives and federal legislation.

Links to welfare-related web sites:

● **Electronic Policy Network.** Web site: *http://epn.org* Links to many liberal-oriented groups.

● **Nieman Foundation.** Web site: *http://www.Nieman.harvard.edu/Nieman/welfare.html* A wide range of links, many of them annotated.

● **Town Hall.** Web site: *http://www.townhall.com* Links to many conservative-oriented groups.

Assistance in compiling this list was provided by the Casey Journalism Center for Children and Families at the University of Maryland. Its web site is *http://casey. umd.edu*

---

cause that person is working?"

The legislation has focused the attention of foundations, research groups, nonprofit organizations, businesses and others on such tasks as helping to make welfare recipients more self-sufficient or trying to document the law's impact.

The welfare law's list of intended purposes extends far beyond a welfare-to-work effort, including promoting marriage and reducing out-of-wedlock pregnancies.

Its advocates hope that instilling more of a work ethic among welfare recipients and requiring school-age recipients to attend school can change their self-image.

Teenagers from low-income families are a particular concern. If they become more optimistic about their prospects, they may better prepare for their future — and may postpone pregnancies.

Researchers have shown that many factors are involved in out-of-wedlock births to teenagers, which have been linked to prolonged stays on the welfare rolls. But conservatives have contended that the guarantee of a welfare check has acted as an incentive for teenagers from low-income families to have children. That guarantee no longer exists.

"When women understand that the government is not going to pick up the role of the other spouse," California's

Anderson said, "they will say, 'I'm not having any more children.'"

More broadly, welfare initiatives will be evaluated for their impact on neighborhoods that until now have largely depended on government aid as income security. With renewed reliance on work and an emphasis on making welfare into temporary aid, said Michael Kharfen, an HHS spokesman, "that changes the whole character of a community."

The prospect of using the federal legislation to lift not only individual families but whole neighborhoods out of poverty is certainly enticing. Whether it is asking too much of a single piece of legislation remains to be seen. ■

Trade Agenda Left in Limbo By Failure of Fast Track

Supporters weigh options after scheduled vote is pulled; some see hope for narrower measures next session

The demise of President Clinton's bid to regain fast-track trade negotiating authority leaves U.S. trade policy adrift and Clinton and free-trade supporters in Congress in a quandary over what to do about it.

In the short term, the failure to pass the fast-track legislation has little evident impact. But free-traders say it sends an ominous signal about this country's commitment to opening global markets and threatens the ability of the United States to preserve its dominant role in trade in the rapidly growing South American and Asian markets.

"Right now, our trading partners take the view that the death of fast track means the end of trade talks," said a former official in the Office of the U.S. Trade Representative. "If none of our trading partners talk with us, it's a huge deal."

House Republican leaders and Clinton shelved the fast-track bill (HR 2621) in the early hours of Nov. 10, after an all-out lobbying blitz failed to produce enough votes to pass it. Arm-twisting by GOP leaders over an unusual weekend session produced more Republican votes than had been promised, but Clinton was unable to move enough Democrats to clinch the victory.

House Minority Leader Richard A. Gephardt, D-Mo., led the opposition, with powerful backing from organized labor. Gephardt had vowed to kill fast track unless the bill was modified to make labor and environmental conditions within the borders of trading part-

REUTERS

White House Chief of Staff Erskine Bowles, left, and Vice President Al Gore flank Clinton on his way to comment on the postponement Nov. 10.

ners a principal focus of trade talks.

"The real question before us now is whether we can connect our values of environmental quality, worker and human rights to our economic policy," Gephardt said after the decision to pull the vote. "Americans want a trade policy that ensures that future trade agreements address all these issues."

Gephardt and other fast-track opponents played up complaints that the administration has failed to live up to promises made to win votes in 1993 for the North American Free Trade Agreement (NAFTA). The sources of such complaints ranged from Floridians upset over fruit and vegetable imports to members of the Hispanic caucus frustrated by underfunding of the North American Development Bank. *(1993 Almanac, p. 171)*

But fast track also fell victim to bipartisan grousing about Clinton's past legislative accomplishments, won with cobbled-together coalitions of moderates that offended both liberal Democrats and conservative Republicans. *(Weekly Report, p. 2817)*

"Every complaint that a member has had in the last four years has been stated in the last 10 days — NAFTA, the budget, welfare reform," said Rep. Robert T. Matsui of California, a leading pro-fast-track Democrat. "I was surprised."

Beyond the blow to Clinton's prestige, the defeat has the potential to unravel the future U.S. trade agenda, which includes potential pacts with Chile and other South American countries, as well as industry-specific negotiations aimed at boosting exports of agricultural goods, services and intellectual property. Further in the future are trade agreements with Asian nations such as Singapore and Indonesia. *(Agenda, p. 112)*

U.S. trade policy has been inexorably moving toward open markets since the Great Depression, and by denying the president fast-track authority, Congress has taken an implicit step in the direction of protectionism, trade experts said.

"I think the Chileans have given up any hope of a free-trade agreement," said John Sweeney, an expert on Latin America with the conservative Heritage Foundation. "We've lost that opportunity now. It's dead. It's road kill. . . . By the time people up here wake up to the fact that we've shot ourselves in the foot, it will be too late."

Fast track requires that trade agreements be awarded quick up-or-down votes in Congress, without amendments that could unhinge such pacts. Without fast track in place, trading partners generally are unwilling to negotiate for fear members of Congress will reopen the deals to seek parochial concessions.

Pacts Pending

The White House and U.S. Trade Representative Charlene Barshefsky identified three key sets of trade negotiations that could be slowed or canceled by the failure to renew exclusive presidential trade negotiating authority. They are:

• **Ongoing World Trade Organization (WTO) talks.** Upon its creation in 1995, the WTO set a timetable for worldwide negotiations aimed at easing tariffs and rules in major market sectors that include intellectual property in 1998, agriculture in 1999 and trade in services in 2000.

• **'Emerging Economies.'** At the 1994 Summit of the Americas in Miami, President Clinton pledged to begin working toward a hemispheric Free Trade Area of the Americas, with a 2005 target for implementation. The first step was to be the expansion of the North American Free Trade Agreement to Chile, which is scheduled to host the next Summit of the Americas in April.

Also, Clinton has announced a goal of a broad free-trade pact with the 17 other members of the Asia Pacific Economic Cooperation Forum, including China, by 2010.

• **Expansion of the Information Technology Agreement.** This global pact should result by 2000 in tariff reductions totaling $5 billion on semiconductors, computer software and other telecommunications equipment, of which U.S. companies are the major producers. The administration had hoped to use this framework to pursue tariff reductions in eight other market sectors, including energy equipment and services and medical equipment and services.

The most contentious ongoing negotiations — the "open skies" talks seeking greater access to Japanese airports for U.S. airlines — are not affected by the lack of fast track.

Little Solace in Sight

The decision to pull the bill leaves free-traders mulling their options, none of which are particularly appealing at this point.

Opinions were mixed about whether Clinton and GOP leaders can mount a successful attempt to pass the measure next year. One widely held view was that fast track has hit its high-water mark and that it will be no easier to pass as the 1998 election nears.

"After this massive effort, after the Senate doing its part, and after all the work that went into trying to get the votes in the House, I don't see it happening [next year] at this point," said Senate Majority Leader Trent Lott, R-Miss. "So it would appear to me that it's dead."

Yet some supporters held out hope that some sober reflection on the demise of fast track, combined with a bit of tinkering with the legislation, might revive it.

"I don't think it's happy talk to say that we're going to bring it up in the spring," said Matsui. "It's an absolute necessity."

Another option under consideration is to craft fast-track authority that is limited to upcoming World Trade Organization negotiations on agriculture, government procurement and financial services. Questions on labor and environmental standards generally do not apply to such talks. Another candidate for narrow fast-track authority is a pact allowing Chile to join NAFTA.

"Next year, I intend to develop a narrower bill that will address issues in upcoming negotiations that are critical to our own interests," said Senate Finance Committee Chairman William V. Roth Jr., R-Del.

But there is no consensus that a slimmed-down fast-track bill is a good idea.

"I think that should be an absolute last resort," said Rep. Jim Kolbe, R-Ariz., a big player on trade issues. But even Kolbe admitted that "it's going to be tough" to revive the broader fast track next year.

Any attempt to bring the measure to the floor in 1998 would require another major push by Republican leaders and the White House, with no guarantee of success. In fact, several House Republicans described this effort to pass fast track as the most intense lobbying job House GOP leaders had undertaken since they took control in 1995.

For days, a steady stream of Republicans who were undecided or likely to oppose the bill trooped into House Speaker Newt Gingrich's suite of offices in the Capitol. The Georgia Republican led a united leadership in enticing, cajoling and threatening the rank and file to support the bill.

The bill was originally scheduled for a vote on Friday, Nov. 7, but vote counts were way too light. As of midday, only 38 Democrats were solid supporters of fast track, which meant almost 180 Republicans would have had to vote for the bill. *(Weekly Report, p. 2751)*

In the rush to adjournment, leaders scheduled Saturday and Sunday sessions to finish up remaining business — and to keep members in town to keep the pressure on for fast track.

No Easy Converts

The GOP vote total grew slowly over the weekend of Nov. 8-9, but Clinton was making almost no headway with Democrats. By Sunday afternoon, the White House had secured only a half-dozen or fewer additional Democrats despite offers of presidential visits to raise campaign funds and other inducements, said members and staff aides on both sides of the Democratic tally.

With Clinton so anxious to win fast track, many Republicans sought to use his desperation to wring concessions on the four remaining fiscal 1998 appropriations bills.

Republicans were pleased with compromises that curbed Clinton's plans for national educational testing and to use statistical "sampling" techniques in the 2000 census, but the White House would not yield to conservatives who wanted to block overseas family planning groups that receive U.S. aid from performing abortions or lobbying foreign governments to liberalize their abortion policies.

In the end, the latter provision was decisive to a critical bloc of conservative opponents of fast track who might have supported the bill if their demands on abortion were addressed.

Those following the overseas abortion controversy came away with different impressions of whether the administration was thinking about yielding on the issue. But in the end, it was clear the White House would not budge enough on abortion to win additional GOP votes.

"Because we didn't have more Democratic votes, we had to get a bigger share of the Republican vote. Now, that brought into play the controversy over international family planning," Clinton said Nov. 10. "Had we been able to resolve that, I think we could have gotten enough votes on the Republican side, to

Is Clinton's Loss Foreign Leaders' Gain?

President Clinton's failure to secure fast-track trade negotiating authority will encourage some countries to cut their own deals while giving other nations an excuse to slow or abandon current negotiations, experts say.

In the wake of Clinton's Nov. 10 decision to withdraw the legislation or face certain defeat, Canada, for one, showed no signs of letting up in negotiating its own free-trade agreements.

Following recent pacts with Israel and Chile, Canadian Trade Minister Sergio Marchi is expected to sign a deal with Mercosur — the trading coalition of Brazil, Uruguay, Argentina and Paraguay — in January.

"There is no doubt some countries will use this [fast-track failure] as an occasion to go slow or stop on trade, or seize the initiative and make a deal," said Robert Herzstein, who was under secretary for international trade in the Commerce Department during the Carter administration and an adviser to Mexico during negotiations on the North American Free Trade Agreement.

Clinton's inability to gain fast-track authority casts doubts on the prospects for inclusion of Chile in NAFTA, which includes Canada, Mexico and the United States. Chilean President Eduardo Frei said his country will move ahead on trade negotiations, including talks with the European Union.

"This is not Chile's problem. This is the United States' problem," Frei said Nov. 10 of fast track's failure. "What has to happen is that the United States must define its trade policy — whether it will play a leading role in the coming years on this issue, or whether it will simply remain undecided."

While the president's failure could have a far-reaching impact, there are certain factors that the Clinton administration can take solace in.

Frei

Although he is the first president since Gerald R. Ford to be without fast-track authority, Clinton still has the constitutional power to negotiate with foreign countries. In pursuing fast-track power, he was seeking an agreement with Congress to avoid amendments to any deal.

I.M. Destler, a professor at the University of Maryland School of Public Affairs and author of a book on fast-track legislation, points out that while this administration has negotiated more than 200 trade agreements, in only two cases has Clinton used fast-track authority.

The United States also has the appeal of being the market everyone wants to deal with and a longstanding reputation as a free trader.Clinton is scheduled to travel later this month to Vancouver, British Columbia, for a meeting of the 18-nation Asia Pacific Economic Cooperation Forum, and then in April to Santiago, Chile, for the next Summit of the Americas. And although he will not have fast-track authority, both sessions will provide him with high-profile opportunities to make his case for regaining the power.

"He can use it as a bully pulpit," said Kim Elliott, a research fellow at the Institute for International Economics.

But those trips will be a stark contrast to Clinton's Asia Pacific meeting in Seattle in 1993 and the last Summit of the Americas in Miami in 1994, when he arrived fresh off his victory in Congress on NAFTA.

"It will raise a larger question of, 'Does he have any power left?' " Destler said.

---

go with the Democrats' votes we had, to pass the bill."

Republicans, both publicly and privately, were not pleased that Clinton seemed to assign blame for the loss on anti-abortion activists.

"His own party, for all the wrong reasons, renounced his leadership," Lott said. "The House pro-lifers were ready to compromise, but even with their votes, the president couldn't get over the top."

Tomatoes, Wheat, Peanuts

Late Sunday, most people thought the vote would finally occur, and supporters were beginning to believe that they might pull it off.

But the Rules Committee meeting required to issue a rule that would permit the bill to come to the floor was postponed repeatedly as negotiations dragged on. A proposed "manager's amendment" would have made mostly minor changes to the bill, including pro-

visions to enforce restrictions on imports of Mexican tomatoes, add Customs Service inspectors and establish "Special 301" procedures against countries that unfairly block U.S. agricultural exports. Other promises, such as actions to curb "dumping" of underpriced wheat by Canada and to protect U.S. peanut growers, came via letter.

"There were discussions about modifying the bill up until 11 p.m. on Sunday," said a GOP Rules Committee aide.

The decision to call off the vote came after Gingrich and Clinton spoke twice and Gingrich apprised Clinton of the final whip count.

According to several sources familiar with the GOP tally, GOP leaders had solid support from perhaps 156 Republicans. They felt fairly confident of another six to eight members. Then there was a list of more than a dozen "Hail Marys" that might get the GOP total as high as 170.

"If everything broke exactly right,

we were within five votes," Kolbe said. "But I think the dynamic of when that vote starts and what happens was just very dicey."

Top Gephardt aide George Kundanis insisted that it was not that close: "They didn't have 15 to 18 people to work with, and they were 15 to 18 short."

If the effort to pass fast track does resume next spring, it will require another big, tiring and perhaps futile push. One glimmer of hope was a group of about two dozen Democrats who said they could vote for fast track if it could be modified to provide greater aid for U.S. workers displaced by trade.

Clearly, more Democrats will have to climb on board before Republicans take the bill up again.

Said GOP Rep. Dennis Hastert of Illinois: "I don't want to . . . have us move heaven and Earth beyond what we thought we could get and then have the Democrats say, 'We can only get 40 votes.' " ∎

<u>WOMEN IN THE MILITARY</u>

Women in the Military: Mission in Progress

Recurrent cases of sexual misconduct force Congress to reassess its handling of gender integration in armed forces

On a winter's morning in 1980, five nervous young women sat beneath the lights of a hearing room on Capitol Hill and told a House military subcommittee how they had been badgered, propositioned, fondled, humiliated and even assaulted at an Army training base in nearby Maryland.

For Lori Lodinsky, fresh out of junior college, the problems began on her first day at Fort Meade when a platoon leader slipped her a note angling for a date. The harassment would drive her from the Army after only a year.

Members of the Armed Services Personnel subcommittee expressed concern that day but went no further, accepting the testimony of military leaders that while harassment no doubt existed, it was not commonplace and certainly was not condoned.

Seventeen years later, the almost weekly revelations of sexual misconduct and coercion are forcing Congress to face an issue it had long trusted the Pentagon to allay.

For the past half-century, Congress has gradually but steadily opened the nation's armed forces to women, who now number nearly 200,000 in almost every job except ground combat and submarines.

However, Congress has been notably reluctant to tackle the consequences of its legislation. The problem, as many experts see it, is that Congress, like the vast majority of Americans, remains ambivalent about giving women an equal share of the power and responsibility of the military.

"I think it says something about human nature," said former Rep. Marjorie S. Holt, R-Md., who instigated the 1980 hearing on harassment. "Until we fix the situation so there is equal power between the sexes, I think we will see this kind of thing go on."

CQ Weekly Report Aug. 16, 1997

DOUGLAS GRAHAM

Women Marines undergoing officer candidate training haul a 30-pound ammunition box across a 25-foot tower at the Corps' Quantico, Va., base.

The Army is so concerned, in the wake of a scandal where drill instructors preyed on young recruits, that it put off releasing a vast new study of sexual harassment until it could come up with some solutions in September.

Defense Secretary William S. Cohen publicly worries about whether the hunt for sexual misconduct, which has extended into the Joint Chiefs of Staff, perhaps "goes too far."

Veteran lawmakers such as Sen. Robert C. Byrd, D-W.Va., worry that the scandals could be a "danger sign that sexual integration complicates an army's fighting capabilities."

Women's rights advocates worry that conservatives in Congress might use the scandals to punish women by again segregating them in the services.

"I think [the congressional] committees are really seriously trying to figure out what to do," said Nancy Duff Campbell, co-president of the National Women's Law Center. But "some people in Congress have an agenda to roll back women's rights."

Necessities of Life

With Congress' decision to end the draft and move to an All Volunteer Force in 1973, the military found itself having to rely on women for the first time outside of a war to help fill its ranks. At the time, there were fewer than 50,000 women in uniform, nearly 2 percent of the active duty forces. Since then, the number has quadrupled, and women now make up more than 13 percent of the force, according to the latest Defense Department figures. *(Chart, p. 115)*

Recruiting women brought other practical benefits — on the whole, they scored higher than men on tests and caused fewer disciplinary problems. As the armed forces moved to a more mechanized and electronic standard of warfare, women proved adept.

Today, as in 1973, the armed services would be hard-pressed to meet their enlistment quotas or force requirements without women.

Having "women in the military has nothing to do with political correctness; it is a readiness issue," said Judith Youngman, chairman of the Defense Advisory Committee on Women in the Services, established in 1951 to advise the Defense secretary on policies and personnel issues concerning women and widely known by its acronym, DACOWITS.

Slowly Opening the Gates

Before and during World War II, women served in segregated military units, such as the Women's Army Corps (WAC) or as nurses. Over the last 50 years, Congress has gradually but steadily lowered the barriers for women. Following are the milestones in that effort:

● **1948** — Women's Armed Services Integration Act (62 Stat. 356-75) brings women into the regular military services but with strict ground rules: Women can make up no more than 2 percent of any one service and can rise no higher than lieutenant colonel or Navy commander. If they later adopt children, marry someone with children or become pregnant, they will be discharged. Women cannot fly in combat planes, nor can they serve at sea, except on hospital ships and transports. Ground combat is not mentioned.

● **1967** — Women Officers Act (PL 90-130) removes 2 percent and promotion ceilings.

● **1973** — Supreme Court rules (*Frontiero v. Richardson*) that dependents of military women can receive the same entitlements offered for the dependents of military men.

● **1974** — Women are allowed to enlist without parental consent at the same age (18) as men (PL 93-290).

● **1975** — Stratton Amendment to the fiscal 1976 defense authorization bill (PL 94-106) opens the Army, Navy and Air

Women in the Military
(As of June 30, 1997)

	Number of women (%)	% Career fields open to women
Army	69,514 (14.5)	91
Navy	49,167 (12.5)	97*
Air Force	65,293 (17.3)	99
Marines	9,140 (5.3)	93
TOTALS	**193,114 (13.6)**	

* Navy officers: 92 percent

SOURCE: Department of Defense

Force academies to women. Coast Guard and Merchant Marine academies had already been opened by administrative action.

● **1978** — Fiscal 1979 defense authorization act (PL 95-485) allows women to serve on all non-combat Navy ships and do temporary duty on warships not on combat missions. *(1978 Almanac, p. 321)*

● **1988** — Defense Department adopts "risk rule" excluding women from non-combat units or jobs if the risk of exposure to direct combat, hostile fire or capture is the same or greater than for associated combat units.

● **1991** — Fiscal 1992-93 defense authorization act (PL 102-190) lifts restriction on assignment of women to combat planes in Air Force and Navy. *(1991 Almanac, p. 414)*

● **1993** — Fiscal 1994 defense authorization act (PL 103-160) lifts ban on women serving aboard combat ships. Congress requires 30 days' notice of policy changes on assignment of women to combat units or ships not already open to them and 90 days' notice of any change in ground combat prohibition. *(1993 Almanac, p. 463)*

● **1994** — Defense Department issues new rule that excludes women from direct ground combat units, defined as those that "engage an enemy on the ground with weapons, are exposed to hostile fire and have a high probability of direct physical contact with the personnel of a hostile force."

Beginning in 1991, Congress removed legal barriers to women flying combat planes and serving on combat ships, and the Pentagon adjusted its policies accordingly. Only the taboo on women in ground combat has remained in place, never written into law, always a matter of military policy. *(Legal history, box, this page)*

In recent years, the debate over women in combat has been overtaken by the equally visceral issue of sexual harassment. And neither the Pentagon nor Congress has been able to cope.

Running the Gantlet

The Tailhook scandal shook the Navy and the public's image of its armed forces in 1992 — dozens of drunken Navy and Marine Corps fliers groping, insulting, humiliating at least 26 women, half of them officers, in the corridor of a Las Vegas hotel.

Congress was appalled. Senate leaders held up Navy promotions for a time to force action against the culprits.

But the problem was more deeply rooted. Half the women in the military said they felt sexually harassed at one time or another.

In November 1996, the Army disclosed that a captain and two sergeants training auto mechanics at the Aberdeen Proving Ground in Maryland had coerced young recruits into having sex. One non-com called it a "game" to see who could bed the most women. A sergeant was subsequently convicted of rape and sent to prison; 12 were ultimately relieved of their duties.

The scandal spread to other training bases, including Fort Leonard Wood in Missouri.

In February, The New York Times revealed that Sergeant Major of the Army Gene C. McKinney, the Army's top enlisted man, had been accused of sexual harassment by a former subordinate. By August, six women had come forward to accuse McKinney of mistreating them, and his preliminary hearing was still under way.

During hearings in February before a Senate Armed Services Committee, Olympia J. Snowe, R-Maine, expressed a frustration many of her colleagues shared.

"Women in the armed services today deserve to know right now that this problem is going to be taken care of," she told Army officials.

The service has been quick to respond. "The Army learned a lesson from Tailhook," said Rep. Tillie Fowler, R-Fla., a member of a House task force set up to study the sexual misconduct problems.

When the Aberdeen scandal surfaced, the Army promised to investigate all allegations. It set up a toll-free hotline for complaints and launched two studies of sexual harassment, one by the Army's inspector general and another by a panel of Army officials and civilians.

The studies were expected to be released in July, but publication was put off until September to give Pentagon leaders time to draft solutions, officials said.

Fowler, who was briefed on the two

Women IN THE MILITARY CHRONOLOGY

1948: Congress integrates women into the armed forces but limits their numbers and bans them from combat planes and ships.

1951: Concerned about low enlistments by women, Secretary of Defense George Marshall forms the Defense Advisory Committee on Women in the Services (DACOWITS).

1970: Elizabeth P. Hoisington and Anna Mae Hays become the Army's first female brigadier generals.

1971: Jeanne Holm is first woman in the Air Force to reach the rank of brigadier general. Holm later writes "Women in the Military: An Unfinished Revolution."

1972: The Navy announces plans for women to be assigned to general overseas duty stations.

1973: Six Navy women become the first women to be designated naval aviators.

1974: Congress allows women to enlist at the same age as men (18) without parental consent; it had been 21.
Naval aviator Jill Brown becomes the first black woman pilot in the military.
Lt. Sally Murphy becomes the first female helicopter pilot in the Army.

1975: The Army announces that all female recruits must qualify with an M-16 rifle.

Defense Department decides that women may remain in the military if they become pregnant.
Congress opens military academies to women.

1977: Coast Guard assigns women to ships.
Twenty-two female Marine officers begin combat training in Quantico, Va.
Secretary of the Army opens many new jobs to women, including tactical missile crews and non-combat helicopters.

1979: Coast Guard Lt. Ingalls Moritz takes command of patrol boat Cape Current.

1980: Military academies graduate 212 women.
Naval officer court-martialed for sexual harassment after four women sailors on his ship file complaint.

1983: 170 women participate in Grenada invasion, mainly in air crews.

Army reports, said they appear to have uncovered many of the same problems that her task force, led by Rep. Steve Buyer, R-Ind., discovered and discussed in a recently released report — that drill instructors are not adequately screened or supervised, that basic training has grown weaker, that some commanders take sexual misconduct more seriously than others.

However, The New York Times, in a July 31 story, quoted an Army official as saying the Army studies found widespread bias against women.

The House National Security Committee included language in its fiscal 1998 defense authorization bill (HR 1119) requiring the Army to institute reforms aimed at improving the selection and training of drill sergeants. The bill, among other things, requires the Army to conduct psychological screening of all drill sergeant candidates and to provide drill sergeant trainees with an opportunity to work with new recruits in initial entry training before graduating.

Buyer, who heads the House National Security Military Personnel Subcommittee, said he plans to hold hearings this fall on the Army's findings.

Back to Basics

Some members of Congress blame the sexual harassment problems on the the Army's decision in 1994 to mix men and women during basic training. The Navy began integrated basic training that same year, while the Air Force has had mixed-gender basic training since 1977. The Marines still keep men and women apart during training.

The Army tried gender-integrated basic training in the late 1970s and early 1980s, and while the service says there are no records on whether the effort was a success or failure, critics say it did not work and that is why the Army ended the practice.

"My conversations with people who ran [those gender-integrated] units said there were serious problems," said Robert Maginnis, a retired Army lieutenant colonel now with the socially conservative Family Research Council. "The only reason [the Army later] jumped on board was because it was politically correct."

"The purpose of basic training is to change a civilian into a soldier," said Charles Moskos, a military sociologist at Northwestern University. "That means there should be a sharp break with the civilian environment. One way is by having sexual segregation."

In the wake of the Aberdeen scandal, 123 House members — nearly a quarter of the House — rushed to co-sponsor a bill (HR 1559) by Maryland Republican Roscoe G. Bartlett that would ban mixed-gender basic training outright.

"It's like putting sparks and gas together and being surprised there is a fire," Bartlett said of training men and women together. "The sexual dynamic is . . . distracting and disruptive."

Sen. Byrd went further, telling colleagues at an Armed Services Committee hearing on June 5, "The scandals that we're seeing in the training commands must be taken as a danger sign that sexual integration complicates an army's fighting capabilities."

"The effect of confined environments where men and women work and live in close quarters certainly involves sexual issues," Byrd said. "It is laughable to assume otherwise."

But neither Bartlett nor Byrd pressed his case. Bartlett planned to offer his bill as an amendment to the defense authorization bill but backed off when there was not enough support in the National Security Committee.

Instead, he supported Buyer's provision for a commission to study whether basic training is adequately preparing recruits and whether mixed-gender training is worthwhile.

Byrd had indicated he would launch a similar effort on the Senate's defense authorization bill but opted instead for an amendment, co-sponsored by Armed Services Personnel Subcommittee Chairman Dirk Kempthorne, R-Idaho, calling for a commission to study the issue.

Kempthorne said that while it is important to ensure women have equal opportunity for advancement and promo-

1988: Department of Defense issues memorandum that sexual harassment "will not be condoned or tolerated in any way."

1989: About 770 women participate in Operation Just Cause in Panama. Army Capt. Linda Bray leads members of a military police unit in a firefight with Panamanian forces.

Naval Academy midshipman Gwen Dreyer is handcuffed to a urinal and photographed by male classmates. Men involved are given minor punishments.

1990: Navy Cdr. Rosemary Mariner becomes the first woman to command a fleet jet aircraft squadron.

1991: Some 40,000 female soldiers are deployed in the Persian Gulf and play integral combat-support roles during the war.

Congress lifts ban on women flying combat aircraft.

At least 26 women, half of them officers, are forced to run a gantlet of drunken Navy and Marine officers at Tailhook Association convention in Las Vegas.

1992: Lt. Col. Ann E. Dunwoody becomes the first female battalion commander in the 82nd Airborne Division.

General Accounting Office releases first of five reports on sexual harassment at the military service academies.

1993: Defense Secretary Les Aspin lifts policy ban on women flying combat aircraft. Congress lifts ban on women serving aboard combat ships.

Nation's first women's war memorial is dedicated, recognizing the women who served in Vietnam.

1994: Lt. Jeannie Flynn becomes the first Air Force female combat pilot, flying F-15s.

Navy issues orders for 60 women to serve aboard the aircraft carrier USS *Dwight D. Eisenhower*.

1996: Pentagon survey finds 55 percent of women in the United States military reported some form of sexual harassment in the past year, including rape, assault, groping and pressure for sexual favors.

Army discloses instances of sexual abuse at Aberdeen Proving Ground training center involving drill instructors. Army moves quickly to deal with the scandal, which has spread to Fort Leonard Wood and other training bases.

1997: Sergeant Major of the Army Gene C. McKinney is accused by several women of sexual harassment. Hearing is in progress.

tion, "Also remember the one purpose of our military is to keep a strong defense. So we can do nothing that in any way hampers cohesion, readiness, et cetera."

Separate but Equal?

Sexual harassment problems have "nothing to do with integrated training," said Snowe. Sexual harassment in the military, she said, "is absolutely a failure of leadership."

Studying the issue is one thing, said Rep. Jane Harman, D-Calif., a member of Buyer's task force, but she is concerned that it not lead to a " 'Women Are Not Welcome' sign on the military."

"Where it logically leads to is two separate militaries," Harman said, "and that is a foolish idea."

Supporters of integrated training point out that a Defense Department survey released in July 1996 found that women in the Marine Corps, which has segregated basic training, had the highest reported levels of sexual harassment in the military —64 percent reported one or more instances of unwanted or uninvited sexual attention.

"It's fair to take another look at it," said Sen. Joseph I. Lieberman, D-Conn., a member of the Armed Services Committee, "but boy I really believe that you've got to put the burden of proof on anybody who would say you should go back to the old way."

"Just because we have some prob-

lems that really relate mostly to the behavior of men doesn't mean we should punish women by depriving them of equal opportunity," Lieberman said.

In addition to the commission that Congress may set up to study the issue, Defense Secretary Cohen announced June 27 that he was establishing a task force, headed by former Sen. Nancy Landon Kassebaum, R-Kan., to study gender-integrated training.

In outlining the task force's goals, Cohen cautioned that the Pentagon is "not going to turn back the clock. We don't intend to."

But he added that "the problems at Aberdeen and elsewhere have raised questions about the success of gender-integrated training and about the treatment of women in the military."

Bowing to Pressure

Some women's rights advocates argue that Congress has been too willing to second-guess its own decisions, rather than pressing the Pentagon to rid the services of discrimination.

"They don't want to get to the conclusion of just saying 'time out.' We've done it over and over again. Women are here . . . They're essential," said former Rep. Patricia Schroeder, D-Colo., a leading proponent of removing the combat exclusions. "It's pretty discouraging. It must be even more discouraging for women in the military who wonder how

many times they have to prove" themselves.

When Congress lifted the bans on women in combat planes and ships, it also voted for a presidential commission to study the issue. As a result, then-Defense Secretary Dick Cheney said he would wait until the commission issued its report before deciding whether to change the services' policies.

The report, which was generally ignored, offered a mixed recommendation to allow women to serve on combat vessels, except submarines and amphibious ships, but to continue the ban on their flying combat aircraft.

Some conservatives, on the other hand, contend that the military has bowed to political pressure from Congress and from feminist activists who want to use the military to pursue a social agenda.

"The perception is that if you cross the feminists, they will hurt you," said Elaine Donnelly, head of the Center for Military Readiness in Michigan and a longtime opponent of an expanded role for women in the services. "There is an element of sexual politics" in a lot of the decision-making by the Pentagon and Congress, she said.

Donnelly and other conservatives are concerned that the military is compromising its central role in national defense to placate women's groups.

"The politicians won't go out on a

limb to say the emperor has no clothes," Maginnis said.

"Where problems occur," said Tillie Fowler, "is when standards get lowered and women are perceived rightly or wrongly as being treated differently and resentment builds" among men. "I think some [military leaders] are so worried about being politically correct, they may be bending the rules."

She added that it "really backfires on women who made it on their own."

A Warrior Culture

Retired Air Force Maj. Gen. Jeanne Holm, in her book "Women in the Military: An Unfinished Revolution," writes that when women were banned from combat, they were "automatically excluded from participation in the primary mission of the armed forces, and their second-class status was thus assured."

For military officers, the path to promotion and true power leads through combat. Pilots control the Air Force; seagoing officers lead the Navy; combat veterans command the Army and Marines.

Women's rights advocates say that only when the last combat exclusion is lifted can women achieve equality and the respect necessary to quell harassment.

During an appearance in late November on ABC's "This Week" program, Army Secretary Togo D. West Jr. agreed an argument could be made that women should have access to all the jobs in the military.

But West and others also noted that there appears to be little support in Congress for the military to take this step. According to Harman, "Society is not ready for it."

House National Security Chairman Floyd D. Spence, R-S.C., who has served in Congress for 26 years, said he is "not sure if it's my heritage" but he firmly believes that women do not belong in ground combat. He is quick to add, however, that this is "not to say there isn't a place — and a big place — for women in the military."

The traditional view is that combat is reserved for warriors, but not for women. America's military, in fact, has long trained its warriors partly by denigrating women. Recruits who cannot keep up, who show weakness, are called "girls" or worse. Cadence chants are rich in sexual bravado.

"Women were little more than trophies in contests of male bravado," Linda Bird Francke writes in her new book, "Ground Zero: The Gender Wars in the Military."

"In such a group-driven male cul-

Sexual Harassment, Circa 1980

A series of articles in the Baltimore Sun in December 1979 reported that "an epidemic of sexual harassment . . . has accompanied the rapid influx of women into the lower ranks of the U.S. Army." The newspaper focused on a unit at Fort Meade, Maryland, where a number of women complained of blatant harassment.

On Feb. 11, 1980, five of those women testified before the House Armed Services Personnel Subcommittee on their experiences. They were followed by Army officers, including the base commander. Following are excerpts from that testimony.

Private Sarah L. Tolaro: I have been on Fort Meade for almost three years, and I have suffered nothing but sexual harassment, just frankly because I am a female . . . I have never seen people treated the way they have been treated on Fort Meade.

Rep. Marjorie S. Holt, R-Md.: Treated by your —

Tolaro: By superiors, by peers. It really doesn't matter. It is just a general, a general outlook on females in the services. They are not regarded very highly by most people, not everyone.

Holt: How does this manifest itself? . . .

Tolaro: Among talking dirty and nasty, I have had several very bad experiences. One, among others, is getting pushed into a corner by two NCOs [noncommissioned officers] and have them exposing themselves to me and then laughing. And I have never had that happen to me before anywhere. . . .

Specialist Jimi V. Hernandez: Once you are in the Army, you learn to have to deal with these things, because while I was in basic training, the same thing happened to me. I had another private come up to me and try to mess with one of my other troops . . . and I told him that Army regulations states that you are not supposed to do this, and he politely told me that his drill sergeant told him, or told everyone in his unit that women specifically came in the Army for that reason.

Del. Antonio B. Won Pat, D-Guam: It is natural of course for women to attract men. Some women attract, you know, more, some less. That is probably not a fault. That is human nature. But when you go into the military, of course, you undergo training and discipline, and as such then that is how you are measured. What I am trying to get at is whether women in the service could do just as well as men. . . .

Jacqueline Lose: Yes, definitely. But the men don't think so. Just the fact that you ask the question puts us on the defensive. It is, like, you know, we went in, we did the training just like the men did. We did it with the men. We did everything they did and usually better.

ture," Francke continues, "the sexual harassment directives from the Pentagon were doomed to sink like stones."

A recently retired Marine major, when asked how long it would take for women to be truly accepted in the Corps, replied: "Generations."

So ingrained is the culture that some Army recruiters, according to The Wall Street Journal, openly worry that diluting the military's masculine image could hurt enlistments.

So far, though, the prospect of hostility and the evidence of harassment has not affected female recruitment, which has remained steady throughout the services through the first half of the fiscal year (October-March) compared with last year.

Even the Army, which has suffered the most adverse publicity, has yet to see a drop in female recruitment from last year's figures, although overall recruiting for the Army has fallen short of its target.

Some women who currently serve in the military say they do not believe the problem of sexual harassment is as bad as it is portrayed in the media.

"You have good units and you have your idiots," said Staff Sgt. Catherine Grossman, the lone female member of the 82nd Airborne field artillery unit at Fort Bragg, in Fayetteville, N.C. "You always hear it. [But] you hear it in the civilian world. I don't think it's worse here than in the civilian world. It's just highly publicized." ∎

Appendix

The Legislative Process in Brief

Note: Parliamentary terms used below are defined in the glossary.

Introduction of Bills

A House member (including the resident commissioner of Puerto Rico and non-voting delegates of the District of Columbia, Guam, the Virgin Islands and American Samoa) may introduce any one of several types of bills and resolutions by handing it to the clerk of the House or placing it in a box called the hopper. A senator first gains recognition of the presiding officer to announce the introduction of a bill. If objection is offered by any senator, the introduction of the bill is postponed until the following day.

As the next step in either the House or Senate, the bill is numbered, referred to the appropriate committee, labeled with the sponsor's name and sent to the Government Printing Office so that copies can be made for subsequent study and action. Senate bills may be jointly sponsored and carry several senators' names. Until 1978, the House limited the number of members who could cosponsor any one bill; the ceiling was eliminated at the beginning of the 96th Congress. A bill written in the executive branch and proposed as an administration measure usually is introduced by the chairman of the congressional committee that has jurisdiction.

Bills — Prefixed with HR in the House, S in the Senate, followed by a number. Used as the form for most legislation, whether general or special, public or private.

Joint Resolutions — Designated H J Res or S J Res. Subject to the same procedure as bills, with the exception of a joint resolution proposing an amendment to the Constitution. The latter must be approved by two-thirds of both houses and is thereupon sent directly to the administrator of general services for submission to the states for ratification instead of being presented to the president for his approval.

Concurrent Resolutions — Designated H Con Res or S Con Res. Used for matters affecting the operations of both houses. These resolutions do not become law.

Resolutions — Designated H Res or S Res. Used for a matter concerning the operation of either house alone and adopted only by the chamber in which it originates.

Committee Action

With few exceptions, bills are referred to the appropriate standing committees. The job of referral formally is the responsibility of the Speaker of the House and the presiding officer of the Senate, but this task usually is carried out on their behalf by the parliamentarians of the House and Senate. Precedent, statute and the jurisdictional mandates of the committees as set forth in the rules of the House and Senate determine which committees receive what kinds of bills. An exception is the referral of private bills, which are sent to whatever committee is designated by their sponsors. Bills are technically considered "read for the first time" when referred to House committees.

When a bill reaches a committee it is placed on the committee's calendar. At that time the bill comes under the sharpest congressional focus. Its chances for passage are quickly determined — and the great majority of bills falls by the legislative roadside. Failure of a committee to act on a bill is equivalent to killing it; the measure can be withdrawn from the committee's purview only by a discharge petition signed by a majority of the House membership on House bills, or by adoption of a special resolution in the Senate. Discharge attempts rarely succeed.

The first committee action taken on a bill usually is a request for comment on it by interested agencies of the government. The committee chairman may assign the bill to a subcommittee for study and hearings, or it may be considered by the full committee. Hearings may be public, closed (executive session) or both. A subcommittee, after considering a bill, reports to the full committee its recommendations for action and any proposed amendments.

The full committee then votes on its recommendation to the House or Senate. This procedure is called "ordering a bill reported." Occasionally a committee may order a bill reported unfavorably; most of the time a report, submitted by the chairman of the committee to the House or Senate, calls for favorable action on the measure since the committee can effectively "kill" a bill by simply failing to take any action.

After the bill is reported, the committee chairman instructs the staff to prepare a written report. The report describes the purposes and scope of the bill, explains the committee revisions, notes proposed changes in existing law and, usually, includes the views of the executive branch agencies consulted. Often committee members opposing a measure issue dissenting minority statements that are included in the report.

Usually, the committee "marks up" or proposes amendments to the bill. If they are substantial and the measure is complicated, the committee may order a "clean bill" introduced, which will embody the proposed amendments. The original bill then is put aside and the clean bill, with a new number, is reported to the floor.

The chamber must approve, alter or reject the committee amendments before the bill itself can be put to a vote.

Floor Action

After a bill is reported back to the house where it originated, it is placed on the calendar.

There are five legislative calendars in the House, issued in one cumulative calendar titled *Calendars of the United States House of Representatives and History of Legislation*. The House calendars are:

The Union Calendar to which are referred bills raising revenues, general appropriations bills and any measures directly or indirectly appropriating money or property. It is the Calendar of the Committee of the Whole House on the State of the Union.

How a Bill Becomes Law

This graphic shows the most typical way in which proposed legislation is enacted into law. There are more complicated, as well as simpler, routes, and most bills never become law. The process is illustrated with two hypothetical bills, House bill No. 1 (HR 1) and Senate bill No. 2

(S 2). Bills must be passed by both houses in identical form before they can be sent to the president. The path of HR 1 is traced by a solid line, that of S 2 by a broken line. In practice, most bills begin as similar proposals in both houses.

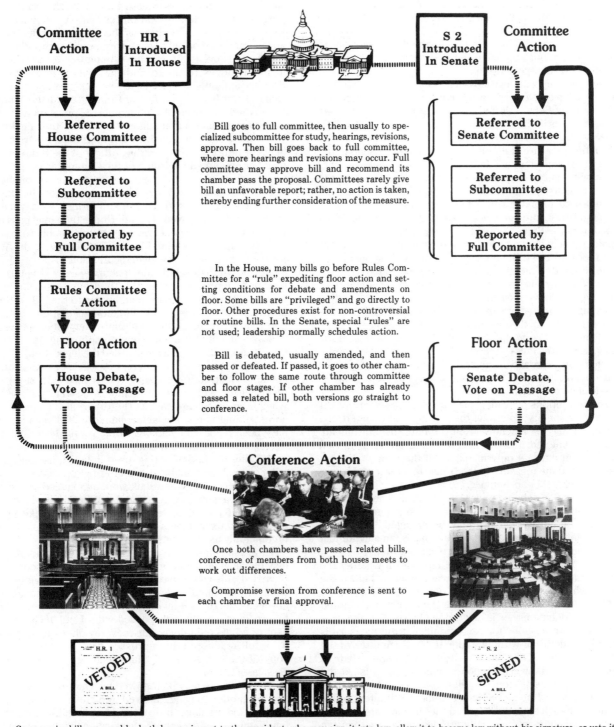

Committee Action

HR 1 Introduced In House

S 2 Introduced In Senate

Committee Action

Referred to House Committee

Referred to Subcommittee

Reported by Full Committee

Rules Committee Action

Floor Action

House Debate, Vote on Passage

Referred to Senate Committee

Referred to Subcommittee

Reported by Full Committee

Floor Action

Senate Debate, Vote on Passage

Bill goes to full committee, then usually to specialized subcommittee for study, hearings, revisions, approval. Then bill goes back to full committee, where more hearings and revisions may occur. Full committee may approve bill and recommend its chamber pass the proposal. Committees rarely give bill an unfavorable report; rather, no action is taken, thereby ending further consideration of the measure.

In the House, many bills go before Rules Committee for a "rule" expediting floor action and setting conditions for debate and amendments on floor. Some bills are "privileged" and go directly to floor. Other procedures exist for non-controversial or routine bills. In the Senate, special "rules" are not used; leadership normally schedules action.

Bill is debated, usually amended, and then passed or defeated. If passed, it goes to other chamber to follow the same route through committee and floor stages. If other chamber has already passed a related bill, both versions go straight to conference.

Conference Action

Once both chambers have passed related bills, conference of members from both houses meets to work out differences.

Compromise version from conference is sent to each chamber for final approval.

H.R. 1 VETOED A BILL

S. 2 SIGNED A BILL

Compromise bill approved by both houses is sent to the president, who may sign it into law, allow it to become law without his signature, or veto it and return it to Congress. Congress may override veto by two-thirds majority vote in both houses; bill then becomes law without president's signature.

The House Calendar to which are referred bills of public character not raising revenue or appropriating money.

The Corrections Calendar to which are referred bills to repeal rules and regulations deemed excessive or unnecessary when the Corrections Calendar is called the second and fourth Tuesday of each month. (Instituted in the 104th Congress to replace the seldom-used Consent Calendar.) A three-fifths majority is required for passage.

The Private Calendar to which are referred bills for relief in the nature of claims against the United States or private immigration bills that are passed without debate when the Private Calendar is called the first and third Tuesdays of each month.

The Discharge Calendar to which are referred motions to discharge committees when the necessary signatures are signed to a discharge petition.

There is only one legislative calendar in the Senate and one "executive calendar" for treaties and nominations submitted to the Senate. When the Senate Calendar is called, each senator is limited to five minutes' debate on each bill.

Debate. A bill is brought to debate by varying procedures. If a routine measure, it may await the call of the calendar. If it is urgent or important, it can be taken up in the Senate either by unanimous consent or by a majority vote. The majority leader, in consultation with the minority leader and others, schedules the bills that will be taken up for debate.

In the House, precedence is granted if a special rule is obtained from the Rules Committee. A request for a special rule usually is made by the chairman of the committee that favorably reported the bill, supported by the bill's sponsor and other committee members. The request, considered by the Rules Committee in the same fashion that other committees consider legislative measures, is in the form of a resolution providing for immediate consideration of the bill. The Rules Committee reports the resolution to the House where it is debated and voted on in the same fashion as regular bills. If the Rules Committee fails to report a rule requested by a committee, there are several ways to bring the bill to the House floor — under suspension of the rules, on Calendar Wednesday or by a discharge motion.

The resolutions providing special rules are important because they specify how long the bill may be debated and whether it may be amended from the floor. If floor amendments are banned, the bill is considered under a "closed rule," which permits only members of the committee that first reported the measure to the House to alter its language, subject to chamber acceptance.

When a bill is debated under an "open rule," amendments may be offered from the floor. Committee amendments always are taken up first but may be changed, as may all amendments up to the second degree; that is, an amendment to an amendment to an amendment is not in order.

Duration of debate in the House depends on whether the bill is under discussion by the House proper or before the House when it is sitting as the Committee of the Whole House on the State of the Union. In the former, the amount of time for debate either is determined by special rule or is allocated with an hour for each member if the measure is under consideration without a rule. In the Committee of the Whole the amount of time agreed on for general debate is equally divided between proponents and opponents. At the end of general discussion, the bill is read section by section for amendment. Debate on an amendment is limited to five minutes for each side; this is called the "five-minute rule." In practice, amendments regularly are debated more than ten minutes, with members gaining the floor by offering pro

forma amendments or obtaining unanimous consent to speak longer than five minutes.

Senate debate usually is unlimited. It can be halted only by unanimous consent by "cloture," which requires a three-fifths majority of the entire Senate except for proposed changes in the Senate rules. The latter requires a two-thirds vote.

The House considers almost all important bills within a parliamentary framework known as the Committee of the Whole. It is not a committee as the word usually is understood; it is the full House meeting under another name for the purpose of speeding action on legislation. Technically, the House sits as the Committee of the Whole when it considers any tax measure or bill dealing with public appropriations. It also can resolve itself into the Committee of the Whole if a member moves to do so and the motion is carried. The Speaker appoints a member to serve as the chairman. The rules of the House permit the Committee of the Whole to meet when a quorum of 100 members is present on the floor and to amend and act on bills, within certain time limitations. When the Committee of the Whole has acted, it "rises," the Speaker returns as the presiding officer of the House and the member appointed chairman of the Committee of the Whole reports the action of the committee and its recommendations. The Committee of the Whole cannot pass a bill; instead it reports the measure to the full House with whatever changes it has approved. The full House then may pass or reject the bill — or, on occasion, recommit the bill to committee. Amendments adopted in the Committee of the Whole may be put to a second vote in the full House.

Votes. Voting on bills may occur repeatedly before they are finally approved or rejected. The House votes on the rule for the bill and on various amendments to the bill. Voting on amendments often is a more illuminating test of a bill's support than is the final tally. Sometimes members approve final passage of bills after vigorously supporting amendments that, if adopted, would have scuttled the legislation.

The Senate has three different methods of voting: an untabulated voice vote, a standing vote (called a division) and a recorded roll call to which members answer "yea" or "nay" when their names are called. The House also employs voice and standing votes, but since January 1973 yeas and nays have been recorded by an electronic voting device, eliminating the need for time-consuming roll calls.

Another method of voting, used in the House only, is the teller vote. Traditionally, members filed up the center aisle past counters; only vote totals were announced. Since 1971, one-fifth of a quorum can demand that the votes of individual members be recorded, thereby forcing them to take a public position on amendments to key bills. Electronic voting now is commonly used for this purpose.

After amendments to a bill have been voted upon, a vote may be taken on a motion to recommit the bill to committee. If carried, this vote removes the bill from the chamber's calendar and is usually a death blow to the bill. If the motion is unsuccessful, the bill then is "read for the third time." An actual reading usually is dispensed with. Until 1965, an opponent of a bill could delay this move by objecting and asking for a full reading of an engrossed (certified in final form) copy of the bill. After the "third reading," the vote on final passage is taken.

The final vote may be followed by a motion to reconsider, and this motion may be followed by a move to lay the motion on the table. Usually, those voting for the bill's passage vote for the tabling motion, thus safeguarding the final passage action. With that, the bill has been formally passed by the cham-

Examples of
Legislative Documents

ber. While a motion to reconsider a Senate vote is pending on a bill, the measure cannot be sent to the House.

Action in Second House

After a bill is passed it is sent to the other chamber. This body may then take one of several steps. It may pass the bill as is — accepting the other chamber's language. It may send the bill to committee for scrutiny or alteration, or reject the entire bill, advising the other house of its actions. Or it simply may ignore the bill submitted while it continues work on its own version of the proposed legislation. Frequently, one chamber may approve a version of a bill that is greatly at variance with the version already passed by the other house, and then substitute its contents for the language of the other, retaining only the latter's bill number.

A provision of the Legislative Reorganization Act of 1970 permits a separate House vote on any non-germane amendment added by the Senate to a House-passed bill and requires a majority vote to retain the amendment. Previously the House was forced to act on the bill as a whole; the only way to defeat the non-germane amendment was to reject the entire bill.

Often the second chamber makes only minor changes. If these are readily agreed to by the other house, the bill then is routed to the president. However, if the opposite chamber significantly alters the bill submitted to it, the measure usually is "sent to conference." The chamber that has possession of the "papers" (engrossed bill, engrossed amendments, messages of transmittal) requests a conference and the other chamber must agree to it. If the second house does not agree, the bill dies.

Conference, Final Action

Conference. A conference works out conflicting House and Senate versions of a legislative bill. The conferees usually are senior members appointed by the presiding officers of the two houses, from the committees that managed the bills. Under this arrangement the conferees of one house have the duty of trying to maintain their chamber's position in the face of amending actions by the conferees (also referred to as "managers") of the other house.

The number of conferees from each chamber may vary, the range usually being from three to nine members in each group, depending upon the length or complexity of the bill involved. There may be five representatives and three senators on the conference committee, or the reverse. But a majority vote controls the action of each group so that a large representation does not give one chamber a voting advantage over the other chamber's conferees.

Theoretically, conferees are not allowed to write new legislation in reconciling the two versions before them, but this curb sometimes is bypassed. Many bills have been put into acceptable compromise form only after new language was provided by the conferees. The 1970 Reorganization Act attempted to tighten restrictions on conferees by forbidding them to introduce any language on a topic that neither chamber sent to conference or to modify any topic beyond the scope of the different House and Senate versions.

Frequently the ironing out of difficulties takes days or even weeks. Conferences on involved appropriations bills sometimes are particularly drawn out.

As a conference proceeds, conferees reconcile differences between the versions, but generally they grant concessions only insofar as they remain sure that the chamber they represent will accept the compromises. Occasionally, uncertainty over how either house will react, or the positive refusal of a chamber to back down on a disputed amendment, results in an impasse, and the bills die in conference even though each was approved by its sponsoring chamber.

Conferees sometimes go back to their respective chambers for further instructions, when they report certain portions in disagreement. Then the chamber concerned can either "recede and concur" in the amendment of the other house or "insist on its amendment."

When the conferees have reached agreement, they prepare a conference report embodying their recommendations (compromises). The report, in document form, must be submitted to each house.

The conference report must be approved by each house. Consequently, approval of the report is approval of the compromise bill. In the order of voting on conference reports, the chamber which asked for a conference yields to the other chamber the opportunity to vote first.

Final Steps. After a bill has been passed by both the House and Senate in identical form, all of the original papers are sent to the enrolling clerk of the chamber in which the bill originated. He then prepares an enrolled bill, which is printed on parchment paper. When this bill has been certified as correct by the secretary of the Senate or the clerk of the House, depending on which chamber originated the bill, it is signed first (no matter whether it originated in the Senate or House) by the Speaker of the House and then by the president of the Senate. It is next sent to the White House to await action.

If the president approves the bill, he signs it, dates it and usually writes the word "approved" on the document. If he does not sign it within 10 days (Sundays excepted) and Congress is in session, the bill becomes law without his signature.

However, should Congress adjourn before the 10 days expire, and the president has failed to sign the measure, it does not become law. This procedure is called the pocket veto.

A president vetoes a bill by refusing to sign it and, before the 10-day period expires, returning it to Congress with a message stating his reasons. The message is sent to the chamber that originated the bill. If no action is taken on the message, the bill dies. Congress, however, can attempt to override the president's veto and enact the bill, "the objections of the president to the contrary notwithstanding." Overriding a veto requires a two-thirds vote of those present, who must number a quorum and vote by roll call.

Debate can precede this vote, with motions permitted to lay the message on the table, postpone action on it or refer it to committee. If the president's veto is overridden by a two-thirds vote in both houses, the bill becomes law. Otherwise it is dead.

When bills are passed finally and signed, or passed over a veto, they are given law numbers in numerical order as they become law. There are two series of numbers, one for public and one for private laws, starting at the number "1" for each two-year term of Congress. They are then identified by law number and by Congress — for example, Private Law 21, 97th Congress; Public Law 250, 97th Congress (or PL 97–250).

The Budget Process in Brief

Through the budget process, the president and Congress decide how much to spend and tax during the upcoming fiscal year. More specifically, they decide how much to spend on each activity, ensure that the government spends no more and spends it only for that activity, and report on that spending at the end of each budget cycle.

The President's Budget

The law requires that, by the first Monday in February, the president submit to Congress his proposed federal budget for the next fiscal year, which begins on October 1. In order to accomplish this, the president establishes general budget and fiscal policy guidelines. Based on these guidelines, executive branch agencies make requests for funds and submit them to the White House's Office of Management and Budget (OMB) nearly a year prior to the start of a new fiscal year. The OMB, receiving direction from the president and administration official, reviews the agencies' requests and develops a detailed budget by December. From December to January the OMB prepares the budget documents, so that the president can deliver it to Congress in February.

The president's budget is the executive branch's plan for the next year — but it is just a proposal. After receiving it, Congress has its own budget process to follow from February to October. Only after Congress passes the required spending bills — and the president signs them — has the government created its actual budget.

Action in Congress

Congress first must pass a "budget resolution" — a framework within which the members of Congress will make their decisions about spending and taxes. It includes targets for total spending, total revenues, and the deficit, and allocations within the spending target for the two types of spending — discretionary and mandatory.

Discretionary spending, which currently accounts for about 33 percent of all federal spending, is what the president and Congress must decide to spend for the next year through the thirteen annual appropriations bills. It includes money for such activities as the FBI and the Coast Guard, for housing and education, for NASA and highway and bridge construction, and for defense and foreign aid.

Mandatory spending, which currently accounts for 67 percent of all spending, is authorized by laws that have already been passed. It includes entitlement spending — such as for Social Security, Medicare, veterans' benefits, and food stamps — through which individuals receive benefits because they are eligible based on their age, income, or other criteria. It also includes interest on the national debt, which the government pays to individuals and institutions that hold Treasury bonds and other government securities. The only way the president and Congress can change the spending on entitlement and other mandatory programs is if they change the laws that authorized the programs.

Currently, the law imposes a limit or "cap" through 1998 on total annual discretionary spending. Within the cap, however, the president and Congress can, and often do, change the spending levels from year to year for the thousands of individual federal programs.

In addition, the law requires that legislation that would raise mandatory spending or lower revenues — compared to existing law — be offset by spending cuts or revenue increases. This requirement, called "pay-as-you-go" is designed to prevent new legislation from increasing the deficit.

Once Congress passes the budget resolution, it turns its attention to passing the thirteen annual appropriations bills and, if it chooses, "authorizing" bills to change the laws governing mandatory spending and revenues.

Congress begins by examining the president's budget in detail. Scores of committees and subcommittees hold hearings on proposals under their jurisdiction. The House and Senate Armed Services Authorizing Committees, and the Defense and Military Construction Subcommittees of the Appropriations Committees, for instance, hold hearings on the president's defense budget. The White House budget director, cabinet officers, and other administration officials work with Congress as it accepts some of the president's proposals, rejects others, and changes still others. Congress can change funding levels, eliminate programs, or add programs not requested by the president. It can add or eliminate taxes and other sources of revenue, or make other changes that affect the amount of revenue collected. Congressional rules require that these committees and subcommittees take actions that reflect the congressional budget resolution.

The president's budget, the budget resolution, and the appropriations or authorizing bills measure spending in two ways — "budget authority" and "outlays." Budget authority is what the law authorizes the federal government to spend for certain programs, projects, or activities. What the government actually spends in a particular year, however, is an outlay. For example, when the government decides to build a space exploration system, the president and Congress may agree to appropriate $1 billion in budget authority. But the space system may take ten years to build. Thus, the government may spend $100 million in outlays in the first year to begin construction and the remaining $900 million during the next nine years as the construction continues.

Congress must provide budget authority before the federal agencies can obligate the government to make outlays. When Congress fails to complete action on one or more of the regular annual appropriations bills before the fiscal year begins on October 1, budget authority may be made on a temporary basis through continuing resolutions. Continuing resolutions make budget authority available for limited periods of time, generally at rates related through some formula to the rate provided in the previous year's appropriation.

Monitoring the Budget

Once Congress passes and the president signs the federal appropriations bills or authorizing laws for the fiscal year, the government monitors the budget through (1) agency program managers and budget officials, including the Inspectors General, who report only to the agency head; (2) the Office of Management and Budget; (3) congressional committees; and (4) the General Accounting Office, an auditing arm of Congress.

This oversight is designed to (1) ensure that agencies comply with legal limits on spending, and that they use budget authority only for the purposes intended; (2) see that programs are operating consistently with legal requirements and existing policy; and (3) ensure that programs are well managed and achieving the intended results.

The president may withhold appropriated amounts from obligation only under certain limited circumstances — to provide for contingencies, to achieve savings made possible through changes in requirements or greater efficiency of operations, or as otherwise provided by law. The Impoundment Control Act of 1974 specifies the procedures that must be followed if funds are withheld. Congress can also cancel previous authorized budget authority by passing a rescissions bill — but it also must be signed by the president.

Glossary of Congressional Terms

Act — The term for legislation once it has passed both houses of Congress and has been signed by the president or passed over his veto, thus becoming law. *(See also Pocket Veto.)* Also used in parliamentary terminology for a bill that has been passed by one house and engrossed. *(See Engrossed Bill.)*

Adjournment Sine Die — Adjournment without definitely fixing a day for reconvening; literally "adjournment without a day." Usually used to connote the final adjournment of a session of Congress. A session can continue until noon, Jan. 3, of the following year, when, under the 20th Amendment to the Constitution, it automatically terminates. Both houses must agree to a concurrent resolution for either house to adjourn for more than three days.

Adjournment to a Day Certain — Adjournment under a motion or resolution that fixes the next time of meeting. Under the Constitution, neither house can adjourn for more than three days without the concurrence of the other. A session of Congress is not ended by adjournment to a day certain.

Amendment — A proposal of a member of Congress to alter the language, provisions or stipulations in a bill or in another amendment. An amendment usually is printed, debated, and voted upon in the same manner as a bill.

Amendment in the Nature of a Substitute — Usually an amendment that seeks to replace the entire text of a bill. Passage of this type of amendment strikes out everything after the enacting clause and inserts a new version of the bill. An amendment in the nature of a substitute also can refer to an amendment that replaces a large portion of the text of a bill.

Appeal — A member's challenge of a ruling or decision made by the presiding officer of the chamber. In the Senate, the senator appeals to members of the chamber to override the decision. If carried by a majority vote, the appeal nullifies the chair's ruling. In the House, the decision of the Speaker traditionally has been final; seldom are there appeals to the members to reverse the Speaker's stand. To appeal a ruling is considered an attack on the Speaker.

Appropriations Bill — A bill that gives legal authority to spend or obligate money from the Treasury. The Constitution disallows money to be drawn from the Treasury "but in Consequence of Appropriations made by Law."

By congressional custom, an appropriations bill originates in the House, and it is not supposed to be considered by the full House or Senate until a related measure authorizing the funding is enacted. An appropriations bill grants the actual money approved by authorization bills, but not necessarily the full amount permissible under the authorization. The 1985 Gramm-Rudman-Hollings law stipulated that the House is to pass by June 30 the last regular appropriations bill for the fiscal year starting the following Oct. 1. (There is no such deadline for the Senate.) However, for decades appropriations often have not been final until well after the fiscal year begins, requiring a succession of stopgap bills to continue the government's functions. In addition, much federal spending — about half of all budget authority, notably that for Social Security and interest on the federal debt — does not require annual appropriations; those programs exist under permanent appropriations. *(See also Authorization, Budget Process, Backdoor Spending Authority, Entitlement Program.)*

In addition to general appropriations bills, there are two specialized types. *(See Continuing Resolution, Supplemental Appropriations Bill.)*

Authorization — Basic, substantive legislation that establishes or continues the legal operation of a federal program or agency, either indefinitely or for a specific period of time, or which sanctions a particular type of obligation or expenditure. An authorization normally is a prerequisite for an appropriation or other kind of budget authority.

Under the rules of both houses, the appropriation for a program or agency may not be considered until its authorization has been considered. An authorization also may limit the amount of budget authority to be provided or may authorize the appropriation of "such sums as may be necessary." *(See also Backdoor Spending Authority.)*

Backdoor Spending Authority — Budget authority provided in legislation outside the normal appropriations process. The most common forms of backdoor spending are borrowing authority, contract authority, entitlements, and loan guarantees that commit the government to payments of principal and interest on loans — such as Guaranteed Student Loans — made by banks or other private lenders. Loan guarantees only result in actual outlays when there is a default by the borrower.

In some cases, such as interest on the public debt, a permanent appropriation is provided that becomes available without further action by Congress.

Bills — Most legislative proposals before Congress are in the form of bills and are designated by HR in the House of Representatives or S in the Senate, according to the house in which they originate, and by a number assigned in the order in which they are introduced during the two-year period of a congressional term. "Public bills" deal with general questions and become public laws if approved by Congress and signed by the president. "Private bills" deal with individual matters such as claims against the government, immigration and naturalization cases, or land titles and become private laws if approved and signed. *(See also Concurrent Resolution, Joint Resolution, Resolution.)*

Bills Introduced — In both the House and Senate, any number of members may join in introducing a single bill or resolution. The first member listed is the sponsor of the bill, and all subsequent members listed are the bill's cosponsors.

Many bills are committee bills and are introduced under the name of the chairman of the committee or subcommittee. All appropriations bills fall into this category. A committee frequently holds hearings on a number of related bills and may agree to one of them or to an entirely new bill. *(See also Report, Clean Bill, By Request.)*

Bills Referred — When introduced, a bill is referred to the committee or committees that have jurisdiction over the subject with which the bill is concerned. Under the standing rules of the House and Senate, bills are referred by the Speaker in the House and by the presiding officer in the Senate. In practice, the House and Senate parliamentarians act for these officials and refer the vast majority of bills.

Borrowing Authority — Statutory authority that permits a federal agency to incur obligations and make payments for specified purposes with borrowed money.

Budget — The document sent to Congress by the president early each year estimating government revenue and expenditures for the ensuing fiscal year.

Budget Act — The common name for the Congressional Budget and Impoundment Control Act of 1974, which established the current budget process and created the Congressional Budget Office. The act also put limits on presidential authority to spend appropriated money. *(See Impoundments, Budget Process.)*

Budget Authority — Authority to enter into obligations that will result in immediate or future outlays involving federal funds. The basic forms of budget authority are appropriations, contract authority, and borrowing authority. Budget authority may be classified by (1) the period of availability (one-year, multiple-year, or without a time limitation), (2) the timing of congressional action (current or permanent), or (3) the manner of determining the amount available (definite or indefinite).

Budget Process — Congress in 1990 made far-reaching changes in its 1974 budget process law, called the Congressional Budget and Impoundment Control Act. The law continues to provide for congressional approval of budget resolutions and reconciliation bills, two mechanisms created by the 1974 law. *(See Budget Resolution, Reconciliation.)* The 1990 changes discarded provisions of 1985 and 1987 amendments to the act that automatically cut federal spending in certain areas when pre-determined targets were exceeded. Those amendments, collectively known as Gramm-Rudman-Hollings for their congressional sponsors, were intended to balance the federal budget by fiscal year 1991. Soaring deficits made the goal unachievable, threatening federal programs with almost random and massive cuts.

Congress stepped back from that brink and provided, instead, for spending caps in three categories: defense, domestic, and international for 1991–93; for the following two years the 1990 changes set overall discretionary spending caps. Each cap will increase automatically with inflation plus — for domestic spending only — an extra $20 billion. Moreover, spending that exceeds the cap due to factors beyond the control of Congress, such as a recession, will not trigger auto-

matic cuts. Entitlement spending, such as for Medicare, was put on a "pay as you go" basis, requiring any expansion be paid for by a corresponding entitlement cut or revenue increase. Also, any tax cut must be paid for by a compensating tax increase or entitlement cut. But if all these provisions failed, automatic spending cuts could still occur. *(See Sequestration.)*

Budget Resolution — A concurrent resolution passed by both houses of Congress, but not requiring the president's signature, establishing the congressional budget plan. The resolution sets forth various budget totals and functional allocations. Its deadline is April 15 but if missed the Budget committees must report spending limits for the Appropriations committees based on discretionary spending in the president's budget.

By Request — A phrase used when a senator or representative introduces a bill at the request of an executive agency or private organization but does not necessarily endorse the legislation.

Calendar — An agenda or list of business awaiting possible action by each chamber. The House uses five legislative calendars. *(See Corrections, Discharge, House, Private, and Union Calendar.)*

In the Senate, all legislative matters reported from committee go on one calendar. They are listed there in the order in which committees report them or the Senate places them on the calendar, but they may be called up out of order by the majority leader, either by obtaining unanimous consent of the Senate or by a motion to call up a bill. The Senate also uses one nonlegislative calendar; this is used for treaties and nominations. *(See Executive Calendar.)*

Calendar Wednesday — In the House, committees, on Wednesdays, may be called in the order in which they appear in Rule X of the House, for the purpose of bringing up any of their bills from either the House or the Union Calendar, except bills that are privileged. General debate is limited to two hours. Bills called up from the Union Calendar are considered in Committee of the Whole. Calendar Wednesday is not observed during the last two weeks of a session and may be dispensed with at other times by a two-thirds vote. This procedure is rarely used and routinely is dispensed with by unanimous consent.

Call of the Calendar — Senate bills that are not brought up for debate by a motion, unanimous consent, or a unanimous consent agreement are brought before the Senate for action when the calendar listing them is "called." Bills must be called in the order listed. Measures considered by this method usually are noncontroversial, and debate on the bill and any proposed amendments is limited to a total of five minutes for each senator.

Chamber — The meeting place for the membership of either the House or the Senate; also the membership of the House or Senate meeting as such.

Clean Bill — Frequently after a committee has finished a major revision of a bill, one of the committee members, usually the chairman, will assemble the changes and what is left of the original bill into a new measure and introduce it as a "clean bill." The revised measure, which is given a new number, then is referred back to the committee, which reports it to the floor for consideration. This often is a timesaver, as committee-recommended changes in a clean bill do not have to be considered and voted on by the chamber. Reporting a clean bill also protects committee amendments that could be subject to points of order concerning germaneness.

Clerk of the House — Chief administrative officer of the House of Representatives, with duties corresponding to those of the secretary of the Senate. *(See also Secretary of the Senate.)*

Cloture — The process by which a filibuster can be ended in the Senate other than by unanimous consent. A motion for cloture can apply to any measure before the Senate, including a proposal to change the chamber's rules. A cloture motion requires the signatures of 16 senators to be introduced. To end a filibuster, the cloture motion must obtain the votes of three-fifths of the entire Senate membership (60 if there are no vacancies), except when the filibuster is against a proposal to amend the standing rules of the Senate and a two-thirds vote of senators present and voting is required. The cloture request is put to a roll-call vote one hour after the Senate meets on the second day following introduction of the motion. If approved, cloture limits each senator to one hour of debate. The bill or amendment in question comes to a final vote after 30 hours of consideration (including debate time and the time it takes to conduct roll calls, quorum calls and other procedural motions). *(See Filibuster.)*

Committee — A division of the House or Senate that prepares legislation for action by the parent chamber or makes investigations as directed by the parent chamber. There are several types of committees. *(See Standing and Select or Special Committees.)* Most standing committees are divided into subcommittees, which study legislation, hold hearings and report bills, with or without amendments, to the full committee. Only the full committee can report legislation for action by the House or Senate.

Committee of the Whole — The working title of what is formally "The Committee of the Whole House [of Representatives] on the State of the Union." The membership comprises all House members sitting as a committee. Any 100 members who are present on the floor of the chamber to consider legislation comprise a quorum of the committee. Any legislation taken up by the Committee of the Whole, however, must first have passed through the regular legislative or Appropriations committee and have been placed on the calendar.

Technically, the Committee of the Whole considers only bills directly or indirectly appropriating money, authorizing appropriations or involving taxes or charges on the public. Because the Committee of the Whole need number only 100 representatives, a quorum is more readily attained, and legislative business is expedited. Before 1971, members' positions were not individually recorded on votes taken in Committee of the Whole. *(See Teller Vote.)*

When the full House resolves itself into the Committee of the Whole, it supplants the Speaker with a "chairman." A measure is debated and amendments may be proposed, with votes on amendments as needed. *(See Five-Minute Rule.)* The committee, however, cannot pass a bill. When the committee completes its work on the measure, it dissolves itself by "rising." The Speaker returns, and the chairman of the Committee of the Whole reports to the House that the committee's work has been completed. At this time members may demand a roll-call vote on any amendment adopted in the Committee of the Whole. The final vote is on passage of the legislation.

Committee Veto — A requirement added to a few statutes directing that certain policy directives by an executive department or agency be reviewed by certain congressional committees before they are implemented. Under common practice, the government department or agency and the committees involved are expected to reach a consensus before the directives are carried out. *(See also Legislative Veto.)*

Concurrent Resolution — A concurrent resolution, designated H Con Res or S Con Res, must be adopted by both houses, but it is not sent to the president for approval and therefore does not have the force of law. A concurrent resolution, for example, is used to fix the time for adjournment of a Congress. It also is used as the vehicle for expressing the sense of Congress on various foreign policy and domestic issues, and it serves as the vehicle for coordinated decisions on the federal budget under the 1974 Congressional Budget and Impoundment Control Act. *(See also Bills, Joint Resolution, Resolution.)*

Conference — A meeting between the representatives of the House and the Senate to reconcile differences between the two houses on provisions of a bill passed by both chambers. Members of the conference committee are appointed by the Speaker and the presiding officer of the Senate and are called "managers" for their respective chambers. A majority of the managers for each house must reach agreement on the provisions of the bill (often a compromise between the versions of the two chambers) before it can be considered by either chamber in the form of a "conference report." When the conference report goes to the floor, it cannot be amended, and, if it is not approved by both chambers, the bill may go back to conference under certain situations, or a new conference must be convened. Many rules and informal practices govern the conduct of conference committees.

Bills that are passed by both houses with only minor differences need not be sent to conference. Either chamber may "concur" in the other's amendments, completing action on the legislation. Sometimes leaders of the committees of jurisdiction work out an informal compromise instead of having a formal conference. *(See Custody of the Papers.)*

Confirmations — *(See Nominations.)*

Congressional Record — The daily, printed account of proceedings in both the House and Senate chambers, showing substantially verbatim debate, statements, and a record of floor action. Highlights of legislative and committee action are embodied in a Daily Digest section of the *Record*, and members are entitled to have their extraneous remarks printed in an appendix known as "Extension of Remarks." Members may edit and revise remarks made on the floor during debate, and therefore quotations from debate reported by the press are not always found in the *Record*.

The *Congressional Record* provides a way to distinguish remarks spoken on the floor of the House and Senate from undelivered speeches. In the Senate, all speeches, articles, and other matter that members insert in the *Record* without actually reading them on the floor are set off by large black dots, or bullets. However, a loophole allows a member to avoid the bulleting if he delivers any portion of the speech in person. In the House, undelivered speeches and other material are printed in a distinctive typeface. *(See also Journal)*

Congressional Terms of Office — Normally begin on Jan. 3 of the year following a general election and are two years for representatives and six years for senators. Representatives elected in special elections are sworn in for the remainder of a term. A person may be appointed to fill a Senate vacancy and serves until a successor is elected; the successor serves until the end of the term applying to the vacant seat.

Continuing Resolution — A joint resolution, cleared by Congress and signed by the president (when the new fiscal year is about to begin or has begun), to provide new budget authority for federal agencies and programs to continue in operation until the regular appropriations acts are enacted. *(See Appropriations Bill.)*

The continuing resolution usually specifies a maximum rate at which an agency may incur obligations, based on the rate of the prior year, the president's budget request, or an appropriations bill passed by either or both houses of Congress but not yet enacted. In recent years, most regular appropriations bills have not cleared and a full-year continuing resolution has taken their place. For fiscal 1987 and 1988, Congress intentionally rolled all 13 regular appropriations bills into one continuing resolution.

Continuing resolutions also are called "CRs" or continuing appropriations.

Contract Authority — Budget authority contained in an authorization bill that permits the federal government to enter into contracts or other obligations for future payments from funds not yet appropriated by Congress. The assumption is that funds will be available for payment in a subsequent appropriation act.

Controllable Budget Items — In federal budgeting this refers to programs for which the budget authority or outlays during a fiscal year can be controlled without changing existing, substantive law. The concept "relatively uncontrollable under current law" includes outlays for open-ended programs and fixed costs such as interest on the public debt, Social Security benefits, veterans' benefits, and outlays to liquidate prior-year obligations. More and more spending for federal programs has become uncontrollable or relatively uncontrollable.

Correcting Recorded Votes — Rules prohibit members from changing their votes after the result has been announced. But, occasionally hours, days, or months after a vote has been taken, a member may announce that he was "incorrectly recorded." In the Senate, a request to change one's vote almost always receives unanimous consent. In the House, members are prohibited from changing their votes if tallied by the electronic voting system. If the vote was taken by roll call, a change is permissible if consent is granted.

Corrections Calendar — Members of the House may place on this calendar bills reported favorably from committee that repeal rules and regulations considered excessive or unnecessary. Bills on the Corrections Calendar normally are called on the second and fourth Tuesday of each month at the discretion of the House Speaker in consultation with the minority leader. A bill must be on the calendar for at least three legislative days before it can be brought up for floor consideration. Once on the floor, a bill is subject to one hour of debate equally divided between the chairman and ranking member of the committee of jurisdiction. A vote may be called on whether to recommit the bill to committee with or without instructions. To pass, a three-fifths majority, or 261 votes if all House members vote, is required.

Cosponsor — *(See Bills Introduced.)*

Current Services Estimates — Estimated budget authority and outlays for federal programs and operations for the forthcoming fiscal year based on continuation of existing levels of service without policy changes. These estimates of budget authority and outlays, accompanied by the underlying economic and policy assumptions upon which they are based, are transmitted by the president to Congress when the budget is submitted.

Custody of the Papers — To reconcile differences between the House and Senate versions of a bill, a conference may be arranged. The chamber with "custody of the papers" — the engrossed bill, engrossed amendments, messages of transmittal — is the only body empowered to request the conference. By custom, the chamber that asks for a conference is the last to act on the conference report once agreement has been reached on the bill by the conferees.

Custody of the papers sometimes is manipulated to ensure that a particular chamber acts either first or last on the conference report.

Deferral — Executive branch action to defer, or delay, the spending of appropriated money. The 1974 Congressional Budget and Impoundment Control Act requires a special message from the president to Congress reporting a proposed deferral of spending. Deferrals may not extend beyond the end of the fiscal year in which the message is transmitted. A federal district court in 1986 struck down the president's authority to defer spending for policy reasons; the ruling was upheld by a federal appeals court in 1987. Congress can and has prohibited proposed deferrals by enacting a law doing so; most often cancellations of proposed deferrals are included in appropriations bills. *(See also Rescission.)*

Dilatory Motion — A motion made for the purpose of killing time and preventing action on a bill or amendment. House rules outlaw dilatory motions, but enforcement is largely within the discretion of the Speaker or chairman of the Committee of the Whole. The Senate does not have a rule banning dilatory motions, except under cloture.

Discharge a Committee — Occasionally, attempts are made to relieve a committee from jurisdiction over a measure before it. This is attempted more often in the House than in the Senate, and the procedure rarely is successful.

In the House, if a committee does not report a bill within 30 days after the measure is referred to it, any member may file a discharge motion. Once offered, the motion is treated as a petition needing the signatures of 218 members (a majority of the House). After the required signatures have been obtained, there is a delay of seven days. Thereafter, on the second and fourth Mondays of each month, except during the last six days of a session, any member who has signed the petition must be recognized, if he so desires, to move that the committee be discharged. Debate on the motion to discharge is limited to 20 minutes, and, if the motion is carried, consideration of the bill becomes a matter of high privilege.

If a resolution to consider a bill is held up in the Rules Committee for more than seven legislative days, any member may enter a motion to discharge the committee. The motion is handled like any other discharge petition in the House.

Occasionally, to expedite noncontroversial legislative business, a committee is discharged by unanimous consent of the House, and a petition is not required. *(Senate procedure, see Discharge Resolution.)*

Discharge Calendar — The House calendar to which motions to discharge committees are referred when they have the required number of signatures (218) and are awaiting floor action.

Discharge Petition — *(See Discharge a Committee.)*

Discharge Resolution — In the Senate, a special motion that any senator may introduce to relieve a committee from consideration of a bill before it. The resolution can be called up for Senate approval or disapproval in the same manner as any other Senate business. *(House procedure, see Discharge a Committee.)*

Division of a Question for Voting — A practice that is more common in the Senate but also used in the House, a member may demand a division of an amendment or a motion for purposes of voting. Where an amendment or motion can be divided, the individual parts are voted on separately when a member demands a division. This procedure occurs most often during the consideration of conference reports.

Division Vote — *(See Standing Vote.)*

Enacting Clause — Key phrase in bills beginning, "Be it enacted by the Senate and House of Representatives . . ." A successful motion to strike it from legislation kills the measure.

Engrossed Bill — The final copy of a bill as passed by one chamber, with the text as amended by floor action and certified by the clerk of the House or the secretary of the Senate.

Enrolled Bill — The final copy of a bill that has been passed in identical form by both chambers. It is certified by an officer of the house of origin (clerk of the House or secretary of the Senate) and then sent on for the signatures of the House Speaker, the Senate president pro tempore and the president of the United States. An enrolled bill is printed on parchment.

Entitlement Program — A federal program that guarantees a certain level of benefits to persons or other entities who meet requirements set by law, such as Social Security, farm price supports, or unemployment benefits. It thus leaves no discretion with Congress on how much money to appropriate, and some entitlements carry permanent appropriations.

Executive Calendar — This is a non-legislative calendar in the Senate on which presidential documents such as treaties and nominations are listed.

Executive Document — A document, usually a treaty, sent to the Senate by the president for consideration or approval. Executive documents are identified for each session of Congress according to the following pattern: Executive A, 97th Congress, 1st Session; Executive B, and so on. They are referred to committee in the same manner as other measures. Unlike legislative documents, however, treaties do not die at the end of a Congress but remain "live" proposals until acted on by the Senate or withdrawn by the president.

Executive Session — A meeting of a Senate or House committee (or occasionally of either chamber) that only its members may attend. Witnesses regularly appear at committee meetings in executive session — for example, Defense Department officials during presentations of classified defense information. Other members of Congress may be invited, but the public and press are not to attend.

Expenditures — The actual spending of money as distinguished from the appropriation of funds. Expenditures are made by the disbursing officers of the administration; appropriations are made only by Congress. The two are rarely identical in any fiscal year. In addition to some current budget authority, expenditures may represent budget authority made available one, two, or more years earlier.

Federal Debt — The federal debt consists of public debt, which occurs when the Treasury or the Federal Financing Bank (FFB) borrows money directly from the public or another fund or account, and agency debt, which is incurred when a federal agency other than Treasury or the FFB is authorized by law to borrow money from the public or another fund or account. The public debt comprises about 99 percent of the gross federal debt.

Filibuster — A time-delaying tactic associated with the Senate and used by a minority in an effort to prevent a vote on a bill or amendment that probably would pass if voted upon directly. The most common method is to take advantage of the Senate's rules permitting unlimited debate, but other forms of parliamentary maneuvering may be used. The stricter rules of the House make filibusters more difficult, but delaying tactics are employed occasionally through various procedural devices allowed by House rules. *(Senate filibusters, see Cloture.)*

Fiscal Year — Financial operations of the government are carried out in a 12-month fiscal year, beginning on Oct. 1 and ending on Sept. 30. The fiscal year carries the date of the calendar year in which it ends. (From fiscal year 1844 to fiscal year 1976, the fiscal year began July 1 and ended the following June 30.)

Five-Minute Rule — A debate-limiting rule of the House that is invoked when the House sits as the Committee of the Whole. Under the rule, a member offering an amendment is allowed to speak five minutes in its favor, and an opponent of the amendment is allowed to speak five minutes in opposition. Debate is then closed. In practice, amendments regularly are debated more than 10 minutes, with members gaining the floor by offering pro forma amendments or obtaining unanimous consent to speak longer than five minutes. *(See Strike Out the Last Word.)*

Floor Manager — A member who has the task of steering legislation through floor debate and the amendment process to a final vote in the House or the Senate. Floor managers usually are chairmen or ranking members of the committee that reported the bill. Managers are responsible for apportioning the debate time granted supporters of the bill. The ranking minority member of the committee normally apportions time for the minority party's participation in the debate.

Frank — A member's facsimile signature, which is used on envelopes in lieu of stamps, for the member's official outgoing mail. The "franking privilege" is the right to send mail postage-free.

Functions (Functional Classifications) — Categories of spending established for accounting purposes to keep track of specific expenditures. Each account is placed in the single function (such as national defense, agriculture, health, etc.) that best represents its major purpose, regardless of the agency administering the program. The functions do not correspond directly with appropriations or with the budgets of individual agencies. *(See also Budget Resolution.)*

Germane — Pertaining to the subject matter of the measure at hand. All House amendments must be germane to the bill being considered. The Senate requires that amendments be germane when they are proposed to general appropriation bills, bills being considered once cloture has been adopted, or, frequently, when proceeding under a unanimous consent agreement placing a time limit on consideration of a bill. The 1974 budget act also requires that amendments to concurrent budget resolutions be germane. In the House, floor debate must be germane, and the first three hours of debate each day in the Senate must be germane to the pending business.

Gramm-Rudman-Hollings Deficit Reduction Act — *(See Budget Process, Sequestration.)*

Grandfather Clause — A provision exempting persons or other entities already engaged in an activity from rules or legislation affecting that activity. Grandfather clauses sometimes are added to legislation in order to avoid antagonizing groups with established interests in the activities affected.

Grants-in-Aid — Payments by the federal government to states, local governments, or individuals in support of specified programs, services, or activities.

Hearings — Committee sessions for taking testimony from witnesses. At hearings on legislation, witnesses usually include specialists, government officials, and spokespersons for individuals or entities affected by the bill or bills under study. Hearings related to special investigations bring forth a variety of witnesses. Committees sometimes use their subpoena power to summon reluctant witnesses. The public and press may attend open hearings but are barred from closed, or "executive," hearings. The vast majority of hearings are open to the public. *(See Executive Session.)*

Hold-Harmless Clause — A provision added to legislation to ensure that recipients of federal funds do not receive less in a future year than they did in the current year if a new formula for allocating funds authorized in the legislation would result in a reduction to the recipients. This clause has been used most frequently to soften the impact of sudden reductions in federal grants.

Hopper — Box on House clerk's desk where members deposit bills and resolutions to introduce them.

Hour Rule — A provision in the rules of the House that permits one hour of debate time for each member on amendments debated in the House of Representatives sitting as the House. Therefore, the House normally amends bills while sitting as the Committee of the Whole, where the five-minute rule on amendments operates. *(See Committee of the Whole, Five-Minute Rule.)*

House — The House of Representatives, as distinct from the Senate, although each body is a "house" of Congress.

House as in Committee of the Whole — A procedure that can be used to expedite consideration of certain measures such as continuing resolutions and, when there is debate, private bills. The procedure only can be invoked with the unanimous consent of the House or a rule from the Rules Committee and has procedural elements of both the House sitting as the House of Representatives, such as the Speaker presiding and the previous question motion being in order, and the House sitting as the Committee of the Whole, such as the five-minute rule pertaining.

House Calendar — A listing for action by the House of public bills that do not directly or indirectly appropriate money or raise revenue.

Immunity — The constitutional privilege of members of Congress to make verbal statements on the floor and in committee for which they cannot be sued or arrested for slander or libel. Also, freedom from arrest while traveling to or from sessions of Congress or on official business. Members in this status may be arrested only for treason, felonies, or a breach of the peace, as defined by congressional manuals.

Impoundments — Any action taken by the executive branch that delays or precludes the obligation or expenditure of budget authority previously approved by Congress. The Congressional Budget and Impoundment Control Act of 1974 was enacted after frequent use of impoundments by President Richard Nixon. In addition to creating the budget process currently used, the 1974 law established procedures for congressional approval or disapproval of temporary or permanent impoundments, which are called deferrals and rescissions.

Joint Committee — A committee composed of a specified number of members of both the House and Senate. A joint committee may be investigative or research-oriented, an example of the latter being the Joint Economic Committee. Others have housekeeping duties such as the joint committees on Printing and on the Library of Congress.

Joint Resolution — A joint resolution, designated H J Res or S J Res, requires the approval of both houses and the signature of the president, just as a bill does, and has the force of law if approved. There is no practical difference between a bill and a joint resolution. A joint resolution generally is used to deal with a limited matter such as a single appropriation.

Joint resolutions also are used to propose amendments to the Constitution. They do not require a presidential signature but become a part of the Constitution when three-fourths of the states have ratified them.

Journal — The official record of the proceedings of the House and Senate. The *Journal* records the actions taken in each chamber, but, unlike the *Congressional Record*, it does not include the substantially verbatim report of speeches, debates, statements, and the like.

Law — An act of Congress that has been signed by the president or passed over his veto by Congress. Public bills, when signed, become public laws, and are cited by the letters PL and a hyphenated number. The two digits before the hyphen correspond to the Congress, and the one or more digits after the hyphen refer to the numerical sequence in which the bills were signed by the president during that Congress. Private bills, when signed, become private laws. *(See also Pocket Veto, Slip Laws, Statutes at Large, U.S. Code.)*

Legislative Day — The "day" extending from the time either house meets after an adjournment until the time it next adjourns. Because the House normally adjourns from day to day, legislative days and calendar days usually coincide. But in the Senate, a legislative day may, and frequently does, extend over several calendar days. *(See Recess.)*

Legislative Veto — A procedure, no longer allowed, permitting either the House or Senate, or both chambers, to review proposed executive branch regulations or actions and to block or modify those with which they disagreed.

The specifics of the procedure varied, but Congress generally provided for a legislative veto by including in a bill a provision that administrative rules or action taken to implement the law were to go into effect at the end of a designated period of time unless blocked by either or both houses of Congress. Another version of the veto provided for congressional reconsideration and rejection of regulations already in effect.

The Supreme Court June 23, 1983, struck down the legislative veto as an unconstitutional violation of the lawmaking procedure provided in the Constitution.

Loan Guarantees — Loans to third parties for which the federal government in the event of default guarantees, in whole or in part, the repayment of principal or interest to a lender or holder of a security.

Lobby — A group seeking to influence the passage or defeat of legislation. Originally the term referred to persons frequenting the lobbies or corridors of legislative chambers in order to speak to lawmakers.

The definition of a lobby and the activity of lobbying are matters of differing interpretation. By some definitions, lobbying is limited to direct attempts to influence lawmakers through personal interviews and persuasion. Under other definitions, lobbying includes attempts at indirect, or "grassroots," influence, such as persuading members of a group to write or visit their district's representative and state's senators or attempting to create a climate of opinion favorable to a desired legislative goal.

The right to attempt to influence legislation is based on the First Amendment to the Constitution, which says Congress shall make no law abridging the right of the people "to petition the government for a redress of grievances."

Majority Leader — The majority leader is elected by his or her party colleagues. In the Senate, in consultation with the minority leader and his colleagues, the majority leader directs the legislative schedule for the chamber. He also is his party's spokesperson and chief strategist. In the House, the majority leader is second to the Speaker in the majority party's leadership and serves as his party's legislative strategist.

Majority Whip — In effect, the assistant majority leader, in either the House or Senate. His job is to help marshal majority forces in support of party strategy and legislation.

Manual — The official handbook in each house prescribing in detail its organization, procedures, and operations.

Marking Up a Bill — Going through the contents of a piece of legislation in committee or subcommittee to, for example, consider its provisions in large and small portions, act on amendments to provisions and proposed revisions to the language, and insert new sections and phraseology. If the bill

is extensively amended, the committee's version may be introduced as a separate bill, with a new number, before being considered by the full House or Senate. *(See Clean Bill.)*

Minority Leader — Floor leader for the minority party in each chamber. *(See also Majority Leader.)*

Minority Whip — Performs duties of whip for the minority party. *(See also Majority Whip.)*

Morning Hour — The time set aside at the beginning of each legislative day for the consideration of regular, routine business. The "hour" is of indefinite duration in the House, where it is rarely used.

In the Senate it is the first two hours of a session following an adjournment, as distinguished from a recess. The morning hour can be terminated earlier if the morning business has been completed. Business includes such matters as messages from the president, communications from the heads of departments, messages from the House, the presentation of petitions, reports of standing and select committees, and the introduction of bills and resolutions. During the first hour of the morning hour in the Senate, no motion to proceed to the consideration of any bill on the calendar is in order except by unanimous consent. During the second hour, motions can be made but must be decided without debate. Senate committees may meet while the Senate conducts morning hour.

Motion — In the House or Senate chamber, a request by a member to institute any one of a wide array of parliamentary actions. A member "moves" for a certain procedure, such as the consideration of a measure. The precedence of motions, and whether they are debatable, is set forth in the House and Senate manuals.

Nominations — Presidential appointments to office subject to Senate confirmation. Although most nominations win quick Senate approval, some are controversial and become the topic of hearings and debate. Sometimes senators object to appointees for patronage reasons — for example, when a nomination to a local federal job is made without consulting the senators of the state concerned. In some situations a senator may object that the nominee is "personally obnoxious" to him or her. Usually other senators join in blocking such appointments out of courtesy to their colleagues. *(See Senatorial Courtesy.)*

Obligations — Orders placed, contracts awarded, services received, and similar transactions during a given period that will require payments during the same or future period. Such amounts include outlays for which obligations had not been previously recorded and reflect adjustments for differences between obligations previously recorded and actual outlays to liquidate those obligations.

One-Minute Speeches — Addresses by House members at the beginning of a legislative day. The speeches may cover any subject but are limited to one minute's duration.

Outlays — Payments made (generally through the issuance of checks or disbursement of cash) to liquidate obligations. Outlays during a fiscal year may be for the payment of obligations incurred in prior years or in the same year.

Override a Veto — If the president disapproves a bill and sends it back to Congress with objections, Congress may try to override veto and enact the bill into law. Neither house is required to attempt to override a veto. The override of a veto requires a recorded vote with a two-thirds majority in each chamber. The question put to each house is: "Shall the bill pass, the objections of the president to the contrary notwithstanding?" *(See also Pocket Veto, Veto.)*

Oversight Committee — A congressional committee, or designated subcommittee of a committee, that is charged with general oversight of one or more federal agencies' programs and activities. Usually, the oversight panel for a particular agency also is the authorizing committee for that agency's programs and operations.

Pair — A voluntary, informal arrangement that two lawmakers, usually on opposite sides of an issue, make on recorded votes. In many cases the result is to subtract a vote from each side, with no effect on the outcome. Pairs are not authorized in the rules of either house, are not counted in tabulating the final result, and have no official standing. However, members pairing are identified in the *Congressional Record*, along with their positions on such votes, if known. A member who expects to be absent for a vote can pair with a member who plans to vote, with the latter agreeing to withhold his or her vote.

There are three types of pairs: 1) A live pair involves a member who is present for a vote and another who is absent. The member in attendance votes and then withdraws the vote, announcing that he or she has a live pair with colleague "X" and stating how the two members would have voted, one in favor, the other opposed. A live pair may affect the outcome of a closely contested vote, since it subtracts one "yea" or one "nay" from the final tally. A live pair may cover one or several specific issues. 2) A general pair, widely used in the House, does not entail any arrangement between two members and does not affect the vote. Members who expect to be absent notify the clerk that they wish to make a general pair. Each member then is paired with another desiring a pair, and their names are listed in the *Congressional Record*. The member may or may not be paired with another taking the opposite position, and no indication of how the members would have voted is given. 3) A specific pair is similar to a general pair, except that the opposing stands of the two members are identified and printed in the *Record*.

Petition — A request or plea sent to one or both chambers from an organization or private citizens' group asking support of particular legislation or favorable consideration of a matter not yet receiving congressional attention. Petitions are referred to appropriate committees.

Pocket Veto — The act of the president in withholding approval of a bill after Congress has adjourned. When Congress is in session, a bill becomes law without the president's signature if the president does not act upon it within 10 days, excluding Sundays, from the time he gets it. But if Congress adjourns sine die within that 10-day period, the bill will die even if the president does not formally veto it.

The Supreme Court in 1986 agreed to decide whether the president can pocket veto a bill during recesses and between sessions of the same Congress or only between Congresses. The justices in 1987 declared the case moot, however, because the bill in question was invalid once the case reached the Court. *(See also Veto.)*

Point of Order — An objection raised by a member that the chamber is departing from rules governing its conduct of business. The objector cites the rule violated, the chair sustaining the objection if correctly made. Order is restored by the chair's suspending proceedings of the chamber until it conforms to the prescribed "order of business."

President of the Senate — Under the Constitution, the vice president of the United States presides over the Senate. In his absence, the president pro tempore, or a senator designated by the president pro tempore, presides over the chamber.

President Pro Tempore — The chief officer of the Senate in the absence of the vice president; literally, but loosely, the president for a time. The president pro tempore is elected by the senators, and the recent practice has been to elect the senator of the majority party with the longest period of continuous service.

Previous Question — A motion for the previous question, when carried, has the effect of cutting off all debate, preventing the offering of further amendments, and forcing a vote on the pending matter. In the House, the previous question is not permitted in the Committee of the Whole. The motion for the previous question is a debate-limiting device and is not in order in the Senate.

Printed Amendment — A House rule guarantees five minutes of floor debate in support and five minutes in opposition, and no other debate time, on amendments printed in the *Congressional Record* at least one day prior to the amendment's consideration in the Committee of the Whole. In the Senate, although amendments may be submitted for printing, they have no parliamentary standing or status. An amendment submitted for printing in the Senate, however, may be called up by any senator.

Private Calendar — In the House, private bills dealing with individual matters such as claims against the government, immigration, or land titles are put on this calendar. The private calendar must be called on the first Tuesday of each month, and the Speaker may call it on the third Tuesday of each month as well.

When a private bill is before the chamber, two members may block its consideration, which recommits the bill to committee. Backers of a recommitted private bill have recourse. The measure can be put into an "omnibus claims bill" — several private bills rolled into one. As with any bill, no part of an omnibus claims bill may be deleted without a vote. When the private bill goes back to the House floor in this form, it can be deleted from the omnibus bill only by majority vote.

Privilege — Relates to the rights of members of Congress and to the relative priority of the motions and actions they may make in their respective chambers. The two are distinct. "Privileged questions" deal with legislative business. "Questions of privilege" concern legislators themselves.

Privileged Questions — The order in which bills, motions, and other legislative measures are considered by Congress is governed by strict priorities. A motion to table, for instance, is more privileged than a motion to recommit. Thus, a motion to recommit can be superseded by a motion to table, and a vote would be forced on the latter motion only. A motion to adjourn, however, takes precedence over a tabling motion and thus is considered of the "highest privilege." *(See also Questions of Privilege.)*

Pro Forma Amendment — *(See Strike Out the Last Word.)*

Public Laws — *(See Law.)*

Questions of Privilege — These are matters affecting members of Congress individually or collectively. Matters affecting the rights, safety, dignity, and integrity of proceedings of the House or Senate as a whole are questions of privilege in both chambers.

Questions involving individual members are called questions of "personal privilege." A member rising to ask a question of personal privilege is given precedence over almost all other proceedings. An annotation in the House rules points out that the privilege rests primarily on the Constitution, which gives a member a conditional immunity from arrest and an unconditional freedom to speak in the House. *(See also Privileged Questions.)*

Quorum — The number of members whose presence is necessary for the transaction of business. In the Senate and House, it is a majority of the membership. A quorum is 100 in the Committee of the Whole House. If a point of order is made that a quorum is not present, the only business that is in order is either a motion to adjourn or a motion to direct the sergeant-at-arms to request the attendance of absentees.

Readings of Bills — Traditional parliamentary procedure required bills to be read three times before they were passed. This custom is of little modern significance. Normally a bill is considered to have its first reading when it is introduced and printed, by title, in the *Congressional Record*. In the House, its second reading comes when floor consideration begins. (This is the most likely point at which there is an actual reading of the bill, if there is any.) The second reading in the Senate is supposed to occur on the legislative day after the measure is introduced, but before it is referred to committee. The third reading (again, usually by title) takes place when floor action has been completed on amendments.

Recess — Distinguished from adjournment in that a recess does not end a legislative day and therefore does not interrupt unfinished business. The rules in each house set forth certain matters to be taken up and disposed of at the beginning of each legislative day. The House usually adjourns from day to day. The Senate often recesses, thus meeting on the same legislative day for several calendar days or even weeks at a time.

Recognition — The power of recognition of a member is lodged in the Speaker of the House and the presiding officer of the Senate. The presiding officer names the member who will speak first when two or more members simultaneously request recognition.

Recommit to Committee — A motion, made on the floor after a bill has been debated, to return it to the committee that reported it. If approved, recommittal usually is considered a death blow to the bill. In the House, a motion to recommit can be made only by a member opposed to the bill, and, in recognizing a member to make the motion, the Speaker gives preference to members of the minority party over majority party members.

A motion to recommit may include instructions to the committee to report the bill again with specific amendments or by a certain date. Or, the instructions may direct that a particular study be made, with no definite deadline for further action. If the recommittal motion includes instructions to "report the bill back forthwith" and the motion is adopted, floor action on the bill continues; the committee does not actually reconsider the legislation.

Reconciliation — The 1974 budget act provides for a "reconciliation" procedure for bringing existing tax and spending laws into conformity with ceilings enacted in the congressional budget resolution. Under the procedure, Congress instructs designated legislative committees to approve measures adjusting revenues and expenditures by a certain amount. The committees have a deadline by which they must report the legislation, but they have the discretion of deciding what changes are to be made. The recommendations of the various committees are consolidated without change by the Budget committees into an omnibus reconciliation bill, which then must be considered and approved by both houses of Congress. The orders to congressional committees to report recommendations for reconciliation bills are called reconciliation instructions, and they are contained in the budget resolution. Reconciliation instructions are not binding, but Congress must meet annual deficit targets to avoid the automatic spending cuts of sequestration, which means it must also meet the goal of reconciliation. *(See also Budget Resolution, Sequestration.)*

Reconsider a Vote — A motion to reconsider the vote by which an action was taken has, until it is disposed of, the effect of putting the action in abeyance. In the Senate, the motion can be made only by a member who voted on the prevailing side of the original question or by a member who did not vote at all. In the House, it can be made only by a member on the prevailing side.

A common practice in the Senate after close votes on an issue is a motion to reconsider, followed by a motion to table the motion to reconsider. On this motion to table, senators vote as they voted on the original question, which allows the motion to table to prevail, assuming there are no switches. The matter then is finally closed and further motions to reconsider are not entertained. In the House, as a routine precaution, a motion to reconsider usually is made every time a measure is passed. Such a motion almost always is tabled immediately, thus shutting off the possibility of future reconsideration, except by unanimous consent.

Motions to reconsider must be entered in the Senate within the next two days of actual session after the original vote has been taken. In the House they must be entered either on the same day or on the next succeeding day the House is in session.

Recorded Vote — A vote upon which each member's stand is individually made known. In the Senate, this is accomplished through a roll call of the entire membership, to which each senator on the floor must answer "yea," "nay," or, if he or she does not wish to vote, "present." Since January 1973, the House has used an electronic voting system for recorded votes, including yea-and-nay votes formerly taken by roll calls.

When not required by the Constitution, a recorded vote can be obtained on questions in the House on the demand of one-fifth (44 members) of a quorum or one-fourth (25) of a quorum in the Committee of the Whole. *(See Yeas and Nays.)*

Report — Both a verb and a noun as a congressional term. A committee that has been examining a bill referred to it by the parent chamber "reports" its findings and recommendations to the chamber when it completes consideration and returns the measure. The process is called "reporting" a bill.

A "report" is the document setting forth the committee's explanation of its action. Senate and House reports are numbered separately and are designated S Rept or H Rept. When a committee report is not unanimous, the dissenting committee members may file a statement of their views, called minority or dissenting views and referred to as a minority report. Members in disagreement with some provisions of a bill may file additional or supplementary views. Sometimes a bill is reported without a committee recommendation.

Adverse reports occasionally are submitted by legislative committees. However, when a committee is opposed to a bill, it usually fails to report the bill at all. Some laws require that committee reports — favorable or adverse — be made.

Rescission — An item in an appropriations bill rescinding or canceling budget authority previously appropriated but not spent. Also, the repeal of a previous appropriation by Congress at the request of the president to cut spending or because the budget authority no longer is needed. Under the 1974 budget act, however, unless Congress approves a rescission within 45 days of continuous session after receipt of the proposal, the funds must be made available for obligation. (See also Deferral.)

Resolution — A "simple" resolution, designated H Res or S Res, deals with matters entirely within the prerogatives of one house or the other. It requires neither passage by the other chamber nor approval by the president, and it does not have the force of law. Most resolutions deal with the rules or procedures of one house. They also are used to express the sentiments of a single house such as condolences to the family of a deceased member or to comment on foreign policy or executive business. A simple resolution is the vehicle for a "rule" from the House Rules Committee. (See also Concurrent and Joint Resolutions, Rules.)

Rider — An amendment, usually not germane, that its sponsor hopes to get through more easily by including it in other legislation. Riders become law if the bills embodying them are enacted. Amendments providing legislative directives in appropriations bills are outstanding examples of riders, though technically legislation is banned from appropriations bills. The House, unlike the Senate, has a strict germaneness rule; thus, riders usually are Senate devices to get legislation enacted quickly or to bypass lengthy House consideration and, possibly, opposition.

Rules — The term has two specific congressional meanings. A rule may be a standing order governing the conduct of House or Senate business and listed among the permanent rules of either chamber. The rules deal with issues such as duties of officers, the order of business, admission to the floor, parliamentary procedures on handling amendments, and voting and jurisdictions of committees.

In the House, a rule also may be a resolution reported by its Rules Committee to govern the handling of a particular bill on the floor. The committee may report a "rule," also called a "special order," in the form of a simple resolution. If the resolution is adopted by the House, the temporary rule becomes as valid as any standing rule and lapses only after action has been completed on the measure to which it pertains. A rule sets the time limit on general debate. It also may

waive points of order against provisions of the bill in question such as non-germane language or against certain amendments intended to be proposed to the bill from the floor. It may even forbid all amendments or all amendments except those proposed by the legislative committee that handled the bill. In this instance, it is known as a "closed" or "gag" rule as opposed to an "open" rule, which puts no limitation on floor amendments, thus leaving the bill completely open to alteration by the adoption of germane amendments.

Secretary of the Senate — Chief administrative officer of the Senate, responsible for overseeing the duties of Senate employees, educating Senate pages, administering oaths, handling the registration of lobbyists, and handling other tasks necessary for the continuing operation of the Senate. (See also Clerk of the House.)

Select or Special Committee — A committee set up for a special purpose and, usually, for a limited time by resolution of either the House or Senate. Most special committees are investigative and lack legislative authority — legislation is not referred to them and they cannot report bills to their parent chamber. (See also Standing Committees.)

Senatorial Courtesy — Sometimes referred to as "the courtesy of the Senate," it is a general practice — with no written rule — applied to consideration of executive nominations. Generally, it means that nominations from a state are not to be confirmed unless they have been approved by the senators of the president's party of that state, with other senators following their colleagues' lead in the attitude they take toward consideration of such nominations. (See Nominations.)

Sequestration — A procedure to cancel (or withhold) budgetary resources. Originally approved under the 1985 Gramm-Rudman-Hollings deficit reduction law, as amended in 1987, it threatened massive across-the-board cuts in federal programs in 1990 and later. Congress in late 1990 changed the law to provide a set of three sequesters, each of which kicks in 15 days after Congress adjourns. One offsets discretionary appropriations for the coming year that exceed statutory limitations and only affects discretionary spending. The second is triggered if Congress enacts entitlement spending increases or revenue decreases during the year and affects "non-exempt" entitlements. The third offsets an increase in the deficit above the limit set in law if the first two sequestions have not eliminated the excess deficit; it will cover all non-exempt spending. (See Budget Process.)

Sine Die — (See Adjournment Sine Die.)

Slip Laws — The first official publication of a bill that has been enacted and signed into law. Each is published separately in unbound single-sheet or pamphlet form. (See also Law, Statutes at Large, U.S. Code.)

Speaker — The presiding officer of the House of Representatives, selected by the caucus of the party to which he or she belongs and formally elected by the whole House.

Special Session — A session of Congress after it has adjourned sine die, completing its regular session. Special sessions are convened by the president.

Spending Authority — The 1974 budget act defines spending authority as borrowing authority, contract authority, and entitlement authority for which budget authority is not provided in advance by appropriation acts.

Sponsor — *(See Bills Introduced.)*

Standing Committees — Committees permanently established by House and Senate rules. The standing committees of the House were extensively reorganized in 1995 by the 104th Congress. The last major realignment of Senate committees was in the committee system reorganization of 1977. The standing committees are legislative committees — legislation may be referred to them and they may report bills and resolutions to their parent chambers. *(See also Select or Special Committees.)*

Standing Vote — A nonrecorded vote used in both the House and Senate. (A standing vote also is called a division vote.) Members in favor of a proposal stand and are counted by the presiding officer. Then members opposed stand and are counted. There is no record of how individual members voted.

Statutes at **Large** — A chronological arrangement of the laws enacted in each session of Congress. Though indexed, the laws are not arranged by subject matter, and there is no indication of how they changed previously enacted laws. *(See also Law, Slip Laws, U.S. Code.)*

Strike From the Record — Remarks made on the House floor may offend some member, who moves that the offending words be "taken down" for the Speaker's cognizance and then expunged from the debate as published in the *Congressional Record.*

Strike Out the Last Word — A motion whereby a House member is entitled to speak for five minutes on an amendment then being debated by the chamber. A member gains recognition from the chair by moving to "strike out the last word" of the amendment or section of the bill under consideration. The motion is proforma, requires no vote, and does not change the amendment being debated.

Substitute — A motion, amendment, or entire bill introduced in place of the pending legislative business. Passage of a substitute measure kills the original measure by supplanting it. The substitute also may be amended. *(See also Amendment in the Nature of a Substitute.)*

Supplemental Appropriations Bill — Legislation appropriating funds after the regular annual appropriations bill for a federal department or agency has been enacted. A supplemental appropriation provides additional budget authority beyond original estimates for programs or activities, including new programs authorized after the enactment of the regular appropriation act, for which the need for funds is too urgent to be postponed until enactment of the next year's regular appropriation bill.

Suspend the Rules — Often a time-saving procedure for passing bills in the House. The wording of the motion, which may be made by any member recognized by the Speaker, is: "I move to suspend the rules and pass the bill . . ." A favorable vote by two-thirds of those present is required for passage. Debate is limited to 40 minutes and no amendments from the floor are permitted. If a two-thirds favorable vote is not attained, the bill may be considered later under regular procedures. The suspension procedure is in order every Monday and Tuesday and is intended to be reserved for noncontroversial bills.

Table a Bill — Motions to table, or to "lay on the table," are used to block or kill amendments or other parliamentary questions. When approved, a tabling motion is considered the final disposition of that issue. One of the most widely used parliamentary procedures, the motion to table is not debatable, and adoption requires a simple majority vote.

In the Senate, however, different language sometimes is used. The motion may be worded to let a bill "lie on the table," perhaps for subsequent "picking up." This motion is more flexible, keeping the bill pending for later action, if desired. Tabling motions on amendments are effective debate-ending devices in the Senate.

Teller Vote — This is a largely moribund House procedure in the Committee of the Whole. Members file past tellers and are counted as for or against a measure, but they are not recorded individually. In the House, tellers are ordered upon demand of one-fifth of a quorum. This is 44 in the House, 20 in the Committee of the Whole.

The House also has a recorded teller vote, now largely supplanted by the electronic voting procedure, under which the votes of each member are made public just as they would be on a recorded vote.

Treaties — Executive proposals — in the form of resolutions of ratification — which must be submitted to the Senate for approval by two-thirds of the senators present. Treaties are normally sent to the Foreign Relations Committee for scrutiny before the Senate takes action. Foreign Relations has jurisdiction over all treaties, regardless of the subject matter. Treaties are read three times and debated on the floor in much the same manner as legislative proposals. After approval by the Senate, treaties are formally ratified by the president.

Trust Funds — Funds collected and used by the federal government for carrying out specific purposes and programs according to terms of a trust agreement or statute such as the Social Security and unemployment compensation trust funds. Such funds are administered by the government in a fiduciary capacity and are not available for the general purposes of the government.

Unanimous Consent — Proceedings of the House or Senate and action on legislation often take place upon the unanimous consent of the chamber, whether or not a rule of the chamber is being violated. Unanimous consent is used to expedite floor action and frequently is used in a routine fashion such as by a senator requesting the unanimous consent of the Senate to have specified members of his or her staff present on the floor during debate on a specific amendment.

Unanimous Consent Agreement — A device used in the Senate to expedite legislation. Much of the Senate's legislative business, dealing with both minor and controversial issues, is conducted through unanimous consent or unanimous consent agreements. On major legislation, such agreements usually are printed and transmitted to all senators in advance of floor debate. Once agreed to, they are binding on all members unless the Senate, by unanimous consent, agrees to modify them. An agreement may list the order in which various bills are to be considered, specify the length of time bills and contested amendments are to be debated and when they are to be voted upon, and, frequently, require that all amendments introduced be germane to the bill under consideration. In this regard, unanimous consent agreements are similar to the "rules" issued by the House Rules Committee for bills pending in the House.

Union Calendar — Bills that directly or indirectly appropriate money or raise revenue are placed on this House calendar according to the date they are reported from committee.

U.S. Code — A consolidation and codification of the general and permanent laws of the United States arranged by subject under 50 titles, the first six dealing with general or political subjects, and the other 44 alphabetically arranged from agriculture to war. The *U.S. Code* is updated annually, and a new set of bound volumes is published every six years. *(See also Law, Slip Laws, Statutes at Large.)*

Veto — Disapproval by the president of a bill or joint resolution (other than one proposing an amendment to the Constitution). When Congress is in session, the president must veto a bill within 10 days, excluding Sundays, after receiving it; otherwise, it becomes law without his signature. When the president vetoes a bill, he returns it to the house of origin along with a message stating his objections. *(See also Pocket Veto, Override a Veto.)*

Voice Vote — In either the House or Senate, members answer "aye" or "no" in chorus, and the presiding officer decides the result. The term also is used loosely to indicate action by unanimous consent or without objection.

Whip — *(See Majority and Minority Whip.)*

Without Objection — Used in lieu of a vote on noncontroversial motions, amendments, or bills that may be passed in either the House or Senate if no member voices an objection.

Yeas and Nays — The Constitution requires that yea-and-nay votes be taken and recorded when requested by one-fifth of the members present. In the House, the Speaker determines whether one-fifth of the members present requested a vote. In the Senate, practice requires only 11 members. The Constitution requires the yeas and nays on a veto override attempt. *(See Recorded Vote.)*

Yielding — When a member has been recognized to speak, no other member may speak unless he or she obtains permission from the member recognized. This permission is called yielding and usually is requested in the form, "Will the gentleman yield to me?" While this activity occasionally is seen in the Senate, the Senate has no rule or practice to parcel out time.

Constitution of the United States

We the People of the United States, in Order to form a more perfect Union, establish Justice, insure domestic Tranquility, provide for the common defence, promote the general Welfare, and secure the Blessings of Liberty to ourselves and our Posterity, do ordain and establish this Constitution for the United States of America.

ARTICLE I

Section 1. All legislative Powers herein granted shall be vested in a Congress of the United States, which shall consist of a Senate and House of Representatives.

Section 2. The House of Representatives shall be composed of Members chosen every second Year by the People of the several States, and the Electors in each State shall have the Qualifications requisite for Electors of the most numerous Branch of the State Legislature.

No Person shall be a Representative who shall not have attained to the age of twenty five Years, and been seven Years a Citizen of the United States, and who shall not, when elected, be an Inhabitant of that State in which he shall be chosen.

[Representatives and direct Taxes shall be apportioned among the several States which may be included within this Union, according to their respective Numbers, which shall be determined by adding to the whole Number of free Persons, including those bound to Service for a Term of Years, and excluding Indians not taxed, three fifths of all other Persons.][1] The actual Enumeration shall be made within three Years after the first Meeting of the Congress of the United States, and within every subsequent Term of ten Years, in such Manner as they shall by Law direct. The Number of Representatives shall not exceed one for every thirty Thousand, but each State shall have at Least one Representative; and until such enumeration shall be made, the State of New Hampshire shall be entitled to chuse three, Massachusetts eight, Rhode-Island and Providence Plantations one, Connecticut five, New-York six, New Jersey four, Pennsylvania eight, Delaware one, Maryland six, Virginia ten, North Carolina five, South Carolina five, and Georgia three.

When vacancies happen in the Representation from any State, the Executive Authority thereof shall issue Writs of Election to fill such Vacancies.

The House of Representatives shall chuse their Speaker and other Officers; and shall have the sole Power of Impeachment.

Section 3. The Senate of the United States shall be composed of two Senators from each State, [chosen by the Legislature thereof,][2] for six Years; and each Senator shall have one Vote.

Immediately after they shall be assembled in Consequence of the first Election, they shall be divided as equally as may be into three Classes. The Seats of the Senators of the first Class shall be vacated at the Expiration of the second Year, of the second Class at the Expiration of the fourth Year, and of the third Class at the Expiration of the sixth Year, so that one third may be chosen every second Year; [and if Vacancies happen by Resignation, or otherwise, during the Recess of the Legislature of any State, the Executive thereof may make temporary Appointments until the next Meeting of the Legislature, which shall then fill such Vacancies.][3]

No Person shall be a Senator who shall not have attained to the Age of thirty Years, and been nine Years a Citizen of the United States, and who shall not, when elected, be an Inhabitant of that State for which he shall be chosen.

The Vice President of the United States shall be President of the Senate, but shall have no Vote, unless they be equally divided.

The Senate shall chuse their other Officers, and also a President pro tempore, in the Absence of the Vice President, or when he shall exercise the Office of President of the United States.

The Senate shall have the sole Power to try all Impeachments. When sitting for that Purpose, they shall be on Oath or Affirmation. When the President of the United States is tried, the Chief Justice shall preside: And no Person shall be convicted without the Concurrence of two thirds of the Members present.

Judgment in Cases of Impeachment shall not extend further than to removal from Office, and disqualification to hold and enjoy any Office of honor, Trust or Profit under the United States: but the Party convicted shall nevertheless be liable and subject to Indictment, Trial, Judgment and Punishment, according to Law.

Section 4. The Times, Places and Manner of holding Elections for Senators and Representatives, shall be prescribed in each State by the Legislature thereof; but the Congress may at any time by Law make or alter such Regulations, except as to the Places of chusing Senators.

The Congress shall assemble at least once in every Year, and such Meeting shall [be on the first Monday in December],[4] unless they shall by Law appoint a different Day.

Section 5. Each House shall be the Judge of the Elections, Returns and Qualifications of its own Members, and a Majority of each shall constitute a Quorum to do Business; but a smaller Number may adjourn from day to day, and may be authorized to compel the Attendance of absent Members, in such Manner, and under such Penalties as each House may provide.

Each House may determine the Rules of its Proceedings, punish its Members for disorderly Behaviour, and, with the Concurrence of two thirds, expel a Member.

Each House shall keep a Journal of its Proceedings, and from time to time publish the same, excepting such Parts as may in their Judgment require Secrecy; and the Yeas and Nays of the Members of either House on any question shall, at the Desire of one fifth of those Present, be entered on the Journal.

Neither House, during the Session of Congress, shall, without the Consent of the other, adjourn for more than three days, nor to any other Place than that in which the two Houses shall be sitting.

Section 6. The Senators and Representatives shall receive a Compensation for their Services, to be ascertained by Law, and paid out of the Treasury of the United States. They shall in all Cases, except Treason, Felony and Breach of the Peace, be privileged from Arrest during their Attendance at the Session of their respective Houses, and in going to and returning from the same; and for any Speech or Debate in either House, they shall not be questioned in any other Place.

No Senator or Representative shall, during the Time for which he was elected, be appointed to any civil Office under the Authority of the United States, which shall have been created, or the Emoluments whereof shall have been encreased during such time; and no Person holding any Office under the United States, shall be a Member of either House during his Continuance in Office.

Section 7. All Bills for raising Revenue shall originate in the House of Representatives; but the Senate may propose or concur with Amendments as on other Bills.

Every Bill which shall have passed the House of Representatives and the Senate, shall, before it become a Law, be presented to the President of the United States; If he approve he shall sign it, but if not he shall return it, with his Objections to that House in which it shall have originated, who shall enter the Objections at large on their Journal, and proceed to reconsider it. If after such Reconsideration two thirds of that House shall agree to pass the Bill, it shall be sent, together with the Objections, to the other House, by which it shall likewise be reconsidered, and if approved by two thirds of that House, it shall become a Law. But in all such Cases the Votes of both Houses shall be determined by yeas and Nays, and the Names of the Persons voting for and against the Bill shall be entered on the Journal of each House respectively. If any Bill shall not be returned by the President within ten Days (Sundays excepted) after it shall have been presented to him, the Same shall be a Law, in like Manner as if he had signed it, unless the Congress by their Adjournment prevent its Return, in which Case it shall not be a Law.

Every Order, Resolution, or Vote to which the Concurrence of the Senate and House of Representatives may be necessary (except on a question of Adjournment) shall be presented to the President of the United States; and before the Same shall take Effect, shall be approved by him, or being disapproved by him, shall be repassed by two thirds of the Senate and House of Representatives, according to the Rules and Limitations prescribed in the Case of a Bill.

Section 8. The Congress shall have Power To lay and collect Taxes, Duties, Imposts and Excises, to pay the Debts and provide for the common Defence and general Welfare of the United States; but all Duties, Imposts and Excises shall be uniform throughout the United States;

To borrow Money on the credit of the United States;

To regulate Commerce with foreign Nations, and among the several States, and with the Indian Tribes;

To establish an uniform Rule of Naturalization, and uniform Laws on the subject of Bankruptcies throughout the United States;

To coin Money, regulate the Value thereof, and of foreign Coin, and fix the Standard of Weights and Measures;

To provide for the Punishment of counterfeiting the Securities and current Coin of the United States;

To establish Post Offices and post Roads;

To promote the Progress of Science and useful Arts, by securing for limited Times to Authors and Inventors the exclusive Right to their respective Writings and Discoveries;

To constitute Tribunals inferior to the supreme Court;

To define and punish Piracies and Felonies committed on the high Seas, and Offences against the Law of Nations;

To declare War, grant Letters of Marque and Reprisal, and make Rules concerning Captures on Land and Water;

To raise and support Armies, but no Appropriation of Money to that Use shall be for a longer Term than two Years;

To provide and maintain a Navy;

To make Rules for the Government and Regulation of the land and naval Forces;

To provide for calling forth the Militia to execute the Laws of the Union, suppress Insurrections and repel Invasions;

To provide for organizing, arming, and disciplining, the Militia, and for governing such Part of them as may be employed in the Service of the United States, reserving to the States respectively, the Appointment of the Officers, and the Authority of training the Militia according to the discipline prescribed by Congress;

To exercise exclusive Legislation in all Cases whatsoever, over such District (not exceeding ten Miles square) as may, by Cession of particular States, and the Acceptance of Congress, become the Seat of the Government of the United States, and to exercise like Authority over all Places purchased by the Consent of the Legislature of the State in which the Same shall be, for the Erection of Forts, Magazines, Arsenals, dock-Yards, and other needful Buildings; — And

To make all Laws which shall be necessary and proper for carrying into Execution the foregoing Powers, and all other Powers vested by this Constitution in the Government of the United States, or in any Department or Officer thereof.

Section 9. The Migration or Importation of such Persons as any of the States now existing shall think proper to admit, shall not be prohibited by the Congress prior to the Year one thousand eight hundred and eight, but a Tax or duty may be imposed on such Importation, not exceeding ten dollars for each Person.

The Privilege of the Writ of Habeas Corpus shall not be suspended, unless when in Cases of Rebellion or Invasion the public Safety may require it.

No Bill of Attainder or ex post facto Law shall be passed.

No Capitation, or other direct, Tax shall be laid, unless in Proportion to the Census or Enumeration herein before directed to be taken.[5]

No Tax or Duty shall be laid on Articles exported from any State.

No Preference shall be given by any Regulation of Commerce or Revenue to the Ports of one State over those of another; nor shall Vessels bound to, or from, one State, be obliged to enter, clear, or pay Duties in another.

No Money shall be drawn from the Treasury, but in Consequence of Appropriations made by Law; and a regular Statement and Account of the Receipts and Expenditures of all public Money shall be published from time to time.

No Title of Nobility shall be granted by the United States: And no Person holding any Office of Profit or Trust under them, shall, without the Consent of the Congress, accept of any present, Emolument, Office, or Title, of any kind whatever, from any King, Prince, or foreign State.

Section 10. No State shall enter into any Treaty, Alliance, or Confederation; grant Letters of Marque and Reprisal; coin Money; emit Bills of Credit; make any Thing but gold and silver Coin a Tender in Payment of Debts; pass any Bill of Attainder, ex post facto Law, or Law impairing the Obligation of Contracts, or grant any Title of Nobility.

No State shall, without the Consent of the Congress, **lay** any Imposts or Duties on Imports or Exports, except what may be absolutely necessary for executing it's inspection Laws: and the net Produce of all Duties and Imposts, laid by any State on Imports or Exports, shall be for the Use of the Treasury of the United States; and all such Laws shall be subject to the Revision and Controul of the Congress.

No State shall, without the Consent of Congress, lay any Duty of Tonnage, keep Troops, or Ships of War in time of Peace, enter into any Agreement or Compact with another State, or with a foreign Power, or engage in War, unless actually invaded, or in such imminent Danger as will not admit of delay.

ARTICLE II

Section 1. The executive Power shall be vested in a President of the United States of America. He shall hold his Office during the Term of four Years, and, together with the Vice President, chosen for the same Term, be elected, as follows

Each State shall appoint, in such Manner as the Legislature thereof may direct, a Number of Electors, equal to the whole Number of Senators and Representatives to which the State may be entitled in the Congress: but no Senator or Representative, or Person holding an Office of Trust or Profit under the United States, shall be appointed an Elector.

[The Electors shall meet in their respective States, and vote by Ballot for two Persons, of whom one at least shall not be an Inhabitant of the same State with themselves. And they shall make a List of all the Persons voted for, and of the Number of Votes for each; which List they shall sign and certify, and transmit sealed to the Seat of the Government of the United States, directed to the President of the Senate. The President of the Senate shall, in the Presence of the Senate and House of Representatives, open all the Certificates, and the Votes shall then be counted. The Person having the greatest Number of Votes shall be the President, if such Number be a Majority of the whole Number of Electors appointed; and if there be more than one who have such Majority, and have an equal Number of Votes, then the House of Representatives shall immediately chuse by Ballot one of them for President; and if no Person have a Majority, then from the five highest on the list the said House shall in like Manner chuse the President. But in chusing the President, the Votes shall be taken by States, the Representation from each State having one Vote; A quorum for this Purpose shall consist of a Member or Members from two thirds of the States, and a Majority of all the States shall be necessary to a Choice. In every Case, after the Choice of the President, the Person having the greatest Number of Votes of the Electors shall be the Vice President. But if there should remain two or more who have equal Votes, the Senate shall chuse from them by Ballot the Vice President.][6]

The Congress may determine the Time of chusing the Electors, and the Day on which they shall give their Votes; which Day shall be the same throughout the United States.

No Person except a natural born Citizen, or a Citizen of the United States, at the time of the Adoption of this Constitution, shall be eligible to the Office of President; neither shall any Person be eligible to that Office who shall not have attained to the Age of thirty five Years, and been fourteen Years a Resident within the United States.

In Case of the Removal of the President from Office, or of his Death, Resignation, or Inability to discharge the Powers and Duties of the said Office,[7] the Same shall devolve on the Vice President, and the Congress may by Law provide for the Case of Removal, Death, Resignation or Inability, both of the President and Vice President, declaring what Officer shall then act as President, and such Officer shall act accordingly, until the Disability be removed, or a President shall be elected.

The President shall, at stated Times, receive for his Services, a Compensation, which shall neither be encreased nor diminished during the Period for which he shall have been elected, and he shall not receive within that Period any other Emolument from the United States, or any of them.

Before he enter on the Execution of his Office, he shall take the following Oath or Affirmation: — "I do solemnly swear (or affirm) that I will faithfully execute the Office of President of the United States, and will to the best of my Ability, preserve, protect and defend the Constitution of the United States."

Section 2. The President shall be Commander in Chief of the Army and Navy of the United States, and of the Militia of the several States, when called into the actual Service of the United States; he may require the Opinion, in writing, of the principal Officer in each of the executive Departments, upon any Subject relating to the Duties of their respective Offices, and he shall have Power to grant Reprieves and Pardons for Offences against the United States, except in Cases of Impeachment.

He shall have Power, by and with the Advice and Consent of the Senate, to make Treaties, provided two thirds of the Senators present concur; and he shall nominate, and by and with the Advice and Consent of the Senate, shall appoint Ambassadors, other public Ministers and Consuls, Judges of the supreme Court, and all other Officers of the United States, whose Appointments are not herein otherwise provided for, and which shall be established by Law: but the Congress may by Law vest the Appointment of such inferior Officers, as they think proper, in the President alone, in the Courts of Law, or in the Heads of Departments.

The President shall have Power to fill up all Vacancies that may happen during the Recess of the Senate, by granting Commissions which shall expire at the End of their next Session.

Section 3. He shall from time to time give to the Congress Information of the State of the Union, and recommend to their Consideration such Measures as he shall judge necessary and expedient; he may, on extraordinary Occasions, convene both Houses, or either of them, and in Case of Disagreement between them, with Respect to the Time of Adjournment, he may adjourn them to such Time as he shall think proper; he shall receive Ambassadors and other public Ministers; he shall take Care that the Laws be faithfully executed, and shall Commission all the Officers of the United States.

Section 4. The President, Vice President and all civil Officers of the United States, shall be removed from Office on Impeachment for, and Conviction of, Treason, Bribery, or other high Crimes and Misdemeanors.

ARTICLE III

Section 1. The judicial Power of the United States, shall be vested in one supreme Court, and in such inferior Courts as the Congress may from time to time ordain and establish. The Judges, both of the supreme and inferior Courts, shall hold their Offices during good Behaviour, and shall, at stated Times, receive for their Services, a Compensation, which shall not be diminished during their Continuance in Office.

Section 2. The judicial Power shall extend to all Cases, in Law and Equity, arising under this Constitution, the Laws of the United States, and Treaties made, or which shall be made, under their Authority; — to all Cases affecting Ambassadors, other public Ministers and Consuls; — to all Cases of admiralty and maritime Jurisdiction; — to Controversies to which the United States shall be a Party; — to Controversies between two or more States; — between a State and Citizens of another State; — between Citizens of different States; — between Citizens of the same State claiming Lands under Grants of different States, and between a State, or the Citizens thereof, and foreign States, Citizens or Subjects.

In all Cases affecting Ambassadors, other public Ministers and Consuls, and those in which a State shall be Party, the supreme Court shall have original Jurisdiction. In all the other Cases before mentioned, the supreme Court shall have appellate Jurisdiction, both as to Law and Fact, with such Exceptions, and under such Regulations as the Congress shall make.

The Trial of all Crimes, except in Cases of Impeachment, shall be by Jury; and such Trial shall be held in the State where the said Crimes shall have been committed; but when not committed within any State, the Trial shall be at such Place or Places as the Congress may by Law have directed.

Section 3. Treason against the United States, shall consist only in levying War against them, or in adhering to their Enemies, giving them Aid and Comfort. No Person shall be convicted of Treason unless on the Testimony of two Witnesses to the same overt Act, or on Confession in open Court.

The Congress shall have Power to declare the Punishment of Treason, but no Attainder of Treason shall work Corruption of Blood, or Forfeiture except during the Life of the Person attainted.

ARTICLE IV

Section 1. Full Faith and Credit shall be given in each State to the public Acts, Records, and judicial Proceedings of every other State. And the Congress may by general Laws prescribe the Manner in which such Acts, Records and Proceedings shall be proved, and the Effect thereof.

Section 2. The Citizens of each State shall be entitled to all Privileges and Immunities of Citizens in the several States.

A Person charged in any State with Treason, Felony, or other Crime, who shall flee from Justice, and be found in another State, shall on Demand of the executive Authority of the State from which he fled, be delivered up, to be removed to the State having Jurisdiction of the Crime.

[No Person held to Service or Labour in one State, under the Laws thereof, escaping into another, shall, in Consequence of any Law or Regulation therein, be discharged from such Service or Labour, but shall be delivered up on Claim of the Party to whom such Service or Labour may be due.][9]

Section 3. New States may be admitted by the Congress into this Union; but no new State shall be formed or erected within the Jurisdiction of any other State; nor any State be formed by the Junction of two or more States, or Parts of States, without the Consent of the Legislatures of the States concerned as well as of the Congress.

The Congress shall have Power to dispose of and make all needful Rules and Regulations respecting the Territory or other Property belonging to the United States; and nothing in this Constitution shall be so construed as to Prejudice any Claims of the United States, or of any particular State.

Section 4. The United States shall guarantee to every State in this Union a Republican Form of Government, and shall protect each of them against Invasion; and on Application of the Legislature, or of the Executive (when the Legislature cannot be convened) against domestic Violence.

ARTICLE V

The Congress, whenever two thirds of both Houses shall deem it necessary, shall propose Amendments to this Constitution, or, on the Application of the Legislatures of two thirds of the several States, shall call a Convention for proposing Amendments, which, in either Case, shall be valid to all Intents and Purposes, as Part of this Constitution, when ratified by the Legislatures of three fourths of the several States, or by Conventions in three fourths thereof, as the one or the other Mode of Ratification may be proposed by the Congress; Provided [that no Amendment which may be made prior to the Year One thousand eight hundred and eight shall in any Manner affect the first and fourth Clauses in the Ninth Section of the first Article; and][10] that no State, without its Consent, shall be deprived of its equal Suffrage in the Senate.

ARTICLE VI

All Debts contracted and Engagements entered into, before the Adoption of this Constitution, shall be as valid against the United States under this Constitution, as under the Confederation.

This Constitution, and the Laws of the United States which shall be made in Pursuance thereof; and all Treaties made, or which shall be made, under the Authority of the United States, shall be the supreme Law of the Land; and the Judges in every State shall be bound thereby, any Thing in the Constitution or Laws of any State to the Contrary notwithstanding.

The Senators and Representatives before mentioned, and the Members of the several State Legislatures, and all executive and judicial Officers, both of the United States and of the several States, shall be bound by Oath or Affirmation, to support this Constitution; but no religious Test shall ever be required as a Qualification to any Office or public Trust under the United States.

ARTICLE VII

The Ratification of the Conventions of nine States, shall be sufficient for the Establishment of this Constitution between the States so ratifying the Same.

Done in Convention by the Unanimous Consent of the States present the Seventeenth Day of September in the Year of our Lord one thousand seven hundred and Eighty seven and of the Independence of the United States of America the Twelfth. IN WITNESS whereof We have hereunto subscribed our Names,

George Washington,
President and
deputy from Virginia.

New Hampshire:	John Langdon
	Nicholas Gilman.
Massachusetts:	Nathaniel Gorham,
	Rufus King.
Connecticut:	William Samuel Johnson,
	Roger Sherman.
New York:	Alexander Hamilton.
New Jersey:	William Livingston,
	David Brearley,
	William Paterson,
	Jonathan Dayton.
Pennsylvania:	Benjamin Franklin,
	Thomas Mifflin,
	Robert Morris,

	George Clymer,
	Thomas FitzSimons,
	Jared Ingersoll,
	James Wilson,
	Gouverneur Morris.
Delaware:	George Read,
	Gunning Bedford Jr.,
	John Dickinson,
	Richard Bassett,
	Jacob Broom.
Maryland:	James McHenry,
	Daniel of St. Thomas Jenifer,
	Daniel Carroll.
Virginia:	John Blair,
	James Madison Jr.
North Carolina:	William Blount,
	Richard Dobbs Spaight,
	Hugh Williamson.
South Carolina:	John Rutledge,
	Charles Cotesworth Pinckney,
	Charles Pinckney,
	Pierce Butler.
Georgia:	William Few,
	Abraham Baldwin.

[The language of the original Constitution, not including the Amendments, was adopted by a convention of the states on September 17, 1787, and was subsequently ratified by the states on the following dates: Delaware, December 7, 1787; Pennsylvania, December 12, 1787; New Jersey, December 18, 1787; Georgia, January 2, 1788; Connecticut, January 9, 1788; Massachusetts, February 6, 1788; Maryland, April 28, 1788; South Carolina, May 23, 1788; New Hampshire, June 21, 1788.

Ratification was completed on June 21, 1788.

The Constitution subsequently was ratified by Virginia, June 25, 1788; New York, July 26, 1788; North Carolina, November 21, 1789; Rhode Island, May 29, 1790; and Vermont, January 10, 1791.]

Amendments

Amendment I

(First ten amendments ratified December 15, 1791.)

Congress shall make no law respecting an establishment of religion, or prohibiting the free exercise thereof; or abridging the freedom of speech, or of the press; or the right of the people peaceably to assemble, and to petition the Government for a redress of grievances.

Amendment II

A well regulated Militia, being necessary to the security of a free State, the right of the people to keep and bear Arms, shall not be infringed.

Amendment III

No Soldier shall, in time of peace be quartered in any house, without the consent of the Owner, nor in time of war, but in a manner to be prescribed by law.

Amendment IV

The right of the people to be secure in their persons, houses, papers, and effects, against unreasonable searches and seizures, shall not be violated, and no Warrants shall issue, but upon probable cause, supported by Oath or affirmation, and particularly describing the place to be searched, and the persons or things to be seized.

Amendment V

No person shall be held to answer for a capital, or otherwise infamous crime, unless on a presentment or indictment of a Grand Jury, except in cases arising in the land or naval forces, or in the Militia, when in actual service in time of War or public danger; nor shall any person be subject for the same offence to be twice put in jeopardy of life or limb; nor shall be compelled in any criminal case to be a witness against himself, nor be deprived of life, liberty, or property, without due process of law; nor shall private property be taken for public use, without just compensation.

Amendment VI

In all criminal prosecutions, the accused shall enjoy the right to a speedy and public trial, by an impartial jury of the State and district wherein the crime shall have been committed, which district shall have been previously ascertained by law, and to be informed of the nature and cause of the accusation; to be confronted with the witnesses against him; to have compulsory process for obtaining witnesses in his favor, and to have the Assistance of Counsel for his defence.

Amendment VII

In Suits at common law, where the value in controversy shall exceed twenty dollars, the right of trial by jury shall be preserved, and no fact tried by a jury, shall be otherwise reexamined in any Court of the United States, than according to the rules of the common law.

Amendment VIII

Excessive bail shall not be required, nor excessive fines imposed, nor cruel and unusual punishments inflicted.

Amendment IX

The enumeration in the Constitution, of certain rights, shall not be construed to deny or disparage others retained by the people.

Amendment X

The powers not delegated to the United States by the Constitution, nor prohibited by it to the States, are reserved to the States respectively, or to the people.

Amendment XI (Ratified February 7, 1795)

The Judicial power of the United States shall not be construed to extend to any suit in law or equity, commenced or prosecuted against one of the United States by Citizens of another State, or by Citizens or Subjects of any Foreign State.

Amendment XII (Ratified June 15, 1804)

The Electors shall meet in their respective states and vote by ballot for President and Vice-President, one of whom, at least, shall not be an inhabitant of the same state with themselves; they shall name in their ballots the person voted for as President, and in distinct ballots the person voted for as Vice-President, and they shall make distinct lists of all persons voted for as President, and of all persons voted for as Vice-President, and of the number of votes for each, which lists they shall sign and certify, and transmit sealed to the seat of the government of the United States, directed to the President of the Senate; — The President of the Senate shall, in the presence of the Senate and House of Representatives, open all the certificates and the votes shall then be counted; — The person having the greatest number of votes for President, shall be the President, if such number be a majority of the whole number of Electors appointed; and if no person have such majority, then from the persons having the highest numbers not exceeding three on the list of those voted for as President, the House of Representatives shall choose immediately, by ballot, the President. But in choosing the President, the votes shall be taken by states, the representation from each state having one vote; a quorum for this purpose shall consist of a member or members from two-thirds of the states, and a majority of all the states shall be necessary to a choice. [And if the House of Representatives shall not choose a President whenever the right of choice shall devolve upon them, before the fourth day of March next following, then the Vice-President shall act as President, as in the case of the death or other constitutional disability of the President. —][11] The person having the greatest number of votes as Vice-President, shall be the Vice-President, if such number be a majority of the whole number of Electors appointed, and if no person have a majority, then from the two highest numbers on the list, the Senate shall choose the Vice-President; a quorum for the purpose shall consist of two-thirds of the whole number of Senators, and a majority of the whole number shall be necessary to a choice. But no person constitutionally ineligible to the office of President shall be eligible to that of Vice-President of the United States.

Amendment XIII (Ratified December 6, 1865)

Section 1. Neither slavery nor involuntary servitude, except as a punishment for crime whereof the party shall have been duly convicted, shall exist within the United States, or any place subject to their jurisdiction.

Section 2. Congress shall have power to enforce this article by appropriate legislation.

Amendment XIV (Ratified July 9, 1868)

Section 1. All persons born or naturalized in the United States, and subject to the jurisdiction thereof, are citizens of the United States and of the State wherein they reside. No State shall make or enforce any law which shall abridge the privileges or immunities of citizens of the United States; nor shall any State deprive any person of life, liberty, or property, without due process of law; nor deny to any person within its jurisdiction the equal protection of the laws.

Section 2. Representatives shall be apportioned among the several States according to their respective numbers, counting the whole number of persons in each State, excluding Indians not taxed. But when the right to vote at any election for the choice of electors for President and Vice President of the United States, Representatives in Congress, the Executive and Judicial officers of a State, or the members of the Legislature thereof, is denied to any of the male inhabitants of such State, being twenty-one years of age,[12] and citizens of the United States, or in any way abridged, except for participation in rebellion, or other crime, the basis of representation therein shall be reduced in the proportion which the number of such male citizens shall bear to the whole number of male citizens twenty-one years of age in such State.

Section 3. No person shall be a Senator or Representative in Congress, or elector of President and Vice President, or hold any office, civil or military, under the United States, or under any State, who, having previously taken an oath, as a member of Congress, or as an officer of the United States, or as a member of any State legislature, or as an executive or judicial officer of any State, to support the Constitution of the United States, shall have engaged in insurrection or rebellion against the same, or given aid or comfort to the enemies thereof. But Congress may by a vote of two-thirds of each House, remove such disability.

Section 4. The validity of the public debt of the United States, authorized by law, including debts incurred for payment of pensions and bounties for services in suppressing insurrection or rebellion, shall not be questioned. But neither the United States nor any State shall assume or pay any debt or obligation incurred in aid of insurrection or rebellion against the United States, or any claim for the loss or emancipation of any slave; but all such debts, obligations and claims shall be held illegal and void.

Section 5. The Congress shall have power to enforce, by appropriate legislation, the provisions of this article.

Amendment XV (Ratified February 3, 1870)

Section 1. The right of citizens of the United States to vote shall not be denied or abridged by the United States or by any State on account of race, color, or previous condition of servitude.

Section 2. The Congress shall have power to enforce this article by appropriate legislation.

Amendment XVI (Ratified February 3, 1913)

The Congress shall have power to lay and collect taxes on incomes, from whatever source derived, without apportionment among the several States, and without regard to any census or enumeration.

Amendment XVII (Ratified April 8, 1913)

The Senate of the United States shall be composed of two Senators from each State, elected by the people thereof, for six years; and each Senator shall have one vote. The electors in each State shall have the qualifications requisite for electors of the most numerous branch of the State legislatures.

When vacancies happen in the representation of any State in the Senate, the executive authority of such State shall issue writs of election to fill such vacancies: *Provided*, That the legislature of any State may empower the executive thereof to make temporary appointments until the people fill the vacancies by election as the legislature may direct.

This amendment shall not be so construed as to affect the election or term of any Senator chosen before it becomes valid as part of the Constitution.

Amendment XVIII (Ratified January 16, 1919)[13]

Section 1. After one year from the ratification of this article the manufacture, sale, or transportation of intoxicating liquors within, the importation thereof into, or the exportation thereof from the United States and all territory subject to the jurisdiction thereof for beverage purposes is hereby prohibited.

Section 2. The Congress and the several States shall have concurrent power to enforce this article by appropriate legislation.

Section 3. This article shall be inoperative unless it shall have been ratified as an amendment to the Constitution by the legislatures of the several States, as provided in the Constitution, within seven years from the date of the submission hereof to the States by the Congress.

Amendment XIX (Ratified August 18, 1920)

The right of citizens of the United States to vote shall not be denied or abridged by the United States or by any State on account of sex.

Congress shall have power to enforce this article by appropriate legislation.

Amendment XX (Ratified January 23, 1933)

Section 1. The terms of the President and Vice President shall end at noon on the 20th day of January, and the terms of Senators and Representatives at noon on the 3d day of January, of the years in which such terms would have ended if this article had not been ratified; and the terms of their successors shall then begin.

Section 2. The Congress shall assemble at least once in every year, and such meeting shall begin at noon on the 3d day of January, unless they shall by law appoint a different day.

Section 3.[14] If, at the time fixed for the beginning of the term of the President, the President elect shall have died, the Vice President elect shall become President. If a President shall not have been chosen before the time fixed for the beginning of his term, or if the President elect shall have failed to qualify, then the Vice President elect shall act as President until a President shall have qualified; and the Congress may by law provide for the case wherein neither a President elect nor a Vice President elect shall have qualified, declaring who shall then act as President, or the manner in which one who is to act shall be selected, and such person shall act accordingly until a President or Vice President shall have qualified.

Section 4. The Congress may by law provide for the case of the death of any of the persons from whom the House of Representatives may choose a President whenever the right of choice shall have devolved upon them, and for the case of the death of any of the persons from whom the Senate may choose a Vice President whenever the right of choice shall have devolved upon them.

Section 5. Sections 1 and 2 shall take effect on the 15th day of October following the ratification of this article.

Section 6. This article shall be inoperative unless it shall have been ratified as an amendment to the Constitution by the legislatures of three-fourths of the several States within seven years from the date of its submission.

Amendment XXI (Ratified December 5, 1933)

Section 1. The eighteenth article of amendment to the Constitution of the United States is hereby repealed.

Section 2. The transportation or importation into any State, Territory, or possession of the United States for delivery or use therein of intoxicating liquors, in violation of the laws thereof, is hereby prohibited.

Section 3. This article shall be inoperative unless it shall have been ratified as an amendment to the Constitution by conventions in the several States, as provided in the Constitution, within seven years from the date of the submission hereof to the States by the Congress.

Amendment XXII (Ratified February 27, 1951)

Section 1. No person shall be elected to the office of the President more than twice, and no person who has held the office of President, or acted as President, for more than two years of a term to which some other person was elected President shall be elected to the office of the President more than once. But this Article shall not apply to any person holding the office of President when this Article was proposed by the Congress, and shall not prevent any person who may be holding the office of President, or acting as President, during the term within which this Article become operative from holding the office of President or acting as President during the remainder of such term.

Section 2. This article shall be inoperative unless it shall have been ratified as an amendment to the Constitution by the legislatures of three-fourths of the several States within seven years from the date of its submission to the States by the Congress.

Amendment XXIII (Ratified March 29, 1961)

Section 1. The District constituting the seat of Government of the United States shall appoint in such manner as the Congress may direct:

A number of electors of President and Vice President equal to the whole number of Senators and Representatives in Congress to which the District would be entitled if it were a State, but in no event more than the least populous State; they shall be in addition to those appointed by the States, but they shall be considered, for the purposes of the election of President and Vice President, to be electors appointed by a State; and they shall meet in the District and perform such duties as provided by the twelfth article of amendment.

Section 2. The Congress shall have power to enforce this article by appropriate legislation.

Amendment XXIV (Ratified January 23, 1964)

Section 1. The right of citizens of the United States to vote in any primary or other election for President or Vice President, for electors for President or Vice President, or for Senator or Representative in Congress, shall not be denied or abridged by the United States or any State by reason of failure to pay any poll tax or other tax.

Section 2. The Congress shall have power to enforce this article by appropriate legislation.

Amendment XXV (Ratified February 10, 1967)

Section 1. In case of the removal of the President from office or of his death or resignation, the Vice President shall become President.

Section 2. Whenever there is a vacancy in the office of the Vice President, the President shall nominate a Vice President who shall take office upon confirmation by a majority vote of both Houses of Congress.

Section 3. Whenever the President transmits to the President pro tempore of the Senate and the Speaker of the House of Representatives his written declaration that he is unable to discharge the powers and duties of his office, and until he transmits to them a written declaration to the contrary, such powers and duties shall be discharged by the Vice President as Acting President.

Section 4. Whenever the Vice President and a majority of either the principal officers of the executive departments or of such other body as Congress may by law provide, transmit to the President pro tempore of the Senate and the Speaker of the House of Representatives their written declaration that the President is unable to discharge the powers and duties of his office, the Vice President shall immediately assume the powers and duties of the office as Acting President.

Thereafter, when the President transmits to the President pro tempore of the Senate and the Speaker of the House of Representatives his written declaration that no inability exists, he shall resume the powers and duties of his office unless the Vice President and a majority of either the principal officers of the executive department or of such other body as Congress may by law provide, transmit within four days to the President pro tempore of the Senate and the Speaker of the House of Representatives their written declaration that the President is unable to discharge the powers and duties of his office. Thereupon Congress shall decide the issue, assembling within forty-eight hours for that purpose if not in session. If the Congress, within twenty-one days after receipt of the latter written declaration, or, if Congress is not in session, within twenty-one days after Congress is required to assemble, determines by two-thirds vote of both Houses that the President is unable to discharge the powers and duties of his office, the Vice President shall continue to discharge the same as Acting President; otherwise, the President shall resume the powers and duties of his office.

Amendment XXVI (Ratified July 1, 1971)

Section 1. The right of citizens of the United States, who are eighteen years of age or older, to vote shall not be denied or abridged by the United States or by any State on account of age.

Section 2. The Congress shall have power to enforce this article by appropriate legislation.

Amendment XXVII (Ratified May 7, 1992)

No law varying the compensation for the services of the Senators and Representatives shall take effect, until an election of Representatives shall have intervened.

Notes

1. The part in brackets was changed by section 2 of the Fourteenth Amendment.

2. The part in brackets was changed by the first paragraph of the Seventeenth Amendment.
3. The part in brackets was changed by the second paragraph of the Seventeenth Amendment.
4. The part in brackets was changed by section 2 of the Twentieth Amendment.
5. The Sixteenth Amendment gave Congress the power to tax incomes.
6. The material in brackets has been superseded by the Twelfth Amendment.
7. This provision has been affected by the Twenty-fifth Amendment.
8. These clauses were affected by the Eleventh Amendment.
9. This paragraph has been superseded by the Thirteenth Amendment.
10. Obsolete.
11. The part in brackets has been superseded by section 3 of the Twentieth Amendment.
12. See the Nineteenth and Twenty-sixth Amendments.
13. This Amendment was repealed by section 1 of the Twenty-first Amendment.
14. See the Twenty-fifth Amendment.

SOURCE: U.S. Congress, House, Committee on the Judiciary, *The Constitution of the United States of America, as Amended*, 100th Cong., 1st sess., 1987, H Doc 100–94.

Index